Reviews of *The Truth Agenda*

'This book is an essential guide to the many mysteries, ;
of 21st century life. Thomas is a highly persuasive
discrepancies and hard evidence, inviting you to draw yc
this utterly fascinating and will be barbecuing out on
...This book is a triple-strength espresso-charged wake u_

'If you've ever thought there was more to prophecies, UFOs, crop circles and other unexplained mysteries, this is the book for you... ...This book is full of important questions, highlighting a need to look much deeper into world events and wake up to what's really going on... ...Rather brilliantly, Thomas explains how we can transform pessimism into positive action, and presents further incredible evidence for the power of collective positive thought. Utterly mind-blowing' [Five-star 'MUST-READ' of the month] — *Spirit & Destiny*

'One of the admirable qualities of The Truth Agenda is the way in which Andy Thomas lays his cards on the table: the book is an ambitious attempt to do exactly what its subtitle proclaims... ...Thomas makes a concerted effort to avoid that reflective, mercury-like quality of so many conspiracy theories, which continually shift position to elude each new rational challenge put before them. With comprehensive notes, links and appendices, this is a useful overview of the current situation regarding some key 'alternative' topics' — *Fortean Times*

'This accessible and comprehensive book is an excellent guide to conspiracy theories, unexplained mysteries and prophecies. It provides detailed and convincing illustrated insights into everything from UFOs to the 9/11 conspiracy theory—the chapter on which I would highly recommend' — *Soul & Spirit*

'[Andy Thomas] does a great job of presenting just about every conspiracy with commendable objectivity – and does our infiltrated civilization a great service by charting the course of a 'truth agenda' that highlights patterns of misinformation, disempowerment, control and surveillance... ...There is no judgement, simply a very good sifting of information and provision of references... ...Thomas' command of the issues is exhaustive and well-referenced, such that anyone could follow the threads and make up their own minds... ...The author ends with a stirring chapter on just how to combat the steady erosion of individual will and creativity and it is clear this is his prime motivation. The truthseekers he wishes to rally must listen carefully to his request for sharp and alert minds and be watchful of their own propensity to project fears of control and desires to believe rather than use their own critical faculties. In this latter respect, the book strikes a good balance of empowerment alongside an array of very disturbing material' — *Caduceus*

'This entertaining book scans a vast timeline from pyramid mysteries, crop circles and UFOs to a collection of modern conspiracy theories, such as the banking collapse, War on Terror, the death of Diana, Princess of Wales, and the Moon landings. For those that question the official line, this is a superb book, full of fascination and wonder... ...Andy Thomas makes no attempt, however, to convince us that we are being hoodwinked. He merely presents alternative views and leaves us to make up our own minds... ...Andy Thomas is a skilful researcher, lecturer and writer and has many successful books about the unexplained to his credit.... ...This book is written with a rare ability to articulate complex ideas in a simple way, is immensely well-researched and is immaculately presented, with over 100 photos. It is exceptional value for money and the best book on the subject I have read' — *Paradigm Shift*

'This book explores a number of contentious topics, asking why so many people now believe in so-called conspiracy theories and what evidence there is to support them... ...This is less wacky than it sounds, as there are interesting connections between a number of these themes, for instance the agenda to bring about a New World Order. Each topic is examined in some depth, and at the end the author suggests how the 'truth agenda' might be applied... ...The author joins the dots in a stimulating overview of our global situation' — *Network Review* (**Scientific and Medical Network Journal**)

'The attractive look and feel of the book... is matched by the clarity and solidity of the writing. This is not a sensationalist work... ...It invites one to pick it up and browse. In terms of its breadth and depth it represents thousands of hours of research and compilation – all handled with a light but serious touch.... ...*The Truth Agenda* is a timely and important book. Buy a copy, read it and pass it on' — *New View*

'A glossy, eye-catching production with scores of topical illustrations and a comprehensive appendix of online resources... ...Intelligent and analytical, Andy Thomas's balanced approach is to steer a middle course between conspiracy theory fanaticism on the one hand and, on the other, general public unawareness of the fascinating but sometimes confusing tapestry of hidden agendas and mysterious events that seem to be secretly shaping our world today... ...A profoundly disturbing but ultimately uplifting handbook for these turbulent times of millennial psychic change' — *Western Daily Press*

'*The Truth Agenda* is just the sort of book you need in order to make sense of the great mysteries and conspiracies of our times... ...Thomas asks why some subjects are considered "respectable" while others are shunned as "fringe nonsense"; his reply is cogent and well-informed... ...This high-quality production, with photos throughout, is well referenced and has plenty of information for further research' — *Nexus Magazine*

'It is impossible to overstate just how vitally important this book is, a true masterwork of its kind and a must read... Buy it, read it, and learn' — *Phenomena*

THE
TRUTH
AGENDA

Making Sense of Unexplained Mysteries, Global Cover-Ups & Visions for a New Era

ANDY THOMAS

Dedicated to all those working for liberty and truth

This US edition published in 2015 by Adventures Unlimited Press,
One Adventure Place, Kempton, Illinois, 60946-0074, USA
Website: *www.adventuresunlimitedpress.com*
E-mail: *info@adventuresunlimitedpress.com*

First published by Vital Signs Publishing, UK,
2009, revised 2011, updated and expanded 2013
Website: *www.vitalsignspublishing.co.uk*

Front cover design by Andy Thomas & Jason Porthouse

ISBN: 978-1-939149-41-1

Other mystery/truth issues books by Andy Thomas:

Fields of Mystery [S B Publications 1996]
Quest for Contact (with Paul Bura) [S B Publications 1997]
Vital Signs [S B Publications 1998, updated 2002 / Frog Ltd (US) 2002]
Swirled Harvest [Vital Signs Publishing 2003]
A Oneness of Mind [Vital Signs Publishing 2003]
An Introduction to Crop Circles [Wessex Books 2006, updated 2011]
Conspiracies: The Facts - The Theories - The Evidence [Watkins Publishing 2013]

CONTENTS

PART FOUR: SOLUTIONS AND INSPIRATIONS

ACKNOWLEDGEMENTS

The author would very much like to thank:

Helen Sewell for her dearest loving support and patience, proofing and inspiration; *Piers Adams* for early proofing, fact-checking and inspired suggestions (investigate *www.redpriest.com* for some truly extraordinary baroque pyrotechnics); *Sue Adams* for the original indexing; *Marcus Allen* for valuable help with the lunar content and his continued support; *Ian R Crane* for early checking and his own support; *Geoff Stray* for scrutiny of the prophecies content; *Terry Boardman* for the Steiner material; *Jason Porthouse* for his work on the front cover montage and other vital aid and friendship over the years; *Jordan Thomas* for suggestions and practical help; all the photographers [see *Picture Credits*], especially *Andreas Müller*, *Tony and Ann Woodall* and *Heather and Ron Thomas*; *Eva-Marie Brekkestø* and *Roy Leraand* for sources on the Norway sky spiral; The several members of the UK 9/11 Truth community, including *Ian Henshall* and *Belinda McKenzie*, who helped with fact checking and image sourcing.

Thanks also to *Martin Noakes* for technical advice and endless vital truth networking, and *Lindsay Woods* of SB Publications for additional help, along with everyone else who has given support and encouragement over the years.

Finally, great acknowledgement is given to the many people out there challenging convention and risking reputations, livelihoods and sometimes actual lives to create a better world, whose work has been wittingly (see Appendices) or unwittingly drawn on in this book.

'A long habit of not thinking a thing wrong gives it a superficial appearance of being right.'

'We are apt to shut our eyes against a painful truth. For my part I am willing to KNOW the whole truth, to know the worst, and to provide for it.'

Thomas Paine 1737-1809

INTRODUCTION

Some years back, I was asked to make an appearance on the BBC's *The One Show*, a popular UK television program, alongside *Nexus Magazine*'s Marcus Allen and UFO investigator John Wickham. The British High Court had just rejected Mohammed Al Fayed's assertions that the tragic demise of his son Dodi, with Princess Diana in a Paris underpass, had been a coordinated assassination. Despite the straightforward verdict that 'gross negligence' from the driver and the paparazzi were all that were responsible, the polls were showing that much of the population still doubted this, and the BBC wanted to examine why a fascination with conspiracy theories persisted.

As ambassadors from the world of mysteries research, the three of us were thus looked after and interviewed at length in a nice London hotel by presenter (and ex-tabloid editor) Kelvin MacKenzie. The discussion took in everything from the paranormal to persisting accusations that the whole truth about 9/11 had not been told. The conversation was affable, comprehensive and balanced.

A day later, finger poised on the recorder button, I watched our interview air on prime-time evening television, knowing that millions would be watching. Well aware from past experience that no more than a few minutes, at best, would remain from the discussion, I braced myself to see what remained from our two hours of recording. 'Minutes' turned out to be very hopeful. Instead, barely *half* a minute remained. I got to mention Guy Fawkes, Marcus asked whether we were alone in the universe, and John said nothing at all. And that was it—all the valuable discussion we had recorded about the more important themes had vanished into the ether. Then it was back to the studio presenters for condescending dismissal.

This sobering experience is a good example of how the so-called fringes of debate are always treated by the mainstream. It is far easier to sweep important issues under the carpet with jocularity and heavy editing than actually confront the reality of why so many people question what they are told to believe by a world that refuses to face uncomfortable questions. Yet a sizeable proportion of its inhabitants have at one time or another witnessed things they cannot understand or make sense of in everyday terms—or have met obstruction while trying to do so. We have it drummed into us time and again that nothing out of the ordinary can really happen, in the face of substantial evidence to the contrary. Those who insist on plying their convictions usually become freak show entertainments for a time, before fading back into obscurity or becoming minor stars in a paranormal research ghetto. Others, whose investigations lead them into mysteries of a more political kind, can find themselves attacked as delusional troublemakers by bitterly defensive press columnists, or even victimized by the state.

Why are things this way? Why are some topics considered 'respectable', while others are shunned as 'fringe' nonsense unworthy of investigation? Is this because they truly are nonsensical—or is it because a nameless stratum of authority would

THE TRUTH AGENDA

rather certain areas were left alone? The evidence, under analysis, suggests the latter as a very real possibility. *The Truth Agenda*, then, is a book concerned with mysteries and cover-ups of many kinds. Some of them reside within the realms of the parasciences, and others very much in the 'real world'—yet both genres appear to be distinctly connected when examined closely. Indeed, the higher echelons and power structures of our entire society seem obsessed with occult knowledge and a belief in the mystical realms, but those lower down the ladder are ridiculed for making a show of investigating them, and often find themselves branded with a sneer as 'conspiracy theorists', a term increasingly employed in an abusive sense. Someone on high seems to feel threatened by these people. The application of a 'Truth Agenda' to these forbidden areas, by the simple method proposed in Chapter I, soon reveals hidden layers more than worthy of investigation.

What this book is *not* is an empty compendium of wacky beliefs listed in order and then unceremoniously debunked, like so many tomes of stocking-filler disinformation clogging up the shelves today. Instead, it tries to build, bit by bit, a coherent picture of the areas that have led people from many walks of life to consider that the times we are now living in are important and that we are not being told the truth about them by hidden levels of authority. Part One lays the groundwork concerning mysteries and conspiracy theories, before Part Two selects three key events in (relatively) recent history to look at how the official evidence for their provenance stands up. Part Three examines the serious social consequences of the mandates engineered by some of the questionable areas exposed, and Part Four provides encouraging evidence that we can collectively turn all of this around to a more positive outlook—if we so choose.

Filming for the BBC's The One Show. *A two-hour television discussion on conspiracy theories resulted in less than half a minute's final broadcast.*

For all the global sweep of the issues revealed by the Truth Agenda, two countries do inevitably feature prominently in this book: the USA and the UK. It cannot be escaped that history and genes inseparably link the two, but beyond this the US, for all its current dilemmas, still just about remains the dominant superpower in the world, hence its recurring profile in the analysis. What happens to America affects everybody, as the global financial crisis so clearly illustrated. I am myself a citizen of Britain, and although this edition of the book has been prepared for a US readership, I have decided to keep some of the text's British perspective intact, which I believe is valuable. The UK has long provided a cultural bridge between the United States and Europe, and what manifests in the 'mother of democracy' still makes a difference to the world. Britain's questionable empire may be long-gone, but many roots of the 'New World Order' began with it. It may even be that the British Isles are being used as a test zone for social engineering planned on a wider scale later.

When people think of 'conspiracy theories', though, it is to the US that minds tend to leap. To some observers, the election of Barack Obama as president saw the old world inhabited by the former Bush administration, with all its uncomfortable roots in 9/11, dubious Middle Eastern wars and 'necessary' restrictions on freedom, conveniently recede into history, all conspiracy theories quietly forgotten in a new world of liberty and joy. Instead, the more realistic pointed out that just three paragraphs

Barack Obama takes his inaugural presidential oath, subject of much controversy in itself [page 21]. *Hopes were high for a new world under Obama, but just minutes after this moment, many of the old agendas were restated, and new conspiracy theories began.*

into Obama's inaugural address—one which bore uncomfortable similarities to his predecessor's first speech—the new president was describing America as a nation 'at war, against a far-reaching network of violence and hatred'. This neatly announced a determination to continue the liberty-crushing 'War on Terror' (in all but name) that some citizens had hoped might indeed recede into history, being a campaign that even the more conservative pundits acknowledge made the world a far *more* terror-filled place to live in, not less. It is also a conflict that had its official beginnings in the baptismal fires of 11th September 2001, a day of events which are mired, like so many other nexus points in history, in doubt, obfuscation and blatant lies, as we shall explore. The passing of the years has not lessened the impact or importance of the issues around 9/11; if anything, it becomes ever-more important to unravel.

Obama's second term saw little change in certain draconian policies, and in fact far more US-sponsored assassinations and drone strikes were recorded than ever before, enhanced by a new ongoing war against fighters of the 'Islamic State', and renewed tensions with Russia. Therefore the need for deep enquiries mounted by 'truthseekers', or conspiracy theorists (a term I doggedly adopt here, rather as Quakers successfully absorbed a name originally intended as an insult) remains entirely valid.

What, though, are these enquiries? This book exists to help untangle some of the matted threads of mysteries research, which can appear impenetrable to those on the outside, and attempts to, as the subtitle suggests, make sense of it all in as straightforward a way as is possible. In so doing, it presents a hypothesis, based on years of interaction and correspondence with those in this world of 'fringe' enquiry, that summarizes and encapsulates its general belief system without gross over-simplification, but also without being the density of a telephone directory, as standard conspiracy texts tend to be. Along the way, some of my own personal fascinations are inevitably woven into the mix, but for the most part *The Truth Agenda* stands as an overview of what a minority—though a sizeable one—believe about their civilization and planetary prospects here in the first quarter of the 21st century. Coming to an absolute judgement on these beliefs is not the purpose of these pages, yet it is striking in their compilation how credible some of them can be made to seem without much effort, even in a hypothetical context.

The core of the conspiracy view is that knowledge of unexplained phenomena and occult beliefs underpin the central philosophy of a secret ruling class that has dominated for millennia, one which may be quietly expecting a potentially disruptive cosmological event to occur to the planet sometime soon, an expectation based on ancient calendars, prophecies and visions. With that in mind, this elite cabal may be installing a regime of control, using any means necessary, to ensure that it retains its power during or after such an upheaval. The odd thing is that, unhinged as some of this may first appear, in summarizing the overall picture the hypothesis takes on a strangely convincing symmetry—even if some of it does eventually turn out to be myth born of collective paranoia. Yet from the darkest of those fears, a number of clear truths do seem to emerge, with the reality of control agendas, vast political lies and the power of hidden ideologies revealing themselves pretty plainly, even if the conclusions drawn by the truthseekers sometimes go too far.

The happy news about all of this is that even if the blackest visions *were* to be confirmed, there is enough human goodness and wisdom available to deal with them —given dedication and positive intent. If all that is achieved by fevered speculation on a hidden world of mysteries and cover-ups is an enhanced appreciation of the freedom and beauty in the lives that people do have—or must create—then none of it is in vain. The empowerment that comes with legitimate questioning, taking nothing at face value about our world or those we allow to govern it, is reason enough to take the journey.

The danger of all such projects is that the very engagement with some of the darker subjects can in itself generate gloom and exacerbate the problem. If all the tracts on positive thinking are correct, campaigning for peace, for instance, is inherently more likely to achieve its aim, on an energetic level, than protesting against war. Yet this cannot be used as an excuse for failing to call to account that which is wrong. Raising full awareness of dysfunctional fixtures, which we can too easily accept due to their sheer familiarity, as one of the opening Thomas Paine quotes suggests, is a vital task if light is to dispel shadows. Hence it is unavoidable that many of these pages are devoted to lifting the layers on subjects which some may find uncomfortable, distasteful or even frightening to question, as we challenge some of history's sacred cows along the way. But challenge we must if we are to break out of the prison of illusion which has been built all around us, whether intentionally or by accident. Only through awareness can we avoid potential disaster; heading for a wall while blindfolded provides merely temporary and delusional security. Opening our eyes to the hard reality of the danger zones is the only way we can avoid their worst excesses. Yet at the end of the journey we take through these pages, something wonderful lies—the realization that collectively we are far more powerful than those so many people credit with having caused the problems.

Egyptian needle and the Moon at the Place de la Concorde, Paris. Ancient mysteries and occult beliefs may still underpin the philosophy of the power structures that run the world today, and big secrets are certainly kept from us.

While readers new to the idea of questioning consensus reality may feel unsettled, the areas covered here will be less startling to seasoned truthseekers with fixed creeds, but alternative analysis needs to reach beyond the front stalls to make a difference, and the broad overview offered here is necessarily streamlined. Numerous sources for more detailed general information are listed in the Appendices.

Any book, naturally, is of its time, but now that we are well into the 'New Era' which prophecies said would begin in 2012, we can get a clearer idea of the wider context of the times of change in which we find ourselves. Few would argue that there hasn't been an tumultuous acceleration of world events in the years since. Many prophetic promises, threats and possibilities could still make themselves known any year or decade now, if they are not already, and we need to stay on our guard and be ready. Some global developments will doubtless overtake the featured material in this tome, especially in such a rapidly altering world where new revelations of previously hidden things seem to be coming to the surface on an almost weekly basis, and with international tensions and conflicts ever in flux—but the broad picture will likely remain relevant for a good while.

Those readers wanting a dedicated history of hardcore conspiracy theories, covering in more detail classic cases such as the JFK assassination, Watergate, Princess Diana, the *Lusitania* incident, Pearl Harbor, the attack on the *USS Liberty* and much more besides, might also like to investigate another of my books, *Conspiracies: The Facts —The Theories—The Evidence* (Watkins Publishing, US, UK & Australia, 2013), which makes for a good companion volume to this one and discusses further the pros and cons of the conspiracy mindset, whilst arguing that truthseekers deserve to be taken far more seriously.

In fact, much of the problem the fringe has in persuading the outside world of the validity of its convictions is that too often those teetering on the edge of interest can be discouraged by what sometimes comes across as partisan overload. With this in mind I have concentrated here on more accessible areas of investigation, whilst omitting others that I feel lack definitive evidence or mask unpleasant racial scapegoating. I have also avoided dissecting the origins of the world's religions and their various claimed misdemeanors. That is too big a task for *The Truth Agenda* and I am assuming that open-minded readers will recognise for themselves the inherent weakness of any mindset that requires blind faith in 'God-given' rights to justify itself. It seems so well established that religions have been misused for authoritarian purposes through the ages, whatever their genuine spiritual values, that the subject doesn't warrant close attention here. Harmful fundamentalism, however, on any side of the debate, religious, political or scientific, is firmly called into question throughout the book.

A degree of moderation, then, is necessary for the purposes of spreading awareness of what may turn out to be the key issues of our times. Its employment should also ensure that each of us remains open-minded, ready to review opinions if discerning evidence is presented, in whatever direction it takes us, towards or away from convention. I have found, from my own experience as a lecturer sharing the mystery realms with mainstream audiences, that people are more comfortable with new ideas when alternative truths are offered, but not sold as absolutes. In that spirit, then, *The Truth Agenda*'s primary purpose is simply to reach out to those who don't feel quite right about the slightly warped society around them and want to look just a little further outside the usual confines of mainstream thinking to see if any answers lie there. Readers must choose their own reality.

At the very least, the journey should provoke thought and discussion. That, if nothing else, should make it worthwhile, even if the reader violently disagrees with the content. It is better to have some opinion than none, with blandness and apathy being particularly virulent weakeners of the human spirit. Strength and substance always comes with healthy debate.

Andy Thomas

Part One:
Mysteries, Miracles and Global Deception

1

I   Making Sense of Our World

Is the somewhat fractured world we live in today just a result of random developments—or a deliberate ploy? And is the picture we are presented with in the mainstream an accurate one? Given that so often it appears not to be, it is inevitable that many have begun to question the very foundations of the society in which they live.

Western Discontent

When a recent poll claimed to have found that a large majority of British people considered themselves to be 'happy', it came as something of a surprise to much of that country's population, and to others looking in. From the evidence of everyday conversation not many people, in the West at least, really seem to be happy with the world we live in today. Perhaps it was just the way the questions were asked, or perhaps the whole poll was some kind of Orwellian exercise in social conditioning, but overall the fair majority of citizens generally appear to hold negative views on the state of things. Notably, the coverage glossed over the not-insignificant finding that over one in four put themselves in the 'anxious' category.[1]

For all our scientific achievements, great discoveries and the many convenience comforts of the modern Western world, there remains a pervading sense that civilization has taken a wrong turn somewhere down the line. Secrets and lies seem rife within governments and institutions, countries go to war on very shaky grounds, and an agenda of control and surveillance appears to have replaced the relative freedom the West once knew. Fear seems to be the main thread—fear of climate change, of terrorism, of flu or Ebola pandemics, of poverty, of immigrants and outsiders, fear of almost everything. All these threats seemingly dangled above us and inflated by media shock merchants mean we increasingly act from a place of threatened security rather than from expansion and joy. The prevailing impression is that we are poised on the brink of political, economic, spiritual and social breakdown as the family unit dissolves and the old foundations of respect and a sense of the sacred dwindle away into disorder, systemic corruption and crime. Meanwhile, savage austerity measures seen in several countries amidst economic turmoil have focused many minds on loss (or, in some cases, simply the fear of loss), rather than abundance.

Positive thinking, then—a vital commodity in unstable times—is currently dwarfed by the seeming enormity of the problems that face us and the coverage given to them. Yet, despite the unquestionable reality of big issues to be dealt with, there is strong evidence that we are disproportionately presented with a negative view of a world that may in truth be much brighter than we are being allowed to see. The version of society we perceive through our screens and newspapers almost unfailingly promotes fear and darkness, and tempts us to give our freedom away, almost as if encouraging hope and liberty would be an irresponsible thing to do.

Almost as if there is some kind of agenda.

The dark things are sometimes real enough—but so is hope and positivity. Yet the latter are without question downplayed as if, to those in control, a divided and unhappy society is far more preferable. Either way, little in our world quite seems to make sense anymore—that is, if one assumes that the world is being run for the benefit of *us*. What if that is not the case?

Some say the current state of our civilization is the result of a series of giant mistakes, the product of error built upon error and rebounds from endless corrective manoeuvres born of desperation, as humankind evolves with depressing slowness. However, an increasing number of people believe that life has become the way it is because a hidden strata of our society *wants it to be that way*. After all, are we really so incompetent as a species? Have we learnt nothing? Many individuals and groups seem enlightened and intelligent, living positive lives and trying constantly to create positive change; yet society as a whole stubbornly refuses to move on from its litany of mistakes, continually repeating the faults of the past.

Understanding Conspiracy Theory

This is where we enter the world of 'conspiracy theory'. It has become an abusive term in recent times, applied by the establishment to marginalize anyone who questions the status quo. An encouraged contempt for conspiracy theorists has allowed these questioners to be pushed neatly to the fringes as sad characters to be shunned, ridiculed or even feared. Books by mainstream journalists (like David Aaronovitch's *Voodoo Histories*)[2], which exist to knock down alternative views on recent history and falsely present all conspiracy theorists as far-right or even anti-Semitic extremists, are given massive media coverage, while the actual evidence presented by those being marginalized is given little or no airing and kept out of polite society. At the same time, fragile 'strawman' theories are forever pushed into the public eye via the tabloids and built up hugely, only to be quickly despatched. Mohammed Al Fayed's clearly doomed attempt —whatever the ultimate

The 'flame of Liberty' above the Pont de l'Alma underpass in Paris, where Princess Diana met her fate. Media hype over the 2008 inquest falsely inflated conspiracy speculation, only for it to be predictably knocked down by the final verdict, cleverly bringing all conspiracy theories into disrepute by association.

truth—to prove in the British High Court in 2008 that Princess Diana was murdered on the orders of Prince Philip provides a good example [pages 91 & 341]. With such an extreme accusation, and with important evidence oddly unpresented or deliberately withheld, it was clear from early on that a verdict to support the conspiracy view would be unlikely; yet certain tabloid newspapers screamed each new clue as sensational fact, before the predictable climb-down or subsequent silence. By loudly fanfaring weaker cases before the inevitable public demolition, all conspiracy theories are brought into disrepute by simple association. Yet the theories for which there is substantial evidence, such as the anomalies surrounding 9/11 [Chapter VIII], are largely ignored or singled out for ignorant dismissal by sneering columnists—usually by failing to address the evidence itself and personally attacking or stereotyping the researchers instead.

Why is there such a stigma against those who question the establishment view? Is it because they are, in fact, asking pertinent questions no-one else dares to about the mysteries and cover-ups that seem to surround us? Even a superficial glance at both history and the patterns of today confirms that

'Bonfire Night' in the UK. The annual 5th November parading of Guy Fawkes commemorates one of the most famous conspiracies of all time—yet we collectively struggle to accept that conspiracies still occur today.

such things have long been indelible components of our world, yet we live in a culture of denial. Indeed, conspiracies and a wide belief in supernatural forces may be underpinning the society we live in to a much greater degree than anyone suspects.

For all the scorn regularly poured upon it, conspiracy theory seems to become perfectly mainstream when it suits a purpose; when British traditions see effigies of Guy Fawkes burnt or exploded each November 5th, for instance, the country commemorates 'The Gunpowder Plot', one of the best-known historical conspiracies, which nearly saw the assassination of King James I. At the other end of the spectrum, the widely accepted—and promoted—belief that bin Laden and Al Qaeda perpetrated the 9/11 attacks is a modern conspiracy theory writ large (yet is never presented as such). And how many people today really believe that John F Kennedy was killed on the whim of a single fanatic with a personal agenda? Conspiracy theory only becomes a pariah when it's turned around and focused on the very people who want us to believe it of someone else.

The *Collins English Dictionary* defines 'conspiracy theory' as:

'The belief that the government or a covert organization is responsible for an event that is unusual or unexplained, especially when any such involvement is denied'.

Given this definition and the lessons that history, both ancient and modern, have to tell us about global deception, who can seriously deny that conspiracies are rife and very real? Theorizing about conspiracies is therefore a perfectly legitimate line of enquiry, and the term 'conspiracy theorist' is interchanged throughout this text with (the sometimes preferred) 'truthseeker' in a firmly non-abusive sense.

However, it is usually the conspiracy theorists that are held up to be the warped components of society, as far as the intellectuals we mysteriously appoint as our moral guardians in the media are concerned. Time and again we read cod-psychological treatise on the inherent dysfunctionality of conspiracy believers, often characterized as ignorant 'deniers' or 'anoraks' with few social skills and probably troubled backgrounds—unlike journalists, of course, who must all, by implication, be impeccable bastions of wisdom. Typical of such scathing negation is this entry from press columnist Polly Toynbee, who writes:

'Conspiracy theory journalism... abounds, assuming anything gleaned through a keyhole or leaked document reveals more truth than the big picture staring you in the face. Healthy skepticism easily tips into the conspiracy mindset, where dark motives lie behind everything... ...If no fact, history or official record can be trusted, then anything might be true and the world ceases to make sense or to be governable by common consent. It is a growing state of mind that, once it takes hold, spreads easily from small things to big beliefs. It needs a firm rebuttal, even when it invades relatively unimportant-seeming things—such as was Shakespeare really Shakespeare?' [3]

... The subtext of which would appear to be 'don't dare to ask questions about anything that isn't obvious'. We clearly shouldn't trouble our undeveloped minds about such things. But why not? Why shouldn't we be curious as to whether Shakespeare really wrote his own plays or whether they were ghost-written, or collaborations? Why wouldn't we want to know why something as huge as the Moon landings appears to have such shaky evidence to support it? Why can't we ask why overt occult symbolism appears in so much architecture and iconography? Why shouldn't it be questioned as to how nearly 3000 people died so easily on 9/11 when normal security procedures should have prevented it? Is the asking of these questions proof of a personality defect? If so, why is it that the people who are now calling society to account come from such a wide cross-section of class and education? Anoraks and fanatics we will always have with us, and they can be loud and undiscerning sometimes, but in recent years the ranks of the challengers have been swelled by a quiet and largely sensible majority.

Toynbee does make an important point to express that if 'anything might be true' then 'the world ceases to make sense or to be governable by common consent'. Many people believe this to be precisely the case, but are not allowed to express it. Suppressing debate isn't healthy and can lead to extremism—something the world has too much of. Toynbee's typical journalistic contempt implies that nothing requires evidence to support it in the conspiracy world and that all who question official dogmas are agitating fantasists. But most self-respecting truthseekers accept the need for clear presentation of reasoned evidence, and it is this approach that we will take here. Much of that evidence is persuasive enough that it deserves a fuller examination. [Interestingly, when this author attended a lecture by Polly Toynbee —renowned for her acerbic pen—and held up 9/11 as an area worthy of more serious study, in the flesh she proved far less willing to defend her views on conspiracy theorists and made vaguely conciliatory noises to avoid a conflict.]

From people tired of such lazy media dismissal, a world of 'truth movements' and campaigns has proliferated in these obvious days of global deception and political obfuscation—a sure sign that we have collectively lost faith in those making the big decisions on our behalf.

New Times, Old Suspicions

Much of this book is necessarily focused on things past, concentrating on events which have shaped the world we live in now. But the temptation to think that new eras leave behind the suspicions of old should be avoided. When Barack Obama had to re-swear his inaugural oath of allegiance as the 44th President of the United States of America the day after fluffing a line during his first attempt in front of millions of viewers on 20th January 2009 [photo, page 13], this was done 'out of an abundance of caution' and to avoid 'conspiracy theories'. This extraordinary action was a tacit acknowledgement of how widespread and influential conspiracy theorizing has become in recent years.

Within hours of Obama's inauguration, in amongst the joyous celebrations from those hailing his historical accession, the Internet was also awash with speculation from those less sure: as Obama hadn't spoken the correct oath (the word 'faithfully' got transposed to a less solid place in a sentence), was he, in fact, really president?[4] Was this a deliberate strategy so that he could not be held technically responsible for his actions if things went awry? With malicious rumors circulating that Obama's birth certificate might have been faked to enable him to take office, unpleasant echoes of the events which marred George W Bush's infamous 2001 presidential election 'victory', with its wide allegations of voting fraud, threatened to undermine the support of a minority, but clearly an influential one. If born outside the USA, Obama would not be eligible as president—some claim his real place of birth was Kenya, with not unreasonable grounds for their doubts given some of the anomalies in the 'official' certificate. The decision to re-take the inaugural oath illustrates that *every* action, no matter how small, is now under scrutiny from those who no longer trust authority; and those in power know it. Not that doing this in any way assuaged the doubts. If anything it raised further questions: Why was the second oath not filmed? Why did Obama not swear on a Bible this time? Were any of the first orders signed by Obama in the hours before the second oath legally binding? And so on.[4]

Such is the climate of doubt we live in today. Let down so many times by a system that, well-meaning or not, appears so often to be corrupt, coldly authoritarian and not running to programs that seem to benefit the common person, people have lost faith in their leaders and confidence is at an all-time low. The modern global financial disaster brought about by supposedly reckless bankers and negligent governments (but see page 73), together with many recent exposures of corruption, have rudely awakened a new and more eclectic portion of the population to considering alternative views on the way the world is run. Those they thought they could trust have proved themselves unworthy of such faith, and the consequences of the betrayal have trickled into everyday lives in a very tangible way, as jobs, savings and pensions have tumbled. The election of new leaders such as President Obama forever seems to raise

The White House, Washington DC. How much difference does a change of occupant really make to the way decisions are made? The presence of the same old faces in the background make many fear that the same old hidden agendas always remain in place.

touching hopes for real change, but rarely does it come, with nearly all politicians cast from the same flawed mould. The elevation of Obama saw supporting masses full of enthusiasm, which bucked the doubting trend for a short while, but the faith was wobbling in some just weeks after his inauguration, and the period after saw a sharp decline in his popularity, despite his second-term election. Who could, after all, live up to such high expectations, argue pundits, especially in a climate where only hard decisions, not crowd-pleasers, can be made?

Yet many outside of the polite mainstream, which had bordered on drooling hagiography during his first presidential electioneering, quickly pointed out that those who helped Obama to power behind the scenes appeared to be precisely the same characters who had helped create previous messes (such as political 'hawk' Zbigniew

Brzezinski, credited by some with actually creating Al Qaeda by masterminding the training of Afghan 'freedom fighters' following the 1979 Soviet invasion), and those Obama appointed to office were, predictably, the same breed of powermonger as before. Even George W Bush's Defense Secretary Robert M Gates, a member of the opposition Republican party, was initially retained from the previous administration.[5] These observations raised legitimate fears: was this just the same old agenda as before? Were the strings still being pulled from mysterious levels above? Those without faith in a system that appears always to be the same behind the scenes, no matter who is in charge, remained unconvinced that a savior had arrived. Indeed, some saw Obama as quite the opposite; a wolf in sheep's clothing. His failure to close the highly contentious Guantanamo Bay detention center [page 188], despite his many vocal promises to do so, for example, and the fact that within a single year he had sanctioned more assassinations in the Middle East than his predecessor had in two terms, only reinforced this view. The massive increase in drone attacks, and the new conflict against 'Islamic State'—the US having mysteriously failed to notice its creep before too late—with many resultant 'collateral' casualties, suggests to some that far from being over, the 'War on Terror' has simply entered a new and deadlier phase.[6]

So the times we find ourselves in now seem no less prone to suspicion and conspiratorial musings than before. Indeed, as economic gloom has continued on, resentment against politicians and, especially, bankers has grown, directly or indirectly encouraging civil unrest in countries such as Greece and also the UK, which saw student rioting in 2010 and an anarchic explosion of urban violence and looting in the summer of 2011 [page 305]. This raises the question in some minds as to whether such responses might be actively stimulated for the purpose of justifying more social control, as we shall explore. Certainly, rather than attempt to understand some of the wider processes that might lead to unrest, not least the huge financial inequalities which have seen class, and often racial, divisions deepen massively, instead those at the bottom of the ladder have effectively been scapegoated as the cause of society's woes, cheaply stereotyped as work-shy scroungers bringing down the economy. Executives at the top, meanwhile, continue to receive enormous bonuses, while everyday folk die from cold, afraid to put the heating on in a world of insane energy prices and falling savings. Such an imbalanced situation, combined with the ingrained culture of blatant political dishonesty, is bound to create a fractured culture. If authorities feel hurt that they are so often the target of conspiracy theories and mistrust, they only have themselves to blame.

Problematically, the age-old response from our leaders to a doubting population seems to be to distract them with bigger events elsewhere. Numerous truthseekers believe, for instance, that the multiple revolutions that swept the likes of Egypt, Tunisia, Libya and especially Syria, amongst other Arab states, with uncertain long-term outcomes, were manipulated from behind the scenes by Western powers either keen to increase their influence or provide useful diversions from problems at home.

Applying the Truth Agenda

If one turns around the naive assumption that the world is run for our collective benefit, and starts to consider just for a moment that it might, in fact, be run instead for the needs of an elite few, with their own murky plans, the uncomfortable result is that everything begins to make a horrible kind of sense and some of the unexplained mysteries and many dark cover-ups begin to form a pattern. Some things are mysteries through the simple absence of an answer. But certain areas may remain obscure because *somebody prefers it to be that way*. The purpose of this book is to explore the possible patterns that might be falling into place before our very eyes in these times of growing doubt and subterfuge. Many thinkers believe we stand at a pivotal moment in human history. Understanding the shape of it all could hold the key to unlocking the cell of ignorance which has perhaps held us imprisoned for far too long.

New York's Times Square announces the death of then Palestinian leader Yasser Arafat amongst its glitz in 2004—geopolitics and commercialism side by side in a world of instant communication. Yet such easy transmission of information also provides a perfect tool of universal propaganda for those who would rule by manipulation.

If there is, then, an underlying global agenda that does not have our best interests at heart, how do we identify and expose it so that mass-awareness and subsequent action might dispel its worst effects? Perhaps, in response, we need to create our own agenda—a 'truth agenda' —a process which simply looks again at the world as presented to us and asks whether the surface glamour and veneer of philanthropic intent holds up to logical scrutiny. Applying the Truth Agenda is a straightforward method of selecting significant events that have shaped our modern world, and starkly and methodically peering just under the veneer to see what lies beneath. In so doing, different underlying motivations to usual surface appearances often present themselves, and many underexposed details are revealed, as this book demonstrates. Such analysis is not original; many other concerned individuals share the task today, and others will doubtless join in. But we appear to live in times where getting to the heart of what is really going on seems to matter more than ever, especially with such sweeping global means of communication, blatant economic manipulation and technological influence now available to those who may have ambitious plans for centralization and concentration of power.

The 2010 WikiLeaks controversy, in which thousands of previously classified international diplomatic and military documents were released without permission on the Internet (and through selected newspapers), caused outrage amongst authorities, but conclusively demonstrated that dishonesty underpins almost every level of decision-making around the world. Yet the WikiLeaks information was merely scratching the surface. Indeed, aside from the doubts and legal complexities surrounding the curious figure of WikiLeaks' founder Julian Assange, many conspiracy believers suspect the organization to be either a victim of, or party to, a manipulation in itself, pointing to the rather selective nature of the subjects exposed. So far, for example, there has been a strange absence of even a sliver of information that might shed light on any aspect of 9/11, either to confirm or deny the official account [see Chapter VIII].[7] However, WikiLeaks has at least served the purpose of further flagging up a different way of looking at the world to a previously dormant public. The more souls who can raise awareness of what might be occurring to our collective detriment, the more chance there is of creating a positive collective solution. This book is but one more small contribution to the process, but the hope here is to encapsulate in an accessible and coherent way many of the key issues, as identified by the world of truthseeking, that can seem confusing and overwhelming to the uninitiated.

Over the years, investigations by many intrepid researchers (including this author) into unexplained phenomena have revealed how a systemic underlying belief in the supernatural and esoterica, and, indeed, participation in conspiracies, has shaped our civilization. This is denied, of course, and paradoxically a veneer of logical scientism is generally presented to us as the foundation of modern society—but the reality is that deeper scrutiny reveals something else altogether. By applying the Truth Agenda to a series of what may at first appear to be unrelated elements, it becomes apparent that there is a linking thread connecting many of the power and belief structures that shape the civilization we live in today. These, in turn, almost certainly play a part in fuelling the control issues that increasingly bind us, as the unfolding of the subsequent chapters will hopefully demonstrate.

THE TRUTH AGENDA: *Doubts about the way the world is being run today are leading an increasing number of people to reconsider 'conspiracy theories' in a new light. If the world is not being run for our benefit, then whose? Changes of political administrations briefly raise hopes for new eras, but the continued policies and inherent dishonesties of old mean that doubts among the public and probing enquiries from truthseekers remain legitimate. Applying a simple process of analysis to the key events of recent history may reveal important hidden layers, offering clues to the real agendas motivating our society.*

The monuments of Giza, Egypt. For all their reknown and the many archaeological guesses, no-one really knows how or why the pyramids were made—yet another mystery we take for granted.

II   MYSTERIES ANCIENT AND MODERN

There are many mysteries around us, which suggest that the world may not be quite as it seems—but as a culture we often like to pretend otherwise. It is always implied that everything is neatly explained and pigeonholed, and we are easily distracted from further investigation by intellectual snobbery or active debunking. Yet becoming more aware of unresolved enigmas can awaken people in unexpected ways. Two mysteries in particular provide good inspiration, one ancient, one modern; the pyramids and crop circles.

The Giza Challenge

Mystery is in the fabric of everything around us, although we soon learn to co-exist with it and, eventually, forget it is there at all. The famous Egyptian pyramids on the Giza plateau stand as a perfect example of a mystery we all live with comfortably. Gigantic, awe-inspiring, they continue to fascinate each generation. Their images adorn calendars, book covers, posters and all manner of merchandise. With blocks so perfectly cut and placed that not even paper can go between them, the pyramids remain the finest example of human architectural genius. Although their original perfection has been marred (their gleamingly smooth outer walls having been largely removed), what we see today would still be a challenge for modern construction techniques. Indeed, the truth is that no-one knows for sure how they were made.

Yet despite this vacuum of knowledge, we continually see television reconstructions of how the pyramids *must* have been made—teams of sweating manual labour hauling massive slabs with ropes and rollers up gargantuan masonry ramps, almost as big as the pyramids themselves. We are more often than not told that ramps are the obvious solution. Indeed, a television attempt to build just a very small modern pyramid a few years ago could find no other way of lifting the blocks to the top. And yet there is no archaeological evidence whatsoever that such ramps were ever built. Their scale and robustness would have been such that surely some trace of their structure would be left today in the sands beneath Giza, but excavations and numerous searches have revealed nothing. One more recent suggestion is that *internal* ramps may have been used, but it all remains highly speculative.[1]

When adventurous souls suggest the possibility that levitation techniques—perhaps using high-frequency sound—might have been used to construct the Egyptian monuments, the intellectuals and archaeological establishment laugh them down, despite some historical suggestions that such an art once existed (even Ian Lawton and Ian Ogilvie-Herald's otherwise skeptical book *Giza: The Truth* accepts the possibility of levitation, but the very act of considering this also pushes them into the realm of the 'alternative' as far as academics are concerned).[2] And so ramps and slaves continue to parade across our screens, and anyone who challenges is described as a 'pyramidiot'. Intellectualism and the darker side of 'peer review', as always, ensure nothing upsets the long-established hypotheses of the academic world—even when they are essentially assumptions and not necessarily supported by facts.

In truth, we do not even know for certain when the pyramids were built, let alone how or why. Traditional Egyptology puts their construction between around 2589 and 2504 BCE during the Fourth Dynasty of the 'Old Kingdom', but less conventional researchers have claimed a date of much greater antiquity. The sphinx, certainly, displays stone weathering perhaps suggestive of a much older, wetter age, though all of this remains in heavy contention—or not. Standard archaeology simply dismisses each of the alternative theories on an equal basis. The dates have been set, the books have been written, and those who question the presumptions of the elder scholars are sidelined and ridiculed.

As to their purpose, the long-held view that the pyramids are simple, if elaborate, tombs continues to pervade the official doctrine, but this simplistic take on these huge structures has been widely challenged, as it fails to take into account many unexplained aspects of their construction and placement. These include possible astronomical features, with a popular belief that the three main pyramids of Giza represent a huge ground plan of the belt of Orion and that thin shafts in the Great Pyramid were once aligned to specific stars.[3] Others vigorously disagree, of course, and there are far too many other alternative theories to explore here, ranging from claims that the structures are 'power-plants', to the concept that they represent geometrical scale models of the planet and stand as a commemoration of a global axis tilt that took place around 10,500 BC. But the plethora of astonishing mathematical correlations and coincidences in the angles and constructions at Giza do seem to demand attention, not least the remarkable fact that the plateau (taking the latitude of 29.5 degrees and longitude of 31 degrees as the 'two lines that cover the most combined land area in the world') stands at the precise center point of all the land masses of the Earth.[4]

The pyramids still stand as the most astounding structures ever built. While academic speculation gives the impression that their construction and purpose is explainable, the fact is that our understanding of them remains very limited—just one more global mystery we live with amongst many others.

While some of the proposals almost certainly do strain credulity, the fact is that a large number of keen researchers believe there is a major hidden

purpose to the pyramids. Some of these ideas, at least, surely deserve a greater level of scrutiny—yet anything that falls even slightly outside the narrow parameters set by the establishment is not acceptable for investigation by the intellectual elite. (To answer a common question here, these qualms do not necessarily equate to a promotion of the idea of extra-terrestrial influence in ancient Egyptian monument building, although some readers may be interested in the biblical references to the mysterious 'sons of God' and the Nephilim in Chapter V).

The Giza plateau stands at the exact center of all the land masses on Earth—surely not a coincidence, but a fascinating observation that remains undiscussed by standard Egyptology.

The ultimate truth of all the pyramidal arguments is not the point here. The Giza challenge is merely illustrative of how the world tends to treat enduring mystery: it simply pretends there isn't any. When the Truth Agenda is applied to the pyramids, definitive answers are not forthcoming, yet the impression is given that all is understood and neatly wrapped-up. When events accumulate too far beyond the mundane and authorities can't pretend anymore, that's when the cover-ups begin (as with UFOs, as we shall see). Some observers, of course, believe the ancient wisdom (if not the technical wizardry), occult knowledge and system of authority displayed by the civilization which worked so hard at Giza *is* preserved and coveted by secret societies and elite bodies who use it to further their own ends in today's world [Chapter V]. Whilst academic protectionism may explain some of the closed-mindedness, other hardcore doubters have alleged the operation of deliberate archaeological cover-ups to conceal humankind's true, and possibly much older, origins.[5]

The Crop Circle Controversy

Another mystery which the mainstream has managed to turn its back on in the hope that it will go away is the ever-enduring phenomenon of crop circles. For years now (indeed, several centuries, according to records), increasingly elaborate shapes have been appearing swirled into crop fields around the globe, with the activity's epicenter being in the English heartlands of Wiltshire. Despite everything routinely espoused about the circles—usually that all of them are made by clever artists, students or drunk farmhands—the absolute truth is that the origins of a large number of them are completely unknown. For all the confirmed or suspected man-made designs, however many, there is a significant proportion of crop formations that seems impossible to explain so simply.

Yet, once again, any sense of mystery is brushed aside by self-appointed intellectuals at one end of the spectrum, and ill-informed journalists and television producers at the other. Seeing in the research community nothing more than speculative talk (largely in favor of a non-human origin) about forces of consciousness, extra-terrestrials or hitherto unknown odd natural processes, it is assumed by establishment pundits that the only real explanation can be the one demonstrated so often in front of cameras —man-made japery with planks, ropes and rollers. But in settling for this weakest of assumptions, skeptics ignore the large amounts of evidence comprising multiple eye-witness sightings of crop circles appearing within just seconds, biological changes of note occurring within the flattened plants, the many reports of bizarre aerial phenomena, the astonishingly complex geometry of a large number of designs, and all manner of very remarkable visual

This staggering crop formation arrived at Milk Hill, Wiltshire, UK, on 12th August 2001. At 800 feet in diameter, it comprises 409 circles and is considered one of the finest works of the phenomenon. The media assure us that all such designs are made by clever jokers, but the evidence does not support this view.

and physiological experiences recounted by numerous people. How are these to be accounted for by the planker hypothesis, which would have it that all formations are of human origin? Repeated manual attempts to recreate many of the less explicable qualities of crop circles have failed or taken unrealistic time and effort, with limited results. Modest man-made formations can take several hours to construct, yet some exquisitely complex designs have been proven to have appeared within prohibitively short periods of time. Nonetheless, heroes are made of hoaxers and the important contrary evidence is simply brushed aside in the mainstream, restoring the cosy order of a 'normal' world with reassuring propaganda that tells us there is nothing in the fields to be interested in (or afraid of).

It is not for these pages to explore the detailed arguments around the crop circle enigma, and this author has written extensively about it elsewhere (see *Appendix 3*).

THE TRUTH AGENDA

Readers must discover and assess the evidence for themselves. However, it is another example of a mystery we live with that is pushed to the fringes, ignored and very possibly covered up. Without wanting to slip into paranoia, there is good reason to believe that some of the voracious debunking which has fallen on the circles has been deliberately organized by hands unknown, anxious that we should not be drawn to a phenomenon that might actually inspire people to *think*—which it does.

The 1991 claims of the two aging pranksters Doug and Dave, that they had invented the entire circle mystery as a novel retirement activity, succeeded in persuading much of the public that nothing of interest was going on. Yet no evidence was ever presented to show that the duo had made more than a few very unimpressive formations. The non-existence of the press agency which put out the Doug and Dave story (the mysterious 'MBF Services' turned out not to be contactable, as a press agency at least, and certain traces led some to suspect MI5 involvement), together with other strange discrepancies and a general lack of conviction, led to a wide view that the whole exercise was a distractive cover-up.[6] If so, it worked well, with a notable fall of interest in the crop circles following the supposed exposé. However, the continuation and grand evolution of the phenomenon long after the comic elderly pair had retired from the scene reawakened a general interest which has endured, if reduced in scale from its previous heights. Some formations *are* clearly man-made, but many defy explanation in such terms. Perhaps that is why further debunking exercises and deceptions still occur from time to time, with new claimants having replaced Doug and Dave since.

Rumors of official government orders to the media to withhold information on the circles and experiments around them persist, and the skeptic stories that do the rounds of press and television have been blamed on everything from the Vatican to the military or CSICOP (the Committee for the Scientific Investigation of Claims of the Paranormal —today known as the Committee for Skeptical Inquiry—a self-appointed Inquisition-like group of savagely fundamentalist academics). A lot of energy certainly seems to have been put into attacking something so

This formation appeared at Boxley, Kent, UK, on 7th August 2006. Although Wiltshire is the epicenter of the crop circle mystery, other English counties also receive patterns, as do other countries around the world.

Mysteries, Miracles & Global Deception

apparently harmless. All of which leads people to wonder why. Does someone on high know something we don't? A study of crop circles by the British Ministry of Defense in the 1980s reportedly concluded that a phenomenon without mundane origins *was* occurring, and tests carried out by ADAS (Agricultural Development and Advisory Service, a division of the British Ministry of Agriculture) in 1995 revealed unexplained anomalies in nitrogen and nitrate ratios in the soil beneath crop formations.[7] The military have also shown a notable interest over the years. It may be that authorities know full well that something of significance is happening in the fields, but they would rather the general populace didn't share their interest.

The fact is that the apparently engineered stigma of ridicule that has grown up around the circle phenomenon has allowed otherwise enquiring minds to be turned away from the potential learning that could be gained from it. Any debunking policies have certainly been successful. Indeed, the very act of including crop circles in this book of generally 'harder' subjects will be used by some to discredit all the other information within it. Perhaps that is why I purposefully include it—because applying the Truth Agenda means being able to look anything and everything in the eye with a fresh perspective. Certainly, it is a fact that some of the truthseekers dealing today with very real-world issues would not be there without the original stimuli of thought provided by these exquisite glyphs, whatever their origins.

Like the pyramids, the awesome presence of the crop glyphs and the subsequent questioning they help stimulate, even through simply contemplating the possibility of higher intervention versus human art, has inspired an advanced level of thinking —and changed the world as a result. Aside from the evolution of consciousness, which seems to arise from the inner debate each person must have when faced with both beauty and enigma, there is also a direct influence, however. Some of the symbolism in the fields clearly echoes ancient wisdoms or archetypal psychological forms, and many aficionados speak of having been 'woken up' inside on a very deep, inexplicable

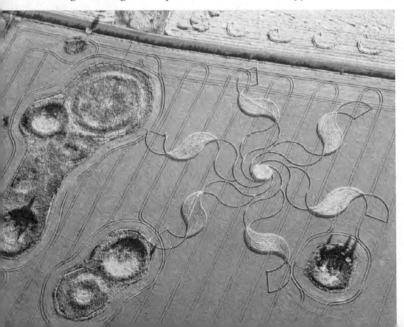

A 750-feet crop formation surrounded by round barrows (burial mounds) near Stonehenge, Wiltshire, UK, 4th July 2002. Ancient sites and underground water seem to attract—or help generate—crop circles, perhaps through natural 'earth energies', leading some to speculate that a combination of forces is at work.

level. The astronomical data contained within other designs has specifically indicated future dates and times which, when they have arrived, have coincided with unusual—and unpredictable—celestial events, sometimes referencing the cycles of the Sun [Chapter XII], factors which may play a key role in our future.[8] Meanwhile, the recurring symbolic references to the ancient prophecies concerning the 'New Era' which began on 21st December 2012—still the subject of much speculation, as we shall see—have led to a broad alternative acceptance of the crop circles as just

one more herald of some imminent and significant event for our planet. Indeed, the hopes and fears surrounding insights into our own future bind together many of the complex mysteries and cover-ups that may well be a major influence in the hidden agendas governing us today.

Other Mysteries

The pyramids and the crop circles are just two examples of mysteries that are lightly dismissed, yet remain entirely unresolved. There are many others which could be listed here, outside of the usual novelties so often inappropriately lumped in with them by a lazy media; Bigfoot, the Loch Ness Monster, big cats, etc., all of which may or may not exist, but hardly carry the same weight of evidence or influence lives on anything like the same profound

Many crop circles display complex detail even at close quarters, such as this tight swirl seen inside part of another formation at Milk Hill, Wiltshire, UK, on 8th August 1997.

level. The more relevant examples include religious apparitions [Chapter IV], out-of-body experiences (verified as more than simple hallucination by much evidence), and ghosts (witnessed by so many reliable people, but scoffed at and sidelined by the 'rationalists'). In any given auditorium, it is fairly easy to find at least two or three perfectly rational individuals with a convincing ghost story to tell.

The latter two phenomena seem strongly to suggest that consciousness can exist outside of the flesh under specific circumstances. Many patients in hospitals have reported finding themselves floating above their own bodies while under general anaesthetic, and have been able to move their disembodied minds around, later describing seeing objects in high places that couldn't possibly have been visible from ground level (as verified by staff). Some researchers have turned this ability into the directed art of 'remote viewing', in which minds are seemingly able to travel to far away or hidden places, often accurately describing layouts or objects, which are later confirmed. That extensive military experiments with remote viewing and other psychic techniques are fully known to have been conducted suggests that this is something taken seriously by higher authorities.

A more physical manifestation of mystery is the disturbing animal mutilation enigma, in which cattle and other livestock are found with specific organs seamlessly and bloodlessly removed, often after sightings of strange aerial phenomena [page 47]. It says something that thousands of cases have been reported over the years, yet most everyday folk have never heard of the phenomenon.

Other seekers are excited by speculation over the origins of the much-debunked but still enigmatic crystal skulls found around the world [see photo], or are fired by the joys of psychic questing and mediumistic channelling. Some researchers explore the possibilities offered by earth mysteries (the ethereal 'energies' around ancient stones and landmarks) and the curious geometrical connections of complexes like Avebury in Wiltshire (site of so many crop circles) with alleged remains of civilizations on Mars. The 'face' and pyramids on the Martian plains of Cydonia have been somewhat reduced in stature by increasingly clear orbital photos which suggest less definite forms, but they are still held by believers to be significant, as are other strange images of what look like buildings and even trees. NASA ignores all such interpretations, but there is evidence that some Martian

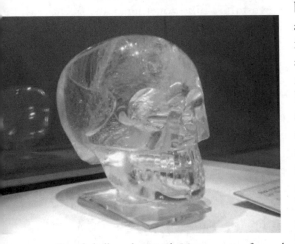

Crystal skull at the British Museum, one of several found across the globe. Although mercilessly debunked and now generally claimed to have been manufactured in 19th century Europe (as opposed to being from Aztec and Maya times, as many believed), the technique behind their astonishingly perfect carving and finish has still never been fully explained.

aerial photographic evidence may well have been edited for public consumption, which raises serious questions as to whether information is being kept from us.[9]

Some mysteries, however, are so much in plain sight that, paradoxically, they are the most quickly forgotten. When a huge and geometrically perfect glowing spiral appeared over the night skies of Norway on 9th December 2009, lasting around twelve minutes, it was witnessed by thousands of observers and widely filmed [see photos]. Even the mass-media couldn't ignore it. However, by compliantly repeating the entirely unproven official explanation that it was a malfunctioning Russian missile (questionable, given the 'supportive' circulated footage of a very different-looking off-course US rocket wobbling across the sky in an unruly fashion), it soon helped wipe the public memory. Few remember it today. Yet other spirals have since been seen across the world (including one at Australia's Gold Coast on 5th June 2010 and another over Israel and Jordan on 7th June 2012), leading to speculation that the testing of some energy weapon device or a spin-off from the HAARP Project [page 70] is more likely to be responsible, especially given the proximity of a HAARP station to the Norway event.[10]

There are many unexplained mysteries to investigate, but we do not need to sift the entire pantheon here. The key point is that the world, which so often presents itself as neatly ordered and understood, may not be quite the tidy package of reason and honesty we are told it is. As such, we need to focus on specific areas that have something important to say about these times of perhaps unparalleled philosophical, social and political change.

Applying the Truth Agenda reveals holes in the official explanations for many of the

The 2009 Norway sky spiral in two of its stages, as witnessed by thousands. Note the curious, if coincidental, resemblance of the 'dark hole' stage [lower] to the Fatima 'Sun' of 1917 [page 58].

mysteries that have been so lightly touched on by the mainstream, and there is good evidence to suggest that full knowledge of them has been continually discouraged by intellectual elitism, distraction or active debunking, as with the crop circles. However, one area in particular shows very good evidence that full-blown cover-ups *are* instigated, and for this we must enter the twilight realm of ufology.

THE TRUTH AGENDA: *Academic elitism and a wide encouragement of skepticism too often prevents warranted enquiry into mysteries and phenomena that could provide valuable information or generate higher aspirations. A closed establishment prevents full investigation of archaeological monuments such as the pyramids, while fervent debunking seems designed to deflect interest away from 'paranormal' enigmas like crop circles, suggesting that important seams of knowledge are being kept from the general populace.*

The legendary military base Area 51, Nevada, USA. This official aerial shot was taken in 1968 and more runways have been constructed since. Many people believe that military technology is being reverse-engineered from recovered extra-terrestrial craft secretly stored here.

III   UFOS

Something strange is flying in our skies. Are UFOs extra-terrestrial or military? Either way, there is clear evidence that full knowledge of them is kept from us. The mystery surrounding this one phenomenon is confirmation that we are clearly NOT told the truth about everything. Yet many people claim to have had encounters with non-human creatures that have left them with a profound sense of expectation about the future.

The Roswell Incident

On 7th July 1947, a New Mexico-based newspaper, *The Roswell Daily Record*, sported an extraordinary headline—*RAAF Captures Flying Saucer on Ranch in Roswell Region.* In that decade this wasn't treated as a joke. Ever-increasing sightings of strange flying objects were being made then and, in a climate of post-war paranoia, any unusual craft or aerial light had the potential to be an unknown external threat. During World War II, bomber pilots even had a nick-name for the peculiar glowing orbs that would sometimes accompany their flight paths—'foo fighters'. These lights, feared at the time to be enemy surveillance devices, were never adequately explained.

Therefore, when a newspaper reported that a flying saucer had crashed in the desert near the town of Roswell, many in 1947 were happy to accept that this was exactly what had happened. Over time, other claimed details began to emerge—bodies of thin, grey alien creatures were reported to have been retrieved from the craft and the area of debris around it, and secretly carried to the local hospital. Military personnel had moved in and cordoned off the area and were planning to retrieve the crashed 'flying disk' for examination. Ever since that fateful headline, the Roswell incident has entered modern mythology; the subject of intense speculation, investigation— and denial. And deny it the authorities did. Alarmed to see news of a direct alien intervention being splashed over the front pages, the Roswell Army Air Field (RAAF) public relations team sprang into action and the next day declared that the crash had involved nothing more than a 'weather balloon'. Soon, the attention around Roswell died down, leaving a vacuum of information which would be gradually filled by the curious, accurately or not, over the next few decades.

One of the RAAF officers who nervously displayed bits of wood and foil from the supposed weather balloon for the press cameras the day after the Roswell incident was Major Jesse Marcel. Marcel had been directly involved with cataloging debris from the crash site and had seen for himself what had been retrieved. Interviewed in 1978 by ufologist Stanton T Friedman, Marcel claimed that the weather balloon story was a decoy and that he had been ordered to front a debunking story. He maintained that he had indeed witnessed for himself unexplained artefacts at Roswell, which appeared to have non-terrestrial origins, and he described strange materials with unusual properties and objects with unrecognizable 'hieroglyphs' on them. In his opinion, an alien craft *was* recovered from the site, and he adhered to this claim until his death. Marcel's children, who were shown some of the debris by their father at the time, continue to support his story today.

As the Marcel testimony became public, so other witnesses from the Roswell event came forward to fill in more details. Although Marcel never saw the full crashed disk for himself, others said they did. Some military personnel and hospital staff claimed to remember five 'alien bodies' being brought in for autopsy, with more than one assertion that one of the creatures was still alive. Several staff reported being intimidated and threatened by sinister officials, who told them to keep quiet about what they had seen.

These are the claims, at least. As the decades have gone by, it has become more difficult to know what really happened at Roswell. Skeptics claim the various testimonies are misremembered minor incidents or full-blown fantasies, while others maintain that a massive cover-up took place. What is certain is that *something* came down near Roswell in 1947, exotic or mundane. It is also interesting to note that the official cover story has altered over the years. By 1995, the innocent weather balloon account had morphed into the object being a secret US government device from Project Mogul, a program to detect sound waves from Soviet atomic tests. Just two years after that it was being suggested that the retrieved 'bodies' might in fact have existed, but were nothing more than crash test dummies being used in an experiment. But why take a crash test dummy to an actual hospital? And what would that have to do with Project Mogul?

For all the clear mythologizing and layers of misinformation regarding the Roswell incident, from both official and ufological sources, the fact is that stories of the event have been instrumental in stirring up interest in the many, many other reports of possible extra-terrestrial intrusions into our world. And what did happen to the supposed disk that was recovered? Some believe they know where it was taken.

The Little A'le'inn *in Nevada, USA, the tourist-face of a subject some believe is a serious business. Just a little way from here is Area 51, a top secret base where many people suspect that the craft retrieved from Roswell—amongst other artefacts—is stored.*

Area 51

UFO folklore has it that the crashed Roswell craft

is stored at a fabled US military base, code-named 'Area 51'. Situated in southern Nevada, and also sometimes known as 'Dreamland', Area 51 does exist, but such secrecy has surrounded its real purpose that it has become the subject of huge conspiracy speculation and has sparked several science fiction bonanzas (of which the alien-invasion blockbuster *Independence Day* is but one cheesy example).

Area 51 is ostensibly a test area for secret weapons and experimental aircraft, and its existence is only periphally acknowledged by the US military. Nothing is known for sure about its real purpose, but a large no-fly zone surrounds it and no-one gets in or out without major security clearance. That security has tightened in recent years. In previous decades it was possible to get close enough to Area 51 for several surreptitious camera crews and UFO investigators to have filmed clearly anomalous flying objects performing highly unusual manoeuvres over the base. Perhaps realizing that it had become an attractive circus for truthseekers, the authorities eventually extended the perimeters beyond visual range.

Groom Lake Road, Nevada, USA. This dusty track leads to the mysterious Area 51, and is about as much as anyone can now see from the ground, its barbed perimeter fences having been greatly extended in recent years.

Anyone trying to get closer today will soon find themselves arrested.

A number of rumors and claims from supposed ex-insiders have surfaced over the years as to the purpose of Area 51 and its nearby bases. The recurring theme of the testimonies is that beneath the grim-looking runways and barracks is an extensive network of hangars holding within them retrieved craft from the likes of Roswell—and more besides, including organic specimens. The supposed intention behind all of this is to examine the extra-terrestrial technology and reverse-engineer it into new devices for military means. Some observers believe secrets from other-worldly technology have already been applied in usable vehicles, such as 'stealth' aircraft, which, oddly enough, bear a slight resemblance to some of the mysterious 'black triangles' that many have sighted in the skies over the years. Others think it has already gone a stage further, believing that most or many of the UFOs seen today are military experiments. Even the Nazis are known to have experimented with primitive flying saucers, so what might be possible today?

It is also speculated that less dangerous alien secrets may have already leaked into mainstream science—some believe the development of microchip and nanotechnology could have been stimulated in the same way. If the US military has been using information from recovered UFOs to gain a military and economical advantage, there is, of course, no reason why other countries might not be doing the same—saucer crashes have been rumored around the world. The whole recent history of technological progress may, in this view, have been influenced, albeit indirectly, by extra-terrestrial intervention if the claims are to be believed. Persistent stories say that governments—the US, in particular—are actually working in cahoots with beings from other worlds, for reasons good or evil. (The hit television series *The X-Files* based much of its central concept around this idea.)

The more incredulous, naturally, dismiss all talk of ETs, and hold that the entire UFO mystery is a product of purely human secret technology, or consider aerial sightings as nothing more than atmospheric phenomena and misreported mundanities. Others, such as Ian R Crane—without dismissing the possibility of real alien presences—have proposed that a deliberately stimulated cultural awareness of ETs is the first stage of a planned *faked* alien invasion [page 47] designed to further the ultimate aims of the global control agenda discussed in this book.

The sign that greets any would-be visitors to Area 51. What does go on inside has never been officially revealed, but the 'deadly force authorized' warnings make it clear that we are not supposed to try to find out.

The important point here is that with Area 51 and the obvious withholding of information on UFOs in general (see below), we have clear evidence of a cover-up, whatever the truth. Although there are plenty of other secret research facilities hidden away in all major countries, there is usually some kind of official explanation to account for their existence. Even if it is just military technology that is being hidden, the fact that so little information about what goes on at Area 51 has been made available, and that all attempts at prising details from authorities are resisted, plainly means that someone doesn't want those on the outside to know what's going on. It would seem that this is but one layer of our society—amongst many others—that is being kept from us, beyond the usual bureaucratic closets, knowledge of which is denied even to the taxpayers that support its existence. All of this secrecy is for our safety and 'national security', we are told.

UFO Evidence

What direct evidence is there that knowledge of UFOs is withheld from us?

Whichever way it is looked at, something strange appears to be flying in our skies, despite the denials of the skeptics. This author, for example, has been approached at lectures many times by commercial pilots who have witnessed craft and other aerial phenomena that seem to defy normal explanation, reports of which are without question kept quiet about in the aviation industry. Numerous people have recounted extraordinary experiences, and many thousands of seemingly rational people around the globe have witnessed flying disks, the aforementioned black triangles, clusters of lights and other objects that all seem to suggest something out of the ordinary is occurring, human or alien. Even when one takes the fantasists, frauds and the merely mistaken out of the equation, there is still a formidable body of highly anomalous sightings that cannot be ignored, and they are taking place all the time. Not everything can be Chinese lanterns or misreported views of Venus (which admittedly make up a certain percentage of sightings), as the likes of cynical TV astronomers would have us believe, and nor has interest in UFOs diminished, despite misleading media coverage which comes around like clockwork every two years or so telling us otherwise, usually when obscure ufology groups break up in favor of using the Internet to network instead; minor developments used to fuel entirely false stories.

UFO 'flaps' (large numbers of reports in one area) have been going on around the world for many years. England had its own in the Warminster area in the 1970s, for instance, and the much-disputed incident at Rendlesham Forest, Suffolk, near RAF Woodbridge in 1980 has become the UK's very own Roswell, equally prone to both denial and mythologizing. United States Air Force (USAF) personnel based there allegedly witnessed a conical craft hovering in the woods, one which supposedly deactivated the nuclear missiles secretly stored nearby, a recurring and striking feature of military UFO reports. Colonel Robert Salas reports a very similar event occurring at the US Malmstrom Air Force Base in 1967, raising some disturbing questions about the apparently omnipotent capabilities of such craft.[1] In the 1990s, Nick Pope, an ex-Ministry of Defense employee, insisted that one of his duties during his employment had been researching UFOs and that the MOD had been actively suppressing information. Although some have accused him of exaggeration (and even of spreading deliberate misinformation), it seems clear that those in power know far more about UFO-related events than anyone is prepared to let on.

It is interesting to note that one of the most pressured extradition cases in recent history, in which the US sought to bring UK resident Gary McKinnon to trial in the States, concerned McKinnon's (admitted) 'hacking' of US military databases, ostensibly to try to find information on UFOs and secret anti-gravity technology. He claimed to have found proof for both by his actions. The disproportionate vigor with which the American legal teams attempted to extradite McKinnon (despite his having been diagnosed as suffering from Asperger's Syndrome, a form of autism) suggested that they were particularly keen to make an example of him, one which might dissuade others from pursuing the truth on UFOs, despite their claim that the concerns merely revolved around 'national security'. More serious espionage had not received such attention, and any prosecutions had previously been allowed to take place in the native countries of the defendants. McKinnon faced a potential 70-year sentence if tried and found guilty in the US. Common sense finally prevailed in 2012, when Britain decided to block any further US extradition attempts, but McKinnon's legal team had to fight its way through both the British High Court and the European Court of Human Rights to achieve this result.[2]

Alleged shot of the classic 'black triangle' variety of UFO, filmed at Wallonia, Belgium, 15th June 1990. Although saucer or cigar-shapes are the most commonly reported objects, the triangles have been seen many times—but are they alien or military?

As far as global UFO sightings go, in recent decades Mexico City seems to have been the center of a quite astonishing series of events. Whole fleets of shining spherical objects and other variations have been seen—and videoed—by many different people across the city at the same time. Aztec and Maya prophecies of coming global change [Chapter XII], and mystical intrigues surrounding the nearby volcanic mountain Popocatépetl, have all added to the portentous sense of mystery which has built up around the flap. Indeed, the Mexican Air Force (Fuerza Aérea Mexicana) is the only authoritative body in the world to have officially acknowledged the existence of the UFO phenomenon as something it is concerned by and interested in, although it remains open as to what the objects are. Other cities around the world have also seen mass sightings, but Mexico and the Southern American countries below it seem particularly prone. In 2013, Canada's former minister of National Defense, Paul Hellyer, went public with his belief that UFOs are real and that ETs are working with the US government, if expressed as a personal rather than an official view.

Previously, the only authorized study of UFOs admitted to by a government was Project Blue Book, carried out by the USAF, which investigated over 12,000 sightings between 1952 and 1969 (and almost certainly beyond, but officially their interest stopped there). Perhaps predictably, the final report in 1970 dourly concluded that UFOs did not constitute 'a threat to national security' and that the vast majority of sightings were 'misidentifications of natural phenomena or conventional aircraft'. It completely brushed over the not insignificant 22% of cases that 'remained unsolved'. The British government has also from time to time (most recently between 2008-2012) declassified reports of UFOs, but with equal lack of commitment or clarity.

However, there are 'Freedom of Information Acts', both in the USA and the

UK. What happens when these are applied and hard-to-get official documents are sought so that the public can make up their own minds on the evidence? Are such documents ever released? Surprisingly, they are, if authorities are compelled enough by dedicated campaigners prepared to go through the layers of red tape. Unfortunately, in most cases where there is even a small suggestion of anything out of the ordinary, what enquirers eventually get presented with are pages with vast swathes of text obscured by black blocks to prevent the crucial details from being read—in the name of protecting the 'national security' that Project Blue Book said UFOs weren't a threat to. So the documents get released, but the secrets stay put.

Campaigners like Dr Steven Greer have soldiered on with efforts such as the Disclosure Project to stimulate governments into releasing the truth by helping 'military, intelligence, government, corporate and scientific' whistleblowers to testify publicly with their UFO and ET technology experiences.[3] However, debunkers do their worst and authorities simply ignore, so it remains an uphill, if noble, struggle that is likely to continue for a while yet before any real recognition is gained, short of an extraordinary event occurring.

With the UFO mystery, then, there is crystal clear evidence of an ongoing cover-up. If the governments of the world aren't going to speak up, however, then we have to turn to civilians who have claimed personal experiences with UFOs and their occupants to see what they have to say. And what some of them report has repercussions that lead us onto an important underlying belief that might be shaping our world today—the expectation of imminent transformational change.

Contactee Experiences

One of the most controversial of all the UFO-related areas is that of 'contactees'; people who claim to have had direct encounters with extra-terrestrial beings. Some describe having been physically abducted onto hovering craft, while others recount being taken from their beds at night by teleportation techniques or through some form of astral projection. Tales of strange physical examinations and even surgical operations being carried out on the abductees by alien creatures are widespread, particularly in the USA, where thousands of claimed abductions have been recorded. The beings described are typically (as at Roswell) the small, slender grey humanoid figures with dark almond-shaped eyes that have become the archetypal extra-terrestrial in the public mind. Other races have also been reported, such as the 'Nordics' (tall, handsome blonde figures), reptilian beings [page 84] and preying mantis-like presences, but the 'greys' remain the most prevalent visitors.

The first contactee story to reach wide public attention concerned Betty and Barney Hill on 19th September 1961. While driving along a quiet road late at night in New Hampshire, USA, they described observing a bright disk-shaped object approach their car. Frightened and curious, Barney stepped out into the road to look more closely. Seeing 'humanoid figures' inside the craft, and feeling threatened by them, the couple decided to drive away, only to enter a strange state of altered consciousness instead. There is uncertainty about what happened next. From information based on disturbing dreams received by Betty after the experience, and hypnosis sessions held later to decipher what had happened during their altered state, they pieced together a scenario familiar from many other contactee accounts since; the medical procedures (which often center around the reproductive organs), fragmented conversations with the beings, and even a moment where Betty was shown an astronomical map outlining the star system from where the visitors had originated.

So many people around the world have had similar experiences—often reported by children, unaware of others having had the same encounters—that it's hard to believe all of it could be lies or imagination. Yet on what level of 'reality' these abductions take place is debatable. Do they occur in the physical dimension, or in the realm of the mind? Are they extra-terrestrial encounters or inner psychotic episodes triggered by psychic or electromagnetic stimuli (which has been shown to give rise to hallucinogenic visions—page 255)?

Extensive investigations by non-ufological enquirers have turned up interesting results. Before his tragic and untimely death in 2004 (run over by a drunken driver, raising inevitable conspiracy speculation), John E Mack, a Harvard professor of psychiatry, endured peer ridicule and academic censure before succeeding in his quest to get the psychological community to acknowledge the scientific validity of the contactee/adbuctee phenomenon. During his studies, he interviewed sixty people and subjected them to rigorous interview and hypnotic regression. Mack found himself convinced that, whatever the exact nature of the contactees' experiences, *they* believed them to be real. With just a few exceptions, he concluded that most of those investigated were well-balanced and reliable witnesses doing their best to describe extraordinary events, which had occurred on at least some level of authenticity. Other studies, including the work of David M Jacobs, have supported these conclusions.

Something, therefore, appears to be happening on a very wide scale, which demands greater attention and not the mainstream dismissal that it usually receives. The similarity to traditional folk tales of people being abducted into the fairy realms, with attendant sexual and psychological overtones, has also not gone unnoticed. Either ETs have been among us for much longer than anyone suspects (and this may be the case—see Chapter V), or there is a mysterious esoteric stimulant at work that produces archetypal experiences for those affected, which are interpreted by individual minds into whatever frame of reference 'works' for them—fairies and demons in old times, aliens today.

Why Would ETs Be Here?

This treatise cannot determine definitively the true nature of the claimed experiences with apparently other-worldly beings. Instead, it is the beliefs and convictions that have resulted from some of these encounters that take us into the next important part of our general hypothesis. Yet there are many who do take the potential presence of ETs seriously, and it is worth a brief summing-up of some of the ideas around this.

If the ETs are real, one must speculate about why they are here. Some believe they are beings that have lost the ability to reproduce and are trying to extract genetic material from humans in an attempt to save themselves (perhaps explaining the fixation on the reproductive organs in many abduction accounts). The breeding of ET-human hybrids is often spoken about by contactees, and has interesting resonance with the ancient myths of the Nephilim [page 86]. The entirely strange and rather disturbing connection of UFO sightings with the many reports of mutilated cattle and other farm animals, in which organs (again, often reproductive) have been carefully removed with almost laser-precision and very little tissue damage, may also play into such an agenda, although secret military experiments cannot be discounted as another possible explanation.[4] Others think the visitors are trying to assess our species to see if we are ready to fit into an intergalactic community—or are weak enough to be invaded. Could there be a number of different ET species vying for control, some benevolent and others less so, with secret deals being made with certain governments? Another view holds that the grey beings are not extra-terrestrial at all, but progressed versions of ourselves from the far future, time-travelling back to regain something vital, which evolution or self-inflicted catastrophe has somehow eradicated.

Traditional flying saucer allegedly photographed at Passoria, New Jersey in 1952. It is easy to be cynical about many of the UFO photographs offered as proof, but the level of eye-witness testimony is substantial, and tales of ET encounters are many.

However, what of the theory that the growing cultural awareness of supposed visits from ETs (nicely debunked for double-bluff purposes) may be part of an ongoing long-term plan to implement a faked alien invasion, as an incentive to create an enforced centralization of power for our protection? This may sound an outlandish concept but, in the light of other controversial evidence we shall explore, the idea of such a massive deception being perpetrated on humanity may not be as entirely unlikely as it sounds. After all, how would the world react to 'visitations' in sensitive areas? This came into focus when several videos were produced showing a glowing object descending to hover over the Dome of the Rock temple in Jerusalem on 28th January 2011. The skeptics cried hoax, naturally, but the reaction to even a potentially anomalous event at one of the most contentious religious spots on the planet showed how powerful the effect of an *unquestionable* and major mass-sighting would be.[5] This point will not have gone unnoticed by those who might rule by manipulation. The fear of an indomitable interplanetary force that humanity needs to unite against (as Ronald Reagan famously postulated) would be a persuasive tool for rapidly forging a centralized global control network. Certainly, talk of 'Project Blue Beam', which is accused of planning holographic projection to falsify either UFO imagery or even a faux Second Coming, is rife in the conspiracy world, although hard information is thin on the ground.[6]

Much discernment and wise contemplation will be required before deciding how to respond if unignorable signs ever do appear in our skies. But how we would be able to know the difference between a real or hoaxed invasion is an argument for another time. What matters here is not so much the authenticity or otherwise of the claimed ET contact experiences, but rather the consequences of how people are affected by them—and the similarity of their visions to beliefs held in many different quarters.

Visions of the Future

As far as the ET contactee accounts go, what takes us towards the unpeeling of the next layer are the oft-repeated claims that their celestial captors, or guides, have shown them visions of the future, either in words, visual images or psychic impressions. In many cases, the visions have been either apocalyptic or at least epic, depicting transformative global events that would come to pass and take humanity onto a new level of evolution—due to occur sometime around *now*.

There are several noted examples of supposed extra-terrestrial prophecy. Claimed (if predictably disputed) contactees such as Billy Meier and Whitley Streiber have described being given information on approaching developments of huge significance including, in Meier's case, an apparent forewarning (in 1987) of 9/11 and the subsequent 'War on Terror', which would come to pass fourteen years later.[7] Ufologist Jon King, meanwhile, claims to have had an entire 'schedule' of how important evolutionary events would unfold (culminating in 'Earthshift'), telepathically transmitted to him during a series of encounters in the early 1980s.[8] At least some of the events made known to King (including an apparent prediction of complex crop formations, or 'energy codings' in Wiltshire) have come to pass, and the general schedule regarding global consciousness appears to tie in with many of the other prophecies made for our times, a crucial phenomenon we shall explore more fully later.

For quick reference, the predictions revolve around a 5,125-year cycle of time recorded by independent cultures around the world, through folklore, prophecies and calendrical systems, all of which seem to indicate that each time the period comes around for renewal, a huge shift for the planet arrives with it. The turning of the most recent cycle, according to the most reliable calculators of the ancient calendars, occurred on 21st December 2012, as was widely publicized at the time. When tangible events failed to take place on that day, the cynics made hay, but this wholly missed the point that almost none of the prophecies had anything to say about that specific day, and most scholars of the predictions never believed it would be the much-mocked 'end of the world', which was largely a media invention in the first place. Instead, the turning of the cycle was always more sensibly assumed by the informed to be the *beginning* of a time of huge shift, in consciousness and evolution, one which might take years, decades, or even centuries to fully manifest—but either way a 'New Era'. Thus, although the mainstream or the disappointed may have pushed it to the back of their heads and moved on since 2012, further speculation should still be rife as to what might transpire [Chapter XII].

Many other supposed ET-related encounters have had similar connotations of impending change for the planet, and 'channelled' messages from all manner of proclaimed other-worldly intelligences have spoken again and again about now and the immediate time ahead as being a crucial nexus point in history. Wherever these visions and messages come from, and whatever the real nature of the abduction experiences, they seem to fit a wider pattern of an upwelling awareness deep within the collective psyche of something big about to happen to the Earth, or at least to our civilization—or even of a simple *need* for something to happen if we are to evolve and expand positively.

This, then, is where we need to investigate other cross-referencing sources to see if there is a wider context into which these insights and prophecies might fit.

THE TRUTH AGENDA: *Secret bases and whistleblowers' talk of recovered extra-terrestrial craft and non-human bodies have created a culture of myth-making and confusion. But it seems clear that there have indeed been direct cover-ups concerning the existence of UFOs, and authorities clearly know far more than they are admitting to, whatever the purpose of these mysterious visitations. There are simply too many reports for all of them to be dismissed, and individuals' encounters with apparently other-worldly beings seem to inspire a greater awareness of the importance of these times, or grant them direct visions of momentous near-future events.*

Statue of Our Lady of the Rosary at Fatima, Portugal, commemorating the remarkable apparitions of 1917. The final 'miracle' of Fatima is still one of the best-documented of its kind. But what was the exact nature of what occurred, and how much are the prophecies made here still influencing powerful people in the world today?

IV MIRACLES AND PROPHECIES

Predictions of future times run through history, and are especially strong within Christianity. Belief in these prophecies, together with information gleaned from clairvoyant sources or direct messages from seemingly religious apparitions witnessed by thousands, may play a quiet but important role in influencing political decisions that affect us all.

Seers and Prophets

A recurring figure in historical and religious sagas is the prophet or soothsayer, one with the supernatural ability to foresee events that will shape the lives of monarchs and nations. The visions are often grand and apocalyptic—and specifically symbolic to the individual or party being addressed. But many believers also take the prophecies literally and apply their meaning directly to global events; hence the fundamentalist Christians currently promoting St John's book of Revelation as an actual prediction of things to come—events that believers claim are about to play out within our lifetime [page 53].

What kind of legacy have the prophets of old left for us, and how seriously should we take the overall picture of the future they have painted? The writings of the French 14th century mystic Nostradamus, for instance, are often held up as examples of successful prophecy, but in truth Nostradamus wrote his quatrains in such cryptic and esoterically multi-layered language that any attempt at interpretation in modern times is entirely subjective. When his words are applied to almost anything, some sort of meaning can be squeezed out, but with no absolute method of verification their usefulness is questionable. As a result, the works of Nostradamus have been much abused. He may have accurately foreseen particular events, but no-one can really be sure. Similar grey areas hover over the writings of those such as Mother Shipton, the well-known prophetess from the same historical period.[1] However, what does emerge from their prose is a sense that *these* times—the end of the 20th century and the early decades of the 21st—would be pivotal times of shift for humanity, and they are not alone amongst seers in suggesting this. Was it merely Millennial superstition at work or was something else being picked up on?

In more recent times, there has been an upsurge of prediction and prophecy, which supports the belief that something of great importance may occur to change the world for those alive today. The disappointment felt in some quarters that this did not all come together in the much-discussed year of 2012 has been allowed, in the public eye, to cloud the notion of a wider, more subtle shift of the age, which those of a less sensationalist mindset always felt was more likely. Yet the signs of change remain, and the popular cultural emergence of clairvoyance and psychic studies from even the late Victorian days onwards has accumulated a deep well of foretellings or channelled messages from the spiritual realms, all with a similar theme concerning our times.

In the early 20th century, the American medium Edgar Cayce became the Nostradamus of his day, anticipating much of the general shape the century would take on as it passed. Supporters claim he accurately predicted the Second World War, the 1929 stock market crash, the subsequent Great Depression and the creation of the State of Israel, amongst other important events.[2] Most significantly, Cayce spoke of a period of devastating 'Earth changes', both climatic and geophysical, which would sweep the world in the last decades of the century. Although such events have clearly played out far more slowly than Cayce foresaw, many aficionados feel that his overall vision may yet be fulfilled. Was he right about everything? Clearly not, and skeptics, naturally, find ways to ignore it all. Yet, some areas are worth further thought. Although, for instance, Atlantis failed to dramatically rise again towards the century's end (at least in any overt fashion—various recently discovered underwater ruins have been claimed as remnants of Atlantis), perhaps Cayce's prediction that it would was fulfilled in a different way—through the growing awareness that ancient wisdom from a once higher civilization (by whatever name) may have been quietly kept alive by secret societies and mystic traditions [Chapter V]. In any case, beyond the more grey areas, numerous soothsayers have agreed with Cayce's overall views on Earth changes.

Edgar Cayce, the famous psychic and visionary, as photographed in 1910. Cayce accurately predicted several of the important events of the 20th century, and his prophecies of significant 'Earth changes' tie in with information received through many other psychic channels.

Many times in more recent decades, channelled messages have been received from all kinds of spiritual realms or apparently extra-terrestrial sources speaking through human contacts—the Pleiadians, the Arcturans, the Council of Nine, the Ashtar Command [page 310], Ascended Masters, *et al*—all giving information and advice on our imminent future. Others have received insights through out-of-body experiences or drug-induced hallucinogenic trips. What trickles through all of these conduits is the assertion that the Earth is about to undergo some kind of shift, either physically, spiritually, or both, and that a period of tribulation and upheaval (as long-standing issues rise to the surface and polarize) will give way to a new 'Golden Age'. Those who practice serious astrology, meanwhile—another statistically significant phenomenon too lightly dismissed by modern academics—believe that as the zodiacal wheel takes us into the Age of Aquarius, and important planetary transits come into play [page 263], dramatic changes will, after a period of upheaval, give rise to a better realm of equality and wisdom, taking us away from the religious strife and shadowy politics that have punctuated the Age of Pisces for the last two thousand years.

How seriously should we take these messages and insinuations? With no way of verifying the claimed sources, should their channellers be trusted? Are all mediums frauds, or self-deluded egotists projecting their own psychological insecurities into fantasies of global change? Or is something genuine rising up in the collective, by whatever means necessary, to alert us to impending transformation? Throw into the mix the visions given to UFO contactees, inspirations gained by contemplation of the more graphic crop circles, and all the multiple layers of the New Era speculation, and there seems to be a clear repeated theme to the insights gained from many contemporary mystical experiences.

Bearing in mind the implications of the ongoing Global Consciousness Project [Chapter XIV], in which some scientists appear finally to be acknowledging the existence of a collective energy field, one that knows no boundaries of time, perhaps we would be wise to take heed of what *could* be a telepathic echo from our own future rippling back towards us from a huge event just around the corner. According to religious sources, especially, those ripples may have been reaching us for a long time.

Religious Prophecies

The most famous examples of future predictions can be found in Judaism and Christianity. Both Old and New Testaments are crammed full of prophets, seers and visionaries crying woe for kings and pharaohs, and hailing messianic figures to come. But the New Testament takes on a more specific theme—'the Day of Judgement', in which the Earthly realm will be cleansed in a series of apocalyptic events, culminating in Christ's return.

Evangelical Christians are pinning a lot of hopes on St John's book of Revelation, in which vivid if rather obscure visions (which some consider might well have come to the author while imbibing hallucinogenic substances) are recorded in very mystical symbolism, believed by many scholars to be encoded as specific messages of encouragement to groups of persecuted early Christians. With their context massively expanded, modern believers are applying the visions as strict predictions of events occurring today—stepping stones to the eventual arrival of the 'New Jerusalem', which will vindicate their faith and leave behind non-believers.

And what of 'The Rapture', in which the devout believe they will be physically floated upwards into the heavens as the apocalyptic events of Judgement unfold? Anticipation for The Rapture, particularly in the USA, is now widespread (despite several false alarms from over-enthusiastic preachers) and has added to the urgency and fanaticism felt by those awaiting the fulfilment of biblical prophecy, even though—perhaps surprisingly—the concept isn't based on any clear reference in the Bible. The Rapture is, in truth, a relatively modern construct, derived from a few disconnected poetic phrases scattered throughout the Old Testament. The origins of the concept's rise into mainstream fundamentalist doctrine is uncertain, though it first found its popularity in the 1800s. Many believers seem convinced it's all in the book of Revelation—but it isn't. Yet strong emotional attachment to Rapture prophecy continues to inspire disturbingly influential people, as we shall see.

Current global events do, however, seem to have a little resonance with what *is* in Revelation, excitedly pointed out by religious eschatologists. Its vision of the 'mark of the beast'—666—branded onto people by a dark regime and without which no-one could buy or sell, is one example. The long-term plan to implant ID microchips into the population could be seen as a fulfilment of this restricted movement and monitoring prophecy [a scheme discussed further on pages 79 and 191]. Together with the universal use of commercial bar codes, stock-monitoring RFID (Radio-Frequency Identification) chips could also be seen in this light, although the oft-quoted conspiracy claim that bar codes incorporate the numbers 666 in the three longer strips that appear in every code is provably untrue.[3] On the environmental front, other believers point to pollution-stimulated algae growths—turning some lakes and rivers around the world a garish red—as a fulfilment of the vision in which 'a third of the sea turned into blood' (Revelation 8:8).

One of Matthias Gerung's (1500–1570) numerous interpretations of the biblical book of Revelation. The lurid and fantastical visions of St John the Divine continue to influence modern Christian thinking today and are widely seen as direct prophecies of our times.

On the other hand, just as with Nostradamus, many of the key phrases in Revelation can be applied to many things and some apparent relevance will emerge if seen through the filters of faith. There may also be deliberate attempts to *fulfil* biblical prophecies, of course, so that believers are seen to be vindicated and ensuring that 'God's will' is implemented, a worrying notion we shall explore further.

Cult interest in the 'Bible Code' has seen another potential layer of religious prediction come to light. First popularized in Michael Drosnin's 1997 book *The Bible Code*, the titular cipher is allegedly to be found by isolating patterns of text characters in original Hebrew versions of the Bible. Doing this apparently reveals secret prophecies, which speak of current events or ones due in our near-future. Some anticipated occurrences are claimed to have already come to pass (the code is said to have foretold the assassination of Israeli Prime Minister Yitzhak Rabin in 1995, for instance), but all of the prophecies are prone to very subjective interpretation and some critics consider the whole thing a hoax. However, once again the biblical code ultimately threatens big transformative disasters to come.[4]

Radical interpretations and 'decodings' of religious texts is a deep and murky area. The key point is that whatever the truth of all this religious revelation, certain people in high positions appear to believe in it—which means that it must be having a profound effect on the world we live in, whether we personally subscribe to the views or not.

As for conventional biblical prophecy, it is clear from scholarly analysis that the writers and (importantly) the many editors of the Gospels and apostolic writings believed that the Second Coming was something imminent, possibly even expected within their lifetimes. Certainly, it is unlikely they thought they would have to wait over another two thousand years for it. Yet, for some hitherto indefinable reason, believers in Christian prophecy seem to be expecting a fulfilment of the prophecies any day now. As a civilization oddly fascinated by numerology and anniversaries of messianic births, the excited build-up to the Millennium [page 239] inevitably played a big role in cementing themes of religious expectation. In certain circles there had been a similar hysteria as the year 1000 approached, of course. Back then, it could perhaps have been attributed to the more simplistic mindset of a medieval population, but a thousand years later little had moved on in this regard. Since nothing of great importance did occur in 2000, much of the focus moved instead to speculation over 2012, for which there was at least a serious body of cross-referencing prophecies and calendrical coincidences that invited some proper consideration [Chapter XII]. With the post-2012 realization that even this marker may have only recorded the beginning of a period of shift, rather than constituting an event in itself, perhaps all along the millennial speculations were in truth about the period ahead of us now, but transposed to an earlier and neater date.

However, Christian expectation of imminent change is not based solely on the word of ancient writings. There are examples of relatively recent prophecies, accompanied by dramatic miraculous phenomena, which have strong implications for a religious power structure that dominates much of the world today.

The Apparition Phenomenon

In October 1917, near the small town of Fatima in Portugal, a remarkable event occurred, which would have lasting repercussions for the Roman Catholic Church. For on that day, something that appeared to be the Sun 'danced' in the sky in front of thousands of spectators—as arranged by the biblical Virgin Mary herself, or at least a being that claimed to be her.

The Fatima events, described below, are generally regarded as the most substantial of all the many 'apparitions' of Mary, or 'Our Lady', which have been reported in relatively modern times, with other significant events taking place around the world, especially in Ireland and, in recent decades, Medjugorje in what is now Bosnia-Herzegovina. Some appearances are to individuals, while others, as at Medjugorje and Fatima, occur before thousands. There is a recurring theme to these experiences; while some see only inexplicable light phenomena, others experience heavenly figures and receive messages and visions concerning the importance of faith and the dangers of losing it in a world about to turn upside down.

What the true nature of these apparitions is has been the subject of much speculation. Many of the Christian faithful accept them at face value as direct visits from divine beings, but others have suspected them of being everything from projections of inner consciousness reacting to natural electromagnetic fields (dowsable 'Earth energy' is often very strong at apparition sites), to extra-terrestrials masquerading as religious figures.[5] It may be that some unknown force is attempting to get its central message across in whatever frame of reference may be necessary to gain attention. Certainly, the communications received resonate strongly with the similar themes transmitted to psychics and ET contactees, albeit with an overtly religious flavour. The message is nearly always one of needing to be prepared, spiritually and practically, for something big. The Fatima prophecies are particularly strong in this regard.

The Three Secrets of Fatima

Although accounts vary, essentially the dramatic events at Fatima began in 1915 when three local shepherd children, Lucia Santos, age nine, and her two younger cousins, Francisco and Jacinta Marto, witnessed a strange transparent cloud 'in the shape of a man' hovering above nearby pine trees. A year later, the cloud was seen again, this time forming fully into what seemed to the children to be an angel. Appearing three times to them and leading the children in devotional prayer, the angel was merely a herald for the strange woman dressed in 'brilliant white' who then appeared before them another year after that, on 17 May 1917. Claiming to be 'from heaven', the as-yet unnamed lady (only in her final apparition did she reveal herself as 'Our Lady of the Rosary') spoke softly and strangely during several meetings with the children, again leading them in prayer, but also divulging three 'secrets' that they must deliver to the Holy Father (the then Pope Benedict XV).[6] Curiously enough, in May 1917, Pope Benedict had made a direct and very public appeal to Mary to intercede to stop the First World War, which was currently tearing Europe apart. Was this his reply?

The first secret was a frightening vision of hell, a warning of what would come to those without faith; the second was an apparent prediction of another World War and a caution about the evils of rising communism. As for the third secret, Lucia was told that it could not be revealed to the Church until after 1960. Lucia became a nun and outlived her cousins, who both died in their youth. She continued to have visions, and decades later dutifully revealed the third secret in a written document. The popes who read it thereafter reportedly appeared deeply shocked. Yet this last secret remained officially hidden until 2000, when the Vatican announced that it was a simple prophecy of the assassination attempt on Pope John Paul II, when a Turkish gunman opened fire in St Peter's Square in 1981. John Paul claimed that his survival was due to the direct intercession of the Virgin Mary; the fact that one of the bullets retrieved after the shooting did curiously appear to perfectly fit a cavity in the crown of one of the iconic Mary statues at the Fatima shrine was used as further evidence that his deliverance must have been the meaning of the last vision. Yet many people doubt that this is the full story of the third secret—after all, why wait so long to reveal something so straightforward and already years past? The nature of the vision, as publicized, was rather vague and esoteric, and certainly open to interpretations other than the one John Paul elected to believe about himself. Even Sister Lucia, before her death at the age of 97, reportedly expressed concerns about how the information was subsequently filtered. In addition, there seemed to be an odd level of official Vatican obfuscation about the issue.

The three children who experienced visions of 'Our Lady of the Rosary' at Fatima, Portugal in 1917. The information shared with them is clearly taken very seriously by the Vatican. Only Lucia Santos (left) survived into old age—her cousins Francisco and Jacinta Marto both died in childhood.

So was the third secret rather more than we were told? The evidence suggests so, for before John Paul's announcement the clear hints that had been dropped by high-level Vatican sources on several occasions about the other aspects of the vision (see below) appeared to speak of a worldwide crisis of Christian faith, and of globally unsettling events due to happen... any time from now.

The Miracle of the Sun

When the children recounted their ongoing experiences at the time, some family members and local villagers were understandably hesitant in accepting the story. With Portugal then under the grip of a fervently secular regime, there was even local political resistance due to the overtly anti-communist flavour to some of the messages. As crowds increasingly gathered to witness the now monthly appearances of the mysterious woman to the children (although it is unclear what the villagers themselves saw at this point), the authorities grew ever-more uncomfortable; at one stage the children were locked up by the local mayor and threatened with execution. Seemingly understanding of their need for proof, the woman promised the children that if they gathered as many people as they could at a certain time around the Fatima pasture-land known as the Cova da Iria (where the apparitions had been taking place), she would perform a miracle that would leave no-one in any doubt as to the provenance of her words. Few could have anticipated the extraordinary events that followed.

On 13th October 1917, with only the word of three children to go on, but in hope for a sign that might liberate them from their agnostic masters, an incredible 70,000 or so believers from the village and its outlying regions gathered in heavy rain to wait for the promised miracle. Sure enough, soon after midday, it came. What appeared to the crowd to be the Sun behind a thin veil of cloud began to perform a series of outlandish and terrifying manoeuvres across the sky, at first revolving rapidly in a Catherine wheel-like manner, throwing out whirls of glowing colors.

Photographs purporting to be of the events at Fatima on 13th October 1917. Above, the gathering crowds wait, as directed by apparently divine messages. Below, a claimed actual shot of the phenomenon seen on the day, photographed from several miles away. Presumed at the time to be the Sun, the object darkened and performed an extraordinary series of acrobatics across the sky. Was this a religious experience, or a classic UFO?

The Lisbon-based (and usually overtly anti-clerical) newspaper *O Dia* reported the events, which were witnessed by the faithful and the doubting alike:

'At one o'clock in the afternoon, midday by the Sun, the rain stopped. The sky, pearly gray in color, illuminated the vast arid landscape with a strange light. The Sun had a transparent gauzy veil so that eyes could easily be fixed upon it. The gray mother-of-pearl tone turned into a sheet of silver which broke up as the clouds were torn apart and the silver Sun, enveloped in the same gauzy gray light, was seen to whirl and turn in the circle of broken clouds. A cry went up from every mouth and people fell on their knees on the muddy ground. The light turned a beautiful blue as if it had come through the stained-

glass windows of a cathedral and spread itself over the people who knelt with outstretched hands. The blue faded slowly and then the light seemed to pass through yellow glass. Yellow stains fell against white handkerchiefs, against the dark skirts of women. They were reported on the trees, on the stones and on the serra. People wept and prayed with uncovered heads in the presence of the miracle they had awaited.'

Even Joseph Garrett, a natural sciences professor at Coimbra University, could not doubt what he saw with his own eyes, and reported the final sequence of events thus:

'This was not the sparkling of a heavenly body, for it spun round on itself in a mad whirl, when suddenly a clamor was heard from all the people. The Sun, whirling, seemed to loosen itself from the firmament and advance threateningly upon the Earth as if to crush us with its huge fiery weight. The sensation during these moments was terrible.'

With a 'falling-leaf' like motion and a final sweep across the heads of the by now traumatized thousands, the object appeared to return to its usual place in the sky, as the 'Sun', and normality, was restored—with one interesting feature: the clothes of the rain-soaked people were now completely dry and all the puddles had gone.

Fatima Under Analysis

What really happened at Fatima that day? Clearly the Sun didn't spin out of the heavens, or the whole world might have noticed. But *something* amazing must have occurred to have been recorded so accurately and by so many. One can understand why the faithful might have been convinced by this that the Hand of God had indeed been at work that day. For all anyone knows, maybe it was. But it is also interesting to note that the behavior of an object that at least looked like the Sun was strongly reminiscent of the reported movements of UFOs in some of the more impressive close encounters—which have also included accounts of heat and extreme drying qualities, where nearby water mysteriously vanishes.

Despite predictable cynicism from skeptics, it is very hard to dismiss the Fatima sighting as mass-hypnosis or hysteria, largely because so many people witnessed the 'Miracle of the Sun' at quite some distance, not just amongst the crowded thousands. Indeed, the aerial object was apparently even photographed from some miles away [see opposite]. In the fascinating black and white images that have come down to us today, it resembles an eclipsed Sun, although no eclipse was due that day.

The exact nature of what happened at Fatima may never be truly understood. What is important to this exploration of the Truth Agenda is the identity of the key Vatican figure who spent years investigating and verifying the Fatima phenomenon: Cardinal Ratzinger—who would become better known as Pope Benedict XVI (the only pope of modern times ever to resign his office, prompting the accession of Pope Francis in 2013). As a result of years of research in his capacity as Prefect of the

Congregation for the Doctrine of the Faith (or 'God's Rottweiler', to his critics), this highly powerful mover and shaker within the church believed firmly in the reality of the secrets revealed to the children—the full and true nature of which he stated openly he had been aware of for many years, even before becoming pontiff. Is it a coincidence that the papal name he chose to adopt was the same as the pope at the time of the Fatima apparitions?

If the third secret was merely a premonition of the assassination attempt on John Paul II (based on the rather obscure and very mystical vision related by Sister Lucia), it is hard to see why Ratzinger himself stated in November 1984 that revelation of its contents would cause 'sensationalism' and that it dealt with 'end times'. When pressed on further detail, he stated that 'in the judgement of previous popes, it adds nothing to what Christians must know respecting what is stated in the Book of Revelation'. This all speaks of a secret far bigger than the Vatican is admitting to. Pope John Paul II himself—before the attempt on his life—reportedly told a select group of German Catholics in 1980; 'if you read that the oceans will inundate continents, and millions of people will die suddenly in a few minutes, once this is known, then in reality it is not necessary to insist on the publication of this secret.'

None of this means that any of the revealed Fatima visions, whatever their true nature, are totally or even partially *correct*, any more than other soothsayings, even if they do seem to be prescient echoes of the apocalyptic zeitgeist we live with today. With no way of verifying the real nature of what made itself known in 1917, despite its impressive display, the prophecies remain on a par with any other source of premonition, psychic, paranormal or celestial, and have to be stirred into the general pool of expectation that seems to have bubbled up in our times.

However, the Vatican's inherent acceptance of the Fatima doctrines means that for a long time we have had, and must still have, men at the head of an incredibly powerful global institution who believe that the world we live in is about to enter a period of dramatic change; based on information from apparently supernatural forces. The Fatima events, and prophecies derived from other significant Marian apparitions, are not shouted about, but they must hold a power over the Roman Catholic Church which indirectly influences the entire world.

Further levels being built into the ground beneath the huge Paul VI Pastoral Center opposite the Fatima shrine in 2012. What is the true purpose of this construction? Is it as much a potential apocalypse shelter as it is a Catholic conference hall?

It has even been suggested that the vast Paul VI Pastoral Center, a cavernous and somewhat oppressive conference hall built directly opposite the Fatima shrine, is in truth a deep bunker intended to shelter the Catholic hierarchy from the catastrophic events alluded to in the unpublicized parts of the third secret. Inaugurated by John Paul II in 1982 in gratitude to Mary, its oddly thick walls and underground corridors with locked blast door-like entrances leading to unseen levels, do nothing to deflate this impression. When this author visited in 2012, a collection of strange 'bleeding' handprints on one of the outer steel doors was suggestive of excluded masses on the outside; an interesting symbolism.

There has been a widespread interest in some interpretations of the prophecies from the 12th century seer St Malachy, which suggest that Pope Francis will be the very last pontiff before the final events of the apocalypse, although historians vigorously debunk this. Where Francis stands personally on Fatima and the secrets remains to be seen, but his predecessor was certainly not alone in being a massively influential figure who believes we are entering 'end times'.

Sinister handprints on one of the outer steel doors at the Fatima Pastoral Center. Meaningful commissioned art or casual graffiti, the symbolism feels uncomfortable.

Divine Inspiration in the White House?

Justification of war on religious grounds and claims of divine personal guidance from world leaders have roots as old as human history, but anyone hoping today's civilization might have outgrown this tendency would have been taken aback by the extraordinary statement released in 2005 and attributed to the then US president, George W Bush. Describing his first meeting with Mr Bush, Palestinian Foreign Minister Nabil Shaath gave this account to the BBC of a conversation which took place in June 2003:

'President Bush said to all of us: 'I'm driven with a mission from God. God would tell me, "George, go and fight those terrorists in Afghanistan." And I did, and then God would tell me, "George, go and end the tyranny in Iraq ..." And I did. And now, again, I feel God's words coming to me, "Go get the Palestinians their state and get the Israelis their security, and get peace in the Middle East." And by God I'm gonna do it.'[7]

Although White House spokesmen officially denied that this was ever said, other Palestinian officials also heard Bush make the claim. Why would they make such a strange assertion without some grain of truth to it? Although it is well-known that the evangelical Christian right played a crucial role in Bush's election, however skewed that process may have been, was the president just speaking glibly of his own personal religious conviction here, or of something more specific? Despite the official denials, it is more than interesting that Bush did later attempt to clarify his position to political author Bob Woodward with the following words:

'I'm surely not going to justify war based upon God. Understand that. Nevertheless, in my case, I pray that I will be as good a messenger of His will as possible. And then, of course, I pray for forgiveness.' [8]

President George W Bush meets Pope John Paul II in the Vatican in 2003. Given the clear belief in prophecies and predictions from both Vatican officials and world politicians alike, one can only wonder at the exact nature of the private conversations held at such meetings.

It is clear there is every reason to be nervous. Although many philosophers hold that we all have an inherent connection with a universal consciousness, a president believing he has a personal direct line from God to guide him, together with the always-concerning conviction that any misdemeanor can be overlooked after simple prayers for forgiveness, is surely cause for concern. (Tony Blair's voicing of open religious platitudes since his conversion to Catholicism is another example of a leader who clearly thought God was on his side during his years of power—

see more below.) Many dubious emperors, kings and assorted tyrants have all been there before. Although the Bush years are long behind us, the global legacy of his policies and the influence of those who aided and abetted his administration, both in front of and behind the scenes, will linger for a long time. Much was also made of Barack Obama's own evangelical Christian roots (on his mother's side) during his presidential campaigns.

As for George W Bush—a recovering alcoholic and a 'born-again' Christian—little here needs to be said about the nature of his rise to power that isn't already common knowledge. The election irregularities and disputes over the highly questionable voting that allowed him into the White House in 2000 will never be satisfactorily settled, although some would say we were at least spared the spectre of Al Gore having a position of power beyond environmental sermons (see Chapter XI to see why this might not have been a good thing). With all politicians who come even close to positions of power apparently guided (wittingly or unwittingly) by the same shadowy manipulators, it is likely the outcome of the election would not have made too much difference in the long-run anyway. However, with a clear hard-line neo-conservative push behind him, Bush was plainly their prime candidate and perhaps the perfect puppet to aid the rise of a new US-led empire through strident military expansion and a climate of control born from the events of 9/11.

Interestingly, whatever skulduggery may have taken place, students of astrology believe the 2000 election could not have gone any other way—the position of George Bush's Sun in his birth chart (6 July 1946, 7.26 am, New Haven, Connecticut) sits amazingly at precisely the same degree as the Sun in the birth chart of the USA (usually taken from the Declaration of Independence, 4 July 1776, 17.10 pm, Philadelphia): 13 degrees Cancer. Like it or not, in this view George W Bush was the perfect expression of the North American collective psyche at the time of his election, the hand of destiny seemingly at work in the bizarrest of ways.[9] America's Neptune, meanwhile, seeking redemption, saw Obama's Mars as its savior. Obama and the US share their Venus in Cancer, suggesting a shared ideal of defending the 'homeland', with Venus representing values, and Cancer ruling home and security.

Despite the evidence that the governments behind governments always ensure the 'right' candidate comes to power, George W Bush's particularly strong Christian convictions and underlying religious fervor (presumably held back by aides keen to play this down) do appear to have set him apart from some of his peers. But if God wasn't personally whispering into Bush's ear in the night, instructing him in global policy, where did his claimed divine guidance come from? Is it more likely, in fact, that God was speaking to him through the advices of... one Pastor Ted Haggard?

The Politics of Armageddon

Evangelist Ted Haggard, known as 'Pastor Ted' to his followers, was the founder of the New Life Church In Colorado, as well as being a founder of the Association of Life-Giving Churches and the leader of the National Association of Evangelicals between 2003 and November 2006. His influence in the spiritual life of Christian fundamentalist America was profound—as was his influence in US politics. For it is on record that Haggard was a key advisor to George W Bush.[10] Not only did he rally massive support among evangelicals for both of Bush's 'successful' election campaigns, but Haggard also held weekly telephone conferences each Monday with Bush and his aides, advising them of the religious direction their global policies should be taking. In 2005, author Jeff Sharlet wrote of Haggard that 'no pastor in America holds more sway over the political direction of evangelicalism'.[11] So perhaps this is how God spoke to George W Bush.

The White House was predictably quiet when Haggard resigned from his church in 2006 after admitting involvement in a drugs and gay sex scandal, but that's not so important here. What is of concern is that for several years Ted Haggard—a man with a strong religious conviction that End Times and The Rapture are imminent—

must have had an important hand in directing the course of world politics.

The evangelical 'End-Timers' movement in the US, especially, is now so strong that a significant proportion of North America's population is expecting the Second Coming any minute now—which means that, overtly or candidly, they must be helping to encourage policies and ways of life that not only prepare them for it (in their eyes), but that actively *help bring the prophecies of apocalypse about.* Many End-Timers see global chaos as a good thing, a fulfilment of the predicted 'tribulation' that will eventually pave the way for the New Jerusalem. If the Day of Judgement brings with it the glorious Rapture, every day closer to world peace and stability is a step *away* from what Christian fundamentalists actually want. Dangerously, Islamic Jihadists flocking to the likes of Syria and Iraq today seem to hold very similar convictions. All this is a bit of a problem to those who don't subscribe to such beliefs, and would actually like a path to peace without prophecy-riddled struggle and strife.

The fact is, however, that for eight years we had a born-again Christian president— a man in one of the highest positions on Earth, with a finger on the very button of the machinery of war—being regularly advised by an evangelical preacher not only expecting the end of the world, but who, by definition, must have seen it as his duty to actually help bring about the final battle of Armageddon, leading 'good' against 'evil'. Seen in this context, maybe some of the policies and mandates that seem to have caused such chaos in the Middle East in recent years begin to make a little more sense. Given Barack Obama's strong charismatic Christian leanings (despite having a Muslim father), and claims that Hillary Clinton, for many years arguably the most powerful woman in the world, is a member of the evangelical 'dominionist' group 'The Family', there seems little reason to presume the religious agenda in US politics will be subsiding any time soon.[12] Numerous members of the right wing 'Tea Party' have similar allegiances.

Hillary Clinton waves to supporters at the Veteran's Day parade, New York, 2004, while cautious minders prowl. Clinton is rumored to be part of a strongly evangelical movement known as 'The Family'. Politics and religion seem as inseparable in the US as in the Islamic countries the US often criticizes.

There is, incidentally, one more influential leader who was also advised on occasion by Pastor Ted Haggard—Tony Blair. His 2007 conversion to Roman Catholicism and his overtly public protestations of faith since leaving public office as Prime Minister of Britain leave little doubt that his own political direction must also have been heavily, if quietly, influenced by his private religious convictions. It certainly explains much about his awkward and slyly deflective response to television interviewer Jeremy Paxman's probing question in a 2003 interview about whether he and George W Bush ever prayed together.[13] Blair's much-publicized closed meetings with Pope Benedict XVI, a key holder of prophetic religious secrets, as we have seen, also make the mind boggle at the nature of the conversations that might have taken place between them.

What is clear from recent events—and the whole of history—is that religion and state in the West have always gone together and still go together, with many people suspecting that fundamentalist agendas underlie many of the decisions which are made, through whatever denomination (note the significant number of strict Christians who were in both Tony Blair's and, subsequently, Prime Minister Gordon Brown's cabinets, including Ruth Kelly—a member of the Catholic extremist group Opus Dei). This is not, of course, to say that Christianity, in its moderate form, is in any way wrong or that governments have no right to religious beliefs. In the Islamic countries, the religious fervor within the politics is at least honest and upfront, however misused and dangerous it may sometimes be. In the West the fervor seems equally keen, but it is kept hidden. Many of the fingers that accusingly point to the perils of Islamic fundamentalism appear to be equally fundamentalist in a different direction.

Some conspiracy theorists reject the notion of religious influence in Western politics, claiming it is merely a cover for overtly power-and-money-based scheming. Others even reject the notion of religious influence in places like the Vatican, pointing to the underlying seams of financial corruption and cover-ups of child abuse scandals which have tainted the Roman church and hardly appear to be very spiritual. The evidence would suggest the ultimate motivation of political and religious factions is probably a mixture of exerting influence through money, power *and* belief, perhaps in preparation for expected big changes and the coming fulfilment of ancient—and modern—prophecies.

THE TRUTH AGENDA: *Prophecies of disruptive but transformative events that will befall our planet seem endemic within ancient religious and mystical texts— but they are also welling up through modern clairvoyance and multiple-witness apparitions. People in high places, claiming divine inspiration or authority, appear to be the guardians of secrets that must surely influence the direction of the world we live in today, and undeclared religious agendas underpin Western politics far more than is admitted.*

Genuine Egyptian needle at the Place de la Concorde, Paris, topped with a golden pyramid [page 91]. The ubiquity of such powerful ancient symbolism is seen by some to be a statement of domination from a hidden ruling elite.

V   GRAND CONSPIRACIES

Is the way in which our civilization is run the result of a massive manipulation from elite groups and secret societies with shadowy agendas? With so many people now doubting the true foundation of the West's supposedly democratic principles, what is the exact nature of those doubts and should we pay any heed to them? The speculation of the conspiracy theorists, whatever the final answers, raises important questions about both the world today and the potentially ancient origins of the power structure that may really govern us.

Conspiracy—An Overall Picture

The preceding chapters give a brief overview of just some areas where many people do not trust the motivations, or the words, of those who supposedly lead us. There so often seems to be disturbing evidence of wider agendas, whether power-seeking, religious or esoteric, running secretly beneath the veneer of normality that is presented to us. The media, in particular, is complicit in supporting this veneer by always refusing to rock the boat beyond certain limits; the scandals journalists reveal rarely touch the true levels of intrigue and deception that run far deeper. We are continually kept distracted and dumb by mind-numbing fascination with trivia and materialism so that most of us never have the time or the need to lift the corner of the carpet to see what has been swept underneath. When we do begin to look, our need for cosy comfort often snaps us back into place and our blinkers go on. That, or fear—of exclusion from society, of terrorism, of war, of disease, of climate change, of financial loss, of outsiders—holds us back from challenging our claimed protectors too much. But there is a sense that this is beginning to shift. A minority, yet a significant one, is now challenging many things that have been hitherto taken for granted, and that minority is, by default, implementing the Truth Agenda. The corner of the carpet is being lifted at last and many do not like what they see. The likes of the infamous WikiLeaks 'revelations' barely scratch the surface.

This is where we truly immerse ourselves in the realm of conspiracy theory, a place where polarities and extremism can admittedly run riot. Yet it is also a place where the right questions, at least, do get asked. Certain devotees of truthseeking see *everything* as a conspiracy, viewing the world as a tangled web of deceit, corruption, manipulation and elitism, convinced that someone out there is deliberately trying to make our lives miserable and mundane so that we never rise above the morass to become the powerful beings that we really are. Although for some this may be mere psychological projection (inner personal fears not being dealt with or 'owned', but conveniently disassociated from and projected onto people and events 'out there'), or indeed 'apophenia' (reading meaningful patterns into what are, in reality, random events), it cannot be denied that there is, unsettlingly, actual evidence to support the reality of a number of these concerns. Consequently, they deserve to be taken a little more seriously.

With the many prophecies of massive change clearly believed in some very high places, it may be that someone wants to ensure they maintain the upper hand should anything come to pass that overturns the traditional order of things [Chapter XII]. If we are being treated as sheep, it may be important to our masters that we are kept in our pens while an anticipated storm passes through; or put in the slaughterhouse, according to the grimmest views.

In the conspiracy view, most political decisions, elections, wars, economic crises, fuel shortages, famines and food crises, terrorist atrocities and even natural disasters are used, manipulated and/or specifically coordinated by a relatively small elite group of influential businessmen, industrialists, politicians, monarchs and intellectuals, to forward a secret agenda with occultist leanings that has *their* best interests at heart and not ours. Although the original secret society that adopted the name was a specific Bavarian group, the network of manipulators is now often generically referred to as 'The Illuminati' (Latin for 'enlightened'). Its influence is believed to be maintained through political and business-orientated power structures, international banking, global trading alliances, arms dealers and (especially) the secret societies, which ensure that dynasties, bloodlines and ancient mystical beliefs endure, with knowledge passed on only to the chosen. In this way, the elite's power is never challenged and its grip on the world never weakens. Subscribers to this view maintain that no politician gets anywhere near a position of influence without the say-so of the Illuminati, and believe that elections are determined either with strategic manipulation of funding for campaigns, clever propaganda or, when forced, actual vote-rigging.

As evidence that many big decisions are made outside of parliaments, truthseekers point to the existence of unelected but powerful bodies such as The Bilderberg Group, The Council on Foreign Relations, The Club of Rome, The Trilateral Commission, the World Economic Forum, the Tavistock Institute and all the many other mysterious high-level clubs, think-tanks and 'quangos', often run by well-known political or business figures. Working with rich and influential families like the Rockefellers and the Rothschilds, these bodies launch significant global policies, which affect our lives yet by-pass the usual structures of democracy. It's certainly no secret that strange little boards and committees, accountable to no-one, have long pulled strings that jerk the actions of those supposedly making free decisions on our behalf, and the banking crises of recent years have revealed where many of the really important decisions are made. Other influences, such as interactions at the bizarre annual Bohemian Grove gathering [page 93], may also play an important role.

Weakening the Masses?

At the more extreme end of conspiracy theory, some are concerned that active steps are being taken to ensure we are enslaved to the elite by plans to neuter not only our personal power but also our health, to weaken us all so that we become more controllable, more malleable to the desires of the few. Draconian controls such as the now ongoing EU restrictions on alternative medicines, vitamins and minerals (courtesy of the 'Codex Alimentarius' food safety body—page 209) *do* seem to be taking away healthcare decisions from us, making us ever-more reliant on powerful pharmaceutical industries, which tend to treat symptoms but not the causes of conditions. Meanwhile, poor nutrition and the increased presence of junk food as a staple diet, particularly amongst the young (with sales of fast food rocketing in the wake of economic downturns), has become endemic, for all the lip-service paid towards healthier living, and we are targeted by an endless list of dubious additives in edible products and debatable chemicals in our water, such as fluoride.

Some questioners continue to believe that the vaccination program, MMR (Measles, Mumps and Rubella) and beyond, has also had dramatic negative effects on our immune systems. With both the safety and effectiveness of the procedure having been challenged by more educated health professionals than is reported, hardcore theorists believe this is a deliberate attempt to damage our natural resistance. We are told that immunization has wiped out disease, but many investigators hold firmly that statistics don't support this and that the figures have been misrepresented to support the continuation of the

Many truthseekers believe the science of vaccination has at best been massively misunderstood and at worst is a deliberate attempt to weaken the immune system of the human race. Here, campaigner Trevor Gunn, author of the notably influential Mass Immunization—A Point in Question *[page 337] gives a presentation to raise awareness of the issues.*

program. It is certainly a verifiable fact that most traditional childhood diseases were already in steep decline before vaccines for them were introduced.[1] The ever-growing cocktail of highly questionable substances (including mercury) that make up a number of vaccines are considered by some to have contributed to behavioral and health problems in young people. Those who raise this, however, are quickly vilified in the media and attacked by mainstream professionals—or even accused of fostering a form of child abuse. Certainly, the claims of the questioners need vigorous scrutiny, but the fact is that doubts remain over the accepted science, and these concerns have still not been definitively addressed, despite the impression consistently sold to the public. (See Chapter X for more on immunization, Codex Alimentarius, and fluoridation.)

Others go even further and believe that cell (mobile) phones and many of the new microwave communication transmitters that have gone up around the world may help us talk to each other, but also act as neural suppressers. Then there are 'chemtrails', increased occurrences of unusual high-altitude vapor trails, which are believed by concerned parties to be evidence that governments are secretly seeding the atmosphere with dubious chemicals for reasons of their own (perhaps to do with climate control, or as further poisonous suppressants). There is also HAARP technology (High Frequency Active Auroral Research Program), where US scientists have learnt to manipulate the ionosphere, supposedly for military communications. Doubters see this as a potential mind-control system, energy weapon and weather manipulator, along with other secret Tesla technology, orbiting transmitters and hidden devices that might be used against us. [See also the sky spirals, page 37.] The original HAARP project is now reportedly offline, but its progeny surely continues.

  Much of this is speculation, of course, although the CIA's MK-ULTRA mind control experiments of the 1950s-60s certainly did occur, and President Obama's mentor Zbigniew Brzezinski [pages 25, 275 & 278] has openly advocated the possibilities of using electronic transmissions to 'seriously impair the brain performance of very large populations', which proves that the potential use of such sinister techniques has certainly occurred to those in power. Readers must investigate the evidence for themselves, but the growing numbers of people prepared to believe in all such things is illustrative of the deepening erosion of trust in authority.

  For some concerned minds, even the fear that someone out there wants to weaken humanity is not enough, believing instead that the ultimate aim is in fact to wipe most of us out. We will deal with this tricky area first before moving on to look at other areas of the conspiratorial view.

Reducing the Global Population

A number of gloomier theorists are convinced there are plans afoot for a massive reduction of the world population, to be achieved through epidemics and viruses, deliberately spread. Some say that AIDS was but one lab-engineered attempt to get the ball rolling (although others have claimed it to be an entire fraud, a misunderstanding of a collection of immune diseases used to create more fear).[2] At the very least, a resurgence of eugenics programs and enforced selective breeding might lie just beneath the surface of some curious policies floating around at the moment.

  Wild paranoia? Over-population is claimed to be a serious issue for the governments of the world, with some models predicting a major food, water and energy disaster by 2030—although there are also claims that these fears are a deliberately-spread myth, designed, like other fear stories [Part Three], to be used as a tool of control, and to justify elitist ambitions for a more 'selective' global population.[3] Much was made in the conspiracy world of a lecture given in 2006 at St Edwards University in Austin, Texas, when Dr Eric Pianka of the Texas Academy of Sciences appeared to advocate the merits of thinning out the masses by the release of a genetically-enhanced strain of the Ebola virus. This story was screamed across the web forums as evidence that we were indeed all seen as nothing more than 'useless eaters' by the intellectual elite.

Pianka later denied this interpretation of his speech, saying that his comments had been taken out of context and that he was simply projecting the possibility that such a virus *could* take hold, not that it should.[4] The fact, however, that so many took his comments as they did was a telling sign of the serious misgivings some people harbour in these uncertain times, and the now increasing spread of Ebola hasn't helped.

Concerns—much stimulated by the media despite very low casualty figures thus far—over the likes of Bird and Swine Flu 'pandemics', have been used to create great panic in recent years, which has seen people across the world rushing to have flu jabs and stock up on the oral anti-viral tablet Tamiflu (oseltamivir), even though neither specifically work on either of the two strains. Aside from fears of actual engineered viruses that might aid a program of depopulation, other truthseekers are as suspicious of the cocktail of drugs that are fed to people panicked into demanding them. Dr Leonard Horowitz, author of *Emerging Viruses*, for instance, believes that some anti-virals and vaccines are deliberately designed to weaken our immune systems, not strengthen them, making us more vulnerable to—or actually activating—later, stronger strains of microbiotic threats, be they Ebola, Swine Flu, Bird Flu or something new, tying in with views held by those who doubt the claimed good intentions of the vaccination program.[5] If nothing else, the known side effects of Tamiflu (accepted even in mainstream circles), which can include behavioral problems and hallucinations, should be cause for great apprehension, considering how much of the world population has taken it over the last few years.[6]

At the other end of the spectrum there are claims that Swine Flu in particular was another exaggerated threat to boost the grip—and profits—of the pharmaceutical industries [Chapter X]. In the entirely disproportionate wave of fear that accompanied just the first indications of a pandemic in 2009, the UK government alone spent £100 million (criticized in later official reports) to stockpile enough Tamiflu to be administered to 80% of the population. Assertions that Tamiflu's three-year lifespan meant that, by happy 'coincidence', masses of global stocks had to be used up or destroyed just as the new pandemic was being announced were denied when the sell-by dates were suddenly extended by two years, but many remain doubtful.[7] It is also a fact that Donald Rumsfeld, ex-US Secretary for Defense, considered by many to be a key architect of the darker global agenda, was once chairman of Gilead Sciences Inc., which owns the patent on Tamiflu, and he retains major stocks in the company today.[8] Rumsfeld was also connected with the production and US government approval of the highly controversial sweetener aspartame, which has crept into much food and drink today yet is considered by many to be very harmful [page 355].

It seems rather extreme to consider that there might really be those out there who would want to wipe many of us from the Earth, and perhaps some of these fears do reside in the realms of paranoia, yet certain clues do seem to suggest that such an intention may not be beyond the realms of possibility. The global warming scare may also play into such an agenda [Chapter XI].

The Georgia Guidestones

In 1979, plans for a mysterious monument at Elbert County, Georgia (USA), known as The Georgia Guidestones, were submitted by an unknown designer (under the pseudonym 'R C Christian'). The resulting artwork was erected in 1980. Resembling a Stonehenge-like collection of vertical slabs, carved inscriptions on the stones (in a number of different languages) record a decree of the artist's aspirations for the world, but are seen by some people as euphemisms to represent the ultimate intentions of the Illuminati. These include references to the formation of a 'world court' and utilize phrases implying the necessity for eugenics ('guide reproduction wisely—improving fitness and diversity'). Most unsettlingly, the stones proclaim that humanity should keep its numbers 'under 500,000,000'. If this recommendation was adhered to, it would mean reducing the current population of the world by nine-tenths. Who would have the right to decide who lives and who dies? Consequently, the Georgia Guidestones are often eyed with suspicion as a celebration of something evil—which may explain why they have been vandalized with (somewhat crude) anti-Illuminati aerosol slogans more than once. Certainly, it seems odd that such a public avocation of mass extermination is allowed to stand unchallenged.[9]

The Georgia Guidestones, USA. The inscriptions on this anonymously-erected monument, written in several different languages, appear, worryingly, to advocate wiping out most of the human population.

Paranoia as Legitimate Mistrust?

Some of the beliefs discussed above may have a basis in truth, some of them may not. Perhaps none of them do. However, the fact that so many minds are willing to consider such extreme scenarios does say much about how little we trust those in authority today. But have those authorities earned our trust?

By at least considering the reasoning behind all these conspiratorial assertions, even if we dispense with several of them, it is interesting to note how many valid areas for legitimate investigation remain.

The Aims of Global Conspiracy

What, then, if true, would be the ultimate aim of all this underhand manipulation? According to most conspiracy theorists, the most cherished long-term desire of the Illuminati is to impose upon the globe a 'One World Government', a body intended to supersede all individual sovereignty and administrations, controlled by one central source working to a universal agenda. The political euphemism for this is the 'New World Order' (NWO), an aspiration for which has frequently been voiced in speeches by western politicians (ex-British Prime Minister Gordon Brown was a prolific user of the phrase) as the answer to all our troubles.

In practice, the long-term logical outcome of such a New World Order would seem to be an all-encompassing regime that will ultimately bring one currency, one authority and one mindset to be adhered to by all humankind—perhaps, if the worst fears are realized, with populations reduced in number and rendered harmless by societal controls, all maintained by a small overseeing committee, pontificating from on high. Such a system would render us more controllable, and ensure that a tiny elite would retain its supremacy, untroubled by real democracy, just as George Orwell warned in his novel *Nineteen Eighty-Four*. Thus, the relentless gathering of European countries into one federal superstate, with the euro or its successor as just the beginning [page 76], and (admittedly denied) mutterings of plans to submit the USA, Mexico and Canada to a similar unified currency (sometimes referred to as 'The Amero') as part of a 'North American Union' are seen by many truthseekers as slow but dogged steps towards One World Government—or at the very least a system of much greater regional centralization.[10] Were the three global superstates of Oceania, Eurasia and Eastasia, as visualized in Orwell's cautionary tale, so fictional after all?

George Orwell (real name Eric Blair), one of the key writers of the 20th century. Orwell's nightmare vision of global superstates and a society governed by draconian control and surveillance is considered by some to be anticipatory of our world's current trajectory.

Financial Manipulation?

The 'credit crisis' of 2008, which plunged countries across the world into recession and millions into misery and unemployment, may have been ostensibly due to a banking system out of control, but the fact that this obvious and inevitable situation was allowed to develop at all has led to a belief that it was a contrived plot to benefit the New World Order agenda. For years, many observers of the Western financial system gave loud warnings that the increasingly reckless investments and wild speculating of arrogant bankers, falsely bloating the economy, were guaranteed to hit a brick wall. All were ignored. It has become clear from whistleblowers in Britain, for instance, that several staff, approved personally by Gordon Brown (while Chancellor of the Exchequer) to regulate the UK banking system in the years and months leading to the crunch, knew of the impending financial disaster and where the mismanagement was taking place. However, either they failed to act and/or pass on the information or they were themselves ignored—taking direct responsibility for the situation one step closer to the highest of offices. The situation in the US, where the ripples first began to make themselves known, appears to have been much the same. All the while government coffers were being filled, our supposed guardians were inevitably happy to turn a blind eye to malpractice—yet at the same time, if they truly believed in *sustainable* growth, why did they not intervene at a sensible juncture to ensure a more measured policy to safeguard the future, instead of allowing such a devastating and entirely predictable crash? Hence, when the Truth Agenda is applied to the bigger picture, it is perhaps not too big a leap to imagine that global financial crises might actually be desirable to those with a hidden purpose to their actions. The current global administrations have all predictably failed to impose any genuinely effective regulation that would prevent it happening again, intimidated, it would seem, by those who really hold the purse-strings.

Many campaigners point to international banking as being one of the key tools of the Illuminati, and challenge the very legal legitimacy of entirely unaccountable financial cornerstones such as the US Federal Reserve (the country's central banking system) and other banks around the world. They point out that these are in truth privately-owned companies, which have corralled and misused our money for their own ends, and that they should never have been given such massive influence. One of Barack Obama's first actions as president in 2009 was to give even *more* control to the Federal Reserve.[11] Globalization, questionable trade agreements and the arms trade, meanwhile, increase the West's control of the 'developing world' at the expense of the people living there, and the bankers are never far away from the machinations. The pertinent documentary *The Money Masters: How International Bankers Gained Control of America*, includes two revealing quotes:

'The powers of financial capitalism had a far-reaching plan, nothing less than to create a world system of financial control in private hands able to dominate the political system of each country and the economy of the world as a whole... Their secret is that they have annexed from governments, monarchies, and republics the power to create the world's money...' —Prof. Carroll Quigley, author of *Tragedy & Hope: A History of the World in Our Time*

'Banking was conceived in iniquity and was born in sin. The bankers own the Earth. Take it away from them, but leave them the power to create money, and with the flick of the pen they will create enough deposits to buy it back again. However, take it away from them, and all the great fortunes like mine will disappear and they ought to disappear, for this would be a happier and better world to live in. But, if you wish to remain the slaves of bankers and pay the cost of your own slavery, let them continue to create money' —Sir Josiah Stamp, Director of the Bank of England in the 1920s [12]

If anyone doubted that money is indeed created 'with the flick of the pen', the now ubiquitous tactic of deploying 'quantitative easing' as a risky way of kick-starting economies should have dissolved any illusions. The fact is that we *have* given our power away to the banks, and without any doubt whatsoever this has allowed them to be run and/or manipulated by elite groups with something other than the public's well-being in mind. Money has indeed long been used as a method of social enslavement; today we have it through crushing everyday debts such as mortgages or

(in the UK) student loans, which hamper our freedom from the earliest stages of life. Now the question of who really owns that money—and thus who owns *us*—is coming to the fore for uncomfortable reappraisal. Banks may have appeared to have taken the public rap for having allowed the 2008 crash to occur (with supposedly humbled board members appearing before Senate and parliamentary select committees to shed a few porcelain tears), but this seems to have been a distractive ruse to conceal what was effectively not only

Canary Wharf, London, the financial center of Britain (complete with glass pyramid—see page 92), towering over its surroundings in more ways than one. International banking is widely considered to be behind many global manipulations, according to conspiracy theorists. If nothing else, it is clear that this is where real power resides.

their continuing, but increasing power. Meanwhile, those at the bottom pay dearly with the little they have, while the emphasis of blame for all this has cleverly shifted so that it is the likes of benefit claimants, single mothers, racial minorities and immigrants that are seen to be responsible for all of society's woes instead of those in the glass towers enjoying enormous undeserved bonuses and living lives of luxury at everyone else's expense. Likewise, in some countries energy prices soar while people shiver, and sometimes die, fearful to turn the heating on, a situation that is sold as 'necessary' to sustain the market, even as profits break new records each year.

Under the pressures of the economic crisis, several major governments effectively used taxpayers money to prop up the banking system in an undeclared form of nationalization, creating a further blurring between the jurisdictions of banks and authorities (which may have been a planned calculated risk on the part of the elite puppeteers). As such, banks thus demonstrated the inherent entanglement they have with—and stranglehold they have on—governments. Unwise gambles with this money see some countries risking total bankruptcy, making them more vulnerable to 'persuasion' on certain issues, or susceptible to more centralized international control, as Greece and a number of other European countries have discovered, weakened under the weight of harsh austerity measures. This makes it harder to resist the carrots being offered by those who claim that Europe and its currency would be 'stronger' under a far more federal umbrella, a solution now being persistently fanfared. Thus measures claimed to benefit the NWO are quietly established.

There is also a pervading suspicion amongst the cynical that temporary fixes which can give the appearance that financial crises are over (usually based on the injection of taxpayers' money and vast amounts hastily-borrowed from various international funds, putting countries into crippling debt for decades to come), are in themselves attempts to create a false sense of security that will in time result in a final and devastating global crash, especially if the fluctuating dollar were to collapse. Into the wake of this, say some, will step the NWO, creating a financial system from scratch that will 'rescue' the world—and more closely serve their purposes.

The European Stepping-Stone

In 2009, there was a fear that the notorious MPs' expenses scandal [page 140] might create such a loss of faith in the British parliamentary system that the country might find itself running into the arms of closer ties with Europe as a remedy. Perhaps it was just coincidence that this occurred in the run-up to important Euro-MP elections—taking any discussion of real and serious issues about Europe's creeping influence away from the front pages for several weeks—but it led some cynics to suspect it may have been a coordinated distraction to quietly allow further federal integration. However, if this was a secret elite plan, then it is one that badly backfired—or the blueprint was suddenly altered. For, in actuality, Britain has taken a far *more* Euroskeptic view since, with the rise (in profile not least) of the UK Independence Party, wide public resistance to EU policies, and government promises of a referendum to decide the country's future in the Union. Although some doubters still fear this outward situation is another distractive ruse, any dark intentions for Britain's role in a more tightly controlled Europe would seem to be on the back-burner

The Strasbourg Parliament, France, one of the two European Parliaments (the other is in Brussels) that have growing influence in an increasingly federal-looking EU superstate. Is this just a stepping-stone to an overly-controlling one world government? Many people fear so.

for the time being. Despite this, the ongoing EU agenda remains quietly aided and abetted in the UK and other countries by those working for initiatives such as 'Common Purpose', which promotes federal European aims through insidious (and suspiciously shadowy) infiltration of local government and public services via 'educational' staff courses and financial backhanders.[14]

The unquestionable march to a far more federal EU is widely viewed as a key step to a global state, in which the idea of a small country retaining its own currency (and thus true control over its own policies) will become impossible to sustain. The denials of federalism often heard emanating from the Brussels and Strasbourg Parliaments have been rendered hollow by situations such as the Irish referendum which rejected the overtly federalist 'Treaty of Lisbon' in 2008. Constitutionally, Ireland's rejection should have seen the treaty's implementation being halted; instead the 'no' vote was simply ignored, with the emerald isle bullied into voting again in 2009, this time to give an inevitable 'yes', given that Ireland's economy had by then become very fragile and that a few little 'sweeteners' had been added into the mix. With referenda in France and The Netherlands already having turned down a reworking of the EU constitution in 2005 to little effect, The Treaty of Lisbon has effectively gone ahead anyhow. If other possible single currencies such as the (thus far denied) Amero do threaten to well up, new areas of the world will presumably be able to look forward to their own similar 'unifying' projects.

Many of the suggested solutions to the global financial crisis could lead eventually to the development of a true World Bank. How long, then, will it be before a One World Government is also suggested to go with it? It is interesting to see how often the idea of increased centralization of power is publicly mooted as the answer to all our problems. With the very public trials of the euro in recent years, and fears for the dollar, some say the collapse of either or both could help pave the way to a new, and probably paperless, global currency. An eventual crash of the euro may even have always been deliberately factored in with this end in mind, according to truthseekers, perhaps making a little more sense of its rollercoaster instability. In this view, all the while it serves a purpose it will survive, but when the time comes for bigger steps towards One World Government, then its collapse might be triggered.

Some minds, of course, welcome the idea of globalized central administration. Surely this would end all wars, and create a new era of peace and harmony, such as that envisaged by Utopian writers for centuries (H G Wells and Bertrand Russell amongst them—pages 270-272)? In theory, perhaps it would. Perhaps there are even good intentions of a kind behind all this centralization [Chapter XIII]. The problem comes with observing those who appear to be attempting to implement this system. Can we trust them? Unfortunately their actions so far, together with the lessons of history, suggest that we cannot. There does not yet appear to be anyone enlightened enough to be entrusted with such vast power, but that isn't stopping certain people from trying to attain it.

Many Threads

How could all this elite control operate without it being obvious? Answer: very subtly. Uniformed Illuminati officers would not openly stroll the corridors of power; they wouldn't need to. Merely pulling a few strings from above and having a few contacts in key places would be quite enough to foster their agendas to begin with—and they would be playing a long game, begun decades, perhaps centuries, ago. In any case, truthseekers claim it *is* all obvious—so obvious that the world doesn't take any notice. A simple glance at those openly attending meetings of democracy-averse groups such as the Bilderbergs—often mainstream politicians, bankers, and even royalty—soon makes it clear who the agents of global elitism might be.

It is traditional with this kind of subject matter to list here an unending series of potential conspiracies and manipulations that may be shaping our world, naming names, identifying backgrounds and getting into complex details about plots and schemes. But that would add hundreds of pages. Although specific examples will follow in this book, readers are advised to research the wider picture elsewhere and speculate as they will (this author's own book *Conspiracies: The Facts—The Theories—The Evidence* gives an overview which may be helpful in this regard). There are numerous tomes and websites out there packed with information on just about any thread one wishes to follow, and readers are encouraged to do so (see *Appendix 3* for some useful pointers)—while they still can. With the freedom of the Internet ever under potential threat [Chapter IX], we may have only a limited window left in which this some of this information can be easily shared. Reading *Nineteen Eighty-Four* (or indeed Aldous Huxley's 1932 novel *Brave New World*) will also help to understand the unfortunate blueprint that many of our governments seem to be working to, Illuminati or no Illuminati. What is important here is to apply the Truth Agenda to some of the bigger mysteries and cover-ups that most people can immediately relate to and that *do* appear to have some serious supporting evidence which demands investigation.

Above all, what the conspiracy speculation does incontrovertibly reveal is that an underlying system of creeping control has been foisted upon us in recent years. This, at the very least, appears to be undeniable whichever way it is looked at.

A Society of Control

Since 9/11, initially under the aegis of the 'War on Terror', and for reasons explored later, the Western nations have implemented a series of policies that have progressively whittled away the liberties that formerly held up our society—all in the name of our protection. This is particularly true in the USA and the UK. Our former freedom—of speech, movement and action—has rapidly been replaced with fear-based restrictions and a culture where people no longer feel so relaxed to speak out loud about their concerns. We are continually monitored by cameras and now governed by either laws or systems that give the state the ability to pry into any area of our lives, no matter how private. This is analyzed more fully in Chapter IX.

Defenders of the restrictions contend that someone with nothing to hide has no reason to fear them, and they welcome the idea of an international ID scheme.[15] One was due to be introduced in the UK by the Labour government of the late 2000s, but the subsequent Conservative/Liberal Democrat coalition reversed the decision, apparently in a new spirit of liberty. The coalition certainly seemed less *overtly* controlling than the previous administration, but the motivation may have been fuelled more by finance, in the rush to plunge the country into stark austerity, rather than benefience. It has also been pointed out that, with human microchipping just around the corner in any case, as shall be explored, there may simply have been no need to spend vast amounts on an intermediate scheme. Why have all the bother and inconvenience of a plastic card, when you can have a little chip inserted into your flesh, which can be 'swiped', like superstore bar codes?

As the issue has not gone away, then, but merely been temporarily sidelined, it is worth exploring the mindset behind the claimed benefits of any kind of ID scheme in any country. Whatever form it takes, it would have to involve a system akin to the proposed National Identity Register (NIR). Surely, say supporters of such schemes, if we know who everyone is, all checked and approved, then we will be safer from terrorists, criminals and electoral fraud? On the surface, some justification for a checking system in some form can be found. The problem, once again, lies with the observation that the kinds of minds likely to implement what would amount to stark controls and restrictions have never proved themselves reliable or trustworthy in the past, in addition to the fact that such systems would inevitably be much open to abuse. Many studies show that they would not be immune to fraud, nor prevent all terrorism or crime—but any equivalent system would certainly give authorities a huge crowbar of control and surveillance.

The microchip tags now being pioneered are 'biometric'. This means that they are not the same as glorified passports or consumer loyalty cards, which is the usual defense. Instead, they help exchange DNA information, fingerprints, digitized facial and iris scans and other very personal information that, in the wrong hands, could be widely misused. Multiple categories of personal information would eventually be held on each citizen. When an ID-chip becomes required, as it soon enough will, for every public transport journey, every shopping and bank account transaction and every entry into a public place, then at that point all significant movements, purchases and decisions we ever make will be recorded via the ID system.

Once information goes onto a centralized digital database of any kind, there is no way of indefinitely protecting it. Sooner or later it will become available to any authority, and probably any commercial enterprise that needs that information (such as life insurers keen to root out genetic disorders). No satisfactory answers to these concerns have ever been forthcoming from governments that support ID schemes. The continual 'accidental' losses of authorities' data discs, laptops and other official files containing detailed information on everyday citizens, forever cause public scandal and illustrate how easily private data can be mishandled. However, these 'losses' are a double-edged sword. Decried by some as evidence of why ID systems could never be safe, the reality is that the public outcry actually allows politicians to justify setting up *more secure and controlled* databases for the future—enabling some to talk up microchip tags as a solution to the problem. Which may be the idea.

More serious is what will happen in a tagged culture where performing most day-to-day actions will not be possible without an ID chip. When someone in authority, however unfairly, decides that a member of the public has become a 'subversive' or undesirable element, it will become very easy to remove them from mainstream society, simply by deactivating their entry in the database (or, at some point in future technological development, deactivating the chip). This will restrict movement and essentially reduce the digitally dispossessed to the status of social lepers.[16] In the forthcoming cashless society, even going shopping in person or online won't be an option in this situation. You may not consider yourself a subversive, but if someone decides otherwise on your behalf, there will be little to be done about it. Given the increasingly controlling tendencies of some Western governments since 9/11, how much of a stretch of the imagination is it to foresee a problematic regime coming to power that might be quite capable of making such decisions when faced with political critics? Already we have seen peace protestors, political truth campaigners and otherwise lawful members of society being intimidated by authorities or physically removed from public meetings [page 191]. In a microchipped society, the threatened withdrawal of personal identity may become yet another useful persuader.

Beyond the more conspiratorial side of the issue, what would transpire if one were simply deleted from the ID system by accident? The proposed legislation would place the onus firmly on individuals to prove who they are and fight for reinstatement to the system, invoking the possibility of Kafka-esque nightmares in dealing with a faceless bureaucracy just to regain one's freedom of movement.

A Microchipped Population

How near are we, then, to a full culture of microchip implants? It has, in fact, already begun. Electronic chip schemes have now been pioneered for several years, especially in the USA, with the likes of police, soldiers, students, young children and office workers being used as guinea pigs. Pets are now widely microchipped without any great fuss being raised, and fear of terrorism and crime is already being used to encourage support for the entire human race to be next for the scheme—no more unidentified bombers or shoplifters; no more straying Alzheimer's victims; no more missing children. The hysterically intense and slightly unsavory media fascination with the tragic apparent kidnapping in 2007 of the little girl Madeleine McCann in Portugal (still unsolved at the time of writing) provided just one of many justifications to the nervous as to why we would all be better off chipped. Fear, as ever, makes us consider the darkest of things through colored filters—and it seems that everything possible is being done to keep us in the fear zone [Chapters IX & X].

The thought of a generation united by the presence of their very own microchip makes some people feel safe, but many others sense something inherently wrong with such a system. With little faith in those implementing it, who knows what the chips might really be used for and what they might be capable of? Just the thought that even an innocent moment on your own would not be possible without the authorities knowing where you were and what you were doing, brings to mind poor Winston Smith cowering in the corner just out of view of the telescreen in Orwell's all-too-prescient parable. Already we have clusters of cameras on every main street (with more in the UK than any other country in the world, oddly), but the chips mean there will soon be no escape, not even in little corners of former privacy.

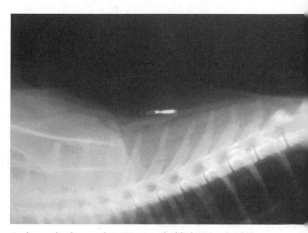

Radiograph of a cat, showing its embedded ID microchip. ID chips for pets are now commonplace, and get us used to the idea of the benefits they can supposedly bring: people are now being chipped too, however, and there are grave areas of concern over the potential misuse of such implants.

It sounds like sci-fi, but it isn't. Some clothing and other goods are already impregnated with RFID chips (Radio-Frequency Identification) for commercial tracking purposes, with the eventual intention that shops will be able to trace their goods from manufacture to sale to final ownership. Even without ID tags, soon every company will know what you bought and where you went with it, allowing them to bombard you with unwanted but specifically targeted advertising and promotional offers, as already happens with online retailers. Vehicles use RFID for toll gates in some countries and a system is also being set up that will track all of our journeys (monitoring speed and driving quality) on government databases. Before long our bodies will be tagged in the same way, the minutiae of our lives available to any authority that wants it. The ID chip will rule everyone's lives—unless a significant number of people stand up and hold out against it, as they admirably did against the card scheme in the UK. But there is only a limited window of time in which the stand can be taken, and the upcoming generation of mobile phone users, social networkers and computer gamers who already interface with technology on a continual basis are far less resistant to the concept of minute-by-minute surveillance. This acceptance will accelerate massively when the Internet is fully available anywhere, anytime through electronic glasses or is (as will in time occur) beamed directly into the eye. All these marvels of science offer astonishing gifts, undoubtedly, but they also bring dangers.

Who, then, are the people who will help make a stand against sleepwalking into a world of state control and systemic monitoring? Who will lead the protests? Why did somebody not warn us about the dangers to liberty that suddenly seem to be upon us? Couldn't somebody have *done* something? These cries will become louder and more ubiquitous as ID schemes and other surveillance measures being developed (such as 'Smart' technology in our homes) finally make themselves fully known.

In truth, there have been several mainstream attempts to alert people to the type of society we are heading into. However, when their brave ambassadors arrive on our living room screens or printed pages, all too often people laugh at them—and we are encouraged to do so. What kind of people are these sacrificial jesters that we might have dismissed rather too easily? Here is one prominent example.

The Fall and Rise of David Icke

When former British TV sports presenter and Green Party spokesman David Icke suddenly announced a spiritual conversion in the early 1990s, it was perfect tabloid fodder. When a former statesman like Tony Blair becomes a Catholic, eyebrows may be raised, but no-one sniggers at the beliefs themselves. But Icke had found a different kind of spirituality, of the New Age persuasion, which, inexplicably, is always seen as fair game for media hounds. Old religions, despite all their foibles, misdemeanors and strange mysticism, seem to command respect, but new belief systems are never afforded the same treatment [page 212]. So when a favorite BBC sports personality started to talk about psychic channelling, higher guidance and our collective connection to a universal consciousness, out came the knives of ridicule.

David Icke, conspiracy messiah to some, laughing stock to others. But many of Icke's predictions have been proven right and his books have a wide global readership.

David Icke's initial penchant for wearing turquoise shell-suits, together with his famous appearance on presenter Terry Wogan's peak-time UK television show to tell viewers that he was the 'Son of God' has somehow lodged in the collective British memory. What few remember is that he did later qualify the latter statement by saying that we are all 'sons of God'—something agreed on by several world religions. But Icke-as-new-Messiah suited the media sensationalists and he was written off as a laughing stock who had just destroyed a promising career. Or had he?

With the turquoise gone, and a little less of the New Age rhetoric, David Icke turned his new-found spiritual insights into something directly practical. His media status, however much it was being used for chuckles, gave Icke an unusually high-profile conduit into the mainstream and he began to find his unconventional views and pronouncements about world events making their way into the global mainstream at a level few others could achieve. As his interest in what could make the planet a better place turned to deep explorations into what had made it so dark in the first place, he found himself becoming labelled a 'conspiracy theorist' and a fighter for liberty and freedom. This enabled the usual journalistic sidelining reserved for such areas, but it also won Icke new attention and support from many despondent truthseekers around the globe, happy to have found someone who could represent them at last.

With those on high perhaps realizing that things were going too far, there were attempts to neuter Icke in the mid-1990s. His risky strategy of quoting the *Protocols of the Elders of Zion*—an apparently forged document of supposedly Jewish plans for world domination created to stir up hatred towards Judaism in 1903—saw Icke receiving very public accusations of anti-Semitism, despite his protestations that he did NOT believe Jews to be behind the protocols. Instead, he openly stated that the sentiments of the document, even if a hoax, were being used as a blueprint for global domination by other groups. His books made this more than clear, but the 'Nazi' accusations stuck for some time before Icke was able to shake them off.

The belief of some that fundamentalist Zionism—as opposed to genuine Judaism—might be a component of New World Order machinations is too often used by the mainstream as a stick with which to beat conspiracy theorists. The curious phenomenon by which a simple rearrangement of the digits in the somewhat bizarre London 2012 Olympic logo created the very clear word 'Zion', for instance, raised many eyebrows amongst truthseekers, but this hardly made them anti-Semitic. The fact is that fundamentalism within nearly all of the Abrahamic religions is almost certainly involved with the global agenda somewhere down the line, as we have already seen, and allegations of anti-Semitism are being wrongly used to close down lines of perfectly legitimate enquiry, especially when it comes to scrutiny of American-Israeli politics, CIA-Mossad operations, or indeed elements of extremist Zionism.

Although misguided protestors stuck in a false past still occasionally turn up at David Icke lectures, eventually most of the negative citations faded and a new respect for Icke's uncannily accurate predictions (see below) won him a wide and dedicated following. Indeed, his PROBLEM-REACTION-SOLUTION equation has become a standard expression in the conspiracy world.

PROBLEM-REACTION-SOLUTION defines the manipulation pattern of the New World Order: 1) Create a problem (for example, encourage, allow or actively promote terrorist attacks—or engineer an economic crisis); 2) This generates a large reaction (the population, through fear or outrage, begs for action); 3) The authorities then happily provide the solution (usually more controls and restrictions, with wider powers granted to them, which is what they wanted all along). PROBLEM-REACTION-SOLUTION is a neat and frighteningly sense-making strategy for the power-hungry, which, once recognized, can be seen in action all around us if we care to look for it.

Over the years, David Icke's prolific books, passionate speeches and website commentaries have become a powerful influence in the pantheon of truth movements and liberty campaigning. He sells out lecture halls and arenas throughout the world and finds his views repeated and pondered on by many other truthseekers. Yet many of those same supporters will not admit openly to having any interest in the man, let alone having had contact with him.

Here's why.

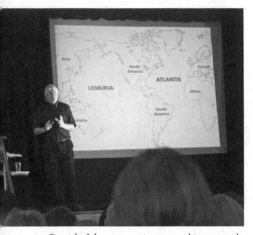

David Icke in action, speaking at the Alternative View conference, 2008. Icke's own all-day seminars can last several hours without a break, but his oratory skills command big audiences.

The Extra-Terrestrial Bloodline

The main contention with the views of David Icke, even amongst some otherwise loyal supporters, has been his belief that... the world is run by an elite group of extra-terrestrial reptilian beings. Icke—and other researchers, it must be said—gradually developed the view, based on alleged (and controversial) eye-witness testimony, ancient legends and clairvoyant sources.

Essentially, the reptile-theory runs that an extra-terrestrial gene was seeded to create a ruling class amongst humankind aeons ago and that this same class—with the British monarchy as its central hub—runs the world today, helping to perpetrate all of the conspiratorial horrors outlined at the beginning of this chapter. According to this view, the reptilian bloodline is diligently maintained, and shape-shifting abilities mask the true nature of its carriers.[17]

If the idea of the Queen being an alien lizard wasn't enough for some, the notion that she and her brethren (including all US presidents) carry out blood sacrifices and ritual child abuse in an extensive occult network was the final straw. This saw many part company with Icke's views, to the point of total denial that they had even looked at one of his books, when, in fact, their shelves were stacked with them.

Why, then, does anyone give David Icke the time of day at all? Is the reptile stuff not evidence enough that he is the madman many proclaim? The reason for Icke's continuing mitigation amongst the loyal—however uncomfortable it may be—is that he has been proven to be right on many things he predicted years ago.

The surveillance state, ID issues, human micro-chipping, a war on terrorism sparked by a massively-orchestrated attack, the rise of a federal Europe, and all manner of global political shifts that have come to pass or are in the planning now—all of these and much more were anticipated by David Icke over a decade before they began in earnest. Perhaps anyone with foresight could have extrapolated the logical conclusion of some of the policies and social trends quietly being implemented in the early 1990s, and Icke has certainly not been alone, nor was he the first, in sounding warnings (see also William Cooper, Alex Jones, Jeff Rense, Jim Marrs, *et al*). Yet Icke's take on it all has turned out to be one of the most fully-formed and shrewd. Hence, for all the disquiet over his more extreme beliefs, many concerned followers of truth and liberty movements have never quite been able to resist tuning into the latest opinions of this sometimes bullish, yet somehow surprisingly grounded modern prophet with formidable skills of oration.

And what of those extreme beliefs? Is the notion of an elite bloodline being passed down through the ages by a ruling class with occult tendencies truly such a hard thing to accept? Royal families and dynasties amongst the wealthy have always guarded bloodlines and performed rituals of a mystical nature. The higher secret societies, which clearly have significant social influence, vet members closely (admitting them with the bizarrest of esoteric ceremonies) and jealously protect their own power and welfare. And it does appear to be true, as any researcher can determine, that many US presidents (and past prospective presidential candidates, such as John Kerry, who would later be elevated to US Secretary of State under Obama's administration) have had direct genealogical links to the British monarchy, including, of course, the Bush family. With even a mainstream research project stating that just 6000 powerful people effectively manage the world, if the extra-terrestrial gene is taken simply as a metaphor, the scenario of the global situation and who might be running it today can still be seen as amounting to much the same thing.[18]

But, for all the controversy, there are those who refuse to fully relinquish the notion that some members of the human race may carry an extra-terrestrial gene. Why? Perhaps because it's explicitly implied in the Bible.

The Genesis Gene
Genesis, Chapter 6, verses 1-4, very clearly implies that humankind once interbred with a race not of our world—the 'sons of God'—and suggests that the influence of that new gene pool continued on through the ages. With a mysterious spin-off hybrid race, 'The Nephilim', also mentioned, the references to possible extra-terrestrial intervention are too compelling to be ignored. The *New American Standard Bible* translates it thus:

'Now it came about, when men began to multiply on the face of the land, and daughters were born to them, that the sons of God saw that the daughters of men were beautiful; and they took wives for themselves, whomever they chose. Then the Lord said, "My Spirit shall not strive with man forever, because he also is flesh; nevertheless his days shall be

one hundred and twenty years." The Nephilim were on the Earth in those days, and also afterward, when the sons of God came in to the daughters of men, and they bore children to them. Those were the mighty men who were of old, men of renown.'

The 'sons of God' clearly implies angelic beings—for which many read extra-terrestrials—interbreeding with humans. They are referred to as 'giants' in some texts. However, some Abrahamic folklore (especially the Ethiopian *Book of Enoch*) has it that the latterly-mentioned Nephilim were the offspring of fallen angels who broke the rules and lusted for human females. Various other biblically-related ancient texts refer to similar stories. Some see the Nephilim as a malign race that God attempted to wipe out with the flood escaped by Noah (the story of which follows on directly from the above quoted passage), although the phrase 'the Nephilim were on the Earth in those days, and also afterward' suggests their bloodline may have survived. Could this be the seed of the so-called reptilian agenda of today? We may never know exactly what this brief passage in the Bible refers to. Perhaps there is an entirely mundane origin (some hold that the Nephilim were simply a race of tall tribal warriors), but it has inevitably led to much speculation amongst those who believe we are still under the influence of the Genesis gene, not least because so many other ancient cultures have similar references to past interference from outside of our Earthly realm.

 A number of old civilizations held that their gods originated from the stars, especially the Egyptians and the Sumerians, whose records have been best preserved. (Tribal traditions also tap the same seam—elders of the African Dogon tribe believe that they are directly descended from beings of the star system Sirius, and some claim they have long known uncannily accurate information about that region of space, although skeptics are predictably dismissive.) The Sumerian legend of the 'Annunaki'—their gods—has many parallels with the story of the biblical Nephilim. The late ancient mysteries speculator Zecharia Sitchin interpreted Sumerian records to read that the Annunaki were, in fact, extra-terrestrial beings from the legendary planet Nibiru, who genetically engineered humankind as a slave race to use for manual labour. Although some scholars have criticized his translations, this interpretation of Sumerian myth, put together with the biblical references, is compelling in its general scope. Sitchin's adherents believe Nibiru is on a long elliptical orbit in our solar system, which will bring it back into close contact with Earth any day now (tying in to some people's interpretations of the 'New Era' prophecies—see Chapter XII). They assert that a pure bloodline left by the Annunaki amongst a dominating class long ago has been waiting in the wings to preserve control for the return of their masters. (Others believe that some of the *same* beings, now incredibly ancient and hidden by their shape-shifting abilities, remain with us today in places of power.) As ever, the truth is less important than the belief in the myth; what matters is that certain people in positions of power may hold these stories to be real, and thus act on them with potentially unfortunate consequences. The Sumerian texts speak of a scenario that could easily be applied to David Icke's reptilian hypothesis. As for Nibiru itself, there have now been several erroneous claims of its imminent arrival back in our local space, usually in the guise of various wandering celestial bodies which turn out to be perfectly normal asteroids and comets, but there are also accusations of massive astronomical cover-ups that may be masking its impending return.

Interestingly, the heart of the Sumerian empire, one of the first great advanced cultures, lay in the area once known as Mesopotamia, sometimes referred to as 'the cradle of civilization'. Is it coincidence that this is where modern Iraq is today—the focus of so much world attention and struggle for control over the last decade or so? During the 2003 invasion, the US military even placed their most major base (Camp Alpha, south of Baghdad) on the precise location of ancient Babylon, destroying important archaeological evidence in the process and causing outrage amongst historians.[19] Perhaps there is more mystical significance to gaining dominance over this area then may at first meet the eye, especially if someone on high is expecting the imminent return of their gods—or the fallen angels—to ancient seats of power.

Sumerian carvings showing the arrival of the Annunaki in spaceship-like vessels. Many ancient myths and legends, including the Bible, record god-like beings arriving on Earth and interbreeding with humankind.

In this context, the information from apparently extra-terrestrial sources, and consequent cover-ups surrounding awareness of UFOs, begins to take on a more important resonance. If our former masters are indeed about to make a comeback, is there a secret plan from those in the know to welcome and re-install them—or to fight them in a slave's revolt?

Aside from all the talk of extra-terrestrial genes, there is certainly evidence that mystical wisdom has been preserved by ongoing channels of occult information and passed down by elite encoding throughout the ages. Even without proof of bloodlines, it is clear that esoteric knowledge from antiquity continues to shape our world today.

The Atlantis Connection

Another Genesis reference may have relevance to the continuation of ancient agendas, albeit more obliquely. Genesis 11, verses 1-9, recounts the story of the Tower of Babel, impressing on the reader how powerful humankind was becoming, post-flood. With 'one language' uniting the peoples of the Earth, plans to build a 'tower with its top in the heavens' attracts the jealousy of 'the Lord', who makes clear his disapproval:

'Behold, they are one people, and they have all one language; and this is only the beginning of what they will do; and nothing that they propose to do will now be impossible for them. Come, let us go down, and there confuse their language, that they may not understand one another's speech.' [20]

Struck down with the unexpected absence of oral communicative skills, humans were scattered across 'the face of all the Earth' and the building of the tower was thus abandoned. (Curiously, the Lord's thoughts here could be seen to sum up the attitude of the Illuminati: a self-aware and united population is inherently powerful and ambitious, so must be kept divided, uncommunicative and distracted—a classic 'divide and rule' policy that ensures nothing solid is achieved and no resistance can grow.) Noting the reference 'let us go down', which again implies beings coming from somewhere above, the tale of the Tower of Babel could be taken as a reference to the Atlantis myth. Again and again, ancient legends (and indeed modern clairvoyance and channellings) speak of today's global culture having originally derived from one centralized advanced civilization, be it Atlantis, Lemuria or Mu. These stories often tell of a fall from enlightenment and a forced scattering of inhabitants, fleeing from a disaster or banishment of some kind.

  Many of the more broad-minded historians believe that the interesting similarities of legends, religious beliefs and construction techniques (pyramids in Egypt, China and South America, for instance), which seem to link otherwise disconnected cultures around the world, speak of refugees or settlers from one previously united civilization setting up anew. Some genetic commonalities also support the idea—plus the similarities of ancient symbolism and belief systems that appear to have seeped down even into modern culture.

Pieter Bruegel's 1563 painting of the Tower of Babel. The story of the tower, halted when God struck down humanity so that men were no longer able to communicate with each other in one tongue, has resonance with the story of Atlantis. Most cultures have myths of a once enlightened but lost civilisation.

Secret Societies

The arcane knowledge, symbols and myths of otherwise lost times are thought by some to be encoded in the writings and teachings of mystic traditions and secret societies, especially amongst the higher echelons of Freemasonry, and ruling-class 'orders' like Skull and Bones, which began at Yale University in Connecticut and has included such alumnae as George W Bush (and indeed his one-time electoral rival John Kerry). This very jealously guarded information may be a fragment of a bygone age preserved for the elite few, believing themselves to be distant descendants of the survivors who were perhaps chosen as guardians of that knowledge for its eventual application in times of upheaval. This is why some conspiracy theorists point to

the likes of Freemasonry as being the core of the dark elite, although it is pretty clear that lower degrees (happy with a bit of ritual, local influence and some nice dinners) wouldn't know much about it, nor would they consider themselves a negative influence in society. Some would also argue that Freemasonry's roots cannot be traced back much beyond a few centuries, and assert that it simply adopted the esoterica of ancient cultures, particularly Egyptian, as an affectation to add gravitas.

Other critics of the secret society-connection have claimed that the likes of Freemasonry's principles would be at odds with those of a born-again Christian such as George W Bush (various religious bodies have attacked Freemasonry as being incompatible with mainstream faiths); however, prominently religious people are known to be members of various 'lodges' and Freemasonry does not discourage belief in God. Indeed, as the mainstream source *Wikipedia* has it:

Original Egyptian needle in situ. Needles and pyramids are still used today to denote power over society.

'Candidates for regular Freemasonry are required to declare a belief in a Supreme Being. However, the candidate is not asked to expand on, or explain, his interpretation of Supreme Being. The discussion of politics and religion is forbidden within a Masonic Lodge, in part so a Mason will not be placed in the situation of having to justify his personal interpretation. Thus, reference to the Supreme Being will mean the Christian Trinity to a Christian Mason, Allah to a Muslim Mason, Para Brahman to a Hindu Mason, etc. And while most Freemasons would take the view that the term Supreme Being equates to God, others may hold a more complex or philosophical interpretation of the term.' [21]

The fact is that membership of secret societies does seem to be a linking thread amongst many influential people on the world stage, and anything hidden is bound to generate fear of cronyism and underhand dealings. Some of Freemasonry's strange and guarded traditions are guaranteed to raise questions from the outside, and the symbols of ancient power that it may share with whatever other questionable forces might be operating do seem to be everywhere.

THE TRUTH AGENDA

It doesn't take much searching to find Masonic and other secret society symbolism in some pretty obvious settings: the profusion of stone 'needles' (often genuine Egyptian imports) and other curious monuments placed at key locations across the world; corporate and political logos with overt mystical references; and, most famously, the 'Eye or Providence' or 'all-seeing-eye' over the pyramid on the dollar bill (amongst other heavy hints on banknotes of many countries). Some researchers believe that the modern layouts of entire cities also incorporate occult significance, with Paris (France) and Washington DC providing particularly good fuel for conspiracy theorists and numerologists alike. With both those cities

The 'Eye of Providence' on a standard dollar bill, with obvious ancient and secret society connotations. The multi-layered meanings of this banknote alone could take a whole chapter to discuss.

having had strong Masonic links during the French Revolutionary years of the late 1700s, the secret society emblems in each do seem to be especially overt, with the requisite needles, pyramids, claimed mystical alignments of street layouts and oddly cryptic and significant architectural proportions provoking huge, if not always accurate, speculation.[22] Pyramids in particular have long been associated with strange properties and used as symbols of dominance (representing the levels of true power, with the ignorant masses at the lowest level). The erection, therefore, of a huge glass pyramid at the Louvre (completed in 1989, the bicentenary of the Revolution), with three smaller pyramidal satellites and also an underground inverted version, was bound to cause the biggest stir of all and remains the subject of much dark muttering amongst fervent anti-NWO factions.

The Washington Monument, Washington DC. Constructed to emulate classic Egyptian architecture, it is the largest obelisk of its kind in the world at (a numerologically curious) 555 feet and five inches tall—and is considered by many to be a straight statement of Masonic domination.

The phenomenal success of Dan Brown's novel *The Da Vinci Code* in 2003 (in which the remains of Mary Magdalene are hinted to lie beneath the Louvre's inverted pyramid, a secret concealed by a series of cryptic clues and conspiracies) compounded the tangled conjecture and gave weight to the urban myth that the main surface pyramid is comprised of 666 glass panes. Although it is a tantalizing fact that the official Louvre brochure did indeed claim this biblically prophetic number during initial construction, a modern count shows that there are in truth at least 673 panes in the completed version. Nonetheless, put together with all the other claimed Parisian occult connections, the arrival of an

actual pyramid in their midst was bound to raise eyebrows —eyebrows which arched even higher when the Egyptian needle at the Place de la Concorde [page 66] was, with great ceremony, mysteriously crowned with a smaller golden pyramid in 1998.

Much of the ancient knowledge kept by today's secret societies and embodied in public architecture is generally believed to have been passed down to modernity by the likes of medieval religious orders such as the

Glass pyramid at the Louvre, Paris, a modern addition to the many mystical symbols across the city. Most of the great cities of the world appear to embody specific layouts and architecture as signs of power.

Knights Templar and the Rosicrucians (bearing secrets learnt during the crusades),

Tip of the inverted pyramid at the Louvre, scene of a fictional conspiracy in The Da Vinci Code, *but full of connotations in its own right.*

with various bloodlines and dynasties sharing many connections. Paris and Washington DC are considered the most prominent examples of that arcane knowledge being given physical form, with all the energetic power such symbolism is believed to hold, but the layout of London is also suspected to have been built with a similar agenda. This is highlighted by the fact that Sir Christopher Wren—a prominent Freemason—had direct influence over the reconstruction of London after the Great Fire of 1666 (the numerology of which has inevitably been seen as more than coincidence).

Paris found itself under further conspiratorial scrutiny when Princess Diana died there in the infamous car crash of 31st August 1997. According to varying claims, the Pont de l'Alma underpass where the shocking incident took place is built either on the site of an ancient Roman temple dedicated, pointedly, to the goddess Diana (the Louvre statue of whom looks oddly similar to the princess), and/or on top of an underground chamber of Merovingian kings (500-751 AD) where ritual sacrifices were once made. The presence above the underpass of the gold 'flame of liberty' monument (now generally presumed by tourists to commemorate Diana's death, but in fact erected in 1987—page 20) gave rise to other fevered speculation from those who believe the Princess's death was essentially an occult-layered assassination. Was a crash engineered at a meaningful sacrificial site to represent an icon of 'liberty' being extinguished? Or is this all fanciful fantasy born of strange coincidence?[23] Others believe that Dealey Plaza in Dallas, Texas, where President Kennedy was shot in 1963, is similarly laden with occult symbolism.

The underpass at the Pont de l'Alma, Paris, where Princess Diana's car crashed in uncertain circumstances that will be debated forever. With the Flame of Liberty monument standing above it, was her death a ritual killing?

Present-day UK architecture seems equally prone to the inclusion of barely-hidden ancient symbolism: Canary Wharf Tower (officially One Canada Square, for years Britain's tallest building), the distinctive skyscraper at a key financial center of London, is topped by a perfect glass pyramid of apparently the same implied geometrical proportions as the Great Pyramid of Giza [Chapter II].[24] Correlation has also been claimed between Canary Wharf and the longitude and latitude of various Egyptian monuments (indeed, an entire global web of Illuminati-inspired mystical alignments is presumed to exist by many theorists), while accusations of occult influence in the local politics of the surrounding borough of Tower Hamlets even reached mainstream news in the 1990s.

This is but a tiny selection of the ancient esoteric knowledge believed to be making its presence felt in the modern world. If it is indeed a conspiracy in operation, those at work on its behalf don't seem to mind boasting about it through overt representation in architecture and public monuments, seemingly rife with multi-layered meaning. Some would say it is a straight thumbing of the nose to the dumb masses.

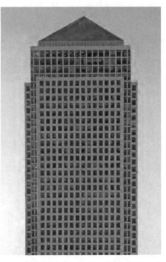

One Canada Square, Canary Wharf, London, topped with a pyramid of its own and allegedly aligned with the longitude and latitude of several ancient sites in Egypt.

Others, of course, laugh at the suggestion that secret societies are the guardians of real power or any kind of ancient wisdom. Is there, after all, any proof whatsoever that they get up to anything remotely worrying or subversive? With this in mind, let us have a look at one such organization in more detail.

The Bohemian Grove Rituals

In 1872, a group of Californian journalists, musicians and artists founded a secret society, which they christened The Bohemian Club, reflecting its then avant-garde roots. As time went by, the club began to attract wealthy businessmen, media moguls and politicians, and this mix soon became its primary focus. Exclusively male, it was the classic fraternal society lampooned more than once by the likes of Laurel and Hardy and *The Flintstones*, with strict vows of secrecy and complex rituals, balanced by 'hi-jinx' and 'low-jinx' entertainments.

Each July, the Bohemian Club would hold an annual summer encampment in beautiful woods outside of Los Angeles purchased especially for its activities. This place became known as Bohemian Grove.

The Cremation of Care ceremony ends with fireworks at Bohemian Grove, California, in 1907. This secret tradition, which bizarrely involves sacrificing the effigy of a child to a giant stone owl, continues today and is attended each year by very high-profile politicians.

At the camp, plays and musical performances would be staged at different arenas throughout the woods, and club members would drink, 'bond', discuss business deals and get up to who knows what else around campfires beneath the stars.

The centerpiece of the summer camp, held on the first Saturday of each three-week event, was a ritual known as 'The Cremation of Care', in which selected members would... *dress in robes and sacrifice the effigy of a child to a giant stone owl*. By so doing, attendees would dispense with the 'dull cares' of the world outside, leaving them free to frolic without conscience.

It might all sound like some eccentric piece of Victoriana, the kind of thing long ago left behind by reason and enlightenment—were it not for the fact that The Bohemian Club is still alive and well and that the Cremation of Care ceremony is to this day conducted each July to massive attendances. Amongst the crowd are always influential politicians, bankers, leading magnates, corporate executives and selected celebrities; the people who shape our society. This, then, is what some of our world leaders do on their holidays: watch effigies of children being sacrificed to large stone owls. Readers may be tempted at this point to dismiss this as mad fantasy. Remarkably, it isn't.[25]

Although it is rarely spoken about in public, it is well-known—and acknowledged—that many key political figures of each generation have made appearances at Bohemian Grove, often upcoming presidents, prime ministers or congressmen; Richard Nixon, Ronald Reagan, Henry Kissinger and Dick Cheney are just a handful of 'names' known to have attended or regularly attended. George W Bush and Tony Blair are also rumored (and generally assumed) to have passed through the Grove, and it is more than likely that Barack Obama and other Western leaders have been there too. With camp attendance figures approaching 3000 in some years, it's a fair bet that many of the aforementioned 6000-people-who-run-the-world will have attended Bohemian Grove at some time or another. Interestingly, Bill Clinton claimed *not* to have ever been there, and famously appeared to mock the Bohemian Club, but if this wasn't a diversionary tactic it might explain why his tenancy in the White House was allowed to be the one of the most publicly vilified in history (despite positive opinion polls), complete with exposed sex scandals and impeachment attempts. Perhaps one is either 'in' or 'out'. [Not that the Clintons should in any way be excused from their own inevitable part in any underlying agendas, especially given the high political profile of former US Secretary of State Hillary Clinton. The ominous string of untimely deaths (around 50, through mysterious suicides, accidents and murders) amongst those with close knowledge of the Clintons' business and political dealings suggests—at the very least—an unfortunate affliction that makes the couple worth avoiding.][26]

How do we know about the Cremation of Care ceremony if it's all so secret? Tellingly, one of the key exposures on the Bohemian Grove activities was made not by a conspiracy theorist, but by UK television and press journalist Jon Ronson. In 2000, whilst researching a book and television series (Channel Four's *The Secret Rulers of the World*), Ronson joined impassioned US truthseeker Alex Jones in breaking into the woods, and successfully filmed parts of the Cremation of Care ritual before having to make a hasty exit as suspicions were aroused. Doubtful at first, but convinced by the evidence of his own eyes, Ronson conceded that the presence of prominent leaders at the Bohemian Grove rituals was at the very least rather odd, and

Actual shot of the Bohemian Grove stage area, which hosts the Cremation of Care ceremony, as seen in 2004. The infamous owl statue can clearly be seen to the left.

devoted a chapter of his bestselling book *Them* to the subject.[27] Was this really what our supposed role models should be doing? His was not the first attempted exposé, nor the last, but certainly the most prominent.

So is the Bohemian ceremony just a harmless pageant (as actor and confessed attendee Harry Shearer has asserted), or something darker? In the ritual, a small boat ferries the effigy across a lake, where it is received by hooded figures and consumed

in fire on an altar beneath the imposing statue of the giant owl, which supposedly signifies 'knowledge'. There has been much speculation about the meaning of the owl, with Alex Jones claiming it is a representation of the ancient Hebrew god 'Moloch' (although Moloch is traditionally a bull-headed creature) and that it has Satanic overtones. In truth, the ritual seems deliberately over-blown and melodramatic, with music and a pre-recorded voice-over from the late television anchorman Walter Cronkite. It's almost laughable. Almost.

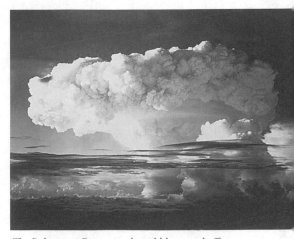

The Bohemian Grove rituals could be passed off as a mere pageant, yet high-level meetings also take place there, away from the prying eyes of democracy and the public. A key early meeting to develop the first atomic bomb is known to have taken place during the Bohemian Club camp of 1942.

If the Bohemian Club rituals were openly spoken of and happily explained away as a jolly distraction for our leaders on vacation, one might be able to accept this as a just another part of the ceremonial fabric of our society. And indeed, when pressed, the little that has been said by club

St John of Nepomuk (by Luigi Crespi, c.1779). Martyred in Bohemia in the 14th century, he is thus patron saint of the Bohemian Club.

members attempts to convey exactly this. But the lack of openness and child abuse symbolism (sacrificing effigies of children seems in poor taste at best) can only create more sinister speculation. The fact that another statue in the Grove shows the club's chosen patron saint, St John of Nepomuk, with a finger held to his lips in a 'keep-quiet' pose, doesn't exactly speak of inclusiveness to the rest of the population.

Claims that it is all a bit of fun, with no meaningful discussion of the outside world around the campfires, is plainly nonsensical, especially given that it is acknowledged that a key preparative meeting for the Manhattan Project, which developed the first atomic bomb, was held during the Grove camp of 1942. It is almost certain that amongst all the admittedly juvenile humour and male-bonding that must go on ('there's no end to the pee-pee and penis jokes, suggesting that these men, advanced in so many other ways, were emotionally arrested sometime during adolescence', wrote Philip Weiss of *Spy Magazine*, who also broke into the Grove in 1989), some pretty serious discussions about global events and underlying agendas must also take place.

All this, put together with the less ritualistic but equally closed meetings at the likes of the aforementioned Bilderberg Group (of which leading politicians and financial leaders from all major Western countries are key attendees), The Council on Foreign Relations, The Trilateral Commission and the many other mysterious high-level 'think-tanks' that influence global politics [page 68], makes it increasingly likely that parliaments and congresses are merely shop-windows for decisions essentially made elsewhere, far beyond the gaze of any who may naively hope that democracy is still a going concern.

A little fuss, at least, is now made at the gates of Bohemian Grove each July by protestors, and Bilderberg gatherings have even started to generate nearby camps of remonstrative truth campaigners. The truthers can take a little heart that their efforts have now helped Bilderberg meetings make mainstream news at last (if dismissively written off as harmless 'business talks'), inspiring semi-maverick MP Michael Meacher to force Kenneth Clarke and Labour shadow chancellor Ed Balls to rather embarrassedly explain their dealings with Bilderberg to the British House of Commons in June 2013.[28] But until a wider public awareness of how the world is really being run begins a serious upward curve of challenge, the elite won't worry too much. The fact that such meetings are not even kept secret anymore, allowing protests to amass, speaks either of the privileged classes' supreme confidence in their own power, or of it all being a peculiar double-bluff. If the former, it demonstrates an arrogance that may yet betray those who wear the robes if a new global consciousness takes hold, something which those who passionately dream of positive change hope is the case. If the latter, it could be that by being more open about its existence the elite hope to normalize their profile and distract attention away from the stranger seams of their activity.

Yet another protest passes the UK Houses of Parliament. But are the world's parliaments really where the big decisions get made, or do allegedly harmless 'business' think-tanks like the Bilderberg Group set the real agenda?

Truthseeker Alex Jones addresses an anti-Bilderberg festival at Watford, UK, June 2013, while the ruling elite meet at a nearby hotel. Although the media generally plays down or denigrates such events, the fact is that the growing movement against such secretive organizations is beginning to seep into the mainstream, vindicating the efforts of campaigners.

Next time you hear of some new grand global policy being announced, consider, then, that it may well have been devised by the type of people who sit around campfires in the shadow of a large stone owl. For this is the reality —not a fiction—that we are dealing with. What the motives and intentions of these people are is far from clear, but perhaps it becomes more obvious as to why so many observers do now subscribe to many of the conspiracy 'theories' stirred by an application of the Truth Agenda. With so much that is so very plainly lied about or at least heavily played down, it really does appear that there are crucial things going on that are actively hidden from us, and not just in the mysterious realms of the paranormal.

Breaking the Illusion

What, then, can we trust? If the illusion we have been fed for so long about the nature of our civilization and those who run it is so very skewed from the reality, is any of our official history reliable or true? Why should we believe *anything* we are told by people who seem to place their interests far above ours? What do we find when we apply the Truth Agenda to the 'authorized' view of even the most major events and achievements?

Here is a test. Stick a pin, while blindfolded, on a chart showing a list of recent historical moments or important global events. Take that randomly chosen selection and then scrutinize it in every detail, spending time looking at the official record versus the reality of what actually happened. Look at the evidence presented to justify the official record and put it through a vigorous analysis of logic, questioning its reliability. Then consider why we are being asked to believe that official record and question who or what benefits most from that belief. This is the Truth Agenda in action.

It is surprising to find from this process that very few things are what they first appear to be. At the very least, the evidence proffered in the mainstream to support an official view is often shockingly fragile, and sometimes plainly deceptive.

As a demonstration, we will look in the next part at three major examples of events either hailed or apparently authenticated by 'consensus reality', but which, under scrutiny, become disturbingly tenuous in terms of the evidence that supposedly supports them. If just one thing we took for granted as a reality can be shown to be even slightly unreliable, then the hypothesis presented in this book moves one step closer to deserving at least some consideration.

THE TRUTH AGENDA: *Mistrust in our leaders and the systems they manage has led many observers to suspect the very worst of both, to the point where some believe a regime of financial and political manipulation is creating a centralized global state designed to maintain power for a small but influential elite. The overt occult symbolism and bizarre rituals employed by those appearing to implement this suggest a firm belief in ancient lore and a total conviction of their right to rule, while the common people are seen as disposable pawns. Those who attempt to expose this scheme are vilified and ridiculed, and may sometimes go too far in their speculation—yet it is hard to dismiss the clear observation that important truths about the way the world is governed are being kept from us. If the fundamental basis of our society is so rooted in deception, why should we trust any story fed to us by officialdom?*

Part Two:
Deconstructing
Consensus Reality

The colossal Saturn V rocket at the Kennedy Space Center, Florida. Rockets such as this were unquestionably seen to take off – but did their payloads really make it to the Moon? If they did, have we been shown the real evidence?

VI   ONE GIANT LEAP..?

The first pin we will stick into the board of famous historical events, for the application of the Truth Agenda, concerns what is often spoken of as humankind's greatest achievement. The Moon landings are frequently held up as an example of the spirit of adventure, ingenuity and determination that gives our sometimes flawed species validation. Yet a surprisingly large number of people doubt the evidence for the lunar expeditions. Has the truth of the Apollo missions really been told, and if not what are the implications for our view of consensus reality?

Growing Doubts Over the Moon Landings

On 20th July 1969, possibly the most famous celebratory moment in modern history occurred when Neil Armstrong, NASA astronaut, landed on Earth's natural satellite and became the first human being ever to stand on another world. Five further missions, with different crews, would follow. In an age of angst, civil unrest and atrocities in Vietnam it was the perfect distraction for a jaded US society, and encouraged all of us to believe there was a better side to the human race that could put triumph above tragedy.

Why, then, have so many people expressed such doubt in the authenticity of the Moon landings? It's one of the most famous conspiracy theories of all, often chuckled about in the mainstream, yet widely discussed. Even in 1969, surveys showed that a surprisingly large proportion of the global population had reservations about what had really happened, with some television viewers phoning in with bizarre claims of seeing Coke bottles on the Moon's surface or catching glimpses of wires and lighting rigs. It was dismissed then as psychological denial from simple folk who couldn't come to terms with the huge technical achievements of the modern world.

However, now many decades on from the NASA Moon missions, not only has the doubt not gone away, it has actually grown. A poll carried out by the journal *Engineering and Technology* to mark the fortieth anniversary of the first lunar foray revealed that a remarkable *25%* of the British public no longer believed we had been to the Moon. Although satellite technology finally photographed the landing sites in aerial shots for the same anniversary, and other orbital images have captured them since, the uncertain smudges purporting to be the original craft and artefacts supposedly deposited by the astronauts have not settled the matter. Given the now easy availability of advanced photo-editing software, the fact is that until the day that independent researchers physically stand on the lunar surface to examine the objects and verify that they are there in the exact same positions and with the exact same lighting conditions, the doubts are going to remain.

Indeed, the previous absence of aerial pictures before 2009, despite the long-established presence of sophisticated lunar orbiters, had already been a puzzle and some doubters believe the time was used to work on good photographic fakes (or even to have secretly flown duplicate equipment up there using automated probes to ensure that items of some kind, at least, would be visible on the surface).

Naturally, not only is the lunar hoax one of the best known conspiracy theories, it is also one of the most attacked. There are vast swathes of the Internet devoted to believers and non-believers battling it out to challenge each other's explanations for anomalies in the NASA record of evidence. Tellingly, however, all this debate has not settled the divisions. Although it seems upsetting to have to question a human achievement held closely to our hearts for so long, sadly we do seem to live in a world of habitual deception where nothing official can be completely relied on. As a consequence, many seemingly unquestionable things do become open to re-evaluation.

Those unwilling to have their higher hopes for humankind dashed tend to get very emotive when the Moon landings are questioned, and bitter exchanges with the heretics are common. Defenders of official records on any subject tend to take on an unhelpful tone of haughtiness and do what is always done when under fire - pick on the weaker areas of the conspiracy theories (the 'strawman' arguments), which indeed *don't* stand up, and ignore the stronger areas, which can then be dismissed by simple association and quietly forgotten about. One example of this regarding the evidence for the Moon landings is the question of why stars can't be seen in the lunar surface photos, a point sometimes shouted by the less sharp of the doubters, and rightly pounced on by defenders. The - in this case quite correct - answer is that the comparatively faint stars wouldn't show up, because of the reduced exposure level necessary to capture the detail of the brighter surface. Such easy knock-downs are trumpeted as being typical of the holes in lunar conspiracy theories. However, the more serious points, such as why the astronauts seem to be standing in anomalous pools of light or have been photographed from impossible angles (as we shall see), are rather conveniently either never addressed, or waved away with explanations that may sound scientific to the lay person ('light scatters differently on the Moon'), but are actually suspect when analyzed.

We will not thrash out every argument around the lunar hoax theory - the interested reader should explore the sources recommended in *Appendix 3* to discover all the many disputed areas - but it is worth looking at some of the major arguments that have simply not been settled or satisfactorily explained by defenders. It is a very complex business, and this chapter is a necessarily simplified look at the main issues to help reveal an important example of something sold as a given which, when put under scrutiny, unfortunately begins to look a little shaky.

The Key Evidence

The NASA Moon landing claims - and they *are* claims - are particularly unusual in the field of human endeavor, because there is so little evidence available to prove what happened. With no accompanying journalists or independent observers, there is simply no outside corroboration of what happened on the Moon - we just have to take the word of a very few people that NASA went there.

What we know for sure is this: huge Saturn V rockets took off (witnessed by tens of thousands), and indeed an unused version of one impressively lies on display today at the Kennedy Space Center in Florida [page 100], so there is no doubt of their existence, nor of a space program in general. At the end of the missions, capsules then sailed down from the sky on parachutes into the Pacific Ocean. This much is certain. What is missing is clear evidence of what occurred in-between.

Approximately 400,000 people were involved in the space missions, most of them sincere, technically-adept personnel, all clearly believing in their work and its aims. The intention to go to the Moon, and the attempted development of the technology to allow it was plainly genuine. Indeed, national prestige was riding on it. In 1961, President John F Kennedy had famously stated his aim of 'achieving the goal, before this decade is out, of landing a man on the Moon and returning him

Exhibits and unused Apollo craft at the Kennedy Space Center, Florida, commemorating the missions to the Moon. How could anyone think that such a huge venture could possibly have been faked? Yet an alarming number of people now question the evidence for the landings.

safely to the Earth'.[1] In the wake of JFK's untimely death in 1963, what respectable US citizen would not want to try to honour that goal?

But what if this lofty aspiration turned out to be unattainable within such a time frame? What if technical disasters and unanticipated problems proved insurmountable? With the Cold War at its height, and an unsavory Asian war going badly, to fail would be a blow beyond measure to the US psyche. What could one do? The conspiracy theorists think they know the answer.

With such a large hole in the demonstrable public record of the Moon landings, outside of take-off and splash-down, we have to rely on three essential pieces of evidence to accept the official story that NASA went to the Moon: the testimony of the astronauts themselves, Moon rocks, and the photographs. It might be imagined that these three key exhibits should stand up to some pretty serious analysis as criteria on which to base our belief in this bold achievement - yet the curious fact is that they don't.

The Astronauts' Testimony

The collected testimony of the astronauts is... interesting. Although some *have* spoken of the profound nature of their experience (more than one 'got' God and became highly religious afterwards), others sometimes sound oddly blasé and matter-of-fact about it; not what you might expect from people who had stood for the first time on another world, looking back up at a now distant Earth. Some, like the late Neil Armstrong, have been strangely quiet about it all, coming forward now and then to make script-prepared anniversary statements, but not with the joy and conviction that might be anticipated. Other testimony is plainly contradictory - some astronauts speak of how bright the stars looked from space (indeed, some of the navigation was achieved by the remarkably archaic method of using a sextant to read the position of stars), while others say they could barely see the stars at all.[2] There are many other inconsistencies and apparent errors in the verbal record, which don't appear to make sense if they had all shared a similar experience, albeit on different missions.

The uncomfortable truth is that people have been known to lie throughout history. Whether it be for patriotic reasons, through respect of oaths, or fear of threats to them and their families, there are many examples of people who have willingly or unwillingly fronted stories to save king and country (Major Jesse Marcel at Roswell being a minor example - page 39). With all NASA astronauts of the 1960s having come from good military stock, patriotic allegiance at the expense of the truth might come easily if they believed the safety and prestige of America was at stake. And if their own families' safety and reputation was also at stake, the compulsion to do their duty might be even stronger.

The crew of the ill-fated Apollo 1. L-R: Virgil Grissom, Edward White and Roger Chaffee. All died during a launch pad fire in 1967. Grissom was a very vocal critic of the Moon missions, loudly questioning their feasibility. Years later, his son Scott uncovered evidence to suggest the crew were murdered.

Surely, though, at least one of the astronauts might have been tempted to blow the whistle if a scam was in operation? Perhaps they tried to; there has been much speculation on more than one NASA figure.

Virgil 'Gus' Grissom, officially the third human to go into space (after Yuri Gagarin and Alan Shepard), in a Mercury capsule in 1961, was originally

scheduled to be the first man on the Moon, not Armstrong. However, reports from colleagues and family show that Grissom - a qualified aircraft engineer - had become an increasingly vocal critic of not only the poor safety specifications of the proposed Moon missions, but even of its entire technical feasibility. With controversy surrounding his own Mercury flight, in which the safety hatch inexplicably blew out on splash-down, there is evidence that Grissom was increasingly seen as a liability.

Grissom felt unfairly blamed for the hatch incident, but he pointed to poor technology as the culprit, beginning a running critique of the space programs he himself was closely involved in. This extended even to hanging a lemon on an Apollo test module in front of press reporters as a sign of his contempt, rating the Moon mission's chances of success as 'pretty slim'. In fact, on the evidence of his first flight (especially when the sunken Mercury capsule, *Liberty Bell 7*, was finally recovered for examination in 1999 and showed no signs of its necessary heat-shield), some doubt that Grissom ever made it fully into space, perhaps explaining further his resentment at having to front something he didn't believe could really work.

The remains of the Apollo 1 capsule after the fire. Scott Grissom later discovered an anomalous metal plate had been deliberately inserted into the wiring, almost certainly causing the fire.

On 27th January 1967, Grissom and his two colleagues Edward White and Roger Chaffee died in a terrible fire that raged through the cockpit of Apollo 1 during training. An inadvisably sealed atmosphere of almost pure oxygen had become ignited by, apparently, poor wiring. Years later, Grissom's son Scott, a qualified engineer, mounted his own investigation and managed to examine the remains of his father's death capsule - and the faulty switch responsible for the fire. He discovered a small and functionless metal plate with it that appeared to fit into the switch - the insertion of which would almost guarantee the production of a dangerous spark. In 1999, Scott went public with his belief that his father was murdered. According to Virgil's wife, Betty Grissom, her husband - who had received death threats he believed came from within NASA - once warned her that 'if there is ever a serious accident in the space program, it's likely to be me'.[3]

Another dubious end awaited one Thomas Ronald Baron, an inspector at Cape Kennedy (now Cape Canaveral) who had compiled a highly critical report on the poor safety record and inefficiency at North American Aviation (NAA - contracted by NASA to work on the Apollo program), which led up to the Apollo 1 tragedy. Stating in front of a congressional subcommittee that one NAA employee 'knew exactly what caused the fire' (although the employee denied this), Baron never got a chance to say more because he and his family died when their car was struck by a train just a week later. Coincidence? The crash was ruled as 'suicide'. With only Baron's short - and highly damning - preliminary paper having been published, the full 500-page report he was compiling before his death never saw the light of day.[4]

Draw your own conclusions. Could it be that someone did indeed do away with a unsettlingly critical astronaut threatening to expose the infeasibility of the Moon missions, and then tried to cover up an all-too revealing inquiry? If so, who would dare try to reveal further shortcomings after Grissom and his colleagues, followed by Baron and his family, met such hideous fates?

Rumors also persist that Apollo 15 veteran James Irwin was about to go public with information about a lunar cover-up, when he died suddenly of cardiac arrest in 1991. Although it is true that Irwin did already have a heart condition, it's interesting that he was the first of the Moon astronauts to pass away.[5] Irwin was also one of the several lunar pioneers who had become evangelical Christian preachers; a response to the wonder of space, or an attempt to find redemption?

The Grissom case illustrates at the very least that there *were* voices raised at the time trying to draw attention to the fact that the Moon mission was far more flawed and risky than the NASA publicity machine was letting on. Nearly all US space shots before the Apollo program, merely low-orbital ones at that, had run into major technical difficulties and had succeeded - just - on a wing and a prayer. Even the formal Apollo training exercises rarely worked properly, with *not one* successful trial of a lunar lander test craft before the real thing set off (Armstrong was nearly killed when such a device span out of control in 1968; he managed to eject just seconds before disaster). Yet six Moon landing missions - with only the highly publicized Apollo 13 as the exception (see below) - seemed to run smoothly and without major error. Getting men in tin cans into low orbit had stretched NASA's capabilities to breaking point, but oddly a voyage to another world was suddenly a breeze.

Neil Armstrong's Lunar Lander Training Vehicle spins to its doom in 1968. Armstrong ejected safely. Not a single LLTV test was ever successful - yet the landers all worked perfectly on the Moon.

The testimony of astronauts, therefore, has to be taken on the same level as the testimony of early mountaineers and explorers (some of whom did fake claims of their conquests) - we simply have to accept their word that they went to the Moon. And perhaps they did, but is the evidence presented for it reliable? This may be a separate issue, for there are plenty of people who believe the missions went ahead, but that the photographic record was faked, for reasons we will discuss later. However, concerns over human survivability in the harshness of space using primitive 1960s technology clouds this compromise theory for others.

At the time (especially before the exposure of Richard Nixon's misdemeanors in 1974, which was a major blow to American faith in the word of prominent figures), few thought to question the word of the astronautic heroes, but in these days of mass-media deceptions, routine political lies, unreliable dossiers that lead us into war [Chapter VII] and buildings that fall down for no convincing reason [Chapter VIII], it is now more understandable why people feel they need a little more substantial back-up for extraordinary claims. So the word of the astronauts, regrettably, is no longer enough to sustain total belief.

We must look, therefore, at the second piece of evidence regularly presented as proof for the Moon odyssey, to see how that stands up to the Truth Agenda.

The Moon Rock Conundrum

If words are not enough, should not a solid piece of geology show that we did actually go to the Moon? When doubts over photographs and testimonies are expressed, rocks retrieved from the lunar surface are usually proffered as the ultimate mitigation. But are they what scientists claim?

There are two major problems with the Moon rock issue. One concerns scientific presumption, and the other, methods of retrieval.

Very few people have ever examined Moon debris. The distribution of material collected by the lunar missions has been extremely limited, and when samples are occasionally released for analysis it is usually only to close associates of NASA or mainstream scientific bodies unlikely to challenge convention. Even then, samples are never allowed to be physically touched, but handled only under strict laboratory conditions. Those who *have* examined rocks or dust have often expressed how similar the samples are to terrestrial geology, with just a few supposed differences. Is this because, as scientists currently claim, Earth and Moon were once joined, split asunder by a massive collision when the solar system was young - or could it be because the samples actually come from Earth itself?

Scientific fraud has been known in many avenues of research. What proof have we that samples released by NASA come from the Moon? If a cover-up of the kind claimed by doubters is in operation, the rocks could come from anywhere. Who would know the difference? Virtually no analysis of lunar materials has been genuinely scientific, because the assumption is always made from the start *that the sample comes from the Moon*. With that very strong impression in mind, it must be hard for even the best laboratory worker to approach their work with a clear perspective. Instead of testing blind samples to see what is there, comparing them to controls without bias (as science claims should always occur), analyses of lunar material always begin with a preconception (rather like the restrictive thinking inherent in mainstream Egyptology as illustrated in Chapter II). In other words, there have been very few, if any, proper investigations to determine whether or not Moon rock is actually from the Moon.

Even when official analysis is conducted within the usual parameters, anomalies still arise, ones that should raise more questions than are ever aired. When eminent UK astrobiologist Andrew Steele of the University of Portsmouth managed to scrutinize Moon material at close quarters, his examinations revealed several components of Earthly contamination; tiny particles of plastic, Teflon and micro-animal remains were clearly present in the samples he was sent. Given the tight strictures over delivery and handling described above, how could such contamination occur? Or was the sample of dirt simply from more terrestrial climes in the first place? In 2009, the Dutch Rijksmuseum in Amsterdam discovered its 'Moon rock' (donated by the US in 1969) was, in fact, merely petrified wood... Thus there are many unanswered questions about where these supposed Moon samples really come from.[6]

Moon rocks, collected by the crew of Apollo 11 - or were they? Could lunar material have been collected by automated probes instead? Some doubt that the rocks even come from the Moon.

But assuming for a moment that most of the rock does come from the lunar surface, the presumption that it could only have been brought back by the astronauts is still a narrow one. Unmanned probes have been a major - indeed, *the* major - part of space exploration since it began. There are far fewer problems accepting the reality of this, because making robotic technology function in deep space is infinitely easier than preserving the fragile life systems of human beings - and there are no clear reasons why anyone would need to fake it.

Several unmanned probes were sent to the Moon before and after the Apollo missions, by both NASA and the Soviet space program. Indeed, as early as 1970, the Soviets claimed to have retrieved small urns of Moon dust, sent back to Earth from an unmanned craft. It is not impossible that scoops of lunar material could have been retrieved by secret NASA probes in the same way. [Similarly, the laser-calibration 'mirrors' left on the Moon by three Apollo crews - another criteria often used as proof that man once stood there - could also have also been placed by unmanned craft (as the Soviets achieved with their own mirrors, twice), although when Gerhard Wisnewski attempted to find out *exactly* where on the lunar surface these mirrors were, no-one was able to tell him.][7] It is even possible that NASA could have bargained with the Soviets for access to lunar soil - not as unlikely as it may sound, despite all the Cold War race-into-space propaganda we were fed in the 1960s and 70s. There is evidence to show that there was quiet cooperation and collusion between the two sides in more than one area [page 127].

Another source of Moon material could be from meteorites. It is now well-known that we have had rocks raining down on us from the planets in our solar system for millions of years, with both Moon and Mars-originated meteorites (we are told) having been clearly identified. Antarctica, for instance, is littered with them. So, if automated probes or outright faking using earthly rocks aren't responsible, this is another way extra-terrestrial geology could be legitimately presented for analysis.

Consequently, lunar rock is not the panacea of authentication that defenders of the official NASA record would wish to us believe. Like the word of the astronauts, it cannot be accepted as definitive proof that we once stood on the Moon.

Two supposedly key pieces of evidence for the Moon landings are therefore more questionable than one might like to believe, with neither astronautic testimony nor geological samples being watertight criteria. All we are left to turn to for final reassurance is the one major area remaining - the photographs and films.

Anomalies in the Photographic Record

They are arguably the most famous photos in history; men standing on another world, crystal-clear images of humankind's gleaming technology set against the grey, barren wastelands of the Moon. They have inspired pride and the spirit of adventure in many seekers - as they did in this author at the time. In my first decade of life while the Moon landings were seemingly taking place, I viewed the astronauts as heroes, and rockets and lunar landers were my transports of delight. This enthusiasm went as far as writing in for James Irwin's autograph when he was in London as an ITV television commentator for one of the later missions, and I was duly rewarded. Whether he scribbled his own name (three times on one piece of paper, oddly), or whether someone in the TV company offices did it to keep a impressionable boy happy, I will never know, but it was a cherished keepsake for many years.

The point here is that it gives this author little pleasure to look now at those photos which so fired the imagination and see... flaws. Like many who first become aware of the potential NASA cover-up, there is shock and a grieving process one has to go through before being able to see the official record more objectively - but once the veil is lifted it is hard to see these iconic images in quite the same way again.

One of the doubters' central accusations against the Moon missions is that some or all of the photos were faked in a studio, or at the very least were taken during legitimate training exercises and presented, with a little doctoring, as the real thing. This idea is so prevalent in the public mind that it has been successfully used as a mainstream source of fiction (the movie *Capricorn One*, in which the Moon is substituted by Mars) as well as satirically lampooned (everything from the James

Bond movie *Diamonds are Forever* to *The Simpsons*), and everyone knows what they are getting at. In fact, the idea is so popularized that this is one of the very aspects used to knock the theory down; it becomes nothing more than a joke after a while. However, could one of the reasons for the high profile of the studio forgery theory be because there is actually a plausible case to be investigated?

It doesn't take too much knowledge of photography to find difficulties in accepting that all of the lunar surface photos were taken in natural light - the central claim of the official story. People with good photographic experience, such as Marcus Allen (who has become one of the key questioners of the NASA claims) - and this author (I have had books of photographs published) - point to very clear anomalies in the lunar photos, which challenge the notion that they were simple snapshots taken on a quick jaunt around the Moon.

So what are these anomalies? Ignoring some of the weaker critiques (debatable shadow angles, the visibility or non-visibility of stars, etc.), we shall explore the stronger evidence that something is not right in these pictures by looking at a few specific examples. Some of the arguments are necessarily of a technical nature, but the issues present themselves clearly enough.

Fig. 1: Apollo 11's 'Buzz' Aldrin standing on the Moon, one of the most iconic and most-reproduced NASA images of all time. But there are several lighting and angle anomalies [see text] that make many people believe it was taken in a studio. The image has not been cropped - this is the exact original. Compare to the NASA Media Services version in Fig. 4 [page 113], where a large slab of black sky has been added in.

The Classic Aldrin Photo

(See Fig. 1): One of the most famous images of all time, often used in NASA publicity and history books, is of Edwin 'Buzz' Aldrin, the second person ever to stand on the Moon, supposedly photographed by Neil Armstrong during the Apollo 11 mission [taken on a Hasselblad 500 EL camera, as all the Moon photos were, using Kodak Ektachrome transparency film, ISO 160 - more on the cameras on page 115]. It's a beautiful composition (in the NASA Media Services version, at least - Fig. 4) and an iconic image, with the foot of the lunar lander just visible to the right.

Anomaly Number One: Despite the quality of the shot, there are four major problems with this picture. The front of Aldrin's suit is lit up very clearly here, apparently by reflected light. According to NASA, the light is being bounced from the lunar surface. This might be believable were it not for some rudimentary rules concerning photography and light. The Sun is very clearly behind Aldrin, to the right of the picture. Given the exposure, which has left his foreground shadow very dark, either the astronaut should look much the same (a stark back-lit silhouette) or his ground shadow should also be lighter and exhibit detail in the dust; instead, we see the full features of his suit, glowing with secondary light, while his shadow is densely impenetrable. The only way to ensure such detail would be revealed on a back-lit standing object (i.e. Aldrin) *without* a great amount of reflected light would be to bring up the exposure of the shot - but this would also bring out detail on the area in his shadow and leave the lit parts of the lunar surface glowing bright. Instead, Aldrin's foreground shadow is completely black and the Moon's lit areas are fairly dull, apart from a peculiar brighter region to the right (see Anomaly Number Two).

With no atmosphere to help redistribute light, it is difficult to explain the visible detail on Aldrin's suit. The lunar surface has the reflectivity of tarmac - the Moon may look bright in our skies, but at close quarters its albedo (degree of reflectivity) is very weak. Reflected light would be unable to account for Aldrin's body detail as we see it here. In other words, it is almost as if some kind of artificial light source has been used to specifically 'fill-in' the parts of the astronaut not in the glare of the bright Sun - but NASA says no extra lighting was used. Some say the fill comes from Earthlight, but (especially as Earth was directly overhead for Apollo 11 - the fill-in light clearly comes from the side, as it does in most of the lunar photos), any such light would be so feeble as to make no photographic difference (and again, even if it did, and even allowing that a space suit is more reflective than Moon dust, why would it not also show up some detail in Aldrin's ground shadow?).

Fig. 2: The same image as Fig. 1, but with the contrast increased (and no other editing). This reveals without doubt that Aldrin is standing with a pool of light behind him to the right - an impossibility if this is natural sunlight.

Anomaly Number Two: Looking at the overall picture, made more obvious when the contrast is adjusted [Fig. 2], we see another clearly observed - and almost entirely inexplicable - phenomenon: Aldrin is in a clear pool of light, a bright spot focused on an area just behind him, to the right (his left). How can this be so, if the only light source is the Sun? The Sun does not produce pools of light in an open space, as can be demonstrated on any clear terrestrial day. Instead, it gives a uniform, evenly-spread light. This would be especially so in a cloudless vacuum. Yet this NASA photo shows a clear fall-off of luminosity toward both the foreground and the background. The horizon is almost in darkness in the increased contrast version, which shouldn't be the case in an even light. Photographing someone standing on a sandy beach or desert (the best equivalent of the Moon we can get down here) does not result in a bright spot in the middle and a darkening to the front and to the horizon.

This is just one of several NASA photos in which an entirely anomalous pool of light is clearly visible. There can really only be one explanation for this - Aldrin (and his counterparts in other pictures) must be lit by spotlights and reflective techniques. But no spotlights or any other lighting equipment were officially taken to the Moon. Interestingly, the photographic bright spots are one of the least-mentioned areas by the many defenders of the official record, yet they are among the most glaring - literally - of all the anomalies.

Fig. 3: Close-up of the reflection from Aldrin's visor, showing Neil Armstrong supposedly taking the picture - but he could not possibly have done so given the high angle of the shot.

Anomaly Number Three: A third major problem with this photo of Aldrin was first pointed out by Mary Bennett and David Percy, authors of the NASA-debunking book *Dark Moon*. The photograph has been taken from a surprisingly high-angle viewpoint (i.e. looking down), clearly revealed by the helmet-level of the background horizon and the visibility of the top of Aldrin's back-pack. This could not have been taken by an astronaut with a camera immovably strapped to his chest (the system used here and in most of the six missions' pictures).

Given the apparently flat lunar surface at this location, whoever took this photo must have been poised with the lens at least at eye level - or higher - and was thus *not* the astronaut visible in Aldrin's visor

Fig. 4: Testing camera levels. Left - photo taken at chest height. Right - photo taken at eye level. Note the line of the background fence and compare to Figs. 1 & 6. Chest-level shots could not possibly result in the horizon lines seen in such lunar images. Yet we are told all the shots were taken at chest height.

reflection (supposedly Armstrong - Fig. 3). Experiments by Bennett and Percy reveal that the horizon line, if taken by a body-strapped camera, should come somewhere around Aldrin's chest, not at the artistically-pleasing level of his visor, which makes for a perfect compositional continuation of the horizon line across and either side of him, a phenomenon seen in a number of NASA images [see also Figs. 4 & 6].[8]

Anomaly Number Four: In fact, aside from all the above issues, the Aldrin portrait is one of the photos that has very definitely been tampered with in PR versions of the same image issued by NASA Media Services [Fig. 5], which have a larger slab of additional black sky above Aldrin's head (making the middle cross-hair, or calibration 'reticle', included on all the lunar images, appear vertically off-center). Comparing with Fig. 1, it can be seen that the original version of the picture shows very little sky above Aldrin (with the cross-hair directly central), and his helmet is uncomfortably close to the top of the frame, which is far less pleasing to the eye, but is as originally taken. If just one image can have been so obviously tampered with, why could it not have happened in more ambitious ways with many of the others? It is claimed, however, that no re-touching occurred.

Fig. 5: The NASA Media Services version of the same classic Aldrin photo, which crops the image and adds extra sky at the top.

This fourth anomaly is fairly explicable, and plainly down to NASA manipulating the image for aesthetic purposes. However, it is hard to find easy solutions for the other troubling difficulties - and this is just one photograph. Others raise similar questions. Whether the classic Aldrin photo was taken on the Moon or in a studio, it seems to have been realized after the fact that this was the best image to be used for PR, despite it being, annoyingly for NASA, one of the very few examples of awkward composition - for it is in itself a mystery how the vast majority of pictures were so perfectly framed on a camera without a viewfinder.

Camera Issues

(See Fig. 6): This photograph of Alan Bean from Apollo 12 shows another very clear example of sunshine seen to one side (left), while fill-in light has seemingly been used to illuminate areas that should be in black shadow (right). Again, the photo has been taken from a high angle to ensure the horizon line reflected in the visor pleasingly continues the one in the background - thus it could not have been taken by the astronaut seen in the reflection. If it was, the horizon behind Bean would run through his chest, so again the photo appears to have been taken by someone else from another, more elevated, angle and the visor image has simply been spliced into the picture (as the contrast differences would appear to suggest).

The angle and extra illumination, however, helpfully reveals for us the Hasselblad 500 EL camera used on all the Moon missions (see also Fig. 7). A normal if expensive camera, only slightly modified for use in the harsh lunar environment, it was attached

Fig. 6: Alan Bean, Apollo 12. Another photo taken from a higher angle than possible if the astronaut in the reflection was taking it. There are also more lighting anomalies. The standard chest-height Hasselblad camera can be seen clearly.

firmly to the chest of the astronauts and had no usable viewfinder. With only basic aperture, focusing and exposure controls operated through thick pressurized gloves, and shots composed by guesswork and body movements alone, all the Moon photos were taken - once again, as with many NASA achievements - on a wing and a prayer. Yet so many of the lunar surface photographs are perfect - rather like studio portraits. This is especially remarkable given that no 'bracketing' of exposures took place (taking three or more shots of the same thing at different light levels to ensure at least one usable image, as practiced by most professional photographers). The unknown photographic conditions on the Moon would have been a particular trial for the Apollo 11 crew who were the first to set foot there.

If one were to spend a day patrolling a dusty wilderness with a camera held firmly at chest-height, photographing friends and their paraphernalia with only basic controls and no viewfinder - and had to achieve this wearing garden gloves - it would soon become clear that gaining usable results would be something of a trial. Most likely, even using a wide angle lens, the odd head might be cut off, the tilt of many of the images might be skewed and the occasional exposure (manual only and unbracketed, remember) would surely be wrong. But on the Moon, none of this seemed to be a problem, beyond a bit of extra sky needing to be added here and there for compositional purposes.

Defenders of the official line state that a large number of lunar photos *didn't* come out well and were held back from publication, but this claim is not supported by the released contact sheets (which supposedly can't be edited) from the original rolls of film. These, despite a few apparent misfires here and there, demonstrate that the majority of shots achieve near-perfection of exposure, focus and composition,

Fig. 7: A Hasselblad 500 EL camera, as allegedly used on the Moon, strapped to the chest with no viewfinder and controls that had to be operated wearing pressurized gloves. The high quality of the lunar photos is truly remarkable.

another mystery of this astonishing historical accomplishment.

The actual films inside the Hasselblad cameras were protected from the extremes of intense heat and deep cold only by a thin layer of 'reflective coating'. But given that lunar temperatures reach over 100°C in direct sunlight, and under -100°C in the shadows (a vacuum doesn't convect heat), and that the Moon is flooded by potentially film-fogging radiation that never gets to earthly environs (more on radiation soon), it is a wonder that any films - vulnerable 1960s stock, not today's more resilient grades - made it back intact at all. Experiments by questioners using ovens, freezers and irradiation suggest severe problems resulting from exposure to these extremes. Some say the films never were usable and that technicians were unable to fix the issue on each subsequent mission, which is perhaps why they might have had to re-stage the photos in a studio or doctor images from training exercises to justify the vast expense of the Moon program; a program that had cost lives as well as money, as with the unfortunates of the Apollo 1 affair and other training personnel. Others, of course, say that far more deception occurred.

Fig. 8: Another clear lighting anomaly. The Sun is behind the LEM, yet all but the ground shadow is brightly lit. Can reflected surface light really be so bright and particular?

Anomalies of the Lunar Lander

(See Fig. 8): In this photo, we see another clear example of fill-in light having been used, and all the same arguments apply as in the previous examples. The lander (or Lunar Excursion Module - LEM) has the Sun visibly behind it to the left, and casts a large jet black shadow towards the bottom right of the photo, in which no detail can be seen at all. Yet the craft itself is brightly lit from the right so that colorful detail can be seen and the United States logo shows up clearly (the latter observation being a notable feature of many of the photos). It is almost impossible to believe that this illumination can be from reflected light, especially given how large the dark area of ground shadow is. Similar issues arise with Fig. 9, in which Buzz Aldrin can be seen descending the ladder of Apollo 11. Given that we are seeing the shadow side of the LEM (i.e. again with the Sun behind it), the levels of light are astonishing - and Aldrin's boot appears to be showing a clear reflection of a single bright light source; a spotlight or flash, perhaps?

Another curious observation regarding images of the six different LEMs is that there appears to be neither blown dust anywhere on the feet of the craft [Fig. 10] nor evidence of the slightest crater or scorch mark beneath the central engines [Fig. 11]. Compare this to the photo of the 2008 Phoenix probe on Mars in Fig. 10, showing clear deposits of dust and soil. It is interesting to note that when the Curiosity rover, another Mars probe, was lowered down from a 'descent stage' in August 2012, the hovering platform left two distinct burnt areas on the martian surface,

Fig. 9: Aldrin descends Apollo 11 on the shadow *side - yet a specific light source creates highlights on his boot.*

even though the engines were a full 20 meters above it. So why not on the Moon?

Official defenders state that most of the thrust to brake the descent of the lunar landers was expended before they reached ground level, but it is interesting to note that from all the pre-mission artwork produced by NASA the craft were *expected* to be descending on huge jets of flame until the surface was reached [page 128]. Even if the defense is partly valid, it seems peculiar that no disturbance of any kind is visible in the Moon dust beneath the craft in any of the six mission photograph sets, and that no scattered dust seems to have been thrown up by what still must have been something of a jolt as they impacted.

There are other anomalies concerning the thrust required to pilot the LEM. Again, pre-mission conceptual artwork suggests that the lifting off of the top part of the craft on departure (leaving the landing gear on the Moon's surface) would produce a notably

Fig. 10: Above - clean foot of Apollo 11. Below - dusty foot of the Phoenix Mars lander in 2008. Is the lack of any scattered Moon dust reasonable?

Fig. 11: The lunar surface beneath Apollo 11 (with refuse sack). In none of the mission shots can disturbance of any kind be seen beneath the LEMs. We are told the thrusters were cut before they touched down, but pre-mission NASA visualizations showed something quite different was anticipated [page 128].

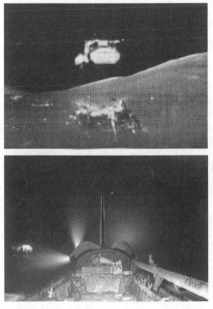

Fig. 12: Above - Apollo 11 lifting off from the lunar surface with no visible exhaust or flame of any kind. Below - the space shuttle firing its main thrusters, with clearly visible effects. Yet the same fuel was used in both. The LEM appears to lift upwards almost as if by crane.

large and visible flame. Even allowing for the fact that thrusters do not burn in a vacuum as they do in an atmosphere, the famous automatic video images of an ascending capsule [Fig. 12] show no light, signs of heat or any visible exhaust at all from such a high temperature rocket - just ejected debris from the explosive bolts. Yet NASA footage of the same thrusters being tested on Earth shows an incredible force being expended; one would expect something to be seen, especially as the fuel used for Apollo was the same as that used for the later space shuttles - which produced very visible effects in a vacuum, filmed on many missions [also Fig. 12].

One would also expect something to be *heard* from the engines; not in silent space, of course, but through the helmet-radios of the astronauts in the cabin of the lunar landers. Given that the astronauts were literally standing on top of incredibly powerful propulsion engines, just feet away from them, it is very strange that no released recordings of astronaut dialogue at the moments when the engines were firing exhibit any background sound at all - instead, all that can be heard are calm voices against silence, with no hint of what at the very least could be expected to be an audible rumble or vibration conducted through the spacesuits, even allowing for the fact that the cabin was reportedly depressurized at the time. [This point raises other questions - how were complex switches, dials and keyboards operated so easily while wearing stiff pressurized gauntlets, when the astronauts' lives depended on very fine accuracy of control? According to legend, Neil Armstrong even turned off the autopilot facility during his own descent, landing manually.]

Everything from the questionable storage capacity of the LEMs, heating/cooling problems [page 124] and their remarkably amateur and fragile-looking construction have been called into question by critics, and not without justification.

Coming back to the photographs, it is alarming to note that many of the problems with the selections under discussion can be detected throughout the entire NASA image record of the Moon landings. There is one potential mitigation, though - what about the video footage? Surely that backs up the veracity of the still shots?

Video Issues

(See Fig. 13): In the left-hand image, we see astronaut John Young from Apollo 16 facing us, leaping up two feet or so off the ground, held in momentary suspension, supposedly using the low lunar gravity to salute the US flag before him in a rather novel way. Looking closely, we can see there is a loose flap on the top of his backpack, sticking up like a little triangle. There is clear space between him and the lunar surface. We can also note the angle of the flag. To the left is the LEM with the wheeled lunar 'rover' in front of it.

This is an interesting example, because the moment the photo was taken was simultaneously recorded on video - presumably from a camera on the rover, from the angles visible in the footage. But instead of being a secondary-source confirmation of the reliability of the pictures, we simply have more anomalies.

In the video version of this moment, seen on the right, the triangular backpack flap, so clearly visible in the photo, is hardly sticking up at all, even allowing for the reverse angle. Also in the video, there is a clearly visible puff of dust thrown up at the moment the astronaut jumps - yet there is no dust at all in the photograph. The flag, meanwhile, is hanging at a notably more sloped angle than in the photo (there

Fig. 13: Left - Still photograph of the Apollo 16 'jump salute', showing John Young leaping up whilst saluting the flag. Right - Video image of the same moment, filmed from a reverse angle. But is it the same moment? The highlighted top of the backpack shows a flap clearly sticking up in the still shot which is absent in the video, the flag is hanging at a different angle and the dust cloud seen in the moving image is not present in its counterpart.

are various anomalies pertaining to flags and their erratic heights and positions throughout the whole image record, in fact - see *Dark Moon* for more). In other words, it seems that the video version of the jump salute was re-staged and not taken at the same time as the photo (or vice-versa). It is not impossible that this was the case, of course, but the point is that we are *told* it is the same moment, when apparently it isn't. Other still shots supposedly taken simultaneously with video footage can be shown to be inconsistent, suggesting that photographs and moving images must have been staged in separate sessions, no matter what is claimed and regardless of whether they were on the Moon or not.

The dust-beneath-the-feet in the jump salute raises another interesting issue. Considering what we are told about the very fine quality of lunar surface material, in such low gravity one would expect any disturbance of it to leave clouds of dust hanging for a short while before re-settling. Instead, in video footage of roving buggies and other astronaut activity (such as the salute) the dust is seen to fall quickly back to the ground. It has also been suggested that in the absence of any moisture at all on the Moon, such clear footprints and tyre-tracks as visible in the photos and films would be unlikely to form in the way seen.

As for the general presence of 'low gravity', this is supposedly proven by the leaden nature of astronaut movement exhibited in the videos. However, some have said that all the apparent gravity effects could be accounted for by the simple act of slightly slowing down normal footage (a technique used in many science fiction entertainments). When tests have been run to speed up Moon videos just a little, it is curious to note that the movements and postures of astronauts and the objects they manhandle suddenly take on quite a mundane appearance - as it would look on Earth, in fact. There are also occasional bright flashes above the astronauts in some of the videos, which the justifiably suspicious have suggested may be wires catching the light. In one scene, an Apollo 16 crew member is clearly seen to stumble, yet is suspended for a brief moment at a miraculously peculiar angle before regaining balance, something unlikely to occur even in reduced gravity.

The videos of the Moon missions shown on our televisions at the time were low-grade versions broadcast by simply pointing a camera at a NASA monitor screen, hence some of the 'ghosting' and general poor image quality that prevented clear viewing of what was going on. Analysis of the original, much higher-resolution, videotapes would have been an obvious line of enquiry to settle some arguments. However, this was not possible for a while. In 2006, it was officially announced that - incredibly, for arguably the single greatest scientific achievement of the 20th century - the original videotapes for all of the Moon missions had been... lost. Lost? Well, possibly misfiled or administratively buried somewhere.[9] So all we had for a while were cruder copies. However, mysteriously enough, the videos were found again just in time for the fortieth anniversary celebrations, so that the legend of NASA's intrepid explorers could be reinforced again - perhaps after judicious edits?

A Studio Hoax?

What is the evidence that a studio could have stood in for the lunar surface, with wires and changed camera speeds used to evoke the feeling of a lower gravity environment? More than one might imagine, in fact. Astronaut training was openly held in quite elaborate mock-lunar landscapes, and huge and very convincing models of the Moon were made for various purposes. Some of the training photographs are uncannily like the claimed real ones, with just a little less detail.

In his 1968 film *2001: A Space Odyssey*, Stanley Kubrick had already demonstrated that special effects could convincingly stand in for real-life space activity. (Indeed, some have attempted to implicate Kubrick and/or his effects team as being part of the lunar deception - others have suggested that Walt Disney, who was a close friend of former Nazi scientist turned NASA rocket-genius Wernher Von Braun from the 1950s onwards, might also have been involved.) With enough time and money, therefore - and with much prestige at stake - it is not too difficult to imagine a studio hoax could be made believable. A convincing replica of a lunar surface had already been built for Apollo 11 training at Flagstaff, Arizona, while a huge assembly of gantries, girders and cranes had been constructed at Langley, Virginia, to simulate low gravity for LEM tests. Both of these sites could easily have been utilized for the purposes of a hoax. In any case, with remote bases like Area 51 available to the US authorities [Chapter III], there would be no shortage of large, secret spaces in which to mount such a venture - if they even needed to be large, that is; the horizons in some of the Apollo photographs do seem rather near, even allowing for the smaller diameter of the Moon as compared with Earth, and hard lines sometimes mark the joining of the ground landscape to distant (and oddly blurry) mountains, almost as if they could be scenery flats creating the illusion of vastness. In some images there is strong evidence of the *same* background scenery being used to represent supposedly different locations, or shifted to be visible in what should be mutually-exclusive compositional shots. Some vistas could also have been convincingly mounted using miniatures, as Kubrick's film makes plain, which might explain the perspective/scale paradoxes and contradictions that present themselves when comparing pictures supposedly taken on the same expeditions.

It is a fact that at least some photographs purporting to show astronauts on the Moon or in space HAVE been fabricated. One much-publicized shot of lunar golf being played [Fig. 15] can be easily unmasked. As Mary Bennett and David Percy write at *www.aulis.com*:

'In the 1994 British hardback version of Moon Shot *by Al Shepard and Deke Slayton there is a large photograph of Al Shepard playing golf on the lunar surface. In this picture is his companion astronaut. A total impossibility if this was a photograph taken on the Moon during the mission* [as no-one else could have been taking the still picture - no automatic Hasselblads were used on the Moon]. *It was not taken at the time. It is a composite of*

Fig. 15: Alan Shepard and Stuart Roosa playing golf during the Apollo 14 mission - except that the photo is a provable composite pasted together from different images, as Mary Bennett and David Percy have shown.

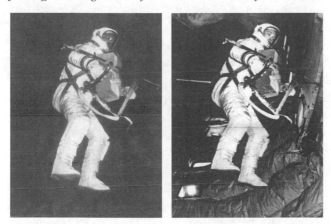

Fig. 14: Left - Michael Collins apparently spacewalking outside Gemini 10, as published in his book Carrying The Fire. *Right - Michael Collins inside a NASA training plane, simulating zero gravity. This is plainly the same photo, with the background replaced by blackness for the spacewalk version and then presented as something it isn't. Some space mission images are easily provable fakes.*

several other NASA pictures. Yet, this fact was not signalled as such within the pages of this particular edition of Moon Shot; it was presented as a photograph of the actual event.' [10]

After this was pointed out, it is curious to note that the photo was omitted from the 1995 paperback version of the said book.

Another famous but unreliable shot shows Michael Collins apparently space-walking, in orbit, outside Gemini 10. This can clearly be proven to be a cut-and-paste image from a terrestrial training mission, reversed and with its background replaced with space-like blackness [Fig. 14].[11] If handy PR shots can be so easily generated and carelessly thrown into the public domain, why might it not be a regular NASA habit?

So is the questioning of humankind's greatest claimed historical conquest the madness it may seem? Or is it a valid concern in response to very obvious inconsistencies and glaring impossibilities, which have never been properly addressed by either NASA or its defenders, despite all their attempts to dismiss the critics?

Choosing the Truth

The depressing reality is that the three main areas of evidence that supposedly support the authenticity of the Moon missions can all be found to be unreliable when analyzed closely. Neither testimony, geology or photography make the solid case we are told exists. So it all comes down to what one chooses to believe.

What about Apollo 13, some say? That mission in 1970 was aborted after an in-flight explosion caused the crew to retreat to the inadequate lunar module to survive, and a landing was never made. Some point to this dramatic event as evidence that the Moon missions were indeed full of genuine peril and unplanned difficulties. Why would anyone hoax that? But even this case isn't clear-cut. With public interest in the Moon waning and budget cuts being threatened (see the conclusion to this chapter to see why that might be more important than at first meets the eye), the Apollo 13 crisis was certainly used as the perfect PR story to re-focus attention onto these gallant pioneers, to justify a few more missions. When Bennett and Percy investigated the location at which Apollo 13 *should* have touched down if it had been successful, they discovered that the lunar region known as Fra Mauro would have been in total darkness throughout the planned time of the trip (hence, in part, their book title *Dark Moon*) - a completely untenable condition for any useful science trip.

If one brushes aside all of the lunar conspiracy theories, one does so in the light of several unexplained and major anomalies. Maybe there really are unusual but mundane explanations for these problems, which haven't yet become clear, even to NASA staff. So defenders attack the doubters' easy targets, but ignore the tougher ones, perhaps because they don't know the answers themselves but assume that explanations will emerge. But what if sensible explanations don't emerge? Those emotionally attached to humankind's achievements in space may never be able to assess objectively the merits or otherwise of the NASA evidence. Thus they will always take part in circular arguments on the Internet and forever be in conflict with those they see as uneducated paranoid deniers, even when their own arguments don't stand up to logical - or scientific - analysis.

The mid-way position taken by some theorists is to believe that we did go to the Moon, but couldn't make the cameras work there. Or perhaps some of the pictures are real, but many of the ones that survived weren't considered good enough to make the case to the world and therefore had to be re-staged? Or did the astronauts see something that they couldn't share with us? There are plenty of UFO-related theories in this area.

In 2008, Edgar Mitchell, lunar module pilot of Apollo 14 in 1971, went on record to say that NASA had covered up UFO reports made by the supposed lunar explorers and claimed that the US had withheld firm knowledge of extra-terrestrials for years.[12] While ufologists celebrated the announcement, stoking more hope for official 'disclosure', as discussed in Chapter III, the more cautious lunar questioners felt that this might be a deliberate distraction in itself. To infer that evidence of aliens was found on the Moon reinforces the view that astronauts *did* land there. This concerns some investigators, for there are also those who feel that we never did go to the Moon, or at least not in the way we were shown.

The Radiation Problem

The notion that astronauts didn't visit the Moon at all seems too much for the hopeful, but there is interesting evidence to be considered here. Radiation, for instance, is a major hazard in space outside of the Earth's protective fields, and on the Moon there is no atmospheric protection. Given that some of the missions took place during high solar activity, when radiation levels were extreme (as Bennett and Percy demonstrate)[13], how did the astronauts survive with just a few millimeters of aluminium between them and space while in the craft (raising also the question of how the capsule survived a cabin pressure of 700 lbs per square foot without exploding), and relatively thin and apparently not radiation-proof suits when outside?[14] Why expose the astronauts to such potentially lethal doses when far less dangerous flight windows could have been chosen? Did NASA really play such a risky game of Russian Roulette with the lives of their heroic front-men?

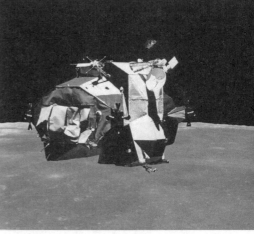

Fig. 16: The Apollo 16 LEM approaches the command module after its trip to the lunar surface. Did men really survive the harsh radioactive environment of space in such flimsy (and in this case apparently beaten-up) tin boxes?

The construction of the lunar lander in particular seems strangely flimsy and ramshackle [Fig. 16], especially given the very substantial and deep walls of radiation protection being proposed for today's developing (and questionable, in the light of these issues) manned Mars missions. Even with these, some of NASA's own former scientists have warned of serious 'health penalties' for travellers to the red planet.[15] Yet the LEM had a 'protective' aluminium skin just three sheets of foil thick. Even the Concorde supersonic airliners carried radiation measuring devices and there have been renewed media concerns of late that regular airplane crews at high altitudes may be exposed to too much radiation. Astronauts working on the International Space Station have also had to develop significant shielding, despite being in a relatively low orbit, safely beneath the Earth's natural protection.

Even before they entered into deeper space, the astronauts would have had to pass through the highly radioactive 'Van Allen' belts that shield us from harmful Sun effects and cosmic rays. Although NASA states that the astronauts' passage through them (for a duration of at least an hour and a half) was too brief to be harmful, independent research - based on official figures of the radiation present there - strongly suggests that the dose received could not possibly leave those exposed to it unaffected. Yet there seems to be no statistical evidence to show that astronauts have been prone to increased cancer or other radiation-enhanced conditions in their later lives.

However, even if the astronauts avoided the radiation problems by some miracle, it is unlikely that the films in the cameras would have remained unaffected, given that they had no special protection. As we have already seen, in the 1960s photographic stock was especially sensitive to damage from radiation of any kind, which was why people would not put undeveloped films through old-style airport X-ray scanners, to avoid the high risk of fogging or the complete obliteration of images. It seems almost impossible that the lunar photos could have been safely returned without a single blemish from exposure to unfiltered solar radiation and cosmic rays. It is interesting to note that as recently as 2001 large-format IMAX film canisters taken into low-level orbit on the space shuttle had to be carefully stored between special protective water containers to prevent the effects of radiation - yet missions to the Moon and back, with zero protection, seemed to pose no problem.

The Heat Problem

Aside from radiation, how the astronauts were protected from the extremes of heat in stark sunlight, and intense cold in the lunar shadows, has never been satisfactorily explained either. The spacesuits used a water cooling system to maintain a comfortable body temperature, yet the LEM itself employed a process that required the occasional expulsion of moisture into the surrounding vacuum. From this, a small cloud of gas or ice crystals could reasonably be expected to be seen venting outside the craft from time to time, but this doesn't seem to have been the case. Marcus Allen writes:

'How was the heat generated in the space craft removed if air conditioning cannot work in the vacuum of space? The lunar landers sat on the Moon's surface for up to 72 hours in direct sunlight, the temperature of which, on the Moon, is higher than the boiling point of water. How did the astronauts keep cool? We are told it was by the use of heat-sinks and the evaporation of water from porous plates, yet no photographic evidence of this occurring has ever been seen.' [16]

The issue of heat regulation, then, is another lunar mystery to add to the long list.

Could a NASA Hoax be Kept Secret?

We are used to believing what we are told to believe. Or at least we agree to believe until events like the Weapons of Mass Destruction debacle unfold [next chapter]. Even now, though, few people like to lift the lid of the Pandora's Box of global deception, because it is too painful and unsettling to consider that those running our world may not be trustworthy. Especially in the slightly more innocent 1960s, and despite some doubts expressed at the time, only a small minority thought to really question something as huge as men landing on the Moon. After all, how could anyone fake something so significant? Even now, in more cynical times, those sceptical of conspiracy believe it would be impossible to maintain a cover-up over something as important as a mission to another world, and argue that there would surely have been whistleblowers. But some researchers assert that there were.

Bennett and Percy hold that some of the peculiar anomalies in the NASA record (and there are many, many more anomalies than we have covered here) were deliberately left or planted there by otherwise silenced personnel, in the hope that someone might spot the errors and begin to question them somewhere down the line - as indeed they have. The late Jack White's detailed analysis of the Moon mission anomalies (including lunar rovers leaving no tyre tracks [Fig. 17], many shadow, lighting and angle problems, clearly manipulated images, inconsistencies with equipment and spacesuit details in photos supposedly taken on the same excursions and, bizarrely, impossibly uncurled photographic prints of previous missions seen lying on a foot of a LEM) can be studied on the *www. aulis.com* website.[17] Even if some of these observances are dismissed or put down to optical illusion, it is hard to feel entirely secure about the official record after perusing them all.

Fig. 17. The lunar rover of Apollo 17. The 'Moon buggy' appears to leave barely any tracks at all in some images, as if it has just been placed into position rather than being driven. Yet clear footprints and dust markings seem to result from all other compressions. The NASA record shows the Apollo 17 rover had already been used before this picture was taken, so it is not, as some have argued, that the lack of tracks is due to its only just having been assembled.

Despite the oft-heard scoffing from defenders of the official story, investigation suggests that it wouldn't actually require many people to operate a mass deception around the Moon landings. Mission Control almost certainly did believe it was communicating with people on the Moon (the signals from the astronauts were relayed in an unusual way, incidentally, which would have made it quite hard to define exactly where they might have been coming from). The multitude of technicians and administrative staff almost certainly worked genuinely towards a goal; rockets took off and capsules splashed down. But if the conspiracy theorists are right, only a limited number of insiders would be needed to perpetrate a studio fake and keep it strictly confidential, even from most of those working in the space program, who would remain unaware. As with the events of 9/11 [Chapter VIII], someone manipulated into perpetrating a tiny but important part of a confusion tactic may not have known themselves that they were doing so. Keeping people rigidly compartmentalized in work environments is a well-established way of maintaining order in the workplace and ensuring that industrial secrets are kept.

If the hoax hypothesis is true, there would have been good enough reason why those few people involved with the Moon missions who *did* know what was really going on would keep quiet, especially if patriotic fervor was strongly instilled, or the known consequence of any betrayal was heavy enough. Perhaps guilt did prey on the perpetrators, though; some of the conversations recorded from astronauts during their missions seem almost cynical in tone, with some of them remarking on more than one occasion that things in space don't look real. As Pete Conrad exclaims loudly during the Apollo 12 mission:

'That Sun's bright, it's like somebody is shining a spotlight on your hands! ... I tell you ... it really is. It's like somebody's got a super-bright spotlight!' [18]

Exuberance on a sunny lunar day, or subtle whistleblowing?

A more famous line may also indicate an interesting Freudian slip. Neil Armstrong, stepping onto the lunar surface for the very first time, notably managed to fumble one of the most iconic lines in history. 'That's one small step for Man; one giant leap for Mankind' *should* have been 'That's one small step for *a* man...' While popular culture has recorded it as a charming (and often unnoticed) blunder in the confusion of great responsibility, some think he was trying to indicate that it really was just a small step for Man.

'Space Race' Secrets

Yuri Gagarin, famously the first man into space. But have we been told the truth about his trip and the entire Soviet/US 'space race'?

But if whistleblowers are notably few and far between, why, then, would the likes of the Soviets, at least, not try to expose NASA if something obviously suspect was going on? Surely it would have been in their interests to have called into question the supposed conquests of their rivals, especially if they knew themselves what was feasible in space and what wasn't? Perhaps not. The acceptance of Yuri Gagarin's history-shattering first-man-in-space flight on 12th April 1961 might have been equally challenged by the US, given that NO evidence whatsoever was presented at the time to prove its reality (and very little has been offered since). Indeed, there is compelling evidence that the early Soviet space program was itself prone to massive fraud and covered-up disasters, with much doubt as to whether it was really Gagarin who made that flight. [19] Yet the US stayed oddly quiet.

The answer to why the space scientists on both sides may have kept hush about each other's possible misdemeanors, for all the 'space-race' front of the Cold War, can

The country of origin was proudly displayed on the Saturn 5 rockets, but President Kennedy himself thought that cooperation with the Soviets was the way forward into space.

probably be derived from observing the kindred spirits of the ex-Nazi scientists who were divided up by the Americans ('Operation Paperclip') and the Soviets to work on their respective space programs at the end of World War II. (Space travel effectively began with German V2 missiles). With each bloc knowing that the conquest - and ultimately the militarization - of space would be crucial to the future balance of power (with long-running plans coming fully to fruition only today, and the majority of space shuttle missions having been quietly military in purpose and responsible for releasing many of the US spy satellites that float above us as we speak), they used the knowledge of those who had once been their enemies. But there seems no reason why the likes of Wernher von Braun and his colleagues, albeit now in different continents, wouldn't still be happy to covertly exchange technological knowledge with each other (as evidence suggests they did). Nor would there be any reason why they would try to expose each other. Old allegiances die hard. Shouting about the potential cover-ups of another might well draw attention to their own.

Shortly before his assassination, it is interesting to note that John F Kennedy, who had long supported the idea of joint space ventures, openly instructed NASA to participate with the USSR space program. His Confidential National Security Action Memorandum (no. 271) of 12th November 1963, headed *Cooperation with the USSR on Outer Space Matters* clearly states:

'I would like you to assume personally the initiative and central responsibility within the government for the development of a program of substantive cooperation with the Soviet Union in the field of outer space, including the development of specific technical proposals.' [20]

Curiously - and true, though it may sound like a conspiracy theorist's fantasy - Kennedy also issued another memorandum the same day asking the CIA to release classified UFO documents to NASA to aid its new era of cooperation with the Soviets (which readers can add to their own list of assassination motives if they wish). When Kennedy was shot dead just two weeks later, the idea of official collaboration seemed to die with him, and the 'Space Race' appeared, publicly at least, to resume - but who knows what lines of communication had already been set up?

Why a Lunar Deception?

There are numerous other concerns that have been raised over the Moon missions, from the ability of the Saturn V rockets to carry the payloads claimed, to the sheer wonder that any of the primitive technology, scorned by even the likes of Gus Grissom, worked at all. But the point has been made here - the solidity of something we all take for granted suddenly seems weak and uncertain when put under the microscope, whatever the ultimate truth.

Why would NASA really mount such a huge undertaking, only to have to fake all or part of it? Was it just to look big on the world stage and distract from its darker

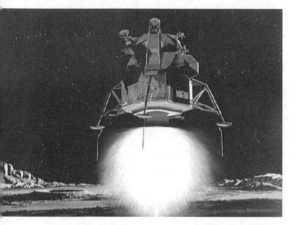

Conceptual Apollo artwork, ironically showing the huge plumes the landers were expected to produce, instead of nothing [Fig. 12]. Were the gung-ho dreams of the early space age genuine, soured by the need to cover up failure? Or was public excitement for unfeasible missions used to generate huge military black budgets?

activities? To honor a dead president's wishes? Or was it something more sinister? Gerhard Wisnewski's book *One Small Step* points out that the huge fiscal allowances approved and supported on the back of public enthusiasm for the Moon missions and subsequent manned orbital programs have enabled massive amounts of cash to fall into military budgets (and almost certainly secret 'black-op' developments) that might otherwise never have been generated or sanctioned. A deception could not endure forever, but perhaps the financial ball was rolling enough by the time of the last mission in 1972 to let its initial spark go. After all, why didn't the Moon program continue, with so many claimed advantages to having bases there?

Perhaps because it was never truly viable in the first place?

There has been much talk of people returning to the Moon (including proposed attempts from several different countries, which could prove interesting), and indeed going on to Mars, so perhaps the technology is at last catching up enough to make it a reality. But at the same time there still seems to be a notable gap between the claimed aspiration to launch new missions and the real will (or ability) to do so, as seemed to be acknowledged in 2010 when President Obama cancelled Constellation, a manned lunar project, because, notably, it was 'behind schedule and lacking in innovation'. The 'private sector' is instead being encouraged to help develop technologies that might actually be technically - and financially - possible in austerity times when the US public might not be quite as behind such a low-priority venture as once they might have been.[21] The truth is that any serious renewed initiative to return to the Moon will now almost certainly be military at heart, whatever impression the PR may give.

It is clear that NASA today is essentially a military outfit, despite the cosmetic appearance of being a civilian operation. Black budgets, kicked off by all the gee-whizz aspirations for the 'final frontier' encouraged so massively in the 1960s, may have been used, while they could be, to develop secret weapons planned to give the US (and, presumably, the wider governments behind the governments) armed domination of our skies - and control over our lives. Already the ionosphere is clogged with non-commercial satellites, the purposes of which are entirely unknown to the general public, leading to much worried speculation from hardcore truthseekers. For all the supposed restrictions of the 1967 Outer Space Treaty (which outlawed the deployment of orbiting weapons of mass destruction), there is little doubt (and little official denial) that loopholes have been found. Thus, space armories and questionable energy emitters are being developed above our very heads, to join the all-seeing spying devices that have long served as the eyes in the sky.

Once again, we're back at the idea of an unfolding agenda of control. Something as seemingly innocent as the idea of putting a man on the Moon - even if it *was* just an idea - may have been part of a wider remit, one that fits into all the theories of elite plans for intense centralization and global domination.

With belief in the Moon landings so integral to our faith in the recent historical record, and to our self-image as a civilization, becoming aware of the evidential anomalies can make people deeply upset and shakes them to their core. It is a profound process that has woken many seekers up to a new awareness that they might have been lied to in other areas too. Investigating huge and traumatic events such as 9/11, something else which has been used to enhance the elite's ability to dominate, shakes people's faith in authority in a similar, if more sinister, way. Distressingly, 9/11 is one more example - and a major one - where the official version falls apart when put under the most rudimentary analysis, as we shall see.

But should we really be so surprised at the concept of such massive deceptions? As a prologue to looking at 9/11, let us first remind ourselves of a very clear-cut instance in which very few are in doubt that the world was deceived - something that was originally fired by those events of September 2001.

THE TRUTH AGENDA: *Mankind's greatest achievement is supported by surprisingly flimsy evidence, and we have to take the word of unreliable authorities that it occurred at all. Something of unquestionable veracity should be self-consistent - yet the anomalies around the Moon landings are impossible to ignore. Better official explanations are deserved, but questioners are brushed aside as delusional. If we did go to the Moon, it seems that the whole story has not been told and that parts of the evidential record, at least, have been tampered with or fabricated. Why? Was support for the Moon missions necessary to generate black budgets for secret projects, masking yet another tier of a control program? Awaking to credible doubts over something as familiar as the Moon landings makes people more open to the possibility that they may have been lied to in other important areas.*

The annual Veteran's Day parade passes the Empire State Building in New York, as troops commemorate genuine bravery and service - but the event is also a statement of US military might, much of its impetus now dedicated to fighting a never-ending war against 'terrorism'.

VII   WEAPONS OF MASS DECEPTION

As another example of a key global event that doesn't stand up to the Truth Agenda, we can look to a public deception that has actually has been widely exposed. The invasion of Iraq, courtesy of a US/British-led alliance in 2003, was based on a claim that turned out to be palpably false. Through fear of 'weapons of mass destruction', people were cowed into lowering their opposition to a disastrous war that has since opened many eyes, in a very real-world way, to an awareness of how popular opinion is manipulated. Trust in authority fell even lower, in Britain at least, when the MPs' expenses scandal was exposed and then government policy was found to be unhealthily influenced by powerful media moguls.

Peeling the Layers of Trust

Just occasionally, an unmistakable mass-deception breaks out of the realm of conspiracy theory and enters the mainstream (whereby, of course, it is suddenly classified as something else). When this happens, it peels off a layer of public trust in our leaders that can take many years to grow back. Sometimes it never does.

The revelations concerning Richard Nixon's Watergate misdemeanors in the early 1970s, for example, notably reduced the average American's confidence in their leaders (with the result that every public scandal since has had the word 'gate' affixed to it - more on this and its possible connections to the JFK assassination can be found in this author's book *Conspiracies*). In Britain, the secret machinations that fired the Suez crisis in 1956 (in which the UK and France secretly persuaded Israel to attack Egypt as a ruse to justify annexing the Suez canal, which the Egyptians had just 'nationalized') damaged British public confidence before that, and has been cited as a major step in the final fall of the colonial Empire.[1] There are other historical examples. In more recent decades, however, and with consequences far more dire, the debacle regarding the Iraqi 'weapons of mass destruction' blasted a crucial chink in the facade of trustworthy government. Now everyone was granted an unholy glimpse into how public opinion is manipulated to support questionable global actions. The legacy on this occasion would lead directly to the dubious rise of Islamic State.

The Afghanistan Campaign

From the day that airplanes slammed into major US buildings on 11th September 2001 [next chapter], two countries, Afghanistan and Iraq, were specifically targeted for war by (mainly) the US and the UK under the blanket remit of the new 'War on Terror' - this, despite the fact that neither country could be shown to be directly responsible for the atrocities. This was especially true of Iraq, its alleged links with Jihadist group Al Qaeda being extremely tenuous to say the least. The public wave of grief and anger over 9/11 enabled obstacles to military action in both these nations to be removed with ease. In any case, both operations had long been in the planning, with an Afghan invasion actually poised to go even before the attacks, as many military sources have confirmed. Fortuitous mistrust of Islamic nations was now cemented firmly in the public mind, enabling first Afghanistan, and then Iraq, to be effectively annexed, with a hanging threat over the other Muslim member states of the 'axis of evil'. It was surely no mistake that George W Bush, a fundamentalist Christian, described the War on Terror as a 'crusade'. We still live with the messy and terrible results of that crusade today.

The operation in Afghanistan could, on one level, be sold as a positive and necessary action. Told that Osama bin Laden and his fundamentalist supporters were responsible for the horrors of 9/11 (despite the Bush and bin Laden families having many proven business connections), people were more easily persuaded into seeing a need for some kind of action in the country where the Al Qaeda chief was allegedly hiding. It took ten years to find him - perhaps. Despite the military incursion supposedly being fired up by his intended capture, incredible as it may seem bin Laden never officially appeared on the FBI's wanted list for 9/11 terror suspects. Tellingly, the official reason given for this was 'lack of evidence'. Many observers suspected the alleged '9/11 confession' video of bin Laden to be faked anyhow. The plumper, darker-skinned character in the fuzzy images released bore little resemblance to the bin Laden seen in previous interviews - who had denied involvement in the attacks.[2] Other confessions, from the likes of Khalid Sheik Mohammed and compatriots, extracted at the Guantanamo Bay detention center using torture and who knows what other brainwashing techniques, are hardly to be relied on either. Given the high-improbability of them ever being released, there is also a fair chance that these characters have played the martyr card for maximum effect. Even if they were involved with 9/11, they are unlikely to have been the major players, as we shall see, whatever the official outcome of their military 'trials'. Yet despite the absence of firm links to the US attacks, the Afghan campaign continued on, with heavy casualties and horrific atrocities on both sides in one of the longest-running conflicts in modern history. Ironically, the world became a far more dangerous place after the War on Terror began, with reprisals and extremism stirred to new heights [Chapter IX].

Western troops in Afghanistan. The 9/11 attacks were used as the reason to enter the country, ostensibly to find bin Laden, but an invasion had long been in the planning and the motives for going in were far more complex.

With no sign of victory

over the Taliban or Al Qaeda and little chance of it ever occurring, despite Barack Obama's 2009 commitment of another 30,000 troops, one has to wonder what the real agenda behind the West's role in Afghanistan was. Predictably, the need to pave the way for a new network of important oil pipelines was one of the likely reasons at least. The US has long made it clear that it would like to see a pipeline running from Turkmenistan, through Afghanistan and into the persecuted Baluchistan (or Balochistan) region of Pakistan, while helping to prevent one being run from Iran, through Baluchistan and into India. (This may help explain the elevation of Pakistan into the big picture in more recent supposed fights against terrorism - page 186). With China also pursuing interests in the region, the growth of a Western 'free Baluchistan' movement has started to grow in the last few years, probably to aid the protection of US influence.[3] Before anything could happen, a foothold was needed in Afghanistan (allowing better access to Pakistan), and the hunt for bin Laden happily provided this.

Osama bin Laden: the hunt for this man supposedly took a whole decade, but the contradictory evidence for his eventual claimed killing only caused more controversy.

The more cynical theorists also see the ensured continuation of Afghanistan's biggest export - opium (a crucial ingredient of heroin) - as another reason for military intervention. Western governments have been accused of secretly creating funds by working with drug cartels, and it is claimed that they actually *protect* the global flow of illegal drugs, for all the public show of opposition. If this seems incredible, it should be remembered that it wasn't too far back in history when Britain went to war with China to openly maintain the opium trade, netting Hong Kong for a century along the way. Could it be that the ruling elite are happier for people to be distracted and marginalized by drugs, as another way of suppressing people's full potential, making money along the way? All this could be dismissed as conspiracy paranoia were it not for the provable fact that Afghan opium production massively soared after the arrival of 'our' troops, leading to inevitable suspicions.[4]

The Killing of bin Laden?

Perhaps conveniently, for Western forces keen to keep going in the area, bin Laden remained elusive for far longer than the public had expected when it reluctantly sanctioned an invasion to right the wrongs of September 2001. Finally, in May 2011, the news was announced that the West's greatest enemy had been tracked down to a compound at Abbottabad in Pakistan and unceremoniously shot dead by US Navy SEALs as he watched television in his underwear.

The triumphant if not-exactly-honourable killing of bin Laden was fanfared as a serendipitous anniversary 'closure' (again) on the 'decade of 9/11'. Obama thus rode high in the polls for a short while, but normal service soon resumed and the reality began to sink in that little on the world political stage was going to change despite the killing. Needless to say, few people in the conspiracy camp believed that the man sacrificed in Pakistan was the real bin Laden anyhow. The late Benazir Bhutto of the Pakistani People's Party - herself assassinated in 2007 - had already stated on live television that he had in fact died of natural causes some years before (a statement backed up by several other sources). The US authorities hardly helped with this perception, by refusing to provide any evidence of bin Laden's shooting and then claiming to have dumped his body at sea afterwards. They also failed to explain the emergence of notably conflicting evidence given by members of the alleged hit squad. The deaths of 22 Navy SEALS from the unit which took out bin Laden, in a helicopter crash just months after the assassination, removed any chance of resolving the inconsistencies and merely added to the dark misgivings around the whole story.

Aside from the details of the event itself, why, in any case, kill a man reportedly discovered unarmed and who presumably could have gifted incredible amounts of useful intelligence to help stop future terrorism and save lives (if the official take on him is to be believed)? Even if it was the real bin Laden in the Pakistani compound, little seemed to have been thought through properly and the whole nature of the action was irresponsible at best.

Iraq and the Weapons of Mass Destruction

Action in Afghanistan at least had a grain of demonstrable justification, as far as the public was concerned. The operation in Iraq was a different matter. In the run-up to the events which would see its borders crossed by a shaky US-led alliance in 2003, the public were visibly unconvinced by the rather vague reasons being given for the necessity of war. The largest peace protests ever witnessed (the numbers played down by governments, naturally) filled the streets of several major cities around the world in February that year, with London alone seeing something approaching two million marchers. The world did not want another war. But it got another war, because the ultimate decision makers, perhaps around the campfires of Bohemian Grove and at the tables of closed cabals, had decided to have one.

With the masses growing ever-more uncomfortable at the impending conflict in the Gulf, George W Bush and his neo-conservative sponsors becoming ever-more gung-ho, and British ally Tony Blair looking ever-more haggard and inwardly-torn by the day, rather oddly the advertised motives for going to war with Iraq kept changing. When humanitarian platitudes and crocodile tears for the undoubtedly oppressed Iraqi population weren't quite enough to convince the masses (after all, why not deal with a few other cruel regimes around the world at the same time?), our secret and not-so-secret rulers reached for the usual solution - the instillation of fear.

When the overwhelming reason for needing to deal with Iraqi leader Saddam Hussein suddenly became his apparent acquisition of 'weapons of mass destruction' (never fully defined), technology which could be called into action to strike Western targets

Iraq's Saddam Hussein, seen here in captivity before his execution. Clearly a tyrant that few miss today, was his removal, however, really only about weapons of mass destruction?

within '45 minutes', some of the global opposition to the war subsided - not much, but it reduced just enough for people *not* to be able to stop all sides of their parliaments, most notably in the UK, voting to give support for what was effectively US action under a very thin smokescreen of an international alliance.

The evidence for these terrible weapons was contained in a British-compiled dossier, supposedly gathered from informed intelligence sources and supported by then US secretary of state Colin Powell. The dossier was loudly proclaimed as the ultimate proof that war against Iraq was now entirely necessary. Yet even while this was occurring, there were clear indications that the weapons did not actually exist. In 2008, Pulitzer prize-winning political journalist Ron Suskind claimed that a key Iraqi intelligence official, Tahir Jalil Habbush al Takriti, had even communicated secretly with US and UK intelligence staff (including then MI6 chief Richard Dearlove) on the eve of war and exchanged credible intelligence that there were no WMDs. Though Dearlove and the US have denied this, other supporting evidence, including damning British government e-mails released in 2009, together with the refusal to release minutes of key cabinet meetings, strongly suggests that the US and the UK knew full well that their given reasons for invading Iraq were bogus.[5]

Nonetheless, what would become known in Britain as the 'dodgy dossier' ('dodgy' meaning unreliable) was held up in both Parliament and Congress as all the evidence needed as to why Iraq must be dealt with (without any of the actual details being revealed, mind), and the machinery of war rumbled unstoppably into life. The neocons got their way and Blair lost his scruples. And so, in March 2003, war against Iraq began, and the rest is... the usual web of deceit and the rewriting of history.

The David Kelly Affair

Yet loud - and qualified - voices *were* publicly raised against the reliability of the crucial dossier, even as the war was raging. When experienced UN weapons inspector Dr David Kelly secretly informed BBC radio journalist Andrew Gilligan that he believed the information in the dossier had been considerably exaggerated ('sexed up', as the suddenly concerned media put it) from its original source, three things occurred: first, someone in high British office surreptitiously released Kelly's name to the press, thus breaking his anonymity, and then Blair's cronies proceeded to besmirch Kelly's reputation, describing him as a 'Walter Mitty'-like fantasist. Following this, cabinet spin doctors, led by unelected 'Director of Communications

THE TRUTH AGENDA

and Strategy' Alastair Campbell, lambasted the BBC as liars (fatally neutering its news output from thereon, ever-fearful of losing the public licence fee) and hounded first Gilligan and, eventually, BBC Director-General Greg Dyke out of their jobs.

And then, on 18th July 2003, Dr David Kelly was found dead in woods near his Oxfordshire home.

With death apparently resulting from a combination of a drugs overdose and wounds to the wrists, it was widely reported that the one official who had dared to speak out against the reasons for conflict in Iraq had taken his own life. But had he? Kelly's death immediately aroused suspicion. Investigations by British Liberal Democrat MP Norman Baker (who bravely voted against action in Iraq and whose 2007 book *The Strange Death of David Kelly* is essential reading) soon revealed serious anomalies in the suicide story.[6] Kelly's body, as officially found, had provably been moved from where it was originally reported to have been, and seemingly rearranged to look more like a traditional suicide. Both the drug intake found in his blood and the wounds to his arteries were far too minor for death to have resulted, and nothing in Kelly's behavior that day or before had suggested suicidal thoughts. Other unexplained aspects, such as a strong police presence near his home *before* Kelly's disappearance and the erection of huge aerials in his garden after, add to the strangeness. (The interestingly-named search for Kelly, 'Operation Mason', is documented in police records as having been mounted nine hours in advance of his being reported missing.) Allegedly compelled to take his own life by depression over the criticism he had received on exposure as the BBC inside source, the reality was that friends and family confirm that Kelly had no reasons to kill himself, nor did he give any signs that he wanted to. He simply went for a walk in the woods one afternoon, and never returned.

Norman Baker MP, whose tireless crusade to get to the bottom of the David Kelly affair made British headlines. Baker concluded that Kelly's death was almost certainly murder and not suicide.

It seems that Kelly himself, neither fool nor fantasist, already had a pretty clear intimation of what might happen to him. Baker writes:

'British diplomat David Broucher told the Hutton inquiry that, some months before Dr Kelly's death, he had asked him what would happen if Iraq were invaded. Rather chillingly, Dr Kelly replied that he "would probably be found dead in the woods".'

Shoehorned by Blairites into supporting the case for proof of Kelly's suicidal intentions, this statement is more realistically seen by most who knew him as his guess at what might be done to shut him up (rather like the intimation Princess

Diana had, expressed in a letter to her ex-butler Paul Burrell and in comments to Lord Mishcon, that someone might try to assassinate her in a staged car crash). If so, it was an accurate prediction.

It seems highly likely from Norman Baker's investigation, and other evidence, that David Kelly was murdered. Baker puts it down to Iraqi dissidents, keen not to stop a regime-changing invasion, but others point the finger of blame closer to home. Either way, the truth about Kelly has plainly not been told, as is strongly suggested by procedural irregularities in the coroner's issuing of the death certificate before the official inquest even concluded, and by Lord Hutton's astonishing 2010 order that medical records of the case not be publicly released for 70 years.[7] Meanwhile, the nauseous hand-wringing of regret from those apparently devastated by Kelly's 'suicide' - the same people who revealed his name to the media - has simply added yet another indignity to the affair.

One thing was for sure; Kelly's grisly demise ensured no other informants would raise any serious voices against the weapons of mass destruction dossier - for a while.

The 2003 invasion of Iraq rages. An astonishing number of people died, were maimed or succumbed to disease because of this action. Yet almost everyone suspected at the time that the war was based on a false premise. Despite this, both Bush and Blair were re-elected to power in the aftermath.

The Aftermath of the Gulf War

Just one year later, however, the mandate for war in Iraq had fallen apart all by itself. No weapons of mass-destruction were found, despite the (claimed) extensive searching. The protestors had been right to question the motives for war, and T-shirts with the slogan 'Tony B-liar' became ubiquitous in the UK. It was to little joy that the unfortunate David Kelly was posthumously vindicated, and much of what was now dismissed as the 'dodgy dossier' was found to have been based on an old student thesis downloaded from the Internet and embellished accordingly. The usual things occurred thereafter. A government-sponsored report into the Iraq action and the Kelly affair (the Hutton Inquiry, published in January 2004) was a predictable whitewash, with all guilty parties effectively acquitted, the WMD promoters having been apparently misled by incompetence on the part of conveniently unnamed intelligence agents. The whole debacle was swept under the carpet - and both the US and the UK public re-voted back into power the very leaders who had taken them into the situation (*un*like the not entirely dissimilar Suez crisis of 1956, over which prime minister Anthony Eden at least had the decency to resign). Between

2009 and 2011, full British hearings on the war (the Chilcot Inquiry) saw many politicians, including Tony Blair, appear to make largely unrepentant excuses in the face of generally insipid questioning. With even mainstream criticism being voiced concerning both the Inquiry's compromised impartiality and its limited powers to overcome government vetoes in some areas (leaving important evidence unaired), the likelihood of any real justice or firmly-directed accountability stemming from the final report - still unpublished at the time of writing - is low.

Meanwhile, Iraq was devastated and reduced to a weakened faction-torn wasteland, its people killed or injured in many thousands and now prone to uncontrolled sectarian violence, while the US and its allies, hidden and overt, had greater access to another country's oil reserves. Tellingly this oil was now sold in dollars again, and not in euros - according to some, one of the main undeclared issues that led to the war (and another element that may be firing up continuing, if inconsistent, US hostility towards Iran, which has also ceased to use the dollar as its sole trading currency). The West also gained a stronger political foothold in the Middle East, at the very heart of 'the cradle of civilization', where some mystic traditions say the gods first arrived on Earth [page 87]. The siting of a US military camp directly on top of the historical remains of Babylon (where legend has it the Tower of Babel once stood) outraged archaeologists, but the gesture may have been highly symbolic.

The mainstream view holds that the invasion of Iraq, carried out without a clear plan for any power structure to replace the Hussein regime, was a massive debacle stemming from more 'incompetence'. Some observers, however, believe that not even the Bush administration could have been that short-sighted. Was the destabilization of the region all part of a wider plan, deliberately helping to enable devastating civil war in Syria and the eventual and suspiciously 'unanticipated' arrival of Islamic State? Is this a calculated chaos to benefit the NWO? Events are certainly following a pattern long predicted by worried truthseekers. With so many religious end-timers [Chapter IV] having influence over US policies, are they also yet another unfortunate blow to the prospect of a peaceful Middle East or actually a happy step closer to The Rapture?

Why the WMD Lie?

Why was the weapons of mass destruction issue focused on so intensely if those pushing for war in 2003 knew it to be a bogus criterion? Why expose themselves so clearly as liars? Some have used this as evidence that it was a genuine mistake on the part of the warmongers, but there is another aspect to consider: bad intentions aren't forgiven very lightly, but human error can be overlooked.

Perhaps those behind the action gambled that the public would grant them absolution for their apparent sloppiness - the usual mitigation, as with the supposed intelligence 'errors' that allowed the 9/11 attacks to occur. If the West had gone into Iraq with all guns blazing for anything even slightly ideologically questionable, the necessary support might not have been there. Taking action to protect us all from potential harm, however, was something far harder for peaceniks to challenge. It has been wondered why a few weapons weren't just surreptitiously planted in Iraq to justify the war, but that might have raised too many enquiries and exposed uncomfortable trails of responsibility. Far better to rely on the public granting forgiveness for mistakes, which, shockingly, it did - to a degree.

Faith and Mistrust

Despite voter forgiveness (or at least apathy), the weapons of mass-destruction disaster did seriously challenge the faith of many people that their leaders were reliable and trustworthy. That faith has not yet recovered, which may be why support for military action in Syria was so firmly resisted by the Western public in 2013, although 'mission creep' against Islamic State is now providing new opportunities, which some fear may have part of the

Not everyone forgave George W Bush and Tony Blair so easily. Here, children's shoes are piled up at London's Cenotaph memorial at a protest march a few years later. The shoes and the mock coffin say it all.

plan - surreptitiously allowing IS to grow to sanction new action in the region. Reluctant public support has without question been greased by the rise of IS, raising fears that further underhand measures might be employed elsewhere to 'manufacture consent', as Noam Chomsky aptly puts it. Meanwhile, Iran's alleged potential to create nuclear weapons has been another fear factor, amidst accusations of its early interference in the Syrian war (although many Western countries were themselves almost certainly involved behind the scenes even before officially deciding to support rebel factions). The blurred lines of allegiances over Syria and IS have forced changes in tone towards Iran from Barack Obama (who has the novel distinction of being a US president with a Muslim father), but Israel's increasingly vocal threats against its nuclear facilities seem to suggest *its* sights are still trained on Tehran at least.

So, despite doubts, the collective weakening of confidence resulting from the Iraq WMD scandal doesn't seem to have prevented a kind of lazy pseudo-trust being reinvested in governments. People's memories are alarmingly short, something surely relied on by those in power; the blind optimism that our leaders might get it right next time always allows the same old faces to continue on. If not, how did Bush and Blair get a second chance in the polls, with so many thousands of men, women and children tragically and unnecessarily dead, injured or sick (particularly through the obscene and much covered-up use of depleted uranium, since used *again,* in the 'liberation' of Libya) as a direct result of the policies they ushered through? The irony of an unapologetic Blair now being the West's Middle East 'peace envoy' seems lost on some people, and his subsequent religious platitudes are hard to swallow.

Nonetheless, for all the blind eyes being turned by voters, the Iraq catastrophe *has* helped create a sizeable demographic that now questions the power structures that shape our world. Sturdy campaigners like the late Brian Haw, who camped outside the British Houses of Parliament with protest stalls for an incredible ten years (despite many attempts to evict him), have helped keep the flame of awareness alive.[8]

Further Breaches of Trust

In the early summer of 2009, the UK's *Daily Telegraph* broke a story that had a further devastating effect on public confidence in politicians in the West's 'mother of democracy'. Outrages involving Lords admitting that they would accept bribes to influence legislation the year before had already hinted at unsavory cracks in Westminster's facade of virtue (with yet more revelations in 2013).[13] However, when a whistleblower leaked details of individual MPs' erratic expenses claims it revealed systemic seams of financial corruption ranging from untenable payments for garden manure and pornographic videos to less forgivable abuses such as mortages being claimed for when they had already been paid off. The huge wave of public anger saw MPs resigning (including, remarkably, the Speaker of the House), paying back what was effectively stolen public money, and making embarrassing apologies.

It is perhaps ironic that the unjustified spending of public cash appeared to raise more lasting outrage than the unnecessary deaths of thousands, but the expenses exposure did lasting damage to public faith in our leaders, in Britain at least, as if more evidence was needed of their inadequacies. There is a view that the denigration of the UK Parliament is in fact an attempt to demolish true democracy in an institution that, if clearly far from perfect, has spent centuries of strife being built up and has inspired most other democracies around the world. By losing faith in what we have, although it has probably always been vulnerable to manipulation from the puppet masters (and the expenses situation certainly needed sorting out), we risk outside intervention coming along to 'put things right' and could become more prey to the future machinations of a New World Order offering a fresh, glorious system.

Already the very low voter turnouts in most British elections give the impression to the higher powers there that no-one really cares how they are governed or who does the governing. This is dangerous. Granted, it is often hard to see what real difference votes make in a manipulated democracy and it has not gone unnoticed that when polls frequently demonstrate that a majority of the public wants one thing, our politicians usually vote for the opposite. It is clear that the firms and forces that they lobby for come a long way before the needs of constituents. Nonetheless this parliamentary system is currently the *only* one Britain has. Events that create further undermining apathy leave the path more open to a complete replacement of that system with something even less democratic, and people in all countries should be on their guard for things that make them stop caring, lest they avert their eyes, lose all engagement and fall into distraction - which is when illusionists work their tricks.

Some illusions were - briefly - exposed in 2011 following the disclosure that media mogul Rupert Murdoch's UK News International newspapers had hacked the phones of everyone from celebrities to politicians and even murder victims. The media circus of the following Leveson Inquiry, which grilled public figures at length to little useful effect (with Leveson's main recommendations effectively sidestepped by both the media and Parliament), was conveniently allowed to eclipse the biggest revelation to emerge from it - the overbearing influence of Murdoch on successive governments of both the UK *and* the US. It quickly became clear that the many surreptitious meetings and quiet social links between Murdoch staff and MPs (including David Cameron and Tony Blair, the latter of which was revealed to be godfather to one of Murdoch's children) went far beyond what might be considered reasonable, and amounted to secret rule from above. With Murdoch seen by most truthseekers as being from the same pool as the Rockefellers, Rothschilds and other fairly obvious NWO operatives, it seemed that a crack in the facade had momentarily opened. Yet all this was hurriedly sidelined by the media, predictably enough, and things soon returned to normal.

Fairy Tales

Fairy tales such as the WMD debacle, and even the tiniest glimpses into what must be firmly embedded corruption, are solid pieces of evidence that we are indeed regularly deceived (even with the deceptions written off as ineptitude). What more proof do we need that we are consistently misled into supporting situations that benefit the agendas of the few against the wishes of the many?

The invasion of Iraq was a direct offshoot of the War on Terror that began with the dramatic events of 9/11. But if no-one now trusts the reasons given for the war in Iraq, why should anyone trust those given for the War on Terror in the first place? Sure enough, by applying the Truth Agenda to the events that put the world on the road to today's control programs, we soon find clear anomalies that demand reappraisal.

THE TRUTH AGENDA: *The weapons of mass destruction catastrophe very tangibly illustrates how easily public opinion falls prey to deception. The wide feeling of doubt at the time, and the evidence revealed since, make it clear that Western governments knew very well that the reasons given for invading Iraq were false. Somebody was even prepared to kill to ensure that information was not exposed, as Dr David Kelly discovered. The campaigns in Iraq and Afghanistan were seen by many as necessary steps in the New World Order plans. With such a plainly underhand lie being employed to win popular consent, can anyone seriously doubt that a manipulation of the masses is taking place?*

The World Trade Center in its heyday. How could such an important complex be attacked and destroyed so easily?

VIII   9/11

The events of 11th September 2001 turned the world upside down and generated the 'War on Terror', which encroached on our lives in ways that many still don't appreciate. Yet the official story of 9/11 is full of holes and anomalies, to a degree that makes it almost impossible to believe when scrutinized in detail. Shocking to behold, the lies and cover-ups surrounding this epochal moment in history reveal even more clearly than the WMD fraud that a significant deception must have taken place. With 9/11, however, authorities and the media have done their utmost to keep a lid on a widespread - and justified - continuing public unease.

The Official Story

On the bright morning of 11th September 2001, four jet liners were hijacked in north-eastern US airspace. Now piloted by Middle Eastern terrorists working for Osama bin Laden's Al Qaeda terrorist network, two of the planes were flown into the World Trade Center in Manhattan, destroying its twin towers completely; another struck the Pentagon, damaging one side of it, and another crashed into woods in Pennsylvania, apparently after passengers attempted to wrestle control back from the hijackers. Around 3000 people died in the attacks.

That is the story that has been told to the world, the one which apparently unfolded before our very eyes on that awful day, and the one to which most people subscribed as the truth - at least to begin with.

As we have already seen, under the mandate of 9/11 the War on Terror was ushered in, ensuring an ongoing conflict that would swell defense budgets and allow battles on foreign shores which might never otherwise have been acceptable to the electorate of America and Europe. Under that mandate, regardless of subsequent changes of presidents and governments, real freedom of speech, belief and movement has been crushed out of all recognition, with many seeing this as a stage towards the New World Order of centralization and domination.

But what if it could be shown that what we are told happened that day is unreliable? The grim conclusion reached by applying the Truth Agenda to this example of a high-profile, yet deeply questionable, occurrence is that the official story of 9/11 may be one of the most serious lies ever told in history. For, shockingly, the details of the 'orthodox' version of events, as set against what actually happened, simply don't stand up to scrutiny.

The Central Allegations

Are the main allegations of those who doubt what we have been told about 9/11 just paranoid sensationalism? The evidence says not, and the caliber of the doubters is formidable. Far beyond the predictable conspiracy community, an increasing number of well-educated scholars, scientists and academics (not to mention film directors, celebrities and artists), from an impressive range of respected professions, have raised very loud voices to call attention to glaring anomalies concerning 9/11. By doing so, they challenge not only obvious lies and suspicious discrepancies in the record, but also events that appear to subvert both the laws of physics and common sense. For the tenth anniversary of the attacks, global polls demonstrated the remarkable trend that around half the world's population no longer believes in the official narrative of 9/11.[1] This is highly significant. Not for nothing has the 9/11 truth movement become one of the most solid bastions of political activism in modern times, with countless groups around the world campaigning for a truly independent inquiry to reveal what really happened. The official inquiry, effectively sponsored by the Bush administration, is hardly to be relied on, as we shall see. Only mainstream journalists seem gullible enough to still accept its very demonstrably skewed findings in full today and their undying complicity has allowed the myth of the orthodox version to propagate, raising serious questions about the media's true impartiality.

With 9/11 increasingly at risk of fading into the general soup of history - as is almost certainly hoped for by all those who stood to gain from it - there is more need than ever to intensify its analysis. The Obama tenancy of the White House, for all the cosmetic changes, has been no less rooted in the global mandate begun on 9/11 than the previous Bush administration, and thus attempts to conveniently consign the attacks to 'the history books' (a desire voiced by several pundits following Obama's accession and then again in the wake of the claimed assassination of bin Laden) should be firmly resisted. The devastating political and social reverberations from 9/11 are still far too strong to be moved on from lightly.

The central accusation of the doubters is that the evidence demonstrates that the 9/11 attacks could *only* have occurred with the aid of insiders holding advantageous roles within the Bush administration and/or the US military intelligence systems. The plotters either comprised a small rogue element acting in isolation or, worse, represented an institutional conspiracy conducted from the highest of places. Many more fear the latter, but either way we have reasons to feel very uncomfortable, especially given that some of the

The World Trade Center in happier times. Little could anyone guess that both towers and the surrounding complex would eventually be entirely destroyed. 9/11 changed the world - but have we been told the true story?

names and faces from the Bush era still remain in places of influence today.

Some investigators say bin Laden's agents were merely 'patsies', unsuspecting martyr-fanatics surreptitiously set up by the real plotters to indict the Muslim world, while others believe the entire scheme was conducted from within the US. It's a shocking charge for those new to the concept, and the knee-jerk reaction is to dismiss the notion that anyone could do such an appalling thing to 'their own people', as most journalists and mainstream pundits tend to do. Yet the unsettling truth is that history is littered with similar examples [Chapter IX] of extreme actions that sacrifice citizens in the name of a higher cause or hidden agenda.

It is worth remembering here that the 9/11 accusations may have a direct precedent. Emad Salem, an FBI agent who infiltrated the Arab terrorist group that detonated a truck bomb in the basement car park of the World Trade Center on 26th February 1993, openly accused the FBI of giving genuine explosives to the group in place of the dummy ones that were supposed to help to frame them.[2] According to Salem, instead of preventing it, the attack (which has mostly been forgotten by the public in the shadow of the 2001 events) was inexplicably allowed to take place, killing six people and injuring over a thousand. Although the allegation was denied by US authorities, it is hard to dismiss the testimony in the light of the 9/11 qualms. Was this an earlier failed attempt to covertly engineer a situation (with the apparent aim of toppling one tower into the other) that finally succeeded eight years later?

What, then, are the key reasons to question the official story of 9/11? There are many areas of doubt, deep and complex, which cannot be covered in full here, and readers must follow-up other sources to get the wider picture, but by again concentrating on some of the more solid and seemingly inexplicable anomalies, a new perspective can nonetheless be gained on the dark day that changed our world.

The Key Evidence

So widely televised and repeated that the images are burned indelibly in our minds, one might think, given the sheer availability of indisputably clear visual evidence of 9/11, that the nature of the events would be beyond any doubt. Yet in many ways this has been the very thing that has enabled greater concerns over the truth to emerge. Like the NASA images, full independent analysis can be made by any informed observer using recordings of what can be seen happening, but what makes 9/11 different is that most people (a minority of 'hologram'/special-effects theorists aside), thanks to the multiple-witnesses, are happy to accept that the bulk of the images themselves are not fake. Thus much of the central argument over the 9/11 story (with the exception of the mysterious Flight 93) becomes not one of pondering the entire authenticity of what we are seeing, but instead of questioning the exact nature of what we are *told* we are seeing.

We are told we see the twin towers pancaking down into dust because a combination of the airplane impacts and subsequent fires weakened the structures to the point of collapse. We are told that the hole in the Pentagon is the result of a Boeing 757 having crashed into it. We are told that Building Seven of the World Trade Center fell down due to fire damage initiated by falling debris from its neighbors. (In fact, for several years, we were not told much at all about Building Seven, but we will come to this.)

There are multiple reasons, beyond the more iconic features, to doubt the official account of 9/11, some of which we will look at later, but these three very visible factors have been key to igniting the arguments. Superficially, what we are *told* to believe at first appears to make sense - until one starts to look a little closer, and thinks with a little less of a tabloid mentality, breaking out of conditioned convention. This is when the veil lifts and the facade of artifice carefully built up in the mainstream begins to crumble under the Truth Agenda.

With this in mind, let's examine the major areas that first ignited the challenges to what people were being told they were seeing.

i) The Pentagon

THE HOLE: One of the first discrepancies to be noticed regarding the very visual evidence of the 9/11 attacks was the impact damage to the Pentagon. Supposedly the hole where Flight 77 (a hefty 228-passenger Boeing 757) entered the building, what we actually see in the early shots (Fig. 1 - before the upper wall collapsed in shortly after) is a horizontal scar, at ground floor level, with a central entry-point of little more than twenty feet across and perhaps twenty feet high. Either side of the hole, there is an extended area of lesser damage approaching a maximum of 120 feet. It didn't take too long for a number of websites, alternative radio stations and eventually the whole world of conspiracy theory and beyond, to wonder, quite justifiably, how a jet liner with a wingspan of nearly 125 feet and a vertical tail of 44 feet in height could have left such a relatively small area of impact.

Fig. 1: The main area of impact at the Pentagon, shortly after the strike (before the roof fell in). The general area of main impact (center) is remarkably small - and the circular objects in front of it are cable spools that were there before the crash. The spools are untouched and there is no visible debris on the lawn. Did a Boeing 757 really hit this building?

Basic trigonometry alone suggests that the width of the entire area of damage should be at least 164 feet across, not 120 feet. The second floor of the Pentagon is hardly even damaged, with *unbroken* windows clearly visible in the immediate post-impact photographs. Why didn't the tall vertical tail tear a scar into the second floor? And how could the bulk of such a large aircraft enter the building through such a tiny central area?

Government-sponsored studies provide computer reconstructions in which the wings of the aircraft are seen to simply melt away into the infrastructure of the Pentagon as the aircraft strikes, as if the vaporization of airplanes were an everyday feature of air crashes. Other official explanations suggest the wings somehow folding back against the fuselage as it enters the building - yet the widely-shown footage shows this very plainly didn't occur when the planes hit the World Trade Center. In most well-publicized air disasters, wing-parts are usually very visibly scattered in the debris field, but not at the Pentagon. It is hard to see how such little visible entry damage could have resulted when Flight 77 hit the building.

LACK OF DEBRIS AND FIRE DAMAGE: A central observation that has been made regarding the Pentagon crash concerns the remarkable lack of airplane remains. In most photographs of the impact zone, there is barely any wreckage visible near the walls or on the lawn. Indeed, large cable spools being used by workmen who were - curiously - restoring that very block of the Pentagon when the plane struck are very clearly visible in front of the entry point, undamaged and barely misplaced by what must have been a significant explosion. There is no evidence of a huge 757 tail lying anywhere, no engines or wing parts.

We are told that most of the debris distributed itself inside the building, and there are a few photographs showing some of this. But these images raise more questions than they answer: what purport to be components of the jet engines, for instance, are far too small to have come from a 757, as many informed aircraft enthusiasts have pointed out. Even credible eye-witnesses on the day have spoken of the remarkable lack of large debris even inside the Pentagon.[3] The very few shots that do exhibit small crumpled parts of the fuselage on the outer lawn make it look as if they have just been neatly placed there for show. Also, as we are told that most of the plane was absorbed into the building (including all of both wings), how did these bits suddenly find themselves far outside?

Photographs showing the entry point *after* the top walls have collapsed (tellingly, the ones most publicized, perhaps because the initial damage looks worse that way) also display another curiosity. Very clean severing of the infrastructure can be seen, with offices on one side of the collapse suddenly exposed to the elements. Yet there is almost no visible fire damage to these rooms. Famously, one of these offices clearly displays a stool with a book or papers still on it, not even displaced or singed [Fig. 2]. Given that a large jet liner, loaded with highly inflammable fuel, had just plunged

Deconstructing Consensus Reality

into the building only feet away, this is rather extraordinary, especially when one considers how much the authorities have made of the extensive 'fireballs' and intense heat from subsequent burning, which supposedly brought down the twin towers.

With these observations and more, doubters have found themselves speculating that what hit the Pentagon must have been something far smaller than a Boeing 757, with much less fuel onboard and a notable clean-strike capability.

Fig. 2: Close-up of the Pentagon damage. Even allowing for the fact that the roof has collapsed in on top of the entry damage, tearing the walls open to expose offices to the elements (rather than it being a direct result of the explosion) it is still hard to see how a stool with papers on it (highlighted) survived a fireball just feet away as Flight 77 struck.

HOW WAS THE PLANE MANEUVERED?: Even if one considers the official view that what hit the Pentagon *was* a 757, this in itself raises many unexplained questions, particularly concerning how it was maneuvered down to an incredibly low position at such a high velocity. We are told that the plane entered the building at a speed of around 500 mph, supposedly taking down street lamps on the nearby freeway as it came in (which some people, interestingly, described as looking as if they had been unscrewed from the ground, seemingly confirmed by a taxi cab driver witness who has claimed 'it was planned').[4] However, simulations of how this flight path could have been attained, when coming from the plane's original altitude, raise serious questions.

To get the 757 down to the virtually lawn-skimming height described, the plane would need to have executed what has been described as one of the most extraordinary acrobatic turns in aviation history, with an extremely tight curve in a very small area of airspace, simultaneously dropping 7000 feet within two minutes. Jet aircraft are built to achieve certain speeds only at very high altitudes where the air pressure is very different, and do not function in the same way at ground level. How, then, did the 757 continue to perform well enough to execute the maneuver and maintain the claimed speed of 500 mph, without stalling or breaking up, as it came in? And how - and why - was it positioned so exactly as to hit precisely the block it did (a largely unstaffed one under restoration), when it would have been much easier to plow into the inner rings of the building from the top? Did someone only want limited damage and casualties here? 125 fatalities at the Pentagon was bad enough, but was it as bad as it should have been if Al Qaeda had really wanted to make their point?

At the helm of the 757, we are told, was Al Qaeda terrorist Hani Hanjour, a man so inept at flying even light aircraft that, at the time he was having lessons, more than one of the US flight instructors who unsuspectingly trained him expressed the view that he 'could not handle basic air maneuvers'. Yet on 9/11, just months later, Hanjour somehow managed to improvise one of the most astonishing aerial feats ever performed.

WHAT DID REALLY HIT THE PENTAGON?: All this doubt leaves a big puzzle - if not a 757, what then did strike this most guarded of buildings, and how? The Pentagon is said to be surrounded by a sophisticated missile defense system which, puzzlingly, was not employed that day, even though by the time it was struck the twin towers had already been hit and it was known that hijacked airplanes were in the skies. How could the US military have left themselves so unprotected as to allow a 757 to descend upon their headquarters? (See Norman Mineta's chilling testimony on page 169 for one possibility.) Or was it not such a large aircraft? Even in the small-plane scenario, however, it should have been successfully intercepted.

The eye-witness accounts are very contradictory. It seems that a large airplane did fly close to the Pentagon just before the much-witnessed explosion, perhaps giving rise to the assumption that it was this that hit the building. But plenty of other people have described a much smaller plane coming in underneath it - or perhaps even a missile. If whatever did hit the Pentagon was indeed flying at around 500 mph, at ground level no-one would be able to say for sure what they saw as it would simply be too fast for the brain to register. However, *told* that it was a 757, perhaps their minds filled in the rest.

The many security cameras clustered around the Pentagon should surely have put the matter to rest? But even here there is confusion and obfuscation. The very few image frames ever released from these security videos show simply a flash of

Fig. 3: A frame from the CCTV video showing the moment of impact at the Pentagon. Officials claim the very few frames ever released from this tape show Flight 77 entering the building - but the vague object is impossible to identify. With the Pentagon surrounded by cameras, why has definitive footage of the crash never been released?

Deconstructing Consensus Reality

something, which might be an airplane, coming in, followed by an explosion [Fig. 3]. Nowhere is there irrefutable evidence that the craft was a 757. The very lack of publicized security images raises great suspicion. With so many cameras trained on the building, one would expect there would be irrefutable visual proof of what happened - but this has not been shared. The authorities seemed eager that the world should see images of exactly what happened at the World Trade Center, but not, strangely, at the Pentagon. Neither is any civilian proof of the Pentagon impact available, as on the day of the attack all local businesses in the vicinity had their security footage taken away by government agents, and none of it was ever returned. Now, so long after the event and with such sophisticated image-manipulation software available, any seemingly convincing images that do ever get released will understandably not be accepted by questioners.

Fig. 4: The final exit hole inside the Pentagon. The object that managed to pierce several rings of the building would appear to be more the result of something sharply penetrative rather than the soft nose of a Boeing 757. And what did really happen to the wings on its way through?

Official shots of the aftermath showing the damage further inside the Pentagon reveal something else of interest. From these images, it can be seen that the front of the impacting craft managed to make its way through three protective rings (blocks with large open courtyards between them) of the building, finally exiting in a neat hole around ten feet in diameter [Fig. 4]. This suggests something of great penetrative power having struck, rather than the relatively light construction of a 757 nose.

So was it a cruise missile or a smaller aircraft, perhaps of military specifications, that really took down the walls of the Pentagon? Most theorists are increasingly drawn towards the latter, but investigation continues, with much speculation centering on the little-known A3 Sky Warrior fighter plane, parts of which seem to match some of the debris that *is* visible in the wreckage. For certain, there is not much evidence to show that Flight 77 was what hit the Pentagon on 9/11. It would seem there is a high chance it was substituted by a more suitable vehicle, perhaps something guaranteed to make a more 'surgical' strike - less devastating than what was needed at the twin towers, but enough to look impressive and make the point. (What, then, did happen to the hijacked Boeing? Some ideas are explored on page 171.) With this act, the world was left in no doubt that, on the surface at least, Islamic fundamentalists could now threaten the very core of US stability and its military protectors.

ii) The Twin Towers

IMPACTS AND COLLAPSES: The overriding image of 9/11 imprinted in most people's minds is of Flight 175 striking the south tower of the World Trade Center (WTC) at 9.03 am. With the north tower already having been hit by Flight 11 at 8.46 am, all cameras were trained on the WTC for this astonishing event, making it probably the most televised live disaster in history. Soon after, further devastating scenes scarred themselves into our collective consciousness as both towers collapsed from their tops downwards in horrific tumbles into their own footprints.

With these images now so familiar, and the message pounded into us (even before the dubious evidence was presented) that this was the work of Al Qaeda terrorists, one might consider what happened at the WTC to be beyond question. However, the more these images are viewed in a spirit of open-minded analysis, the less the official scenario makes sense.

Before 9/11, no modern building had ever collapsed due to fire damage. Yet on this day, *three* huge structures came down in their entirety at the WTC complex, effectively due, we are told, to weakened infrastructures and fire. We will concentrate on the twin towers here and then look at the third tower in the section titled *WTC 7*.

DID FIRE MAKE THE TOWERS FALL?: The official explanation for the falling of each tower can be summed-up thus: the impact of the planes damaged core supports and removed fireproofing insulation, enabling the subsequent build up of heat from the resulting fires to weaken the steel infrastructure, resulting in the collapses we all know so well. Yet there are so many problems with this hypothesis - widely disseminated as fact - that the rest of this book could be devoted to discussing it. But here are some of the key issues.

Whether fireproofing really was removed from the core supports by the initial impact of the airplanes, and if so how much, can never be known. The damage was never observed by survivors up close, let alone forensically examined, during or after the disaster, so most of the official theories are based on supposition and unsettlingly unscientific experiments by the likes of the National Institute of Standards and Technology (NIST), which simply arrived at its estimates by 'firing shotgun rounds at steel plates in a plywood box'.[5] NIST and the US technology magazine *Popular Mechanics* have been the key defenders of the science of the official story (and effectively acted as mouthpieces for the Bush administration to many minds), but as truth-campaigning author David Ray Griffin devastatingly demonstrates in his indispensable books on 9/11, too often they play with figures and twist semantics to make the incredible sound credible.

Even assuming that fireproofing was removed, exposing steel to heat, it has become clear that the constant high temperatures required to weaken the steel supports could never have been reached by the types of fires we see burning in the available footage.

Deconstructing Consensus Reality

Simplifying things, steel begins to seriously weaken at about 2732°F [1500°C], but despite deceptive insinuations from the likes of NIST, there is no evidence to show that the kerosene fires from the exploded jets could have burned for long enough to reach anywhere near that temperature. The fiercest kerosene blazes might just reach around 1832°F [1000°C] at the very most, even with added fuel from office furniture, carpets, etc.[6] Defenders of the official account use the notion of lashings of jet fuel running down the corridors and lift-shafts to justify all of the structure-weakening damage they say occurred, but this doesn't make sense under scrutiny, especially as the shafts were staggered and no single one ran the entire height of the buildings. Even some official sources acknowledge that the very black smoke that pours from the towers is evidence that the fires there in fact burned at relatively low, oxygen-starved levels. Most of the kerosene fuel can be seen flaming itself out almost immediately in the huge orange fireballs resulting from the initial airplane strikes, so the subsequent fires were probably composed of building material smouldering at much lower temperatures than a continuous kerosene burn.

The orange fireball seen as Flight 175 strikes the south tower (above) shows that most of the kerosene jet fuel burnt itself out in the initial impacts, leaving relatively low temperature fires, as demonstrated by the black smoke (below). It is a mystery how such temperatures could have weakened steel supports to the point of collapse.

Although it is clear that some of the tragic victims in the towers found the heat in their areas unbearable, and chose to leap to a quicker, if appalling, end, the visual evidence suggests far less of a 'raging inferno' (the standard employed terminology) than has been promoted. In one heart-rending news image, a woman can be seen standing at the very edge of an airplane-torn scar, forlornly looking outwards. Although she is at the center of the initial destruction, the heat has clearly died down enough to allow her this reflective moment. This does not suggest temperature levels that would weaken steel to the massive extent required.

HOW DID THE STEEL SUPPORTS FAIL?: To result in the type of collapse we see, floor neatly coming down upon floor, each level's core support would have to fail at exactly the same time. Is this credible? Independent analysis from qualified physicists such as Dr Steven Jones and architects like Richard Gage suggests it isn't - without an artificially introduced force.[7] Even accepting the possibility of heat weakening the steel beyond durability in certain places, there is a problem. With clearly uneven and relatively sparse fires seen to be burning in the towers, what could generate such a previously unheard-of simultaneous structural failure?

The weakness of the original 'pancaking' theory, which holds that the added weight of each floor descending then brought down the next and so on, as the floors became disconnected from the support columns, has even been acknowledged by the likes of NIST, but its tinkering with alternative plays on the idea are barely more convincing (it now says that 'global collapse' occurred, precisely because the support columns did *not* become disconnected, thus progressively dragging each one inwards). Whichever way officials say the collapses occurred, we are still being asked to believe that buildings specifically designed to withstand the impact of more than one Boeing 707 (the largest plane at the time the WTC was constructed), were, in fact, little more than card houses with no serious inner support structure.

It is interesting to note that the initial authorized computer models of how the towers collapsed, widely disseminated to the media in the wake of 9/11, managed to omit the key central support columns completely, showing instead just an empty void in the middle of the tower, and floors mysteriously sliding down around them. This was clearly manipulative. In fact, as the eventual release of the WTC blueprints in March 2007 confirmed (suspiciously held back from public view from the attack date until then), each tower had 47 core columns and 240 perimeter (exterior) columns.[8] Even allowing that several of these columns may have been damaged by the initial impact, the fact is that the buildings were designed to withstand the severing of many of them and they should not have fallen in the way we see. MIT professor Thomas Eagar - generally a supporter of the official view - was himself puzzled by this, writing:

'The number of columns lost on the initial impact was not large and the loads were shifted to remaining columns...'[9]

It is clear, for instance, that Flight 175 actually impacted WTC 2, the second tower to be hit, near the corner of the building. This should have caused far less damage to the central supports than occurred at WTC 1, which was struck nearer the center of its north face - yet WTC 2 collapsed *first*, after only 56 minutes (WTC 1 fell after 102 minutes). How did this occur?

In any case, why wasn't the progressive collapse of each tower eventually halted, or at least hindered and slowed, by the floors below, which had not been damaged by fire or impact? How could *every* previously undamaged support on *every* floor fail all at the same time as the one above came down, even given the combined weight tugging on the supports in the revised 'global collapse' theory?

Many independent physicists (i.e. not connected to the US authorities) who have analyzed the falls of the towers have severely challenged the official explanation. Sooner or later the collapse should have halted itself by the simple laws of gravity, density and mass, as Richard Gage has demonstrated.[10] If nothing else, one might expect to see some kind of uneven descent at work, even if its progression was relatively swift. Instead, what actually occurs is a virtually 'free-fall' total failure of both towers (i.e. falling at the rate that something would drop, without resistance, in normal gravity), each entire structure unstoppably coming down within ten seconds. This is something unheard of in architectural history - apart from in controlled demolitions.

Wreckage at 'Ground Zero'. How did so many support columns and beams fail so utterly? Many qualified professionals believe that only strategically placed explosives could have resulted in such total devastation.

WERE THE TOWERS DESTROYED BY CONTROLLED DEMOLITION?:

Aside from all the many other areas of dispute, the most discussed aspect of the 9/11 anomalies are the claims that the bizarre collapse of the twin towers indicate the strong likelihood of controlled demolition techniques being employed that day. This is a serious contention, because it unequivocally implies that the towers must have been laced with explosives before the attacks - something which could not, presumably, have been achieved by the direct presence of Middle Eastern terrorists, and would also require time and qualified skills. Accepting this scenario demands that some kind of 'insider' assistance must have been involved to ensure the successful destruction of the WTC. What, then, is the evidence to support the demolition view?

The entire nature of the tower collapses is anomalous. For instance, as the South Tower falls, we clearly see the first thirty floors or so begin to topple over steeply towards the ground, only for the leaning block to unexpectedly *correct itself* (or at least just dissolve into dust) and fall instead into the 'footprint' of the rest of the building. We also see the tall crowning transmission antenna on the North Tower suddenly descend inwards into the center of the falling roof at a rate slightly *faster* than the general collapse going on around it. Neither of these oddities, nor any of the other strange phenomena observed during the collapses (see below), are consistent with what would be expected from a natural fall, nor with any variation of either the pancaking or global collapse theory. Instead, they strongly suggest that forces within the building are being engineered to disintegrate the internal support columns, thus accounting for the angle correction and the unexpected acceleration of the transmission tower. Only explosives or other destructive devices placed within the building could credibly account for this.

Critics of truthseekers ask how such devices could have been placed without anyone noticing - but it could have been a long and slow process, masked by any kind of maintenance procedure. Indeed, Scott Forbes, an office worker at the WTC (attacked as a fantasist by official defenders), has claimed there was a thirty-hour 'power down' of the WTC on 8-9th September 2001 for a 'cabling upgrade', during which electricity was sporadically off and CCTV cameras did not function. There are also reports that the status of 'heightened security alert' was lifted just two days before that, with reports of sniffer dogs being abruptly removed from the premises. These claims remain unconfirmed, but even if this information is ignored Richard Gage has suggested that extensive lift-shaft maintenance work carried out in the months before 9/11 could have comfortably masked the planting of explosives, and believes that the shafts would have given good access to critical structural points. The truly cynical may also wish to note that Marvin Bush, one of George W Bush's brothers, was at one point a co-owner of Securicom, the company in charge of security at the WTC.

When all is said and done, however, any arguments over the 'how' must be looked at in the light of the available *direct* evidence that explosive technology might have been used to bring down the twin towers - and that evidence is persuasive.

EVIDENCE OF EXPLOSIVE DEVICES: In truth, the word 'collapse' is not really accurate for the destruction of the twin towers. Even the most cursory observation of what happens when they fall reveals that they effectively *explode* from the airplane entry floor levels downwards, with substantial amounts of debris being cast far outside of the general collapse area with what must be incredible force, certainly beyond that expected from a simple gravitational fall. Large chunks of rubble and beams were found several blocks away in the aftermath, together with other wreckage, including fragments of human remains on tops of buildings so far away from the WTC site that they were only discovered years later.[11] Applying the laws of physics to the filmed ejections of material demonstrates that the angles and momentum of larger objects seen flying outwards could not occur without an additional force of propulsion - which explosive devices would provide.[12] Evidence that large amounts of heat and energy were expended during the destruction of the towers can be seen from the 'pyroclastic' nature of the clouds of white dust, which so dramatically pursued fleeing citizens through the streets in a far more expansive manner than one might expect from a straightforward fall. The clouds billow upwards and outwards, suggesting to some researchers the presence of a great motivating upsurge, probably from intense heat, just as in a volcanic eruption.

The state of the fallen buildings showed such an extreme level of destruction that the term 'pulverization' was used by several 'Ground Zero' workers - the buildings had not merely collapsed, but had literally been reduced to dust. Barely anything survived the fall. Bobby Gray, a crane operator who was part of the clear-up team, exclaimed:

'I don't remember seeing carpeting or furniture. You'd think a metal file cabinet would make it, but I don't remember seeing any, or phones, computers, none of that stuff... ...Even in areas that never burned we didn't find anything. It was just so hard to comprehend that everything could have been pulverized to that extent. How do you pulverize carpet or filing cabinets?' [13]

All that remained of the towers were sections of the outer lattice at ground level. Clearance workers reported a remarkable lack of actual objects, such as filing cabinets or telephones, almost as if everything had literally crumbled to dust - more evidence that high temperature explosive devices may well have been employed here.

All this can justifiably be considered as evidence that a very intense form of explosive was used to destroy the towers. A divide has opened up in the truthseeker world over this issue, with supporters of Dr Judy Wood[14] and theories of secret energy technology or micro-nuclear devices having been employed on one side, and physicists such as Dr Steven Jones and Dr Niels Harrit on the other, who believe that some kind of more conventional inflammatory substance such as nano-thermite, which enables materials to burn at far higher temperatures than normal, might have been used to weaken the structures. The latter camp has thus far garnered the backing of more scientists, but both sides agree that a natural collapse is conspicuously unsupported by the available evidence.

The application of an artificial weakening process may explain how the steel core supports were able to snap so easily, once a final explosive impetus was applied. A clue that might suggest the presence of nano-thermite, or some other intensifying process, would be visible molten metal - and sure enough we see molten metal literally running down from the smoking towers in some footage, despite the relatively low

Everything was pulverized to a very fine and highly poisonous dust at Ground Zero, as this fireman discovers - how could a natural physical collapse cause this? The firemen were hailed as heroes on 9/11, but the authorities were happy to send their heroes back into the danger zone long before the toxicity had settled, causing severe health problems - and deaths - since.

temperature fires caused by the plane impacts, which couldn't possibly have altered the nature of steel in this way. Large amounts of molten metal (which official mouthpieces have tried to suggest is glass, but there is too much eye-witness evidence to the contrary from wreckage clearance crews) were found in the rubble even days after the collapses, and subsequent aerial thermal imaging revealed very high lingering temperatures at Ground Zero, far above that which could be explained by the remnants of jet fuel fires. Energy device adherents believe their science would explain this better, although it is, of course, possible that several kinds of technology might have been used at the same time. Certainly, compelling evidence of nano-thermite has been claimed in an analysis of the dust from the destruction of the towers, carried out by seven scientists, including Jones, published in April 2009 in the paper *Active Thermitic Material Discovered in Dust from the 9/11 World Trade Center Catastrophe*. Gregg Roberts of Architects and Engineers for 9/11 Truth reports:

'The team analyzed dust samples that were collected from four locations near Ground Zero. One sample was collected ten minutes after the North Tower exploded, so it could not have been contaminated with particles from the cleanup efforts. All four samples contained the same unusual, tiny red/gray chips, which turned out to consist not only of the ingredients of conventional thermite but also carbon, silicon, and other elements.' [15]

[Even without the thermite, the issue of toxic dust, containing many other dangerous contaminates, is another outrage of 9/11. Firemen, rescue workers and New York civilians were inexplicably assured by authorities that it was safe to re-enter the area long before it actually was, almost certainly leading to health issues and many subsequent deaths caused by respiratory conditions and other problems.] [16]

Another notable feature suggesting the use of explosives to bring down the towers, which can clearly be seen in photographs of the WTC rubble, is the remains of steel beams exhibiting ends that seem to have been sliced neatly across at 45° angles, almost as if they have been sawn. Official defenders claim this is simply where recovery crews cut the beams to clear wreckage, but comparing these to stock promotional photos of 'cutter charges' and their results, used in controlled demolitions to take out the infrastructures of buildings in neat portions, one can see that the observed angular slicings are virtually identical. It is certainly noteworthy that nearly all of the steel beams at Ground Zero seemed to fall as neatly severed, manageable and regimented-size pieces that were easy to pick up and take away afterwards. It is hard to imagine that a random structural failure would have produced this level of organization.

DEMOLITION SQUIBS?: One of the most debated visual anomalies in the collapse footage concerns what some describe as 'squibs' - large and vigorous puffs of smoke and ejected material, which can clearly be seen blossoming at different places along the entire height of both WTC towers as they fall, far below the level of the descending disintegration. No adequate explanation has yet been presented for what these are. Defenders have claimed they are the result of an air pressure-wave pushing through the building as the floors come down from above, blowing out glass windows. Others have suggested they are gas canisters or air ducts exploding, but these explanations are little more than empty guesses, especially given that air ducts don't generally explode under pressure, and no industrial gas canisters were present in either of the twin towers. The pressure-wave theory sounds more feasible, but doesn't convince, for two main reasons: 1) the 'puffs' are far bigger and more violent (and in oddly selective places) than such an innocuous term suggests, ejecting large amounts of rubble - more than would result from just air pushing out office materials, as the pressure-wave theory would suggest - and 2) some of the ejections are so far down from the collapsing floors that any pressure-effect could not possibly have yet reached those levels (especially given that each tower is coming down at 'free-fall' velocity for at least part of the descent, the maximum attainable speed).

It is hard to see how the official explanation can account for these phenomena. Yet comparison of these puffs with film of squibs resulting from explosive charges placed in buildings that *have* been brought down by controlled demolition reveals an uncanny likeness between the two, leading many to conclude that what we are seeing as the towers fall are strategically-placed explosives - of whatever kind - going off to weaken each floor, ensuring total collapse.

In addition to the squibs, there is also footage showing rapid flashes of light running in vertical strips along the corners of each tower, like firecrackers - or little explosive charges. All this could be dismissed as electric cables breaking, were it not for the fact that, again, they are actually sizeable discharges and occur at a notable distance below the collapsing floors.

Put together with the fact that many people described hearing and seeing explosions going off in the towers both during and *before* the collapse, there is a substantial case to be answered here.

TESTIMONY OF EXPLOSIONS: In the original news footage of 9/11, as broadcast on the day, it is notable how many firemen, rescue workers and civilians all reported witnessing what seemed like explosions *inside* the twin towers while they were still standing - and then as they came down. TV stations across America reported these in unambiguous terms at the time, with interviews and even live footage of clouds of smoke coming up from the *basement* of one of the towers (before it fell) after a particularly loud boom. Yet in the days after, references to any of this began to be dropped until at last it was as if these reports had never been. There seems to have been a concerted mass-edit ever since, with no mention of internal explosions whatsoever in any of today's available mainstream archive footage (luckily, home video recordings of the live broadcasts, made on the day, preserve the evidence). Indeed, even the French Naudet brothers, who were famously filming New York firemen for a documentary on the day of the attacks (and took the only officially available clear footage of the first tower strike) have, in the reissued version of their tribute film *9/11*, deliberately removed a striking sequence where a group of returning firemen animatedly discuss how the collapsing towers were like explosions taking out the floors ('Boom, boom, boom'). This can only raise further suspicion that a rewriting of history is taking place.

Yet, on record, are astonishing testimonies such as this, from fire captain Karin Deshore, describing (allowing for excited grammar) the phenomena he witnessed at the moment one of the towers fell:

'Somewhere around the middle of the [North Tower of the] World Trade Center, there was this orange and red flash coming out. Then this flash just kept popping all the way around the building and that building had started to explode. The popping sound, and with each popping sound it was initially an orange and then a red flash came out of the building and then it would just go all around the building on both sides as far as I could see. These popping sounds and the explosions were getting bigger, going both up and down and then all around the building.' [17]

This is just one of many similar accounts. Firemen, in particular, being the closest witnesses, documented many such reports. Numerous people confirm descriptions of explosions taking place far below the line of the plane impact damage before and during the falls. It is also clear from fire crew testimony (and the Naudet footage) that explosions *did* occur in the basement of the towers, causing visible damage in the lobby. This is often put down to burning jet fuel pouring down the lift shafts, but given the extreme length of the lift shafts it is hard to see how such extensive damage could occur at ground level from this alone.

The firemen's testimony in all this is crucial to getting to the truth of what happened at the WTC. Yet most firemen will no longer discuss their experiences openly. Why should this be? Perhaps because of the concerns expressed by auxiliary lieutenant fireman Paul Isaac:

'Many other firemen [besides me] know there were bombs in the buildings, but they're afraid for their jobs to admit it because the 'higher-ups' forbid discussion of this fact.' [18]

THE JANITOR'S TALE: In the light of reluctance amongst the rescue services to speak out, we therefore have to turn to civilian testimony for back-up evidence concerning explosives at the WTC, and here one man's story stands out. William Rodriguez was a janitor in the North Tower on the day of 9/11, and was decorated by George W Bush himself for his bravery in re-entering the tower with firemen after the plane strike and helping to release trapped workers by opening fire doors and acting as an informed guide. The testimony of Rodriguez is important, because he is one of those who witnessed a huge explosion in the basement of the North Tower just *before* the plane hit the building.

Rodriguez and his staff were in the first sub-level office at the time, when a large blast rocked the floor below them. A burned and bloodied staff member staggered in, shouting 'Explosion! Explosion! Explosion!' Other co-workers have confirmed the basement blast (describing extensive damage reminiscent of the 1993 truck bomb, which first attempted to bring down the towers).[19] The almost immediate plane strike afterwards, and the subsequent drama, distracted from this event at the time, but Rodriguez didn't forget.

Other basement explosions were described and felt by many witnesses, including the aforementioned live broadcast (since mysteriously removed from media circulation), showing large pre-collapse clouds of smoke coming up from the ground.

In Rick Siegel's interesting amateur footage of the burning towers, taken from one of the wharfs across the water at Hoboken, a mile or so away, the fall of each tower appears to be markedly preceded by a deep boom, which shakes the ground about ten seconds before.[20] Although this remains to be corroborated by other witnesses, in the video smoke can certainly be seen to rise from the basements after each boom. Taking out the roots of a building's basement just before pulling down the infrastructure above it is a known controlled demolition procedure.

William Rodriguez and the firemen with him all heard explosions in the tower around them as they attempted to rescue office workers. They also became aware of strange movements of what sounded like heavy equipment on a service floor usually closed off to normal staff, noises that have never been explained. Managing to survive the final collapse of the tower by incredible chance (protecting himself by diving under a nearby fire truck), Rodriguez was sure that someone would want to document his important testimony when the officially-appointed 9/11 Commission was preparing its reports, but neither he nor his staff were ever called to give evidence:

'I contacted NIST... ...four times without a response. Finally (at a public hearing), I asked them before they came up with their conclusion... ...if they ever considered my

statements or the statements of any of the other survivors who heard the explosions. They just stared at me with blank faces.' [21]

Incensed at the refusal of any authority to acknowledge his experiences, Rodriguez embarked on an ongoing global lecture tour in which he has since shared his full and heartfelt account with thousands, in an attempt to by-pass the clearly partisan establishment filters. As such, he has probably done more than many conspiracy theorists to spread awareness that someone may have placed explosives in the twin towers to help to bring them down.

However, given that no construction has ever fallen due to fire damage in the whole of modern architectural history (including hotels and tower blocks which have burned for up to 24 hours without collapsing, as at Madrid in 2005) it is a remarkable thing that not two, but three buildings apparently did so on 9/11. For most people forget, and have been encouraged to forget, the fall of WTC 7.

iii) WTC 7

At 5.20pm on 11th September 2001, after several harrowing hours since the morning attacks, the fall of one more, unoccupied, office block at Ground Zero was barely noticed. Building Seven - WTC 7 - was just more collateral in a long day of death and destruction.

Yet 9/11 truthseekers believe that the collapse of WTC 7 is one of the most anomalous aspects of all - because it was never hit by an airplane. Partially but not substantially damaged by falling debris from the twin towers, and exhibiting limited fires on one or two floors, its sudden and total collapse into its own footprint seems completely inexplicable.

Official defenders say that both the fires and debris damage were far more extensive than was apparent, but the reality is that in almost no available footage of WTC 7 can anything other than minor impairment and modest burning be observed (new testimony and film was suspiciously held back until broadcast by the BBC in 2008, but have to be taken on trust and still don't prove the case). If major buildings fall down with such little provocation, then every block in Manhattan should have been emptied of occupants then and there for general safety reasons alone. But they weren't. Neither have any fears ever been expressed since that a building might collapse due to fire or exterior damage, even when a light aircraft accidentally struck a New York apartment block in October 2006, causing an extensive blaze on two floors.[22] Neighborhoods were not evacuated.

HOW COULD WTC 7 FALL?: WTC 7 was built specifically to withstand every imaginable hazard, especially as, significantly, it housed a number of important occupants, including Mayor Rudi Giuliani's Emergency Command Center for the City of New York, offices for the US Department of Defense, the CIA and the US

Secret Service. In addition, it also hosted the Inland Revenue Service (IRS) and the Security and Exchange Commission, which were both at that point investigating the unfolding Enron corruption scandal.

How, then, was such a crucial building able to come down so easily, again at free-fall speed and with no unevenness of collapse? How could 24 core and 57 perimeter support columns simultaneously fail, level by level, without even airplane impact damage to explain such a failure, but with only minor structural compromise? Debris hitting the outside of the building could not possibly have removed fireproofing from the internal support columns - one of the central arguments claimed for the fall of the twin towers - so how could modest fires, with not even kerosene to fuel them, have weakened the floors in this way?

Unlike the twin towers, which seem to explode with great force from the top downwards, the fall of WTC 7 in available footage is far more sedate, and much more like a conventional implosion demolition, gracefully descending to the ground with a minimum of fuss. It seems that the twin towers were meant to go down in a dramatic spectacle never to be forgotten, whilst WTC 7 was removed as quietly and as simply as possible. Its disintegration received only limited television coverage, through all the media obsession with the bigger events of the day, and most people forgot that it even occurred. Incredibly, in the final 9/11 Commission report WTC 7's entirely puzzling demise doesn't even warrant a single mention.

The Federal Emergency Management Agency's demonstration of the position of WTC 7 as the second twin tower collapses nearby. Some damage to Building 7 might be expected, but why did it later fall down like a pack of cards when it was never hit by an airplane and exhibited only limited fires?

A large number of physicists with no ties to US authorities have expressed the view that instant structural failure of a building in this way is simply not possible without an explosive impetus. Several demolition companies, shown the footage of WTC 7's fall by 9/11 researchers, who did not at first tell them the time, place or nature of what they were looking at, expressed the view that the images must be film of expert demolition at work. All were amazed when told the real location

WTC 7

and circumstances, and all stated the impossibility of such a collapse resulting from fire or debris damage.[23] NIST itself hesitated in publishing a final report on WTC 7, perhaps because even its own writers were struggling to come up with an official explanation that could make any sense.

In summer 2008, the BBC's *Conspiracy Files* program (which had already launched what amounted to a manipulative debunk of 9/11 truther claims in a previous 2007 episode) broadcast unseen footage supposedly taken by firemen of the 'raging infernos' in WTC 7, together with alleged new testimony that the internal fires were far greater than anyone could see from the outside.

The official NIST report finally followed shortly after in August 2008, saying much the same thing, and describing the building's fall (conveniently) as a 'new phenomenon', in which, floor by floor, the heat-weakened connections to the steel supports simultaneously snapped (rather than being pulled inwards, as in the 'global collapse' explanation for the twin towers). Given the seven years it had taken for this theory to emerge, with its very sparse supportive footage and suspiciously late testimony, many were dubious of the claims. Its science was highly questionable to say the least, depending heavily on the assertion that the shear studs supporting the building snapped as heated beams expanded away from the surrounding concrete - seemingly ignoring the fact that concrete actually expands at almost the

WTC 7 exhibited some fire during the day - but not much. Why should it have so effortlessly fallen down just a few hours later? And why was such an important building, home to several high-profile occupants, including the Mayor's Office of Emergency Management, abandoned to its fate so early in the day?

same rate as steel, which is why the two are so often used together. Worse, the official assessment of the blazes NIST states caused the extreme temperatures was based on computer models of *presumed*, theoretically required, fires - rather than the modest ones that were actually there. Even allowing for the 'more-fire-than-anyone-realizes' excuses, it remains that no modern structure should possibly have fallen in this way due to fire alone. The NIST report is considered by many professional observers (including members of the Institute of Electrical and Electronics Engineers, in a 2014 paper) to be a work of scientific fraud.

Moreover, the evidence that controlled explosives were very probably employed is once again made clear by scrutiny of the footage. Very suspicious puffs can be seen emanating from the side of WTC 7, almost exactly at the moment it begins to fall, with no possibility of their being pressure-wave effects this time (because nothing is yet coming down). A ripple that passes across the main face of the building suggests a blast shockwave of some kind in progress, and witnesses reported seeing glass windows 'busting out' just before it began its straight descent into rubble.

OFFICIAL ACKNOWLEDGEMENT OF DEMOLITION?: There seems to be some confusion amongst even the authorities at the core of the 9/11 events as to what happened regarding WTC 7. Although the official line now says that fire and debris damage caused its collapse, it seems that the idea of admitting deliberate demolition with regard to this block *was* toyed with. Otherwise, how do we make sense of WTC owner Larry Silverstein's now notorious comments on Building Seven in the 2002 PBS television documentary *America Rebuilds*, in which he states the following?:

'I said, "We've had such terrible loss of life, maybe the smartest thing to do is pull it." And they made that decision to pull and we watched the building collapse.'

Given that 'pull it' is a traditional demolition term used to describe the moment that a building is pulled down, at first sight this would appear to be confirmation that WTC 7 was indeed demolished, ostensibly for safety reasons (rather than it just falling down), and Silverstein's comments were leapt on by truthseekers as such. But if WTC 7 could have been destroyed in this way, why not the twin towers also?

All this began to raise uncomfortable speculation. After all, lacing a building with explosives is something that couldn't possibly have been done in an afternoon, in all the chaos of a disaster zone. Controlled demolitions can take weeks to plan. Were office workers always sitting just feet away from officially-sanctioned explosive charges, designed as part of the infrastructure just in case emergency demolition was ever needed (an argument which has also been made for the twin towers)? Such a wild contingency measure would be unheard of. If not, however, how

FEMA's annotated aerial shot showing the remains of the WTC complex. The twin tower areas are just below the bottom of the picture. It can be seen that parts of WTC 5 and WTC 6 survived, but WTC 7 - set back further - didn't.

could WTC 7 have possibly been brought down that day?

With conspiracy theorists now calling WTC 7 the 'smoking gun' of 9/11, and officials perhaps realizing the revealing and potentially disastrous nature of the 'pull it' statement, attempts were made to rescind or at least re-clarify Silverstein's words, which were hastily explained as meaning that he was simply referring to the decision to 'pull' the firemen out of the dangerous building. But this raised more questions than it answered. With demolition experts confirming that the phrase 'pull it' was pretty unambiguous in its industry meaning, to use such a term to refer to removing rescue crews from a danger zone was highly unusual to say the least.

FOREKNOWLEDGE OF WTC 7'S COLLAPSE: Accepting for the sake of argument that Silverstein *was* only referring to the removal of the firemen from WTC 7, this still leaves a major anomaly, because it is very clear that officials knew well in advance that this building would collapse. But how did they know?

WTC 7 was set back some distance from the twin towers, with Buildings Five and Six in-between. Even allowing for the fact that these nine-storey blocks were much lower than Seven's 47 storeys, why would anyone think that WTC 7 was about to come down when there seemed to be no great concern over the potential collapse of these other substantial surrounding blocks of the WTC, which were far more damaged by falling debris? Also, with no steel-frame construction ever having collapsed due to fires on a few floors in the whole history of modern architecture (and with no airplane impact), why did anyone think this would happen now?

Yet officials were plainly aware that WTC 7 would be coming down, up to seven hours in advance, according to the testimony of fire officers. Captain Michael Currid, president of the Uniformed Fire Officers Association, reported Mayor Giuliani's Office of Emergency Management as having warned that WTC 7 was 'basically a lost cause and we should not lose anyone trying to save it'.[24] Other officers received the same message and fire crews were removed from the building and a safety cordon set up several hours before it fell. But why should this be? With firemen having tackled far worse blazes in New York before then, why single out WTC 7 as a 'lost cause', especially for such a vital administrative building?

Given that the building was actually *home* to the command center of the Office of Emergency Management, it seems to have been evacuated extremely early on - even before the towers next to it fell, according to the late City Housing Authority worker Barry Jennings, who claimed that he and Michael Hess, New York's 'corporation counsel', entered the command center shortly before 9.03am (after the North tower was struck, but before the South was hit) only to find it already deserted. Yet the official story says the evacuation did not occur until 9.30am. It should be noted here that Jennings and Hess also reported a large explosion taking place inside WTC 7 as they tried to leave the mysteriously empty building. The blast destroyed the stairs beneath them. Other sounds of explosions followed. If true, this suggests that a

THE TRUTH AGENDA

systematic weakening of the structure may have been taking place throughout the day before WTC 7's eventual collapse in the late afternoon.[25]

Interestingly, some communicative cross-wires seem to have occurred in the hour before WTC 7 did finally come down at 5.20pm, which again speak not only of foreknowledge of its destruction, but also a direct planning of it. In 2007, footage from BBC World News' live coverage of 9/11 re-emerged on the Internet, showing reporter Jane Standley describing the collapse of WTC 7 a full twenty-three minutes *before* it actually fell. Ironically, the still-intact block can be clearly seen in shot on the horizon behind her. All this speaks of a pre-prepared statement accidentally going out a little too soon. Just a mistake on the part of those who had been warned of the building's supposedly dangerous condition, or a demolition schedule going a little awry?

The smoke plume from the fall of WTC 7, exhibiting the 'pyroclastic' flows seen on 9/11. These suggest extensive heat in the dust clouds not typical of natural collapses.

WHY DESTROY WTC 7?: Why bring WTC 7 down as well as the twin towers? Some 9/11 ponderers hold that the events of the day may have been coordinated from WTC 7, with unknown occupants using it as a central hub to control the outcome of the attacks. This belief is held especially amongst those who suggest the planes were guided in by remote control, with command perhaps even taken out of the hands of the supposed hijackers - not as outlandish as it may sound when the evidence is examined, especially given the modern ubiquity of military drone technology.[26] Perhaps, with the job now done, having allowed time to remove all useful items, it was safer and more convenient to destroy the remaining evidence than risk rescue crews and investigators finding incriminating clues in the aftermath.

If nothing else - although this still suggests pre-planning, and therefore foreknowledge of the day's attacks - the rather serendipitous loss of crucial Enron investigation documents (and who knows what else) may have been a good enough reason for someone to bring down the building, in the hope that its destruction might not be noticed in amongst all the tumult. And mostly it wasn't, despite WTC 7 being one of the most mysterious and suspicious elements of 9/11.

Other Areas of Concern

All of the above points, in themselves, stand as good enough justification for a new and totally independent public investigation into 9/11, which is the central aim of most of the truth campaigners. With the official 9/11 Commission having been effectively staffed by close associates of the Bush administration, such an independent inquiry has not yet occurred. These included, as Executive Director of the Commission, Philip Zelikow, a long-time friend and colleague of then National Security Advisor (later Secretary of State) Condoleezza Rice.[27] Anyone in doubt over the obvious partiality of the supposed inquiry should invest in a copy of David Ray Griffin's 2004 book *The 9/11 Commission Report: Omissions and Distortions*, which outlines, point by point, every failure of the Commission to address the truth of what really occurred on 9/11. The book's title - one of several damning volumes by Griffin - tells you all you need to know here about the official report's reliability.

Those who attack 9/11 truthers often accuse them of putting unnatural focus on contentious minutiae taken out of context. However, when challenging the truth of something, one should always look for 'clusters' of anomalies and inconsistencies - and there is more than enough evidence of such clusters with regard to 9/11. Applying the Truth Agenda to this subject reveals some of the largest evidential holes to be found in any historical event. Before we move on to exploring the bigger picture of where all the mysteries and cover-ups discussed in this book are taking us, it would be remiss, therefore, not to touch at least briefly on some other areas of concern.

DO WE REALLY KNOW WHO THE HIJACKERS WERE?: If members of Al Qaeda were involved at all with the attacks, even merely as patsies, were the hijackers the ones we were told about in the news? Mohammed Atta, for example (held to be the ringleader on the day), far from being a devout Muslim as claimed, appears to have enjoyed himself at lap-dancing clubs and casinos in the preceding week - behavior hardly befitting a religious martyr. Also, given that Hani Hanjour could barely handle a light aircraft, let alone a jet airliner, how was he able to execute the extraordinary manoeuvre into the Pentagon (see above) - unless someone else was piloting the plane or remote control had been imposed on Flight 77?

The hijacker Mohammed Atta, supposedly a devout Muslim, was seen cavorting in lap dancing clubs just days before 9/11. Was he really a religious martyr?

The appearance of the supposed hijackers passing through airport gates in security video footage is inconsistent with descriptions given by the ground staff at the time, and security 'time-coding' on the tapes appears to have been tampered with. Although there has been some mysterious and not entirely convincing backtracking on the story since, it is interesting to note that, in the weeks after 9/11, BBC News reported that seven of the alleged hijackers were claiming to be both innocent and alive and well in their native countries.

The identification of the hijackers - as claimed by the US authorities - always seemed fortuitously easy; as well as suspiciously over-incriminating evidence apparently having been left in their parked cars, we are also asked to believe that some of the hijackers' passports were picked up from pavements below the WTC, having survived the huge fireballs of the airplane impacts. Little else escaped intact in the otherwise pulverized remains.

As already mentioned, the 'confessions' of those incarcerated by US authorities and accused of plotting 9/11 cannot be relied upon either, with 'guilty' verdicts always guaranteed, but accusations of both plea-bargaining and brainwashing being rife.

HOW WERE THE HIJACKS SO SUCCESSFUL?: With only boxcutters (standard DIY blades) as weapons, and very restricted access to the cockpits (indeed, some say Flight 77's black box shows the cockpit doors were never opened),[28] is it reasonable to believe that four aircraft were successfully hijacked in the way claimed, and so quickly? Why, for instance, did not one of the pilots have the time or the initiative to press the emergency mayday button just a finger-click away?

In addition, for every plane, the transponders (automatic beacons) were switched off - almost unheard of in any previous hijacking case. Although NORAD (North American Aerospace Defense Command) and the FAA (Federal Aviation Administration) claim this is why they were unable to trace the flight paths of the airplanes, this simply cannot be true, as the craft would have shown up clearly as radar blips at least - otherwise, as David Ray Griffin has pointed out, how has the US ever protected its airspace? Russian bombers, for instance, would hardly have been likely to have been broadcasting convenient transponder signals.

On 9/11, the suspicious NORAD exercise 'Operation Vigilant Guardian', which concerned hypothetical jet liners hitting well-known US buildings (including the WTC), was being conducted *that very day* - amongst several other oddly-timed national drills. This enabled genuine confusion to reign amongst air traffic controllers ('is this real-world or exercise?', says one, when being told of the hijackings), and created a good cover for officialdom to explain why proper intercepts were not made. NORAD's own tapes of air traffic control conversations are controversial in themselves, with inconsistencies and evidence of selective editing having occurred (with changes made to the record in recent years), perhaps to obfuscate the facts about who knew what - and when - about the hijacked planes, raising serious doubts over the official claim that they didn't have enough time to stop the attacks.[29]

Even allowing for genuine disorganization, it is an incredible anomaly that fighter planes - until 9/11, always scrambled within minutes of even a suspected hijack - were not sent up until far too late. No action was taken even after the first WTC tower had been hit and other planes were known to have been hijacked. When fighters were finally launched (and official times are inconsistent as to when this happened, but it was at least thirty minutes after the first tower strike), they flew too slowly, and from a *more distant* base than was available, consequently achieving nothing.

Evidence that the hijacked planes (or their substitutes - see page 171) may indeed have been deliberately permitted to continue to their targets came from an unexpected source during the 9/11 Commission interviews. Norman Mineta, United States

Secretary of Transportation at the time, made the following fascinating statement in his testimony regarding what he experienced in the Presidential Emergency Operating Center as Flight 77 approached the Pentagon:

'There was a young man who had come in and said to the vice president [Dick Cheney], 'The plane is 50 miles out. The plane is 30 miles out.' And when it got down to, 'The plane is 10 miles out,' the young man also said to the vice president, 'Do the orders still stand?' And the vice president turned and whipped his neck around and said, 'Of course the orders still stand. Have you heard anything to the contrary?' Well, at the time I didn't know what all that meant.' [30]

Many consider that they *do* know what it meant, believing that Flight 77, or whatever replaced it, was being allowed to do its worst. Other interpretations might be made of this strange anecdote (and have been), but given that no 'orders' at all seem to have been acted on in the authorized version of events (with no interception nor activation of the Pentagon's defenses), Mineta's testimony seems to confirm that officials knew full-well that a plane was on its way to the Pentagon and that they chose not to intercept it; indeed, it is hard to see what else this exchange could have meant. The fact that the 9/11 Commission failed to document this surely crucial information in its final report also suggests they saw it in the same light.

HOW DO WE KNOW WHAT HAPPENED ON THE PLANES?: Although tales of what supposedly occurred on the hijacked aircraft have now passed into popular folklore, the reality is that there is very little available evidence to support them. This is especially the case given that the Flight Data Recorders ('black boxes') from Flights 11, 175 & 93 were, officially, 'never found', presumed destroyed, so telemetry about the way the planes were handled is unavailable. (Some workers at Ground Zero have claimed the boxes there were indeed recovered, but there has been no official recognition of this.) The Cockpit Voice Recorders for Flights 11 & 175 were also 'never found' but, interestingly, given how much contention there is over what hit it, both

The remains of Flight 175 on the roof of WTC 5. Despite hijackers' passports having survived the fireballs, the Flight Data and Cockpit Voice Recorders at the WTC have never been recovered - officially, at least.

recorders for Flight 77 *were* found at the Pentagon, as if to reinforce confirmation of the presence of a Boeing 757. Only the voice recorder was found for Flight 93, which crashed in woods in Pennsylvania - and from this, and a few phone calls supposedly made by the passengers and cabin crew, has been constructed the heroic story of passengers storming the cockpit ('let's roll'), which inspired so much patriotic fervor in the media.

HOW WERE THE CELL PHONE CALLS MADE?: Almost all we have to prove the presence of Al Qaeda terrorists on the hijacked craft comes from details given in the now fabled cell (mobile) phone calls from frightened passengers and crew. Although in-flight back-of-the-seat calls may have been possible from some of the planes (although there is confusion about this), many questions have been raised about how cell calls - officially the main source of the conversations - could possibly have been made in 2001, when no mechanism then existed to enable them to be used at the altitudes claimed for the hijacked planes. Only in more recent years have commercial systems been introduced to allow this. The biggest doubts have been cast over the Flight 93 conversations, where nine cell calls were allegedly made.

Puzzled at these claims, Canadian science writer A K Dewdney decided to put this to the test with a number of experiments and concluded that the possibility of *any* cell phone connections being successful above a height of 8000 feet was extremely unlikely.[31] Given that the officially-acknowledged altitude of Flight 93 was between 34,000 feet and 40,000 feet, calls from this plane should have been impossible. Perhaps realizing the proven infeasibility of the cell phone claims, in time the FBI mysteriously changed its data to state that in fact all but two of Flight 93's calls were in fact made from seat phones, going against all their previous statements - but even the two remaining cell calls are very unlikely to have taken place.

The odd nature of some of the alleged communications (only a very few of which have ever been publicly broadcast) also raises doubts, as with the transcript of the now infamous call from Flight 93 passenger Mark Bingham to his mother, in which he opens a weirdly stilted conversation with the words 'Mom, this is Mark Bingham'. Would anyone really feel the need to give their surname to their own mother, even under stress? Given that voice-synthesiser technology, which can reproduce basic sentences in an authentic copy of someone's individual tones, is now a scientific reality, is it too extreme to consider that these calls could have been faked? Many researchers, even cautious ones, believe they may well have been.

Most famously, CNN television pundit Barbara Olson reputedly made two calls to her husband Ted (United States Solicitor General at the time of 9/11 and a close Bush supporter), on which much has been based. David Ray Griffin writes of this claim:

'According to this story, Olson reported that his wife had "called him twice on a cell phone from American Airlines Flight 77," saying that "all passengers and flight personnel,

including the pilots, were herded to the back of the plane by armed hijackers." The only weapons she mentioned were knives and cardboard cutters... ...Ted Olson's report was very important. It provided the only evidence that American 77, which was said to have struck the Pentagon, had still been aloft after it had disappeared from FAA radar around 9:00 AM... ...Also, Barbara Olson had been a very well-known commentator on CNN. The report that she died in a plane that had been hijacked by Arab Muslims was an important factor in getting the nation's support for the Bush administration's "war on terror." Ted Olson's report was important in still another way, being the sole source of the widely accepted idea that the hijackers had boxcutters.' [32]*

However, Ted Olson's account has been undermined by the FBI's own data, which records that in truth Barbara Olson attempted just one cell call - one that *didn't connect.* Ted Olson later changed his story to say that the call must have been from a seat-back phone - but American Airlines has confirmed that Flight 77 did not have such facilities. Neither does the Pentagon agree with Barbara Olson's supposed version of what happened on the plane, prompting Griffin to add:

'This rejection of Ted Olson's story by American Airlines, the Pentagon, and especially the FBI is a development of utmost importance. Without the alleged calls from Barbara Olson, there is no evidence that Flight 77 returned to Washington. Also, if Ted Olson's claim was false, then there are only two possibilities: Either he lied or he was duped by someone using voice-morphing technology to pretend to be his wife. In either case, the official story about the calls from Barbara Olson was based on deception. And if that part of the official account of 9/11 was based on deception, should we not suspect that other parts were as well?'

WHAT REALLY HAPPENED TO THE AIRPLANES?: There are even doubts amongst the more ardent questioners as to which planes actually hit the twin towers. These issues are far more contentious, but are included here for the sake of completeness. Several witnesses remarked on the day that the planes at the WTC did not resemble commercial aircraft, and video analysis doesn't rule out the possibility that the hijacked liners may have been switched at some point to similar but augmented military-type versions better suited to the task. (There are many debates about anomalous undercarriage 'pods' visible in some shots of the supposed Flight 175 hitting WTC 2, and curious flashes are visible just before impact both there and in the Naudet footage of WTC 1 being struck, suggesting to some that something is being fired from the planes to ensure maximum penetration). The switched-plane theory is unproven, but, if true, raises the question as to what happened to the real craft and passengers if they were not the ones involved in the strikes? This is a pertinent question, if only for Flight 77, which, in the light of the evidence, is particularly hard to accept as being the object that struck the Pentagon.

Deconstructing Consensus Reality

There have been claims that the actual planes we were told were used in the attacks were, having been switched, just quietly re-fitted, re-registered and sent back into service. One school of thought holds that the aircraft, having been hijacked, landed safely in secret, perhaps at military bases. (On the day of 9/11, US television station WCPO-TV did also report that Flight 93 had landed safely at Cleveland Hopkins Airport, Ohio, although this has since been vigorously debunked as a reporting error.) In this hypothesis, the passengers from all the planes were packed into Flight 93, which was then flown off and dispatched by a missile or fighter over Pennsylvania. An extreme belief, perhaps, but given the many other difficulties with the official story, such potential atrocities cannot be entirely ruled out.

It is certainly curious that every flight involved in the hijackings was unusually very low in passenger numbers that day, with Flight 93 in particular operating at only 19% capacity - just 45 people onboard a plane that seated 239. Was this a deliberate ploy to guarantee that all the hijacked passengers would eventually fit onto one plane? It is also interesting to note that apart from the dubious and inconsistent airport security images of the supposed hijackers, no images have ever been released showing any of the other passengers boarding. In addition, it is said that not one friend or relative of any of the claimed nine local inhabitants due to arrive from Flight 93 was waiting at San Francisco when airport staff tried to inform people of what had happened - almost as if their arrival wasn't expected. This raises curious questions, and to this day no definitive passenger list for any of the hijacked flights has ever been agreed, nor have the names that were allegedly the hijackers' 'false IDs' been revealed.

The bizarrely insignificant impact crater caused by Flight 93 in Pennsylvania. The lack of debris or aircraft parts at the site is highly anomalous, suggesting the bulk of the plane was destroyed before it hit the ground. The authorities deny shooting it down, but the physical evidence and eye-witness testimony speaks differently.

WHAT DID HAPPEN TO FLIGHT 93?: Even dispensing with the more controversial theories, there is huge confusion over the ultimate fate of Flight 93. The government deny shooting it down, even for reasons of protecting the public, and support instead the heroic tale of passengers forcing the plane into the woods while trying to stop the hijackers - yet eye-witness evidence suggests otherwise, with clear reports of pursuing planes and an aerial explosion. The debris field from Flight

93's destruction was spread over several miles and there was almost no visible wreckage or human remains left at all at the plane's supposed final resting place; just an anomalous shallow hole in the ground. The apparently vaporizing force of such destruction seems far beyond that which one would expect from a plane coming down by itself, especially when compared to footage of other air crash sites in recent decades, which usually display noticeably large airplane parts, bodies and artefacts strewn around. At least two Hollywood takes on the Flight 93 story have now firmly cemented the official version in the public mind, but the evidence speaks of something less noble occurring.

WAS THERE FOREKNOWLEDGE OF THE ATTACKS?: On a general level, the Bush administration's weak claims that no-one could have foreseen that planes could ever be used as missiles in such a way were provably false, as intelligence reports had warned more than once that such a ploy might one day be used. Condoleezza Rice, however, claimed that such reports were 'never briefed to us' - leaving responsibility for failure once again with unnamed intelligence staff.[33] The fact that one Samuel Byck had hijacked a plane in a failed attempt to fly it into the White House as early as 1974 (dramatized in the 2004 movie *The Assassination of Richard Nixon*) also seemed to escape attention. An episode of the short-lived *X-Files* spin-off TV series *The Lone Gunmen* had even portrayed a disturbingly prescient fictional attack on the World Trade Center, using a remotely-guided jet liner, just months before something similar happened in reality. So the assertions that such a thing had never been imagined, and thus could not have been protected against, are nonsensical.

It has in any case been publicly admitted that intelligence warnings of specific and imminent airplane attacks *were* received by US authorities in the run-up to 9/11, but their failure to act on them has been sidelined under the same blanket of 'incompetence' and bad communications that somehow always sees politicians being reluctantly forgiven by voters. Some canny minds within the US, however, clearly did take serious notice of whatever was bubbling up from 'deep throat' sources - or acted in the absolute confidence of their own plans - as unusual stock market 'insider trading' in the days before the attacks demonstrates beyond doubt. Beginning a week before, and peaking on 6th September 2001, there was an unprecedented 1200% increase in trading activities on the two airlines used in the attacks, as a large amount of 'put options' (basically, financial 'bets' that the stock of a particular company will go down) were placed on them. Sure enough, in the immediate wake of 9/11, $2.5 million profits were made as the stock fell by 43% on American Airlines and by 39% on United Airlines. Strange trading in connection with other companies that would suffer due to the attacks also occurred. The official investigation into these serendipitous transactions mysteriously absolved the traders in question with the somewhat circular reasoning that they had 'no possible ties to Al Qaeda' - neatly avoiding the point that Al Qaeda may not have been the main players.

Meanwhile, some have pointed out the further serendipity of owner Larry Silverstein taking out insurance against terrorist destruction of the WTC complex just six weeks before 9/11. This was indeed lucky, as even after the previous basement bombing of the North Tower in 1993 no-one had thought to do this. The insurers consequently paid out millions of dollars to Silverstein. The latter example could, of course, be chance, but there is enough general evidence to confirm that there *was* solid information floating around that something big was about to happen. San Francisco mayor Willie Brown, for instance, was reportedly warned to be 'cautious' about flying on September 11th, while civil rights campaigner Dick Gregory was advised by personal sources to avoid New York that day.

Despite all this evidence of foreknowledge in many areas, the media has often preferred to concentrate on the unproven, but much-whispered (especially in the Islamic world, predictably enough) claim that a large Jewish contingent of WTC-based staff didn't turn up for work on 9/11 - thus neatly implying that questioning 9/11 is essentially an anti-Semitic exercise, when it most certainly isn't. It has been asserted that a strangely large number of WTC workers were absent that day, suggesting that some at least had been party to a sixth sense - or a tip-off - but Jewishness probably wasn't a connecting factor. Meanwhile, those who do believe Zionist elements of Mossad may have been involved with whatever unknown criminal cartel was at work on 9/11 can hardly be labelled anti-Semitic for speculating on the possible participation of one of the world's most powerful and shadowy intelligence organizations, which has close links with the not-exactly-spotless CIA.

WHAT DID THE PRESIDENT KNOW?: The much-lampooned and oft-criticized response of George W Bush, on-camera, to the news that America was 'under attack', whispered into his ear by presidential aide Andrew Card, has now entered cultural infamy (much of it courtesy of the sequence's inclusion in Michael Moore's documentary film *Fahrenheit 9/11*). Sat on a chair telling stories to children in a classroom of the Emma E Booker Elementary School in Florida, Bush looks confused and unable to respond appropriately. Instead of excusing himself, politely breaking off to address the nation, he continues to read for several more minutes. What did he really know about the events at this point?

Despite accusations from some quarters, there are those who suspect that Bush may have been initially ignorant about the larger agenda unfolding that day, hence his confusion. If there was knowledge of, or involvement in, the attacks at a government level (many truthers accuse Dick Cheney of being a key architect), was Bush informed a little later in the day, once in the 'safety' of the presidential plane Air Force One? If so, did he go along with the revealed plans willingly, or was there an implicit threat to his safety if he didn't? (It was publicly stated on the day that there was a coded terrorist threat to shoot down Air Force One, but did the threat in fact come from closer to home, as a blackmail strategy? This element of 9/11 has since been played down to the point of denial.)[34]

Further confusion has been added by later comments from Bush, in which he stated that he already knew of the first WTC strike before he entered the classroom - he had seen the footage and thought, with characteristic insensitivity, 'that's one terrible pilot'. But how could Bush or anyone have seen this footage? The only officially acknowledged distinct video of the first impact was taken by the French Naudet brothers - and *wasn't televised on the day of 9/11*, only being released later. The tape stayed trapped within its camera with the film crew as the traumatic day progressed. So how could Bush have seen it that morning? Is he lying about this for some complicated reason, or was there a secret camera weirdly trained on the WTC to capture the moment for inside conspirators? If the latter, this would implicate Bush's involvement from the start, but his reaction in the schoolroom suggests that he may simply be a man who doesn't really know what's going on. Either way, Bush should have then responded to the crash in front of journalists before he entered the class, if only to voice supportive sympathy to the families of the victims.

When the second impact at the WTC occurred, another important thing failed to happen. Given the absolute certainty that America was now indeed under attack, and with Bush surely a prime target and his presence at the school widely revealed by news coverage, why was he not immediately whisked away for his own safety - and to protect the schoolchildren from potential attack? Yet the story of the pet goat continued on. Was this inaction because those in command of the situation (officially or unofficially) knew full well that no airplane would be heading in that particular direction that morning? Questions within questions reveal no obvious answers to any of this, but it is very clear that something is not right.

WHY WAS THE WTC WRECKAGE ILLEGALLY REMOVED?: Given that on 9/11 the WTC became the USA's biggest-ever crime scene, why was no proper forensic examination of the wreckage ever carried out? Instead, it was cleared with almost disrespectful haste, and the remains (including the vital steel supports, which could once and for all have settled the matter of what made them snap) were - quite illegally - removed and hurriedly shipped out to the Far East for recycling, after only the most perfunctory survey by a chosen few. The much circulated assumption seems to have been that as it was a 'fact' that bin Laden and his associates were responsible for the attacks, then why waste valuable time proving what was already known? As a result, the evidence was destroyed and inconvenient questions will now never be answered, at least not through forensic analysis.

Official Debunking

We could go on, and other sources [see *Appendix 3*] provide much more. But enough has been stated here to make clear that at the very least there are many unanswered questions about 9/11 that should seriously concern us. On the events of this day are based the entire rationale of the war against liberty - and actual wars in the Middle East - that we have seen ever since. Yet there is overwhelming evidence of falsity, subversion and distraction from official channels in almost every area concerning this vital keystone of history. Who exactly *was* behind the coordination of the attacks is unknown at this stage (although some fairly obvious prime suspects amongst the US neo-conservatives have been directly cited by researchers like Webster Tarpley), but it is clear there is a substantial case to be re-investigated.

The usual defense - that such a huge fraud couldn't possibly be perpetrated without the knowledge of thousands at a highly involved level - doesn't stand up under analysis (as with the NASA arguments). The suspiciously 'coincidental' NORAD exercises occurring on 9/11 probably helped cover a multitude of sins on the day, with any intentionally dubious decisions neatly lost in the confusion. Only a very few people in the chain of command would have to be involved to ensure that the attacks would be successful - and spectacular enough to rest in the consciousness of civilization forever. Perhaps that's why both towers (WTC 7 aside) had to come down completely - blackened holes in the sides of buildings that could be repaired might not be enough to make the point. The total destruction of one of the most famous landmarks in the world, together with a shocking loss of life, would be.

The aforementioned defense often offered against the inside-help theory - 'how could anyone do such a thing to their own people?' - is also flawed when held up to the depressing legacy of history. There have been many well-documented cases of the power-hungry making what they see as 'necessary sacrifices' for the foment of some wider agenda, as we shall explore in the next chapter. Why should 9/11 have been any different? A halfway-house theory put forward by some people, that perhaps the authorities merely stood back and let the attacks of 9/11 occur for political gain but didn't actively plan it, is also unsatisfactory. There is too much evidence to show proactive manipulation on the part of some hidden cabal with access to high places of authority. But even if the halfway idea is considered, is letting something happen on

The beautiful 'Tribute in Light' is shone from the site of the WTC each year on the anniversary of 9/11. Those who died and suffered are rightly remembered, but until the full story is uncovered, a risk remains of something similar being engineered in the future. The media often states that it is 'disrespectful' towards the victims and their families to question 9/11, but campaigners believe that wilful ignorance is even more disrespectful.

purpose any less lamentable than directly aiding and abetting it?

Official - and highly flawed - attempts at debunking what George W Bush rather richly described as 'outrageous conspiracy theories' (not realizing that the official bin Laden story, even if taken as true, is in itself a conspiracy theory) have become louder and more desperate as the public clamor to get to the reality of 9/11 mounts. But the arguments put forward to combat the outrageous - or, more accurately, out*raged* - theorists are all too often weak and evasive, with the defenders simply ignoring anything embarrassingly stark that can't be answered by the authorized account (read David Ray Griffin's *Debunking 9/11 Debunking* for a convincing point-for-point rebuttal of virtually all of the attempted official defenses).

A Growing Movement

Although the passing of the years may have lessened the momentum a little, the still-growing ranks of the global 9/11 truth movement, the poll results which demonstrate the doubts of enormous numbers of people across the globe, and the ever-high Internet hits on documentaries questioning the official line (with statistics conspicuously cranked down from time to time by seemingly concerned web hosts), are testament to the obvious fragility of the story we have been fed. Despite the US media's usual shock-horror response when the likes of Iran accuses America of self-inflicting 9/11, the fact is that its own surveys suggest that even the majority of the US population itself now doubts the official story, or at least believes that authorities allowed the attacks to occur.[35] There is a not-insignificant network of web-surfing, DVD-swapping and pamphleteering that has already tipped the balance of popular thinking and this will only spread further if convincing answers to the (literally) burning questions are not forthcoming. The hope of those in authority would seem to be that all of this will eventually fade into history, where no real harm to their plans can be done by the doubters, in the same way that many people now assume that JFK's killing was a wider state conspiracy of some kind but are no longer inclined to worry about it. It must be ensured that this hope is forlorn, if we are to protect what is left of freedom and real democracy, and this means speaking out and continuing to spread awareness of the serious issues around the events which are still actively impacting on our world today.

Right now, the word 'fringe' certainly no longer serves to describe the upsurge of people who feel they have had their intelligence insulted for too long by arrogant and evasive authorities, in themselves supported by a complicit (and intimidated?) media, which does everything it can to belittle 9/11 truthseekers. Believing in '9/11 conspiracy' is regularly held up to be proof of eccentricity or delusion, and some US citizens have even found themselves sectioned under mental health laws for publicly expressing this view, suggesting a desperation on the part of authorities. Why should this be the case, though, with so many convincing arguments and perfectly legitimate lines of enquiry to support the doubts? Mainstream pundits have entirely failed the public regarding open-minded analysis of 9/11, with some pompously dismissive columnists (including nemesis of conspiracy theorists David Aaronovitch, and environmentalist George Monbiot, who shamefully described 9/11 questioners as 'morons' prey to an 'epidemic of gibberish') demonstrating a state of smugness and utter denial that merely illustrates the hollowness of popular journalism's supposedly investigative ideals.[36] Television, meanwhile, also produces ignorant dismissals of impressive evidence and omits all of the important details, as ever. In Britain the attacks on truthers have been particularly savage, with the atrocious and misleadingly manipulative entries in both the BBC *Conspiracy Files* and *Conspiracy Road Trip* series providing final proof that, since the David Kelly affair [Chapter VII], this once-great broadcasting institution has been well and truly neutered when it comes to incisive investigation of sensitive areas, specializing instead in debunking documentaries or, at best, weak exposés of relatively trivial matters.

A member of the London 9/11 Truth Campaign shows the determined dedication that many global campaigners have to uncover the real details of the events, spending time distributing leaflets and raising awareness. Why? Because the control agendas still affecting our lives today are inextricably bound up in the legacy of 9/11.

But then 9/11 has had a number of far-reaching consequences, some depressingly mundane and some distressingly massive, which we shall now explore in Part Three before coming to the good news of how easily all this deception and doubt might be turned around at last.

THE TRUTH AGENDA: *The event that created the mandate for the 'War on Terror', a campaign that crushed liberties and created havoc around the world, demonstrates serious anomalies when the details are examined. Important questions about the logic, timing and physics of most of the occurrences on 9/11 have been too lightly dismissed, with plain obfuscation from both authorities and the media. The official 9/11 Commission Report omits crucial evidence that paints quite a different picture to the official view and implies layers of complicity and deception. This troubling and unavoidable conclusion strongly suggests that the attacks were engineered either partially or wholly by a criminal cabal with influence in the US command infrastructure, and possibly beyond. 9/11 presents one of the most powerful cases that the view of the world we are presented with by the mainstream is a manipulated construct that is secretly shaping our lives.*

13

Part Three:
Tools of Control

The Liberty Bell hangs in Philadelphia, Pennsylvania, and was made to represent the freedom of the USA and its people. Yet, in the wake of 9/11, the Patriot Act and other supposed anti-terror legislation wiped away almost overnight many of the old protections of the Constitution. Perhaps the famous crack, which dogged the bell from its first use, was a symbolic omen.

IX   THE WAR ON LIBERTY

The 'War on Terror', might have been better described as the 'War on Liberty', given the mandate of control it created for Western governments, with everyday freedoms previously taken for granted greatly eroded away in less than a decade - through the instillation of fear. Little conspiracy thinking is necessary to see the reality of this process occurring all around us. Are the tools of control that have been created by it being put into place as a key element in the ruling elite's long-term plans?

The Project for the New American Century

If 9/11 was coordinated partially or fully by internal US influences or indeed agents of any secret agenda, what might the aim have been? It is compulsory at this point for all truthseekers to cite the Project for the New American Century (PNAC), a think-tank of fervent US neo-conservatives, which produced a document in the late 1990s entitled *Rebuilding America's Defenses: Strategy, Forces and Resources for a New Century*. In it, the future of American power is discussed with disturbingly frank self-awareness. Amongst its expressions of concern that the US would lose influence without a refreshed conquering spirit and an appropriate mandate for expansion, the following line proved serendipitously prophetic in the wake of the 9/11 attacks:

'The process of transformation, even if it brings revolutionary change, is likely to be a long one, absent some catastrophic and catalyzing event - like a new Pearl Harbor.'

It is notable that within hours of 9/11, George W Bush himself was likening the attacks to the events at Pearl Harbor during World War II, drawing a renewed attention to the original PNAC document from those who knew its contents. Suddenly the desired 'process of transformation' had indeed been boosted by the very kind of catalyzing event it had visualized, and the public references made to 'the new Pearl Harbor' in the rush of patriotic speeches were none-too-subtle for those on the alert. In the wake of the developments that have ensued since, the PNAC musings look ever-more like a blueprint for the new wave of American Imperialism that followed 9/11, and another step in the unfolding journey towards the New World Order.

The Pearl Harbor comparison is eerily resonant in more than one respect; despite cries of outrage from patriots, revisionist investigators have revealed details that make it increasingly likely that covert decisions within the US were involved in 'allowing' the Japanese onslaught to occur in 1941; indeed, it may have been deliberately provoked by the US banning of Japanese oil exports shortly before.[1] Allegations that the best Naval vessels were curiously absent from the docks on the day of the attack, in a situation perhaps analogous with the 2001 strike on the Pentagon seemingly being targeted only at its most expendable block [page 148], have been denied, but if nothing else, as with 9/11, it seems clear that intelligence warnings of the Japanese attack were received, but no action was taken. The spectacular tragedy which unfolded did the trick in raising the necessary impetus for the US to join the global conflict, dissolving the previous public resistance and perhaps helping a further NWO plan unfold.

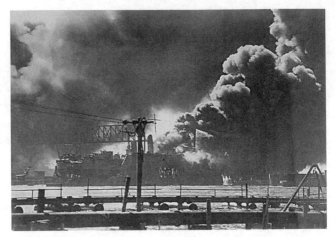

Pearl Harbor, 1941. It is now widely believed that the infamous Japanese attack on the US base was deliberately allowed to occur, as important intelligence warnings were given in advance, but nothing was done to stop it. The evidence shows that this kind of approach to global politics for the foment of grander plans may be disturbingly common.

'False-Flag' Terror

For critics of 9/11 conspiracy theories, the major sticking point is this: how could even the most power-hungry manipulators in such a nationalistic country be persuaded to sacrifice around 3000 of their own people to make a point? Yet the terrible truth is that throughout history this kind of technique has been used time and again to create military and political advantage. The enduring name for such actions - 'false-flag' attacks - stems from the ancient practice of ships attacking their own allies under the flags and colors of their collective enemies, stirring hatred against the foe and giving rise to the required public backing for what might otherwise be unpopular wars and 'necessary' withdrawals of freedom. There have been many variations of mandates being engineered for otherwise unjustifiable actions, and we don't even need to look back to ancient times to find examples.

We have already seen [Chapter I] how it is increasingly believed that the English Gunpowder Plot of 1605 may have been deliberately coordinated by Protestant officials to stir up ill-feeling towards Catholics and thus initiate a new reign of persecution. But even in more recent times there is suspicious evidence of this type of policy being pursued. It is likely, for instance, that the sinking of the luxury liner *Lusitania* in 1915, an event which was instrumental in encouraging public support for the US to join World War I, was manipulated in a not entirely dissimilar manner to the Pearl Harbor incident twenty-six years later. Inexplicably left without its usual warship escorts one day, the *Lusitania* seems to have been deliberately imperilled in waters that were known to be patrolled by German U-boats, leading to its predictable destruction and the loss of over 1200 civilian lives. The key maritime decision-maker of the day, First Lord of the Admiralty Sir Winston Churchill, keen for the US to join the war, had expressed a wish for such a ship to 'get into trouble' only months before. The truly cynical have suggested it may even have been torpedoed by our own vessels, but German log books do record the *Lusitania* as one of their sinkings. British decisions seem to have ensured it was a target, however.

During the Arab-Israeli 'Six-Day War' of 1967, the supposedly accidental air and sea attack by Israel on the American ship *USS Liberty* off the Sinai Peninsula coast is seen by many as a botched attempt to implicate Egypt in its destruction, to encourage a US attack on that country and widen the conflict. When the *Liberty* failed to sink, and too many survivors could testify as to who was responsible, a rapid apology from Israel helped cover-up any darker revelations - but many historians remain dubious and survivors of the attack still campaign for a new inquiry.

The 9/11 resonance most regularly invoked, however, is the burning of the Reichstag parliament building in Berlin in 1933. Blamed on communist forces, apparently led by Dutch insurrectionist Marinus van der Lubbe, the huge fire precipitated an almost overnight suspension of civil liberties that wouldn't be fully restored until after World War II. Yet there is evidence, if not entirely proven, to suggest that the Nazis themselves started the fire, or were at least instrumental in manipulating the communists into action. Whichever, it was a crucial event in the rise to power of Adolf Hitler and was used massively to promote his violent campaign against all opposition. Indeed, the style of rule adopted by Nazi Germany in the years after the fire, with its dissolution of common freedoms and increased militarism, has alarming parallels with what has occurred in the West since 9/11.

Those who react in horror to the notion that the Land of the Free would ever resort to the depths of such false-flag tactics would do well to examine the now freely-available US documents concerning Operation Northwoods in 1962, another 'smoking gun' oft-cited by truthseekers. At the height of North America's long-running stand-off with Fidel Castro's communist Cuba, a plan was put forward to justify a full-scale assault against the country, which involved the staged shooting-down of a dummy US airliner. Although the scheme did not involve the actual killing of US citizens, and was never implemented, the seed of an idea which might have eventually blossomed into the 9/11 attacks can be clearly discerned. Above all, the Operation Northwoods papers categorically demonstrate that our governing administrations (and/or whichever higher powers might be pulling the strings) *will* consider any tactic, however low, if it results in military and political advantage.

Given this, those who suspect inside involvement in 9/11 tend also to doubt that Timothy McVeigh and two other conspirators acted alone in bombing the Alfred P Murrah Federal Building in Oklahoma City on 19th April 1995. That atrocity saw an entire office complex destroyed in a powerful blast that claimed 168 lives - until 9/11, the worst act of terrorism in the US. Supposedly an attack to avenge the victims of the 1993 Waco siege (in which religious guru David Koresh and seventy-

THE TRUTH AGENDA

six others were shot or burned to death by FBI teams, apparently deliberately),[2] many campaigners consider the Oklahoma incident as being an early step towards creating a mandate for liberty infringements through legislations that would be stepped up massively in the wake of 9/11. As with the WTC complex, the extensive damage to the Oklahoma offices suggests to doubters that a single truck bomb could not have caused so much devastation. Open reports of secondary explosions on the day (initially broadcast across the media, and then omitted in later edits), together with audio tapes from office dictation machines, which recorded more than one blast, have also been cited as important evidence of underhand action.[3] The strong conviction that pre-placed explosive charges must also have been deployed at the Alfred P Murrah building has obvious echoes with the concerns over 9/11, and the finger of blame has once again been pointed at inside forces somewhere within the infrastructure of US authority.

The devastation caused at the Alfred P Murrah building, Oklahoma, in 1995. Yet, as with 9/11, there is evidence that pre-placed explosives were also used in addition to the truck bomb blamed for the blast, with more than one detonation recorded on the day. If so, who could have placed them?

Allegations of false-flag actions are not restricted to the West; there are plenty of researchers (including renowned British journalist John Sweeney) who also believe that the 1999 apartment block bombings in Moscow, for example, supposedly perpetrated by Chechen terrorists, were in fact partially or wholly coordinated by Russian intelligence forces to create the necessary mandate for the military incursions into Chechnya which followed.[4]

Going to the trouble of staging a false-flag event may not even be necessary when straight disinformation can sometimes perform the same trick. The Gulf of Tonkin incident on 4th August 1964, a supposed major attack by North Vietnamese forces on US destroyers, was long held up as a key trigger in the horrific war that troubled the world for the next decade. In 2005, the US National Security Agency (NSA) quietly released documents that finally confirmed long-held suspicions that, beyond one minor skirmish two days before the alleged incident, the attacks *never actually occurred*. Once again, the confusion was put down to 'intelligence errors' and sonar irregularities on the night in question. Many people suffered and died for those errors. Sooner or later some kind of trigger for war would doubtless have been found, but error or deliberate ploy, the fact is that maintaining the myth that an attack had indeed occurred was a beneficial justification to keep in the public eye.[5]

Creating the conditions and necessary support for wars and restrictions on liberty - always to 'protect' the population from the enemy - by means of staged, openly provoked or merely claimed atrocities has a long history. There seems no reason to believe that the 21st century is immune to the same games, difficult though it is to accept that anyone could still inflict such engineered horrors. Yet that seems to be the cold reality we must face when the Truth Agenda is applied and the shortcomings of so many official accounts and claimed motivations are exposed.

Even if our elected leaders are not directly creating the harm, those manipulating them from somewhere in the background, be they the Illuminati, elite dynasties, scheming bankers, occultist plotters or merely rogues amongst the rich and influential, would appear to think that carnage and chaos is fully justified in the name of some loftier cause. The nuances of what that cause might be are explored in Chapter XII.

What seems beyond dispute, whatever its impetus, is that the War on Terror also inflicted on us a War on Liberty that has since taken away, day by day, openly or by stealth, many of the joys of being a free human being that we previously took for granted in the West.

The War on Terror

In many ways the War on Terror, launched by the US in the wake of the 9/11 attacks and supported by most Western countries, was a stroke of genius on the part of those behind it. Although the ongoing campaign is never officially described under this name anymore, its legacy clearly persists. With the Soviet Union rather inconveniently dissolved after 1991, leaving no common foe to unite against, the elevation of Osama bin Laden to the role of Public Enemy Number One and the promotion of the lurking threat of Al Qaeda in every country was the perfect replacement. Now, once again, a control agenda and the global economy, so reliant on the unholy manufacture and export of armaments, could be kept bubbling along forever under the umbrella of a war that *could never end*. Who seriously believed, when the War on Terror was launched, that its aims would ever be fulfilled, with Middle Eastern terrorism such a nebulous and apparently insidious fixture?

On the basis of attempting to 'fix' this problem, first Afghanistan, then Iraq, fell to Western corrective procedures, neatly giving our leaders a niche of influence in some useful geographical and energy-rich places along the way. None of this is to say that no action at all should ever be taken in the likes of Afghanistan if evidence truly suggested the need, but that evidence was never forthcoming and the motives remained shadowy at best [Chapter VII]. By 2014, with many men, women and children dead on both sides, the US and its allies finally withdrew most of their forces (even briefly considering talks with the Taliban) and the Afghans regained some kind of self-rule, if very vulnerable to renewed terror assaults. The essential failure of the substantial military Afghan campaign, resulting instead in an actual *spread* of conflict into Pakistan, suggests we are not being told the whole story. Attacks carried out by Pakistani extremists and the ongoing import of Taliban insurgents into that country have also placed India's unstable neighbor under the microscope. US drone strikes, the new frontline method of surreptitious intervention, it would seem, have become commonplace there and in other Middle Eastern sovereign territories, often killing as many civilians as claimed terrorist targets and making it a mystery why more international concern has not been raised so far.

With the more recent arrival of Islamic State as a new and deadly force to usefully kick against, and the grim situation in and around Syria seemingly broadening the chessboard, with the involvement of multiple Shia and Sunni Muslim rival factions, Lebanese Hezbollah forces, Al Qaeda splinter groups, Israeli/US and Russian interests and beyond, the Middle East has become even more of a dangerous cauldron.

Whether Al Qaeda, now highly active in Syria, Pakistan and various North African countries, we are told, was merely a phantom menace or a genuine threat before 9/11 will probably never be resolved. Essentially spawned by the US itself sponsoring the Afghan Mujahideen as freedom fighters to combat the Soviets in the early 1980s [page 25], many people suspect that the Al Qaeda we were all told to fear in the wake of the 2001 attacks was initially a created myth, a convenient catch-all facade thrown up by US intelligence services over an essentially ragged and divided series of tin-pot militias, then of little threat to the West. Even the otherwise toothless post-David Kelly BBC dared to air a series in 2004, *The Power of Nightmares*, very convincingly exposing this frank reality about Al Qaeda, before the channel pretended it had never broadcast it and returned to airing the usual War on Terror propaganda.[6] With Western governments drumming bin Laden's culpability for 9/11 into everyone's heads (despite his own denials - as we have seen, only later very doubtful 'recordings' of someone purporting to be 'bin Laden' made his supposed claim on 9/11 explicit), the irony is that the motley Jihadist groups all now branded 'Al Qaeda cells' actually *became* more powerful and began to play up to the legend being created for them. Even mainstream pundits accept that the world became a far less stable place once the War on Terror began, not a safer one, which would appear to be a self-defeating policy - unless this was the idea all along.

Doubting the origins of Al Qaeda is not to say that Islamic fundamentalism, which seeks to impose its repressive values on everything else through violent means, is not a problem in itself, but its prominence on the world stage has almost certainly been elevated to unimagined heights by the very powers that claim to oppose it. And so the West, for a while, had a perfect replacement for the vanished Soviet threat.

However, recent years have seen a renewed demonization of Russia, beginning with the Ossetia crisis in 2008 and accelerated by the 2014 Ukrainian revolution - both blamed by some on Western interference. The need to rebrand an old enemy, and elevate a new one (IS), may in itself be an acknowledgement that the Al Qaeda 'threat' outlived its usefulness a little too soon. With bin Laden apparently dead, in whatever circumstances, [page 133], a replacement collective foe was required and IS and the re-energized Russia of Vladimir Putin have fitted the bill nicely, with Putin apparently more than happy to take the bait, effectively annexing Crimea along the way. The Ukraine and Middle East stand-offs, meanwhile, with their echoes of Cold War conflict-by-proxy, are believed by many truthers to have been manipulated into being (former French Foreign Minister Roland Dumas stated in 2013 that Britain had been 'preparing gunmen' to help destabilize Syria at least two years before the civil war began).[7] Putin's old-style dictatorial regime does raise genuine concerns, but the West's own record is hardly immaculate. Both sides seem to be playing a dark game. Powerful societies always need outside enemies, as George Orwell knew when he imagined the overarching and engineered threat of the subversive Albert Goldstein and his followers in his all-too prescient novel *Nineteen Eighty-Four*. We in the West now have Russia again, and Russia has us, with IS and Al Qaeda kept going somewhere in-between.

David Icke has long written of an Illuminati-engineered conflict with China that would help bring about the much planned for One World Government, but the West's firmly bonded financial relationship with China has perhaps fogged things for now. The US undoubtedly feels threatened by Chinese dominance in industry and its growing spread of political and economical influence around the world, but it also has to do business with it. Relations are inevitably strained by different views over the Middle East and only time will tell whether the New World Order (which seems primarily Western-driven) decrees that a balance must be struck, or a conflict escalated instead. At the same time, the periodic belligerence of North Korea also offers another convenient and clearly-identifiable enemy, although its rather eccentric nature seems to take it into a different side category, with neither China, Russia or the US really seeming to know what to do with it unless this is just in itself another feigned stance to obfuscate wider plans. Either way, whatever occurs on the world stage in the next few years will be considered by many observers to be part of the ongoing NWO plan, and the War on Terror undoubtedly provided a political and military impetus that continues to tip dominoes today.

The Patriot Act

The political fallout from the War on Terror and the subsequent muscle-flexing of the US and its allies, in Europe and the Middle East, has been pretty clear for all to see. But what of the effect on our everyday lives?

The other major casualty of this war has been the liberty of the individual, that rather annoying little feature for our leaders which is supposedly such a keystone of Western democracy. After 9/11, with the public told that dangerous terrorists were now potentially on every corner, even in mainland America, that liberty could be neatly curtailed in the name of our protection - and it duly was.

The introduction of the entirely misnamed US 'Patriot Act' in the fear-stricken climate of post-9/11 America saw the abrupt removal of rights and freedoms that had been written into US law since 1776. The Bill of Rights, which underpinned the ground-breaking Declaration of Independence, is in many ways a perfect blueprint of how the balance between government and its citizens should be - at least, if it were lived to the letter. Americans have justifiably boasted of the bill's importance over the centuries, in its protection of the individual and the enshrining of basic civil liberties against governmental interference. We'll put aside here the belief of some conspiracy theorists that America was itself founded by the Illuminati as a step towards the New World Order. Either way, it is clear there were some genuinely positive aims in the original Bill of Rights, however warped things might have become. Yet in less than five years following 9/11, incredibly, that crucial bill saw many of its central pillars dissolved or sidelined in the name of protecting US citizens from terrorism. As John Whitehead of the Rutherford Institute writes:

'The Patriot Act violates at least six of the ten original amendments known as the Bill of Rights - the First, Fourth, Fifth, Sixth, Seventh and Eighth Amendments - and possibly the Thirteenth and Fourteenth as well.' [8]

Rushed through as an emergency measure within weeks of 9/11, and finally written into law in 2006, the Patriot Act was a convoluted acronym for 'Uniting and Strengthening America by Providing Appropriate Tools Required to Intercept and Obstruct Terrorism Act of 2001'. This, and the many further legislations that followed it, basically gave US authorities *carte blanche* to pry into all private communications without court orders [perhaps using the PRISM system - page 193], increase blanket surveillance of its citizens, restrict freedom of movement, limit the rights of protest and grant indefinite detention on any immigrant deemed a potential threat. In essence, it enabled the authorities to do whatever they wanted, anywhere, anytime, and allowed them to target anyone they suddenly considered dangerous or undesirable.

Guantanamo Bay in its 'heyday', with inmates bound in restrictive suits to prevent freedom of movement. The physical and psychological pressures put on supposed terror suspects, together with dubious interrogation practices like 'waterboarding' (simulated drowning), are torture by any other name and a blot on a supposedly civilized society. Despite several promises to close the base, it remains active.

The multiple outrages and injustices of Guantanamo Bay and the obscenity of 'Extraordinary Rendition', in which terror suspects are secretly flown to scruple-free countries to evade international laws on torture, are just two of the depressing abuses of these powers we have seen since the new Act was introduced. So far it is prisoners of war and foreign - usually Islamic - suspects who have been the prime targets, but the net has widened. Despite Barack Obama's supposed intention to close Guantanamo, this never happened. It was always doubtful that the powers behind the throne would allow real change. Whatever the cosmetic adjustments, the 'anti-terror' strategies of the preceding administration remained firmly in place, as Obama's inaugural address (see *Introduction*) made clear they would.

As a result of the Patriot Act and its subsequent additions and amendments, many law-abiding US peace protesters and truth campaigners have unexpectedly found themselves at the wrong end of this all-too-flexible law, victimized and intimidated by an administration that, through fear of terrorism instilled in the masses, has been given the foundation of every tool of control it could possibly want. Most senators and congressmen never even read the Patriot Act bill before passing it. Who was likely to, presented with 342 pages full of dense legalese in small print? Fear, and/or the appeal of increased control, seemed to be the primary motivator in pushing the act through, not sensible consideration of its wider implications; something those behind it were presumably banking on.

The Death of Habeas Corpus

New and draconian restrictions on previously acceptable social activities and freedoms were not the sole domain of the US. Some observers believe that Britain is being used as an intense control experiment, and the UK also saw similar post-9/11 withdrawals of liberty, albeit more surreptitious ones. Perhaps realizing that its population wouldn't sit still for such an overt measure as a British Patriot Act, in which people would notice too soon what was being taken away from them, the government introduced the same restrictions through a series of quiet legislations, altered small print and shifted goalposts. In this way, in the last few years the everyday liberties we all once took for granted have been almost eradicated without too many noticing - yet.

When basic legalities that have protected human rights since the Dark Ages are suddenly taken away or twisted beyond all recognition, it is time to start worrying. The official acceptance of *habeas corpus* [literally, Latin for 'you must have the body'] has long protected citizens of civilized countries from tyranny and unlawful imprisonment by preventing authorities from detaining anyone without charge. It was being practiced in England from as early as the 12th century and was definitively enshrined in British law with the Habeas Corpus Act of 1679. Only in extreme times of national emergency or war has it been suspended. By calling the nebulous and seemingly unendable fight against terrorism a 'war', both the US and UK authorities were cleverly able to stretch and abuse habeas corpus beyond recognition when it suited them, effectively dispensing with it in any meaningful sense.

The attempted erosion of this crucial protection reached its culmination in the British House of Commons where (after much dubious tearoom lobbying and deal-making), as part of the 2008 Counter-Terrorism Bill, Parliament voted to extend to forty-two days the period in which terror suspects could be held without charge - an enormous increase on any previous benchmark. All of the many public protests and concerns over the potential abuses of this measure were ignored, and enough of the population, especially after the London bombings of 7th July 2005 [page 199], were fearful enough not to resist the result too much. Only the House of Lords stepped in to prevent this part of the Bill becoming law, refreshingly defeating it by a huge 309 votes to 118.[9] Even a former head of MI5 (of all people), a former Lord Chief Justice and a former Metropolitan Police Commissioner felt it went too far - but the very intention to introduce such a law made clear the direction in which the UK was heading. Climbing down, the then Home Secretary Jacqui Smith subsequently announced that the forty-two day proposal 'would be published in a separate draft Bill that could be voted on in the event of a national emergency'. (The country has, thus far at least, backed away from such approaches since, though some human rights watchers wonder for how long, should new atrocities arise.)

Before the Lords acted, reaction to the crow-barring in of the forty-two day rule was enough to trigger a by-election in the Yorkshire constituency of Haltemprice and Howden in July 2008, when Conservative MP David Davis resigned in protest, supposedly in an effort to draw attention to this further assault on civil liberties.

David Icke during the weeks of his standing in the 2008 Haltemprice and Howden by-election, supposedly called to raise awareness of liberty issues. Only Icke's policies really tackled the issues, but the media ignored them.

Any real issues were neatly sidelined in the media, however, when the main parties declined to put up any candidates, ensuring Davis' return to office but also taking any serious focus away from the campaign. News reports concentrated less on the issues and more on the high financial cost of what they saw as a questionable election, focusing on its wackier and/ or celebrity candidates (including Miss Great Britain). Strangely, there was very little coverage of one of the few candidates who did put himself up for election on the issues, and not for the fun of the circus - one David Icke. Turning down the chance to have a chuckle about alien lizards and conspiracies, the media chose instead to largely ignore him - perhaps because what he said about the liberty issues during his (knowingly) doomed campaign made so much sense.

Human Microchipping Revisited

The most visible reactive measure to be inspired by the War on Terror in the UK was the attempted launch of a biometric ID card scheme and the creation of an interactive National Identity Register (NIR), a central database intended to include all the personal details of every individual, including their DNA profile. Despite the withdrawal of this scheme by the Conservative/Liberal Democrat coalition in 2010, largely as a cost-cutting measure, the ominous shadow of the upcoming ID microchipping program [page 80] remains a serious threat that will doubtless achieve the same end and quickly spread around the world once sold as an attractive and convenient proposition to a generation entirely used to minute-by-minute technological interfacing. Even for objectors, in time the foment of extreme social disadvantages to *not* having an ID chip will make the take-up almost universal.

When a biometric chipping scheme does arrive, however, it will have a huge potential for both direct misuse and simple misadventure by bureaucratic error. A system that has the potential to enable any authority anywhere to know of every movement, every transaction, every genetic detail and personal history of every individual alive is one that can only be operated by wise, well-intentioned and reliable bastions of total integrity. With corruption and intrigue endemic around the world, from the lowest ranks of local government to the higher echelons of parliaments (as regularly revealed in Britain alone by the likes of the otherwise conspiracy-denying *Private Eye* magazine),[10] it is clear from the most cursory application of the Truth Agenda that nowhere in the world do we have anything even approaching, nor showing any signs of becoming, the kind of enlightened management necessary to run a system of this kind. Placing such power into the hands of authorities that are showing disturbing tendencies towards fascistic control cannot be the sensible thing to do. Who knows what régimes may one day come to hold governmental reigns?

The microchip tags currently being developed run a high risk of creating a system which, once it controls entrance to every workplace, shopping mall, station or public building, and is necessary for every monetary transaction, will allow the elimination of any 'undesirables' from mainstream existence simply by selective electronic blocking or deletion. Life could be made terribly hard for any political or social heretics, who could soon find themselves living as down and outs if pushed to the fringes of society by the restriction of ID access.

If the reader is at this point feeling a little put out at the thought that anyone might ever come to think of them as an 'undesirable', it is worth considering that if the current trajectory is not checked, a time may come when the very act of reading a book like this could be considered a subversive act. We already live in a society where the likes of Walter Wolfgang, a loyal 82-year old British Labour Party activist, found himself forcibly ejected by security heavies from a political conference for merely calling out the word 'nonsense' when confronted by then foreign secretary Jack Straw's weak justifications for the Iraq war. He was prevented from re-entering the hall under 'Section 44' anti-terrorism powers, just one more misuse amongst many of these supposedly emergency legislations. It was revealed that of 1,271 arrests made under the same Act between 2007-2008, only 73 were actually for suspected terror offences. The problematic Sections 44 and 47a of the British Terrorism Act 2000 were the basis of outrageous abuses of police powers for a while, with several innocent protestors and civilians wrongfully apprehended under them.[11] Suspect rules under Section 76 of the 2009 Counter Terrorism Act could have also, if implemented to their fullest in a time of crisis, effectively outlawed public photography of police activities, neatly making any visual evidence of police corruption or violence inadmissible in court. The same legislation was actively used to restrict the use of cameras in many perfectly normal places.[12] When in 2010 the European Court of Rights sensibly ruled as unlawful the stop-and-search powers being exerted under the Act, the UK government reluctantly issued remedial orders to clarify some of the murkier areas, but even now cases arise of train and plane-spotters being targeted as possible criminals under anti-terrorism laws, and innocent sight-seers have still found themselves being taken in for questioning. The irony is that while the civilian use of cameras becomes more restricted, the presence of those installed by authorities grows, particularly in British and American public spaces.

The signs are that *all* of us are already held to be potential undesirables, as the myriad of cameras and other surveillance devices that have infested our cities in the last decade or so testify. With measures which effectively sanction the automatic and sustained monitoring (without the need to apply for warrants) of all our e-mail activity, web surfing and telephone calls now firmly embedded in both US and UK society (see next page), even the sanctity of our homes, personal interests and communications is no longer respected. Every one of us is now routinely treated as a potential criminal - and privacy has become a thing of the past.

The Surveillance Society

Mainland Britain now has more security cameras than any other country in the world (although the US is fast catching up) with nearly two million CCTV cameras said to be in operation - one for every 32 people. With these intrusive eyes perched over nearly every main square, every major road and every mall, as well as numerous private premises, it is estimated that an average trip outside our homes sees us being captured on camera around 300 times. But why?

We are told, continually, that these cameras are there for our protection - largely from crime and terrorism. Yet many studies have shown that whilst these images may help identify some faces after an event, there is no evidence that CCTV actually prevents crime or increases our safety. ABC News journalist Marcus Baram writes:

'According to a British Home Office review of dozens of studies analyzing the cameras' value at reducing crime, half showed a negative or negligible effect and the other half

showed a negligible decrease of 4 percent at most. Researchers found that crime in Glasgow, Scotland, actually increased by 9 percent after cameras were installed there.' [13]

So the central, oft-repeated claim that our day to day privacy is only being violated for our own good is not supported by the data gathered by the very authorities who are creating this surveillance state. So we must look for other explanations to make sense of why our rulers feel they need to keep such close tabs on their own citizens.

George Orwell reached his own fairly clear conclusions as to why this might happen way back in 1948, and now that this nightmare vision has become reality (including the cameras that can shout instructions from faceless security teams, which are now being installed in some public places) we must ask ourselves some very stiff questions about the motives of those in charge.

The UK in particular has always had an element of the 'nanny state', its ruling class feeling that it knows better than its apparently plebeian citizens what is best for them, but with an entirely disproportionate fear of terrorism and dark plots being pushed on its citizens

Surveillance cameras are now a common sight across the world, with Britain having more of them than any other country - and this despite statistical evidence that they do not prevent crime. So what are they really for?

daily through media manipulation and government policies, the control agenda is now seriously... out of control. Again, are the British being used in some way?

Outcries over plans to set up a UK centralized database to keep records of all e-mails, Internet visits and phone calls did at least result in a public government climbdown in 2009, but a subsequent 'request' to all communications firms to keep records to be made forcibly available to authorities on request, established the same concept by stealth, something reinforced by a new 'Counter Terrorism and Security Bill' in 2014. This was in itself a spin-off from the proposed 2013 'Communications Data Bill', widely condemned as a 'snooper's charter', an obvious government attempt at a mass surveillance program. But all this had, in truth, already been rendered redundant by widely reported revelations in June 2013 that the US PRISM system (with the cooperation of the UK's GCHQ communications center) had in any case been effectively spying on the general population of the world since 2007. Uncovered by US whistleblower Edward Snowden, it quickly became clear that this had been achieved through unlegislated and therefore totally unlawful electronic Internet and phone surveillance. Companies like Google and Facebook denied that any of their data had ever been volunteered, but stolen or given it was now finally clear, if it wasn't already obvious, that anything sent into cyberspace could never be considered secure. But this didn't make it right. Apologists soon began to defend the right of a state to 'guard' its peoples' safety, as ever, yet the clandestine and illegal nature of the PRISM disclosures (a system which seemed to be a development of the earlier and troubling ECHELON 'signal interception' network) were more suggestive of an intention to deceive and suppress rather than to protect.[14]

Targeting suspected criminals or terrorists by obtaining court orders to allow surveillance of individuals is one thing - blanket monitoring of all citizens is quite another. Now anyone even slightly suspected of being a 'danger' to society may unwittingly find themselves under the microscope. But who gets to decide who and what is dangerous? We may believe ourselves to be law-abiding and undeserving of state suspicion, but what if the state thinks otherwise? Those authorities calling the shots at the moment have hardly proved themselves fair or trustworthy thus far.

Policing Cyberspace

The world of electronic communications has been a gift to those who wish to keep an eye on who we all are. The ubiquity of online social networking where many personal details are routinely exchanged is, to an extent, leading society to a mindset of blanket openness anyway, which some say is a healthy development, while others see it as the gateway to an abyss of state snooping. The success of sites like Facebook has been used in some quarters to denigrate genuine concerns over privacy, implying that people are perfectly happy for the minutiae of their lives to be shared widely. But *choosing* to share information is one thing - having personal details invaded and potentially misused without awareness or the granting of permission is quite another, yet this is what we now seem to have.

In addition to knowing who we are in contact with and when, the new surveillance regime means that every website we look at, and the subject of every search we make, is now available to government databases, with profiles of each individual gradually being drawn up and documented. Reading books instead is not a solution as library records are now routinely given over to authorities on request, while titles ordered from Internet retailers or bought on credit or debit cards are, of course, more than fully documented. Even our over-the-counter transactions are closely monitored, through the same card records or use of loyalty schemes, which is how personalized special offers can be so specifically targeted. Now our everyday habits, fascinations and beliefs are being equally profiled. Cash payments remain the last bastion of retail privacy, but with so much talk of the coming 'cashless society', this option's days are numbered. Soon it will become impossible to live one's truth and have particular interests without its nature being fully known by a very real Big Brother.

The freedom of speech engendered by the unexpected advent of the Internet in the late 1980s is seen by some as a lifeline against any totalitarian force that would prevent us speaking our minds; indeed cyberspace has been a phenomenal opportunity for the airing of truth and liberty issues. But it may prove to be a very short-lived shaft of light if proposed legislation and reforms of the online world go ahead. Aware that some kind of genie of liberation was released from the bottle by the availability of unfettered communication, there is every indication that the powers that be are trying to push it back in again.

Long-term plans may eventually bring the Internet under new regulations, which could see websites treated the same way as television stations. If this were to go ahead, a paid licence would be needed to operate a website, which would have to follow strict guidelines about content and form.[15] This could put non-profit-making hobbyist or campaigning web platforms out of the reach of the average person. Wading through layers of bureaucracy and paying fees just to put up a new piece about flower-arranging or collectable antiques could make running an amateur site unviable, leaving only overtly commercial web pages available. In an era where the right to mount even street protests is becoming harder by the day, having to pass every new entry for a truth website or simple blog through the regulatory channels to see what is permissible would pretty much see the end of the Internet as a campaigning tool. In an increasingly repressive system, the expression of views seen as merely fringe annoyances today could become major heresy tomorrow. More than one neo-conservative or 'Tea Party' right-winger has expounded the - inexplicable and entirely untrue - view that Internet truth forums that promote revisionist views and 'outrageous conspiracy theories' foster and encourage 'terrorism', and these warped characters have done little to conceal their desire to shut down the Internet as we know it today. Real concerns over child pornography and other extreme sites plainly need dealing with (aside from growing issues over the societal effect of general sexual content on young minds), but we need to be very wary of the potential misuse of across-the-board knee-jerk censorship.

The cleverness of the repressive regulations being proposed is that there won't be one key moment where any particular (legal) content or views will be banned or restricted, causing instant adverse reaction. Instead, the same effect is being quietly achieved with the gradual introduction of 'safety features' and apparently beneficial 'improvements', the pill perhaps eventually to be sugared by promises of a faster and easier-to-use system (sometimes dubbed 'Internet 2'). There would reside all the new licensed and regulated sites - by default, largely commercial ones - with slick, flashy and fully interactive facilities, leaving the old Internet looking slow, complex and old-fashioned by comparison and deemed to be full of the old dross, criminal porn and extremist elements that people would be encouraged to think was all that was there, eventually seeing its end.

It is not just at the webmaster end that the way we use the Internet could change. Another proposal already being explored and pioneered by some servers is for website accessibility to be regulated like satellite TV channels are today. Instead of free access to any website anywhere, surfers would be encouraged to sign up for 'packages' of the sites they already like to use, with benefits and good hosting deals offered to make it worthwhile. Viewing sites outside of those signed-up for would see extra charges of a much higher tariff, or they would simply not be accessible, depending on the package selected. In this way, again rather cleverly, the freedom to seek out or accidentally discover little sites with unexpectedly astonishing or hard-to-get information could be greatly curtailed. In the last few years, we have already seen Google agree to block certain human rights websites so as to be able to operate in China (with similar deals struck in other restrictive countries), and in 2014 the European Court forced it to take down links on the orders of powerful individuals. This new philosophy of selective omission is already, therefore, a major weakening factor.

The constant media harassment of the Internet, so often characterized entirely disproportionately as nothing more than a playground for pedophiles and Jihadist groups, is helping to create the climate of fear that will strangle the freedom of legitimate online communities. Any form of communication is open to abuse from a minority, and there is no question that there have been abuses - but in the eyes of many the entirely beneficial and liberating effect of people being able to express their honest opinions about global events and voice apprehension about those running our lives has made living with the relatively few violations of good sense and humanity a necessary price. We must not allow those who would hide reality to succeed here.

Thus caution is advised against the mob-mentality so often stimulated in the tabloid press against the Internet. Given the media's often partisan and complicit role in peddling myths and half-truths (especially in regard to 9/11 and other questionable authorized versions of big events), only online facilities have allowed a public voice to question the propaganda, and they have been a crucial tool of liberation in times of growing oppression. This window of free speech is in danger of closing all-too-soon and it should be used to its fullest while it still can be, to fight for its continued existence as a platform for all, not just the sanitized few.

But, some readers may say here, what about the real threat from terrorism and crime? Surely it cannot all be false-flag action and obfuscation? Do we not need at least a measure of compromised privacy and information filters to protect us all?

Dealing With Real Threats

A trap fallen into by a number of conspiracy theorists is to assume that *every* single terrorist act or political shenanigan must be an engineered step towards an evil New World Order. Some truthers go as far as believing that atrocities such as the Boston marathon bombings of 2013, the Norwegian student massacre of 2011, or various US school shootings, are either the result of unwitting mind-controlled perpetrators under hypnosis or, at the hardest end of the spectrum, even entirely fabricated with actors to encourage repressive legislation into being. But the adherence to believing that such audacious plans could work every time without the truth ever being accidentally revealed perhaps assumes too much power on the part of those who might be behind control agendas, as we shall explore more in the last chapters. There is evidence that mistakes *are* made and that there are squabbling factions even amongst those who might be pulling the global strings - therefore unpredictable elements remain at large in the world, and this may offer a glimmer of salvation.

A basic human nature is still there to contend with, however, and real, raw, unsponsored terrorism is always going to arise in particular circumstances at certain times even without the impetus of any background manipulation. So how do we deal with genuine threats without shutting down our basic human liberties?

Especially in the UK, the War on Terror revealed a fundamental philosophical shift in recent decades as to how authority deals with those who might harm or disrupt us (indicating that there may well be a wider plan at work). British citizens who lived through the 1970s and 1980s will remember the appalling campaign of terror operated by the IRA and opposing

The scar left by the IRA bomb at the Grand Hotel, Brighton, UK, on 12th October 1984. The attempt to wipe out Margaret Thatcher and her cabinet failed - just. Despite this and other audacious attacks during the IRA campaign, the country did not close itself down into the fear-bound siege mentality that was fostered under the War on Terror.

outfits from Northern Ireland. It is interesting to note that whilst there were some restrictions of movement in mainland Britain during those times, and checking of bags in city department stores and public places (especially after the Harrods bomb of 1983), there was *not* that sense of all-pervading fear that was placed on us after 9/11 and, specifically in the UK, '7/7', when an air of sensible caution was replaced by something grimmer and more socially debilitating. This has lessened a little since, perhaps through the passing of the years or because it is simply impossible to keep a nation on high level alert forever, but as a general rule we still appear to be encouraged to allow fear to rule our lives. During the IRA campaign, there was outrage at the killings and injuries that took place, but also a sense of common resistance, of refusing to give in to the coercive tactics of an extremist minority. Even when the UK government was targeted with the Brighton bomb of 1984, which nearly assassinated Margaret Thatcher in her conference hotel, British society did not lock itself into a fearful siege mentality, where everyday freedoms were dispensed with to deal with the evil of the few. In the 'blitz-spirit', necessary care and security was taken, but life and the spirit of liberty went on. Why should that not be the case now?

Even if we dispense with the justifiable inside-job suspicions for a moment and take 9/11 at face value, what we have done by allowing the War on Terror and its subsequent tailwind to dominate Western life since is to capitulate to the intentions of the minority threats that genuinely do exist. By indulging in the very climate of terror they desire, we hand our power over. There is a balance to be struck between common-sense measures and fear-based restriction, but the right balance has still not been achieved at the moment, either because society is going through some strange dark night of the soul, or because it doesn't suit some murkier purpose which still requires justification for foreign wars and control of its own people.

There will always be those who will want to hurt or kill for some fanatical cause. But how common these fanatics are is questionable. Since the IRA ended its attacks, 7/7 has been the only major mainland bombing incident in Britain. Since 9/11, thus far, the US has remained free from any large-scale assaults. Despite the occasional atrocity around the world, we seem to be much safer than we are told. Yet we are continually given the impression that killer terrorists are on every corner, and that only secret intelligence squads and complex police operations, with all their new surveillance powers, keep us protected. The evidence for this is very often unclear, however, and explanations oddly elusive. Public 'Terror Alert' scales go up and down in an abstract dance of mysterious figures, tanks suddenly appear outside airports and then vanish again for no apparent reason, and politicians talk of raised threats and then never mention them again.[16] Bomb plots and discoveries of new 'terrorist cells' make headlines for a few days, and then melt away with no explanation and few apologies for the consternation caused.

There are occasional terrorism prosecutions, which one would expect and even hope for, but official reports themselves conclude that just one in eight terror arrests ever results in an actual conviction.[17] If it is true that we are kept cushioned from the real threats of terrorism by undercover intelligence, as we are continually told, the low conviction rate is a major anomaly, unless people are being quietly executed out of the public eye and outside of the law. But then why shout things to the media about new 'plots' so loudly before being sure, when that intelligence so often appears to be plainly sensationalized - and wrong? It is almost as if someone does want us to be kept in a state of fear.

When it looks like we might be relaxing again about security and control, something always seems to be activated or re-inflated to crank up the alarm again. Hence widely publicized plots involving threats to airplanes being blown out of the sky using water bottles, explosive underpants or shoes mean that we now queue even longer at airports and put up with cold intimidation and intrusive body-scans that would never otherwise be accepted. As well as having obviously harmless containers taken away from us to join the vats of supposedly assault-potential household objects, mothers have also been asked to take sips of their own bottled breast milk to prove its harmlessness, or toddlers forced to take off their sandals. Precautions of some kind are necessary - without question - but a sensible balance has to be struck and the petrified society that has been crafted is no longer operating from a centered place of wisdom.

One of the other areas that leads to conspiracy theories, though, is that we so seldom seem to be given straight answers to glaring anomalies in claimed terror plots.

7/7 Anomalies

When terror attacks do occur, such as the bombings on 7th July 2005, which exploded three underground trains and a bus in London, killing 52 people and injuring hundreds, people naturally fear for the safety of themselves and their loved ones. However, difficult though it has been to voice in a media that denies the existence of conspiracies, it is worth mentioning that even here there are a number of strange anomalies, which have called the origins of this event into question from various truthseekers (crudely 'debunked' as usual by the always-reliable BBC *Conspiracy Files* series), who have once again accused secret forces of background involvement.

Terrified passengers escape from a smoke-filled tube train on the day of the 7/7 bombings. But even with this event, unlikely anomalies and 'coincidences' present themselves.

It seems likely from investigations that Islamic participants were at least partly involved in the events, but doubters base their allegations on a series of errors and contradictions in the official story surrounding the commuter trains that were supposedly caught by the bombers on their way to London, suspicious changes made several times to the official narrative, lack of clear CCTV evidence - and the nature of the explosions themselves.[18] Some witnesses reported blasts seemingly coming up from *beneath* the trains, rather than from the claimed rucksacks, and photographic evidence of the aftermath seems to support this. Strangest of all is the fact that Peter Power, a supposedly independent 'crisis management specialist' and security expert, claimed that his firm, Visor Consultants, was operating a terror alert rehearsal at the *very times and very places where the real attacks occurred*. Broadcast in the UK on BBC Radio 5 Live's *Drivetime* program on the day of the events, the following comments from Power are worth relating:

POWER: ...At half-past nine this morning we were actually running an exercise for, er, over, a company of over a thousand people in London based on simultaneous bombs going off precisely at the railway stations where it happened this morning, so I still have the hairs on the back of my neck standing upright!

PETER ALLEN (DJ): To get this quite straight, you were running an exercise to see how you would cope with this and it happened while you were running the exercise?

POWER: Precisely, and it was, er, about half-past nine this morning, we planned this for a company and for obvious reasons I don't want to reveal their name but they're listening and they'll know it. And we had a room full of crisis managers for the first time they'd met and so within five minutes we made a pretty rapid decision, 'this is the real one' and so we went through the correct drills of activating crisis management procedures to jump from 'slow time' to 'quick time' thinking and so on.[19]

So, just as with 9/11, we are asked to accept that the events of 7/7, by complete coincidence, unfolded simultaneously with a drill that posited almost exactly the same scenario, at the same places. The official Inquest acknowledged a drill days before, but it was clearly not this one. Did the bombers somehow know about the 'exercise' taking place that day, and choose to align their attack with it as some kind of cover? If so, how did they know of the terror rehearsal without inside information or help? Did the individuals involved simply believe they were taking part in an exercise, only to discover too late that their rucksack bombs were real? (This would have resonance with Emad Salem being given real explosives instead of dummies in the alleged FBI set-up of the 1993 World Trade Center truck bomb - see page 145.) The videos we have been shown of some of the alleged 7/7 bombers speaking to camera suggest real martyrdom intentions, but there could be more to the story. Or was the whole thing instigated by black-op intelligences, using patsies and terror drills to create maximum confusion (as on 9/11, it would seem), which would make later attempts at getting to the truth almost impossible?

Only the bus in Tavistock Square doesn't seem to fit with the exercise locations - allegedly the terrorist there had intended to target the nearest underground station, but changed his plan, detonating the bomb nearly an hour after the other explosions. One claimed, if controversial, eye-witness account of what happened on the bus is very at odds with the official version, with talk of it being deliberately 'diverted' into the Square by two unmarked cars, as if it were being set up in some way.[20]

Were the strange circumstances

The 7/7 bombings and the police shooting of an innocent man in the hysteria that followed created an intense climate of fear for commuters and visitors to London - yet life went on. How much are we prepared to sacrifice for a safety we can never in any case guarantee?

surrounding 7/7 and the exercises truly just a bizarre coincidence? The Truth Agenda requires a clustering of anomalies to reveal deeper layers of deception beneath, and 7/7 is certainly far less of a clear-cut case than 9/11, with most of its events having happened deep underground and off-camera. But the odds against coincidence in the terror drill scenario alone suggest something is not quite right. As with Building Seven on 9/11, the official response to this aspect of the events has been to completely ignore it, as if Peter Power never made his very clear statements. Power himself later played down the comments, making the exercises sound much vaguer, despite researchers having since verified that they certainly *were* taking place that day.

Needless to say, the anomalies (and there are many more - see *Appendix 3*) and the predictably selective inadequacies of the official 2010-2011 Inquest (led by Lady Justice Hallett) have left some truthseekers very doubtful about the events of 7/7.

Regardless of the reality, 7/7 was undoubtedly used to bring home to the British public that without the War on Terror and its necessary homeland security restrictions on life and liberty, more of this kind of thing might occur. Spain had already received its own reminder when commuter trains in Madrid were hideously exploded in March 2004. Blamed loosely on Al Qaeda, those attacks seemed intended (though unsuccessfully) to restore a wavering Spanish public to supporting their government's involvement in the Afghanistan and Iraq campaigns. Likewise, events in New York seemed far away to some in the UK, but bombs in London helped bring them 'on message' and encouraged yet more suspicion of the Muslim world, creating further division and social unrest. Not for nothing, perhaps, was 7/7 described several times in the media as 'the British 9/11'.

The police's killing of Jean Charles de Menezes, mistaken for a potential suicide bomber on the London Underground and shot in the head at point-blank range less than two weeks after 7/7, despite being entirely innocent, sent out a further message. The police marksmen claimed that they shouted a warning to de Menezes, and that he advanced 'aggressively' towards them before they opened fire. Not one witness who appeared at the subsequent inquest verified this claim, and it was also rejected by the jury, which accepted that de Menezes was not in fact given a warning and that he did not approach the police first. Disregarding this, the Crown Prosecution Service, in a mockery of justice, refused to allow a verdict of unlawful killing, forcing the return of an 'open' verdict instead. Outraged protests from the jury and de Menezes' family failed to make a difference.[21]

With this edict, it was made quite clear to the population that anything which occurred in the name of fighting terrorism was above the law and not to be questioned, even if unfortunate civilians had their brains blown out in the process. Anyone concluding from this that we were now definitively living in a 'police state' was, of course, merely misguided. Similarly, the global over-use of the control regime's dangerous favorite toy, the Taser stun gun, has resulted in the unnecessary 'accidental' deaths of an increasing number of unarmed civilians with apparently weak constitutions - but these regrettable incidents also reinforce a warning; mess with the authorities and next time it could be you.[22]

A Difficult Choice

We have to make a choice. Terrorism, false-flag or genuine, is something we have to deal with. Some might argue that it makes no difference - it's real, wherever it comes from, and we have to protect ourselves. But what we give away to ensure that protection has to be thought about very carefully. If there must truly be a war on terror, then that war has also to be fought philosophically and

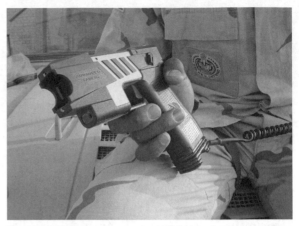

The control state's current weapon of choice, the Taser gun (seen here brandished by a US soldier). Supposedly a humane stun-gun, the high charge electrical shocks administered by Tasers have now killed many people around the world. Their supposedly 'safe' status has encouraged a wide over-use of the gun, often in totally inappropriate situations, against unarmed civilians, disorientated elderly citizens or non-threatening protestors.

in a spirit of defiance. Fundamentalism that kills, be it Muslim, Hindu, Christian, Zionist, or whatever creed of justification, must be challenged and discouraged. But the terrorists win when we change our whole style of life to accommodate them. How far do we want to go down that path? At what point do we decide we must take a risk to preserve our freedom?

We can openly walk down our streets and into shops and offices and say we will take a calculated risk while doing so, for the sake of living the liberty of which the West so often boasts - or we can choose embedded microchips, more security guards and metal-detectors, more cameras and surveillance of our private lives, to save us from religious fanatics. (On one level, of course, we have already seen in Chapter IV that some Western countries are effectively being run by religious fanatics.) We can choose to show contempt for the minority of criminals that demonstrate no respect for life and property, and hold our heads up high and live positive lives in the hope that positive thought proliferates (and it does - see Chapter XIV) - or we can cave into the fear continually drummed into us by press and television that knife crime, shootings and muggings are growing by the day (statistically ambiguous, despite event clusters in certain areas and much increased news *coverage*).[23] Then we demand detection equipment at the doorways of shops and schools and stations, and build our whole lives around trepidation and negativity. Already, some souls live cowering behind their front doors, scared to emerge. In some unfortunate city suburbs this may be justified, but how broadly should it really be applied? We can take wise precautions to protect our children and loved ones, but allow them to live freely and openly and try to build a world where dire concerns are not so necessary - or we can buy into the terror-fuelled myth spread by endless headlines on the likes of poor Madeline McCann [page 80] or other rare and regrettable cases, that *all* our children are in equal danger and that pedophiles and killers lurk in every park and Internet chatroom. By doing this we inadvertently embrace the 'safety' that will come with the microchipping schemes already being pioneered, and keep our children behind closed doors; never again will people be lost, but never again will they be truly free either.

It's all a question of where we choose to draw the line. It is a collective decision that has more power than perhaps we know, as we shall see. What price our safety and security? If we decide to live in darkness and alarm, at the expense of all else, protected but effectively imprisoned in grim police states, then darkness and alarm is what we shall have. But is that really all we want?

Fear must not be given into, or it takes over and proliferates. Positive thinking is a tangible and forceful power as we shall see, not just a New Age concept. Yet fear seems to be the thing most widely encouraged in our current society, and not solely residing within the realms of crime and terror.

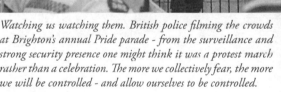

Watching us watching them. British police filming the crowds at Brighton's annual Pride parade - from the surveillance and strong security presence one might think it was a protest march rather than a celebration. The more we collectively fear, the more we will be controlled - and allow ourselves to be controlled.

THE TRUTH AGENDA: *The War on Terror and its legacy has been one of the greatest coups on human liberty ever staged. In the name of our protection, fundamental freedoms have been eroded or taken away, leaving us prone to unhealthy state intervention or surveillance. False-flag terrorism to create states of fear is something with a long history and still seems to be occurring now. But whether the terror and crime we have to deal with is real or false, it is clear that fear of it is being used to control us. Striking the right balance between sensible precautions and a self-defeating climate of alarm is the only way to break free of this trap - which means we must not fall prey to the manipulative culture of fear currently being foisted on us.*

Modern technology has given us many wonderful things... but are we being made too reliant on pharmaceuticals and additives, while natural alternatives are being taken away from us..?

X   CAGING THE HUMAN SPIRIT

With constant fear sustained by a heightened perception of terrorism and crime, other factors in our society also seem primed to control and suppress the human spirit through disproportionate health and safety regulations, the abuse of 'political correctness' and burgeoning restrictions on personal health choices, which enslave us to pharmaceutical solutions and weaken our natural immunity. Is this a further policy being operated to prevent us from stepping into our true power as human beings?

The Bonds of Health and Safety

The erosion of liberties in our day to day lives seems to have been accompanied by another dimension of the control agenda; a crushing of the human spirit, a dampening of our essentially adventurous natures. Under a system that seems to prefer us nicely contained, harmlessly shored up behind our front doors, hypnotized each night by soaps, game shows and electronic entertainment, or depressed into inaction by an endless parade of negative news, the person who stands up and shines, takes a risk or merely ventures out in some proactive way, seems frowned upon. No great laws are required to generate this climate; a simple reliance on concerned jobsworths excited by the minutiae of small print can achieve the same thing.

For our protection, we are told yet again, the exhaustive catalog of health and safety rules that govern our lives, for example, has suppressed the generally harmless everyday activities we once took for granted, watering some of them down to near-pointlessness. Life itself is a risk, and sometimes unfortunate accidents will occur, but taking a risk of any kind is a diminishing option in a system that seems unable to bear anyone taking responsibility for themselves; witness the ever-shrinking equipment at children's playgrounds, all thrills removed, all adventure neutered. No sane person would want to see a child harmed, but in an ever-more litigious world the disproportionate reduction would seem to have more to do with authorities' fears of legal action than a genuine concern for health, as most 'risk assessment' decisions do. Several studies have shown that a surfeit of risk-reduction actually damages child development.[1]

Woods and parks that might once have been packed with adventuring youngsters on sunny days are now often deserted, with children absorbed in electronic worlds instead, or grounded by parental fear sparked by tabloid pedophile hysteria. Now fear of litigation has added to the disconnection with the outside world, with skateboard parks and adventure playgrounds sometimes suddenly removed by order in the middle of the night - beyond the sight of those who might protest. Carried out without discussion or local consultation, these decisions are made by the same authorities who then spend thousands trying to control hooligans at a loose end. But 'Health and Safety' must prevail, and the human spirit must acquiesce.

Thus, beyond the obvious codes of common sense practice offered to the public, have come edicts of the absurd that have encroached on normal folk. Although the worst excesses do thankfully seem to have been pulled back from in more recent times due to public resistance, as a prolific lecturer this author can testify to the still significant number of halls and venues where organizers are not permitted to boil kettles without official caterers being present, or where handbags cannot be kept under seats. Fire safety instructions must be ritually read out to bored audiences who can see for themselves that a room has two obvious exits. Nearly every week the news is full of examples of Health and Safety banning the likes of pencil cases from schools (because they might contain sharp objects) or removing goalposts from local playing fields (because people might run into them and hurt themselves). Invent a bizarre example and it will probably be a reality somewhere. These are the small-minded restrictions that people begin to rebel against, because it credits them with no intelligence and takes away all self-responsibility. If society is increasingly acting in a childish way perhaps we shouldn't be surprised, when even senior citizens are treated like irresponsible children. But is this crushing of the spirit accident - or design? Some truthseekers believe the latter.

Some of the supposed health and safety rules are nothing more than misinterpretations by petty-minded small-time authorities (often the risk-assessors rather than the H&S officers), intent on controlling others, as they themselves are unwittingly being controlled. But there are plenty of demonstrably insane rules that have been officially imposed on things that previously ran without fuss, which appear to make no sense beyond being there to outrage the soul and dull the independent spirit. It can carry a high financial burden for self-employed traders, for instance - who may have worked happily and successfully for years - to get newly required Health and Safety certificates. Thus many independent electricians and plumbers have gone into bankruptcy (especially in economic downturns) because the high costs of licences or certificates to prove the blindingly obvious that are now required to trade are beyond their means. To deter bad workers, the law is threatening the livelihoods of the good at the same time. It is almost as if being self-employed - and therefore less dependent on more easily-regulated bigger companies - is discouraged in today's Western society, which prefers a safer hive mentality, not independence.

All this has been exacerbated - created? - by the tendency to treat people as statistics, not individual souls with feelings. The misplaced obsession with targets, ratings and administration has resulted in a culture where standards are too often twisted or 'dumbed down' to get students through exams, viewers to tune in, shoehorn staff into the right category, or force patients through hospital systems without actually meeting their human needs (leaving far too many reports of people suffering in their own filth while nurses prioritize the tasks that meet tick-box targets). This reductionist approach to life has only generated distancing and dysfunction in society, which some believe is a key part of the elite plan. If the quality of education, social sophistication and human care had provably risen with all the mountains of form-filling, these fears could perhaps be lightly dismissed, but the opposite appears to be true.

Some readers may suspect too much paranoia here, especially those who struggle with the notion that our authorities may not have our best interests at heart. Almost certainly, some repressive regulations are simply good intentions gone too far. However, a look at the wider picture does begin to raise questions as to whether our health and safety really is the primary concern of a system that reduces us to numbers, or whether it actually suits those who may have fascistic plans for the world for people to be enslaved by Kafkaesque restrictions in every stratum of life. For if our good health is genuinely the main focus of the rules and regulations that bind us, some very strange decisions are being made that seem to promote the opposite outcome.

The Battle for Natural Health

In recent decades, one of the largest growth areas in health-care has been the awareness that natural supplements and 'complementary' medicine can have a highly positive influence on our well-being and resistance to disease. Millions testify as to their effectiveness, and have been liberated from reliance on sometimes harmful pharmaceutical solutions. Often the successful results speak for themselves.

One might imagine governments concerned for our health and safety would welcome this development, with its plainly beneficial effects. Instead, there has been a sustained attack on the natural health industry courtesy of a self-elected mainstream body of intellectuals who have declared it quackery unworthy of academic respect. With alarming regularity the media loudly trumpets another supposedly scientific study that discounts any meaningful results from a predictable range of targets, usually high-dose vitamins, health supplements, homeopathy, or all manner of alternative therapies, sneered at in superior tones. At the same time, wonder-drug medical 'solutions' often fill front page headlines of newspapers, telling us we will soon no longer have to worry about niggling things like diet, exercise and lifestyle. Yet the non-effectiveness of many conventional medicines (astonishingly, only a minority of pharmaceutical products can be scientifically proven to be effective) and their many unfortunate 'side' effects seem not to fill the same pages or minutes of air-time to an equal degree. Few people doubt the important and efficacious role mainstream medicine plays in our civilization, but too many of its supporters seem blind to its faults, and are over-fervent in their censorship of alternative methods.

Scientific verification of areas that seem to fall outside of straightforward cause and effect is inevitably going to be controversial, and there is no reason why science shouldn't mount investigations into natural health claims. But the strong impression given with such studies is that a negative outcome is always anticipated from the outset - which, by definition, is an unscientific approach. This is similar to the analyses of Moon rock being flawed by the pre-experiment assumption that it *is* Moon rock in the first place [Chapter VI]. If science doesn't find anything within the usually very narrow parameters it has set for itself, the phenomenon under investigation is declared as non-existent - or fraudulent. Sometimes, as with crop circles (or psi investigation - Chapter XIV), when peer-review science does begin to support the veracity of an unusual area it can suddenly find itself dismissed as 'fringe', and qualified academics are unexpectedly marginalized and even vilified

Herbal medicine has been used successfully for centuries, but creeping legislation is now notably reducing the number of high-dose vitamins and natural supplements available to the public, courtesy of the Codex Alimentarius food safety body.

by the wider scientific community. Given the noted observation in quantum physics that the experimenter is somehow inextricably entangled with the outcome of the experiment itself, perhaps unsurprisingly no supportive results on natural health are ever produced by scientists of a skeptical mindset - and most mainstream tests are inevitably carried out by such people. The fact remains, however, that many sufferers seem to benefit from natural health practices, and double-blind tests carried out by more open-minded investigators (admittedly fewer, largely because they don't receive the same kind of commercial funding as the doubters) *do* show supportive results.[2]

Skeptics assert that any positive effects of non-conventional practices are merely the placebo effect in action (omitting to address the interesting successes reported on animals - and babies - which presumably fall outside this explanation). This ignores the fact that official medicine itself often operates on the placebo principle, as many doctors will confirm. And even *if* the placebo effect is all that is going on with complementary health, it is still *an* effect with a positive outcome. Yet every effort is seemingly being made to stamp out alternative medicine and naturally advantageous products.

There has been a massive rise in obesity and heart disease in our increasingly sedentary Western culture. With so many citizens addicted to junk food and force-fed much-questioned additives such as the sweetener aspartame (or its craftily renamed equivalents), which now laces multiple popular drinks and foodstuffs,[3] the encouragement of healthy diets and good eating from the likes of TV chefs and fitness pundits receives much publicity and gets lip-service support from authorities. Yet, paradoxically, those who believe, based on experience and evidence, that certain high-dose vitamins or natural supplements can also make a huge difference to health and well-being, are now being penalized by international directives, courtesy of the Codex Alimentarius, a long-established food safety think-tank founded in 1963 as part of the Food and Agriculture Organization of the UN, and connected to the World Health Organization. These directives compromise greatly the right to choose a 'holistic' path of dietary care, by notably restricting the availability of certain products and overly tightening rules on their manufacture. The Alliance for Natural Health, which has valiantly fought the Codex Alimentarius, sums the situation up thus:

i) Massive restrictions on allowed ingredients, including vitamin and mineral forms, as well as botanicals
ii) Massive restrictions on maximum permitted doses of vitamins and minerals
iii) Massive restrictions on what can be said about any product with beneficial properties
iv) Imposition of pharmaceutical-type standards, making it difficult for many truly natural products to comply [4]

What the now ongoing international implementation of the Codex directives means is that the quantity of vitamins and supplements that can legally be bought and consumed is being reduced, in some cases to the point where taking the permissible amounts could eventually become pointless. The advertising of any genuine benefits to certain items has also become illegal unless they have been proven by clinical trials (bringing us back to the problem of skeptical experimenters). The availability of commonly used herbal remedies such as St John's Wort and Valerian has already been compromised and even entirely innocuous plants such as garlic and mint could now, in theory, be classified as drugs if promoted as being for health purposes. The reason for these restrictions? - to 'protect' (of course) the public from the potential harm of natural products, the benefits of which have not, in the eyes of Codex, been scientifically verified. The fact that many of these products and substances have been used harmlessly for generations and that they involve far fewer chemical and toxic elements than most conventional pharmaceuticals (which, statistically, are far more provably harmful) seems not to count. Quite astonishing figures show that each year in the USA alone around *800,000* people die due to unexpected effects of normal medication, over-prescription or incorrect diagnosis by doctors, making these the main annual causes of death in the US - yet no outcry demands the kind of draconian measures being proposed for natural medicine, which can barely be shown to have killed anyone in its long history.[5]

There are double standards being employed here. While taking away the easy accessibility of natural health products, Codex is at the same time also weakening the rules on organic food (making it permissible to have certain amounts of non-organic ingredients included in products labelled as organic), relaxing restrictions on genetically modified constituents (which no longer have to be indicated when included in some ingredient lists), permitting higher pesticide residues in vegetable produce, and encouraging irradiation for preservative purposes. How can an authoritative body, which claims to have our health interests at heart, support such policies when so many people have expressed serious concerns over the areas in question? With aspartame accepted as a foodstuff, but St John's Wort restricted as a drug, we have truly entered twisted realms.

Other inconsistent health policies affect our lives in ways that may be directly sinister. For instance, growing global imposition of the highly debatable fluoridation of drinking water - the very stuff of life - presupposes dental benefits that have been challenged even by a number of mainstream science studies (which have suggested *detrimental* effects in particular experiments), but still it continues. Some observers believe this is yet another attempt to poison and suppress our natural immune systems, with fluoride being entirely alien to the human constitution.[6] Yet natural products, which have a long history of positive influence and very few downsides, are being withdrawn. Once again the power of choice and our right to take just small risks is being encroached on by faceless boards, which have decided on our behalf what is good for us and what is not. This is not to say that *no* protective measures should be taken to ensure our food and supplements are safe and sensibly regulated, but the current measures go much too far into draconian - and entirely contradictory - realms. Campaigners like Scott Tips, Ian R Crane, Robert Verkerk and Philip Day have done sterling work in trying to raise public awareness and may well have helped prevent the proposed worst excesses of the Codex-driven agenda from being embedded into international law. Despite this, even some natural health retailers rather blindly seemed not to believe that any measures would ever come to fruition, hence resistance was too little and too slow to halt the entire program.

The irony is that the mainstream scientists branding natural health products and alternative medicine as potentially dangerous are often the same ones who dismiss both as meaningless nonsense. Some of them object on the grounds that alternative health care might dissuade patients from seeking the 'proper' (i.e. pharmaceutical) attention that they may also need, but others contend the issue merely on the basis that fringe methods, in their eyes, simply don't work, mortally offended at what they see as bad science. Yet the attempt to protect us from their possible harm (high-dose vitamins have been especially lambasted in these areas) is surely a tacit acknowledgement that these practices might have a real and verifiable effect of some kind after all - or why try to stop them?

What this is truly all about, as far as many justifiable cynics are concerned, is protecting the interests of the huge pharmaceutical and food industries, which do not benefit from us being healthy. Those who feel this view is too pessimistic might like to consider that official Codex Alimentarius publicity openly acknowledges that all of its meetings (often large conferences) are attended by representatives with 'transnational corporation interests'; i.e. major food manufacturers and pharmaceutical giants (or 'Big Pharma' as truthers dub them). Conspiracy die-hards contend that neither does it suit the wider powers to have a healthy and energetic population, and that the erosion of our personal health choices is yet another part of the program to weaken humanity into submission.

DIPHTHERIA is deadly-

IMMUNISATION is the safeguard

ASK AT YOUR LOCAL COUNCIL OFFICES OR WELFARE CENTRE

Issued by the Ministry of Health and the Central Council for Health Education

Post-war poster promoting the happy benefits of vaccination. Yet if the practice is as safe and effective as advertised, why after all this time are so many people still concerned about possible side effects? Some researchers question the entire science behind immunization. Why are these arguments not yet settled?

Immunization Choices

With what we put into our mouths being regulated by strong-arm tactics, what we put into our bloodstream is increasingly dictated in the same way. The choice as to whether to vaccinate or not is rapidly being eroded, with countries like Australia and some states of the USA already having made it effectively compulsory for most groups. The UK is also heading towards a mandatory MMR program, fuelled by repeated exaggerated measles scares and other claimed epidemics which usually melt away without any solid statistics, dutifully inflated by the media. Yet this push towards legal obligation is occurring despite many concerns over the reliability of the very science of immunization, and the serious side-effects which have been alleged to occur. The alleged malpractice of just one of the questioners, Dr Andrew Wakefield (who proposed a now refuted connection to autism, though he is still fighting his case), has been allowed to eclipse other very serious observations. It is certainly a fact that nearly all diseases supposedly eradicated by vaccination can be shown to have already been on a steep decline before its introduction, and in some cases diseases have *risen* afterwards. There also seems to be no great statistical increase of disease in unvaccinated children, despite much pharmaceutical propaganda (unsurprising, with huge profits at stake).[7]

This is a controversial area, and a very emotive one, but given the still unsettled debates around the issue, the global rush towards compulsory injections of toxic compounds (which can include poisonous mercury) straight into the deepest part of a child's immune system is questionable at best. Again, the *manner* in which we are cajoled into accepting vaccination - nearly always through fear or emotional plays around the issue of 'responsibility' to our children, together with the clockwork rounds of epidemic stories that rarely go any further - takes away the concept of personal choice and suggests that any opinions outside those of government scientists are automatically wrong. With the EU Codex directives, even alternative methods of staying healthy and naturally boosting our immune systems are under attack, making us more vulnerable to control and prone to dependency on a state that seems to prefer chemical-based solutions. Unsurprisingly, then, many doubters suspect that the push to vaccinate (with new vaccines being introduced and promoted with the fear-factor every year, to deal with everything now, from cervical cancer to the latest flu) is as much about protecting the pharmaceutical industries, with all their powerful lobbyists and political influence, than protecting the individual.

Given other possibly detrimental effects of modern living, from effects of pesticides and growing electromagnetic and microwave pollution (both of which some researchers believe are contributing to the very serious disappearance of bees and other important wildlife) to the allegation that our very planetary atmosphere is being tampered with through the 'chemtrails' phenomenon [page 70], it is not so difficult to see why some people have become convinced there is an ongoing and deliberate assault on our physical and mental well-being. But if so, there also seems to be an attack on our spiritual and social well-being. With no frontier seemingly sacred, the 'thought police' of Orwell's nightmare parable may have finally arrived.

Policing Personal Beliefs

The current tendency of governments to think they know better than the individual what is good for them has also extended beyond health and into the realm of the spiritual. The acceptance of the esoteric within long-established religions - and elite infrastructures - is fine, it seems, but anything outside of those traditional parameters has noticeably become a target of persecution.

In May 2008, a new EU law entitled the 'Unfair Commercial Practices Directive' was introduced across Europe. Ostensibly in place to protect consumers from fraudulent traders, it worries those with mystical leanings for it also carries an underlying implication that - if the directive is ever followed to the letter - all practitioners of psychically-based religions such as Spiritualism, all forms of mediumship and mystery arts such as astrology, tarot and divination, must provide empirical proof of their effectiveness. If not, by implication these services must be classified only as 'entertainment' - or not advertised at all.[8] Sensible precautions on one level perhaps, but such blanket discrimination will always disadvantage methods that are impossible to prove in anything that might equate to clinical trials because they lie beyond standard scientific paradigms - paradigms set by minds closed to alternative thinking from the start.

Although some of the initial responses to the new law were admittedly too reactionary, the fact remains that, as with complementary health product regulations, advertisements claiming any genuine benefits to mystical services are now technically in breach of the law. If the European anti-fringe lobby that seems to be growing in influence were to take a greater hold over things (especially given the traditional evangelical opposition to what it calls 'the occult'), it could use powers now firmly in place (albeit hidden in the small print) to see such activities greatly curtailed, without the need for any new public offensive. Despite a little tabloid coverage, this potentially dangerous piece of legislation was allowed to slip through Parliament without resistance, yet it amounted to an attack on the very fundamental freedom of the individual - the freedom to live a personal spiritual conviction.

Religious persecution of one kind or another has plagued history, but the introduction of parliamentary Acts of Tolerance and the creation of the multi-faith society most of the West comprises today was a step towards some form of enlightenment. However, fear of a new dark age of 'occultism', much of it promoted either by the fundamentalist Christianity that would appear to lurk behind certain policies [Chapter IV] or, conversely, by rampant scientism and debunking bodies such as the Inquisition-like CSI (Committee for Skeptical Enquiry), is seeing a new intolerance quietly being inflicted on our society. Major religions can freely shout about their effectiveness through posters and propaganda - yet New Age beliefs or alternative practices, with no less evidence for their provenance, are being singled out as unworthy of the same respect. Already routinely lambasted by the media, now they are under potential attack from the law.

Chicago spiritualists, 1906. Back then it was thought that mediumship and communication with the dead would become accepted as a mainstream religion, but a continued bias against alternative faiths has resulted in increased marginalization, now manifesting in legislation.

What authority on Earth is omniscient enough to be able to pontificate as to which faith and/or spiritual practice is acceptable for promotion and which is not? Why, for example, should those quite happy to accept the belief that wafers and wine can turn into the body and blood of Jesus Christ not also accept the (statistically supported) belief that the motions of the planets can influence moods and psychological profiles? How is it that a system which accepts the belief in spiritual inspiration from heavenly realms cannot also accept the belief in the presence of disembodied entities apparently speaking through mediums? Why should a culture that increasingly speaks of an 'entangled' quantum universe [Chapter XIV], which seems to defy our previous understanding of time and space, close its doors to the belief that such entanglement might enable divinatory processes to work through the principle of the 'holographic universe'? In short, what possible right can anyone have to compel another to describe their cherished convictions as being simply 'entertainment' or something similarly derisive?

Regardless of the alternative world's veracity or otherwise, the growing mainstream resistance to it amounts to a new religious intolerance. It is a policing of the human spirit at its deepest level, and marks the revival of a worrying policy that tyrants and oppressors have used since time immemorial when they have felt threatened by the power of individuality and any who might step outside of the pre-approved authoritarian religions. The Soviet Union and China once heavily suppressed the freedom of faith (although, ironically, China today has a burgeoning Christian movement). Now the West, with its strange paradoxical mix of underlying religious fundamentalism and hard scientism all at the same time (note the huge publicity given to God-baiting biologist Richard Dawkins and the general promotion of atheism in recent years - is this another kind of double-bluff conditioning at work?), is beginning to do the same to those who would choose their own inner path. The 'persecution' is currently very subtle, to be sure, but tidal swells are often hard to notice at first.

If spiritual beliefs were ever to become policed in the way some people fear, it is one clear area that would demand some form of mass civil-disobedience. Martyrs once stood against the crushing of their personal convictions at the cost of their lives. Hopefully such a high price should not need to be paid again in these supposedly more civilized times (any legally-required disclaimers could simply be made in a tangibly sarcastic context, for instance). But who knows where a new witch-hunting mentality could lead? We must be on our guard. Acquiescing without resistance to rules that humble and humiliate private philosophies could lead to a dangerous path.

Political Correctness

The right to choose our beliefs is closely related to the right to hold an opinion, yet this is another area of our lives that has been encroached upon as part of what could be an ongoing attack on our ability to function as fully-rounded human beings. The scourge of 'political correctness' has been a prime suppressor of the freedom to express our inner feelings, and for the last two decades it has notably curtailed the collective's ability to speak its mind, forcing us into a kind of false interaction with others that stifles debate and blocks progress in working through social issues.

Racism and the intimidation or humiliation of any minority group, from the gay community to the disabled is plainly - to all but right-wing fanatics and advocates of eugenics - unacceptable on every level. All such ignorant prejudices should be given the contempt they deserve. But when the misplaced *accusation* of such intimidation is used to denigrate entirely normal expressions, words or terminology that are clearly well-meant or logical ('blackboard' is no longer an acceptable term in schools, for instance, even in the few that still have them), or to quash necessary concerns and important discussions (the issue of immigration, for instance), common sense is replaced by a field of distortion that serves no-one.

The terror of being falsely accused of political *in*correctness, with the accompanying threat of becoming a social pariah, has given birth to a climate where people are afraid to speak what is in their hearts over particular issues, not helped by 'hate crime' laws in some parts of the world, which are ambiguous enough to potentially restrict legitimate questioning on many things, including 9/11. The lightest criticism of extremist Zionism is already enough to have someone marked down by the Anti-Defamation League (the understandably defensive but sometimes over-zealous Jewish rights organization). Consequently, valid concerns and feelings can be pushed into the shadows and fester, where they are sometimes reborn in yet more extremism, albeit of a different kind (almost certainly a factor in the recent rise of many global far-right movements into mainstream awarenes - Golden Dawn in Greece and the English Defense League in the UK, for instance). Other people simply sink into disillusion, where the enthusiasm to fight injustice becomes seriously sapped.

What all this breeds, more than anything else, is resentment - resentment of the very kind of minorities political correctness is supposed to protect. Fear of other cultures, other religions, of other ways of being, are all fostered by this approach, almost as if it is *meant* to, creating more division and disunity amongst communities - and, especially in the case of criticism of Islam, helping to bolster support for the West's debatable Middle Eastern wars. Muslim fundamentalism is a problem that needs dealing with, as all fundamentalism does, but the false notion that Muslim = fundamentalist = terrorist (not helped by the media) has been allowed to grow in part by the block that political correctness has put on serious discussion of the real issues. Did political correctness thus arise through natural filters of society, or was it subtly introduced as part of a deliberate Divide and Rule policy..?

The beauty and wisdom of the Muslim world is too often overshadowed by the media's over-focus on fundamentalism and horror stories of Christmas trees being banned to avoid offending Islam, etc. Whilst occasionally true, it is often those trying to be politically correct, rather than the minorities they are claiming to protect, that are the cause of the problems - thus spreading division. Is this a deliberate ploy?

Community and Family Fracturing

Part Four of this book provides some fairly obvious, yet easily missed solutions to many of the issues raised throughout these pages. At the risk of holding that optimism back a little longer, some of the other ways in which society has allowed itself to be corralled into a divided and distracted state of being need a brief mention here.

Given the devastating lengths to which the ruling elite will seemingly go when it needs to, as discussed in earlier chapters, it is not beyond the realms of possibility that a Divide and Rule strategy is being implemented under a veneer of appearing to nurture the opposite, as seen with the political correctness issue. It is certainly hard to make sense of some of the more peculiar legislation and encouraged social trends that seem to split communities, not unite them. Brian Gerrish, a retired UK Naval officer who began to fight what seemed like simple bureaucracy in his home town of Plymouth, only to uncover a demonstrable layer of infiltration in local government from the dubious federalist-EU initiative Common Purpose, believes that concerted efforts are also being made to split families and dilute community spirit through unnecessary social services interventions and authoritative interference.[9] Gerrish's view even extends to believing that some of the appalling and often sinister civic art that has been foisted on the public in parks, at road junctions and in retail arcades in recent decades is actually designed to lower our spirits, not raise them. If this seems to take concerns a little too far, it is hard to deny that modern culture, for all its multiple communication facilities, does often seem to encourage alienation rather than cohesiveness.

The arrival of television (and to a degree its progeny, the Internet) has been a key factor in this process. On one level it has created a kind of community of its own, but at the same time it has taken people away from each other, holding us in cushioned, enclosed environments, reducing the social interaction previous generations once took for granted. It has also divided families, with a majority of Western children now said to eat dinners on laps in front of televisions without their parents, who eat elsewhere. Family meals occur only on very special occasions, creating schisms and non-communication where once there was social glue.

The fracturing of families has inevitably been a big part of what might be an ongoing social experiment. Divorce, separation and single-parent families may have become unavoidable in the psychological climate of our times, but all the studies show that overall the end product gives us young people far more prone to problems of loneliness, rage, alcohol, drugs and teenage pregnancy. The lack of family role models (especially male ones) is seen as a major problem by some analysts, but the lack of *any* role models is another. With Christianity, especially, having lost its hold in some countries (especially England) - good or bad, depending on your viewpoint, but still a social shock to the system - and now mired in child abuse scandals, and with congresses and parliaments full of particularly uninspiring personalities (now seen as generically corrupt), who should people look up to? Who is setting the standards? Most of the 'celebrities' we elevate to high status to fill this vacuum are hardly beacons of virtue. [See Chapter XV for some possible remedies.]

A nation of the dispossessed may seem like something a ruling class would wish to avoid, but the counter-argument is that people entangled in their own social problems are far less likely to cause trouble in areas further afield, leaving our hidden overlords free to plan a world that doesn't ultimately include the likes of us anyway.

Media Influence and Propaganda

Although sometimes a pleasant diversion (perhaps literally), electronic media, beginning with radio and television, has also been one of the primary tools of our social undoing. For the first time in human history devices have been created that can focus many minds on the same thing at the same time - both a blessing and a curse. These mediums could serve humanity well if put to good use, and there is nothing wrong with a little entertainment for entertainment's sake. Yet even the most perfunctory sift through TV channels on any given evening will reveal the menu of violence, negativity and depression we flood the collective consciousness with every day [page 293] - something that surely cannot be good for the spirit or long-term social stability. The contention that television (and cinema) acts as a necessary catharsis and an outlet for our repressed aggressive tendencies can only be stretched so far. The unstoppable proliferation of computer games, in which the player

Many people watch several hours of television every day. It has transformed the social habits of the Western population; fine in moderation, but its propensity as a tool for propaganda and for creating a distracted and compliant society, easy to control, is dangerously high.

becomes the actual perpetrator of violence, now played by millions of people (especially children) around the world, *has* to raise even more serious questions - but they are for a forum beyond this book. Few would really disagree that it all makes for a more fractured society, if only through the increased physical isolation of those who experience more electronic social networking than direct human interaction. The question here is whether all of this is a vagary of cultural evolution or a deliberate ploy of social engineering from a ruling class adopting a bread-and-circuses policy. There are some campaigners, of course, who believe television is a direct mind-control/surveillance system and won't have one in their home at all.

Television and online viewing are certainly very persuasive mediums. The power of imagery and suggestion is particularly hypnotic (obviously more so than radio, although that outlet is not guiltless) and allows a very selective version of consensus reality to be easily fed to the masses. Like the press, at its core most mainstream broadcasting endorses the official line on almost everything, with only a very few tiny cable or satellite channels having dared to challenge this state of affairs, and they struggle to survive because advertisers won't support them. We may say we are not influenced by what we watch, and program makers will deny that anything they transmit really affects people (in a personal conversation, British media mogul Michael Grade once assured this author, incredibly, that TV has no sway over anyone), but if either of these assertions were true then billions would not be spent on the glitzy commercials that help part us with hard-earned money.

As a propaganda tool, the 'idiot's lantern', as television was once known, is still the primary frontline, given that online viewers are able to choose more selectively what they see (although this can present problems of its own, restricting exposure to at least slightly varied viewpoints). Programs that pretend to question the status quo (i.e. past 'investigative' takes on 9/11 or the Moon landings, etc.) nearly always end up avoiding the real issues and instead simply validate the standard position, usually with the obligatory sneer. Likewise, with just a few notable exceptions, there is now a scarcity of real political incisiveness beyond shallow critiques of surface details (particularly in the UK, after the BBC's neutering in the wake of the David Kelly affair - page 135). Even when major scandals are uncovered, there is usually little sustained questioning of the underlying key issues and things are swiftly moved on from, allowing the deeper implications to go undiscussed.

With the consensus view continually pumped from our screens and thrown into print day after day, it is hard not to be drawn in by it on some level. It *is* eventually possible to watch or read the news with discernment and avoid being conditioned by every underlying agenda slid into our living rooms, but it takes practice and diligence that not everyone finds easy to maintain.

'Dumbing Down'

It is difficult to deny that the phenomenon of 'dumbing-down' has also infected the media. Those who believe that television can be a useful educational tool increasingly despair at the many watered-down psuedo-'documentaries' that have now taken the place of once-great series. Too often, crashing music, thin treatments, inane animations and over-glamorous presenters (lingered on with fawning camera shots) seem to replace depth and informed content. Even late-night news shows would sometimes seem more at home in the childrens' slot. Accurate speech is increasingly degraded by poor pronounciation and very limited vocabulary to accommodate the less sophisticated among us - which on one level seems kind, but it also encourages the dangerous trend of pandering to the lowest levels of culture, instead of trying to offer something potentially better. This questionable approach takes the evolution of consciousness backwards for everyone. But once again, is it evolution - or social engineering? Some minds suspect the latter.

Encouraging hidden talents in those with less fortunate educations doesn't have to be patronizing. Treating people as idiots and bringing everything down to the level of phone-texting or Twitter speak certainly is. The decline of the written and spoken word is already considered to have detrimentally affected the development of speech in young people, a development already hindered by too much television in the early years, according to repeated studies. We are at risk of entering the world of *Nineteen Eighty-Four*'s 'Newspeak', in which subversiveness is stamped out by the deliberate deterioration of language into a kind of baby-talk that makes it *impossible* to express any kind of complex idea that might challenge convention or authority. Meanwhile, attention spans have been greatly reduced to match, by the ever-faster editing of modern media techniques and flickering images which, after prolonged exposure, leave people unable to concentrate on anything for long anyway - hence, in part (on top of the chemical effect from food additives, known to produce hyper-activity), the low boredom threshold of the generations raised on frantic games and quick-fire cuts, and never free from iPods and cell phones.

When young people show signs of reacting to all this over-stimulation with 'difficult' behavior or the tellingly-named Attention Deficit Hyperactivity Disorder (ADHD), the state reaches for pharmaceutical solutions, with an astounding one in ten children in the USA now dosed up with the highly-questionable and potentially dangerous drug Ritalin to keep them docile. An alarming number of adults are also routinely fed antidepressants instead of being offered constructive counselling.[10]

Instead of rousing people to aspiration and helping them to become more than they are, we are currently keeping people in stasis or, worse, reducing the population to an infantile and numbed condition that then demands the presence of a nanny state to look after it - which the authorities duly provide.

In this daze we allow our senses to be dulled and our attention to be diverted from the things that might really matter by media outlets that tantalize with the promise of instant fame and riches from TV quiz shows, talent competitions, and national lotteries ('a tax on the poor'), or eat our time and attention with essentially meaningless football scandals, celebrity gossip and cheap titillation. Mesmerized by these things, we do not see the magician's sleights of hand that are shaping the world in front of our very eyes.

Physical Barriers

One of the serious issues conjured by a media obsessed with titillation is a general debasement of sex and natural human affection, created by negative associations with, or false impressions of, sexuality. This has been greatly accelerated by youthful exposure to online pornography, for which simple solutions remain elusive without falling into the trap of unfair blanket censorship. But many of the portrayals of sex found online and reinforced by general media stereotypes, have undoubtedly diminished its more empowering and enlightening qualities (indeed, sex was once thought in some mystic circles to connect us to higher spiritual powers). The dark shadow of AIDS was one of the first things to turn something wonderful into something dangerous and frightening, and now ubiquitous public information advertisements about all the other apparently rife sexual diseases seem to be doom-laden beyond the call of duty.

The reporting of sexuality in negative contexts has produced a continual run of scare stories over the rapists and pedophiles that apparently stalk every street. The shocking revelations in 2012 that a number of British radio and television personalities, most prominently one Jimmy Savile, had indeed abused many children, with subsequent institutional cover-ups, did not help dispel this negative impression. Pedophilia must unquestionably be exposed and fought, and accusations of abuse rings at work in the highest of places [page 84] still remain to be properly investigated. However, the fear around the issue has been disproportionately and perhaps deliberately allowed to generate a culture where teachers and carers can no longer make physical gestures of the most innocuous kind (permission now has to be sought just to offer first-aid in some schools) and taking photographs of class plays or sports activities invites frowns or demands from parents or staff to stop. [As it happens, few laws actually prevent normal photographs of children in most public places, but the general hysteria around pedophilia has created the *assumption* that there are such laws.] And so, yet more distance is forced between people and we find ourselves policing each other without even the need for edicts from above - a key feature of the world that has been created around us. When parents increasingly dare not take snaps of their own children on a beach for fear of being prosecuted under child pornography laws, we know we are in a society that is being led in a very unhealthy direction.

A general respect for the personal boundaries of those around us, together with wise and balanced sexual behavior, is something sensible; an irrational fear-bound society that sees a human gift as inherently threatening, while continually obsessing over it, is inviting psychosis.

The Caged Society - Evolution or Contrivance?

In all these ways, truthseekers believe we have been tricked. Thus hypnotized, diverted by trivia, controlled by fear, anesthetized by additives and pharmaceuticals and kept in the dark from what is really going on in the world around us, only one more ingredient is needed for the conjurer's final distraction - something provided easily in the shape of rampant materialism. This was accelerated massively in the every-man-for-himself boom years of the 1980s and has never left us since. Even in years of financial crisis, retail therapy is still one of the most popular pastimes. With spiritual matters either placed on the backburner in the modern Anglo-Saxon world, or warped by evangelical fundamentalism of all kinds (another kind of bondage, in the opinion of many free-thinkers), the strings are firmly attached for our role as puppets, as we look for instant, if unenduring fixes in the only cathedrals still packed with people - the shopping malls.

What, then, will we do if an even bigger world economic crisis occurs, bringing everything down with it, as some believe is the plan [page 74]? Like birds unable to fly out when the door is finally opened, if materialism is our cage, then we will look to the same masters to make a new protective prison for us and to bring back the old comfortable fixes. And our masters will surely deliver - albeit with a world finally tailored to their exact needs.

On such fears, the conspiracy world is based. Could all this be just the chance of evolution's trial and error, then, or is the view that it is being intentionally manipulated through social engineering a realistic possibility? The truth, as ever, may lie somewhere between the extremes. Nonetheless, an incohesive and disempowered population is clearly easier to control. But what would all this control really be needed for? Is it just about power for power's sake or is there another, more pressing, reason? We shall explore a strong possibility soon, which will help bring together many of the sometimes seemingly disparate threads discussed in the book so far.

Shopping malls, our new cathedrals. With the world in economic peril, we still distract ourselves with material comforts.

However, there is one more widely-promoted tool of control that is currently having the effect of creating division and alienation that we need to look at first, one flying closely under the radar as something of apparently unimpeachable good intent - that of our growing collective desire to save the planet from impending climate disaster.

THE TRUTH AGENDA: *The diminishment of self-responsibility and choice, even in matters of health, means that we are left at the mercy of those who seem to prefer us hooked on chemical-based symptom suppressors and dubious additives in our food and water, rather than allow us to protect our well-being by natural or common sense methods. The employment of psychological warfare also seems apparent in societal trends, with people reduced to statistics while health and safety, political correctness, family breakdown and the distractions of the media and materialism alienate people from each other and from their own sense of self-empowerment. Many people believe this is a deliberate policy of Divide and Rule, creating a weaker - and therefore more malleable - society.*

Tools of Control

Balancing our energy needs with concerns over the environment and climate change is one of the big discussions of the age - but have we really understood climate change, and is the global warming scenario the correct one? Many people want a real debate, but they are still not being allowed a full voice in the mainstream.

XI THE GREEN DILEMMA

The widely-promoted fear of a major catastrophe due to climate change is increasingly creating a judgmental society of finger-pointing and mistrust. With man-made global warming having been decided on as the primary mechanism of our forthcoming undoing, it might be thought that all the arguments were settled. But are they? Continuing skepticism around this area suggests not. How can we strike a balance? Sensible protection of our planet, its wildlife and its ecosystems is a must, but climate change and green issues do appear to have been hijacked for use as more tools of control through which the hands of freedom are being tied.

Policing Each Other Through Green Concerns

In the darker days of the Soviet Union and its communist associates, one successful method by which behavior was controlled was to sow seeds of doubt and suspicion amongst the general populace by hiring urban spies and encouraging exposure of anyone showing signs of disloyalty to the state. Avoiding the need for expensive monitoring, the people simply policed each other and fear kept dissent down.

Although, as we have seen, mass-monitoring technology is now easily affordable and ubiquitous, this self-policing technique has still crept into Western society in a number of ways, most prominently through the unexpected channel of 'green' concerns. This has manifested in recycling officers sifting through bins in some areas of the USA and UK, fining unfortunates who may have inadvertently thrown away inappropriate items—despite fluctuations in the recycled materials market which too often sees collected waste end up in landfill nonetheless. Some authorities have even placed cameras and other detectors in recycling containers, truly bringing the surveillance state to our doors, via our bins. However, due to genuine and well-intentioned concerns about the perilous state of the planet's ecology, a significant number of people seem to believe such measures are a *good thing*.

The much-encouraged hysterical response to the claimed threat of global warming (see below) and climate change in general has enabled the creation of a culture in which it has become legitimate to criticize and monitor other people's behavior in the name of saving the planet. Because the aspiration seems like a reasonable one, some have gone along with this new green fascism, not because they feel comfortable with it, but through political correctness or fear of ostracism. Raising objections against an apparently virtuous cause risks seeming uncaring and impolite.

Consequently, with all the fears around man-made greenhouse gases contributing to global warming, and the screams that 'peak oil' has been reached and that we are about to run out of the black gold that has fired our modern world, it has seemingly become more acceptable to criticise others for taking a holiday by airplane, or for buying a bigger auto, house, etcetera—or for not recycling properly. One is as likely to come across a street protest against 4x4 vehicles than one about something arguably more crucial like, say, the truth about 9/11 or the growth of surveillance and the loss of freedom. In a very clever way, people have been turned inwards on each other, controlling *themselves* by policing each other's lifestyles in the name of the environment.

Recycling and sensible environmental measures are a good thing; intimidation, social scrutiny and mistrust are not. The resentment towards all this has notably grown in more recent years, and the backlash, expressed in skepticism or indifference towards climate change, would appear at first to be self-defeating to either those who genuinely care for the planet, or to the manipulators trying to use the situation to their own advantage. But is this a serious miscalculation on the part of the ruling elite, or a strand of the divide-and-rule control agenda working out exactly as it should?

Pollution is a problem that needs tackling, but much of the responsibility for doing so seems to have fallen on the everyday person instead of the huge industries that generate much of it, thus neatly deflecting the burden of guilt.

The Guilt of Climate Change

Unquestionably, the main guilt for environmental destruction and climate change has been cunningly placed on the small people—us. Our thoughtless over-use of cars, domestic energy and airplanes is apparently to blame. Yet, for all the climate treaties and uneasy (and possibly unattainable under the current global economy) carbon reduction targets fanfared by leaders keen to be seen to be doing something, the fact is that the real polluters, the industrial giants, chemical plants and power stations, continue belching out emissions into the atmosphere and poisoning the waters while authorities turn blind eyes and society continues to function on the benefits of their doing so. What environmental fuss has been made has often been compromised by weak finances and the need for vote-winning policies (rather than the wider good), seeing reversals of apparent good intentions, as with the US Tea Party, which has never been sold on green rhetoric.

Conversely, as this official reluctance to truly commit to any meaningful action continues, the feeling of personal guilt concerning our own comparatively tiny carbon contributions grows ever-more suffocating, drummed into us by doom-laden television documentaries and pronouncements from government-funded scientific bodies. This transference of guilt is tacitly supported by regimes around the world, either because they are unsure how to balance the needs of a perilous economy and the planet, or because the social controls and coffer-swelling taxes the global warming scare has gifted are too valuable to lose. All the time public collective guilt broods, the *appearance* that something is being done is partly maintained by all the media energy expended over the issue, even though the underlying problems remain unaddressed. So the common people are carrying the lion's share of responsibility instead of those entrusted with finding the solutions, who happily pass the burden back. We too often fail to notice this inequality because we are all too busy believing that dismantling the wood burner or persuading our neighbors not to fly to Hawaii next week could make a major contribution to preventing climate change.

Despite the conspiracy theories, this distractive guilt isn't uniquely placed on us from on high. Those individuals deeply touched by the apparent plight of the Earth can also be relied on to ensure local communities are kept on their environmental toes by the creation of activist groups (like the Transition US/Transition Town initiative), set up to encourage communities to become greener and more self-sufficient, less reliant on oil and other resources that may become scarce.[1] In theory, the aims of such groups are entirely sensible and praiseworthy, but in practice some campaigners' fervent tones, using aggressive words like 'unleashing' to launch environmental initiatives, can risk intimidating those who feel less sure of their ultimate aims. Some green publicity statements give the strong impression that there are those who actually *want* a social apocalypse and a return to a medieval lifestyle, in a kind of non-religious echo of the end-timer philosophy explored in Chapter IV.

Resistance to open debate over issues taken for granted by the likes of Transition groups, such as the man-made causes of climate change or the certainty that oil is about to run out (challenged by leading truth campaigners such as Ian R Crane, who worked in the oil industry for much of his life), has generated a number of heated conflicts on Internet forums and at public gatherings. It has also bred resentment amongst those feeling bullied by new (and often young) boil-in-the-bag enviro-activists, who seem to think nothing of disrupting airports and public spaces while accosting unwitting bystanders with often third-hand platitudes they barely understand themselves but have been trained to parrot. Such public intimidation may win frightened lip-service for a while, but not genuine support. This, surely, is not the way to save the planet. Many green thinkers seem resistant to considering conspiracy speculation, without seeing that they themselves may be some of the very people being manipulated to discourage free-thinking individualism.

The Global Warming Conundrum

The rise of the new green dogma has been fuelled by a huge wave of propaganda concerning man-made global warming. Climate change of some kind would seem to be a fact by simple observation, but the loose way the terms 'climate change' and 'global warming' are so often interchanged to mean the same thing is questionable, because many people believe that global warming—especially that seen as man-made and despite the impression continually given in the media—remains a hypothesis, and is not a proven certainty. Even when accepted as a certainty, the causes of any warming are a debate in themselves.

By accident or design, it has been of great political convenience to finger human-caused greenhouse gases as the primary source of the global warming we are all being encouraged to fight, with all the requisite carbon taxation and added social controls that come with it. It also massively benefits the quietly powerful nuclear industry, which is promoted by some scientists (even by previously green thinkers such as James Lovelock) as the only practical non-carbon answer to slowing the onset of impending global catastrophe. The slew of negative publicity now given to alternatives such as wind farms raises the question of which lobby might benefit most from these attacks, whatever the arguments over the inefficiency and visual impact of wind turbines. A nuclear waste accident could, in the long-run, have a far greater impact, as Japan discovered in the wake of the 2011 tsunami which deluged several nuclear reactors to terrible environmental effect at levels which may well have been covered-up.

As fear of greenhouse gas doom rises—and it is plainly stirred as a fright-based mass-hysteria—we find ourselves giving in to draconian measures and granting assent to very tough carbon targets, which threaten jobs and make everyday life generally harder even as real industrial legislation remains unenforced. All necessary sacrifices, we are told, for the future of the planet. Yet the world is being turned upside down for something which remains unproven, and a very large number of people still question global warming despite the relentless propaganda. Despite the subsequent official whitewash, the 'Climategate' emails of 2009 [page 233] strongly suggested a deliberate withholding of any data which might challenge the man-made warming hypothesis. In 2014, a US poll showed that around 35% of the population remained doubtful about any warming and a further 18% were unconvinced humans were to blame, a figure leapt on by establishment scientists as merely signs of public ignorance—not of their own inability to produce firm proven evidence.[2]

It may be the case that global warming of one kind or another *is* a reality, of course, but the purpose of this book is to make sense of why so many people doubt the veracity of much of what they are told to believe nowadays. Applying the Truth Agenda to this issue yet again reveals valid grounds for questioning and deep areas of confusion that are not being properly acknowledged. It is little surprise that the public remains unsure, when there seems to be such a concerted effort to keep a lid on what is, in truth, a tumultuously boiling debate.

We are repeatedly told that nearly all respectable scientists support the idea of man-made global warming, based on firm evidence. But the truth is that surveys which claim to demonstrate this can often be shown to be flawed or deviously manipulated—and there are many equally respectable scientists who have raised concerns about the 'firm evidence' under discussion.[3] When big names come forward to voice this, however, they suddenly find themselves redefined as 'mavericks' or are accused of secretly working for oil companies or polluting industries, as ex-UK Chancellor Nigel Lawson and TV naturalist David Bellamy, both of whom have widely questioned global warming, found to their cost.[4] Peter Taylor, once an environmental adviser to both the UN and the EU on climate change, as a less famous but equally notable example, eventually resigned when he realized that any statistical results they produced that didn't support the idea of global warming were being ignored, or dismissed as 'instrument error'.[5]

Other government-funded climatologists have reported similar stories. Lawrence Solomon's book *The Deniers* [see *Appendix 3*] lists and interviews around twenty fully-qualified climatologists and scientists who challenge the global warming model. Yet with nearly all official climate research now being funnelled into the concept of man-made global warming, it has become impossible to study much else with financial support—thus skewing both the figures and the weight of mainstream opinion towards one view. It has also opened the world to the disastrously misconceived policy of growing crops for biofuels, which is destroying forests and communities as surely as global warming would.

Peter Taylor, former environmental advisor to the EU and UN, is one of many qualified climatologists who challenges global warming theory and claims that data which supports an alternative scenario is being systematically ignored.

The disproportionately huge siphoning of funds into a climate mono-science has also allowed studies into areas of equivalent importance to be neglected. Research into the potentially devastating disappearance of bees, for example (which, again, would harm the ecosystem as much as global warming), was for years only granted tiny budgets, and when some of the results suggested that neonicotinoid pesticides were very likely to be a major factor, the UK government actually opposed (unsuccessfully) a European moratorium on their use, while US officials have also dragged their heels, making clear their support for chemical companies over the environment.

When the previously-eminent ex-editor of *New Scientist*, Nigel Calder, co-authored with Henrik Svensmark the 2007 book *The Chilling Stars*,[6] proposing that cosmic rays and solar cycles could equally explain climate change and pointing out that past rises in ancient carbon cycles did not directly correlate with changes of global temperatures (there is generally an 800-year or more delay between the two), Calder's pedigree was suddenly erased from memory and he found himself ostracized from the science community. A British Channel Four documentary the same year, *The Great Global Warming Swindle*, based partly on Calder and Svensmark's theories, was equally slammed as entirely worthless because of a number of errors, and claims that some of the scientists interviewed on the program were quoted out of context. However, following up the complaints, the UK broadcasting regulator Ofcom ruled that the program 'did not materially mislead the audience so as to cause harm or offence,' and accepted Channel Four's claim that 'none of the inaccuracies materially affected the argument of the film in any way'.[7]

Despite the official finding in favor of *The Great Global Warming Swindle*, it was nonetheless entirely dismissed by green pundits and quickly buried under the ongoing deluge of global warming propaganda. Yet when one Stewart Dimmock went to the British High Court to challenge the dubious use of Al Gore's hugely influential US 2006 global warming-promoting film *An Inconvenient Truth* as an educational video in schools, and the film was indeed found to be inaccurate on nine major points (see below), this didn't prevent it continuing to be shown to children as a factual documentary. Nor did it slow its seemingly unstoppable cinematic tour of multiplexes, local venues, churches and environmental groups. The film is still quoted today as a work of reliable science, but the court ruling demands attention.

An Inconvenient Ruling

The ruling against the Al Gore movie is worth quoting in full here, because it sums up the types of misrepresentation concerning the global warming hypothesis that are all too rife. The website *www.newparty.co.uk*, key in bringing the case to court, reports the ruling thus:

The decision by the government to distribute Al Gore's film An Inconvenient Truth *has been the subject of a legal action by New Party member Stewart Dimmock. The Court found that the film was misleading in nine respects and that the Guidance Notes drafted by the Education Secretary's advisors served only to exacerbate the political propaganda in the film.*

In order for the film to be shown, the Government must first amend their Guidance Notes to Teachers to make clear that 1) The Film is a political work and promotes only one side of the argument. 2) If teachers present the Film without making this plain they may be in breach of section 406 of the Education Act 1996 and guilty of political indoctrination. 3) Nine inaccuracies have to be specifically drawn to the attention of school children. The inaccuracies are:

1) The film claims that melting snows on Mount Kilimanjaro [is] evidence [of] global warming. The Government's expert was forced to concede that this is not correct.

2) The film suggests that evidence from ice cores proves that rising CO2 causes temperature increases over 650,000 years. The Court found that the film was misleading: over that period the rises in CO2 lagged behind the temperature rises by 800-2000 years.

3) The film uses emotive images of Hurricane Katrina and suggests that this has been caused by global warming. The Government's expert had to accept that it was "not possible" to attribute one-off events to global warming.

4) The film shows the drying up of Lake Chad and claims that this was caused by global warming. The Government's expert had to accept that this was not the case.

5) The film claims that a study showed that polar bears had drowned due to disappearing arctic ice. It turned out that Mr Gore had misread the study: in fact four polar bears drowned and this was because of a particularly violent storm.

6) The film threatens that global warming could stop the Gulf Stream, throwing Europe into an ice age: the Claimant's evidence was that this was a scientific impossibility.

7) The film blames global warming for species losses including coral reef bleaching. The Government could not find any evidence to support this claim.

8) The film suggests that sea levels could rise by 7m causing the displacement of millions of people. In fact the evidence is that sea levels are expected to rise by about 40cm over the next hundred years and that there is no such threat of massive migration.

9) The film claims that rising sea levels has caused the evacuation of certain Pacific islands to New Zealand. The Government are unable to substantiate this and the Court observed that this appears to be a false claim.

Not all of the inaccuracies in the film were fully considered by the court as the judge requested a sample on which to consider the case. Professor Carter's witness statement lists 20 inaccuracies in the film.[8]

Another critic of the film was John Coleman, the founder of the hugely influential Weather Channel (US) but also a very vocal global warming skeptic, who himself at one point considered suing Gore and other proponents of the unproven hypothesis.[9] Coleman has been especially critical of the 'carbon credits' system, a suspect corporate tactic in which companies are allowed to continue to pollute if they simultaneously invest in environmental projects abroad. Investigation has too often revealed misrepresentation and outright fraud concerning the true nature and value of these supposedly balancing projects, suggesting that the credits scheme is yet another distraction to deceive the unassuming, guilt-ridden public.[10]

The ongoing promotion of *An Inconvenient Truth* in British schools despite the High Court ruling, without any of the stipulated conditions being met, neatly illustrated two things: firstly, that the rule of law seems not to apply to people in high positions (i.e. Gore), and, secondly, that our children are provably being educated with propaganda as regards global warming (and who knows what else), not factual material.

The Confusing Data of Climate Change

What jars with those unsure of what to believe as regards climate change is that average global temperatures have actually been on a general *decline* since 1998.[11] This is dismissed as nothing more than a statistical blip, a cycle within a cycle in an otherwise upwards trend, which may yet turn out to be the case—but it can be relied upon that if the temperature had risen in that time instead, such a statistic would now be loudly trumpeted as the final proof of global warming, as indeed were the very marginal global temperature rises which were claimed to have made 2014 the 'hottest' year. Other freak spikes have been used to 'prove' a general warming, yet general data still seems to demonstrate that not

For all the hysteria over carbon pollution contributing to global warming, it can be clearly demonstrated by analysis of ice core samples and other methods that historical carbon variations in the atmosphere have very limited correlation to climate or temperature changes.

only has the claimed overall temperature rise flatlined or even reversed, but also that scientific models which predict devastating consequences within a century may have been vastly overemphasized. Amidst some grudging reassessments, mainstream reports of these significant admissions heavily play them down, with quoted scientists still insisting that damaging man-made warming will strike soon enough regardless.[12] But accepting the reality of climate change does not mean having to accept the warming model. Qualified commentators like Peter Taylor and Australian geophysicist and astronaut Phil Chapman actually believe we may be entering a period of global *cooling*, which could create a new Ice Age, albeit a modest one [see also Chapter XII].[13] If so, the massive reductions of carbon being proposed, if ever implemented, could have entirely the wrong result anyhow, helping to hold back (if very slightly, on the grand scale) a mechanism needed for keeping temperatures *up*.

It may be that confusion was the idea all along. There is evidence to suggest that the global warming hysteria as we know it today had some of its seeds in a conference held in North Carolina in 1975, *The Atmosphere: Endangered and Endangering*, an event that hosted Malthusian-style speakers advocating the need for world depopulation [page 70]—another possible motive for creating a climate scare. An article by Marjorie Mazel Hecht on the website for *21st Century Science & Technology* magazine observes the following:

'[The conference was] *organized by the influential anthropologist Margaret Mead, president of the American Association for the Advancement of Science (AAAS), in 1974. Mead—whose 1928 book on the sex life of South Pacific Islanders was later found to be a fraud—recruited like-minded anti-population hoaxsters to the cause; sow enough fear of man-caused climate change to force global cutbacks in industrial activity and halt Third World development... ...Guided by luminaries like these, conference discussion focussed on the absurd choice of either feeding people or "saving the environment".*

... The North Carolina conference, which took place Oct. 26-29, 1975, was co-sponsored by two agencies of the US National Institutes of Health: the John E. Fogarty International Center for Advanced Study in the Health Sciences and the National Institute of Environmental Health Sciences... ...It was at this government-sponsored conference... ...that virtually every scare scenario in today's climate hoax took root. Scientists were charged with coming up with the "science" to back up the scares, so that definitive action could be taken by policy-makers.

Global cooling—the coming of an ice age—had been in the headlines in the 1970s, but it could not easily be used to sell genocide by getting the citizens of industrial nations to cut back on consumption. Something more drastic and personal was needed.'[14]

Likewise, it is now widely suspected that the once-popular 'hole in the ozone layer' public frenzy was at best a genuine misunderstanding of a natural process with little to do with man-made pollution (the hole periodically opens and closes by itself), and at worse was used as a deliberate deception to further not only the above agenda, but also to benefit industries that made billions from the introduction of CFC-free (chlorofluorocarbons) replacement technology.[15] If the report on the 1975 conference is accurate, it would explain much of the trajectory of climate propaganda we have seen since. It is interesting to note that just two years later the British TV faux-documentary *Alternative 3* posited the notion that government scientists were secretly planning to decamp to Mars and the Moon to escape devastating climate change caused by pollution.[16] Although quickly revealed as a spoof, many viewers felt that the program masked a genuine agenda, and if nothing else it unquestionably helped to seed fear of climate change in the public consciousness.

As for global cooling, as Mazel Hecht's conference report points out, it is true that just a few decades ago it was the environmental cooling model the public was being warned of. Yet many researchers still adhere to that former model, if for different scientific reasons. R Timothy Patterson, professor of geology and director of the Ottawa-Carleton Geoscience Center of Canada's Carleton University is another proponent of global cooling, stating:

'*CO_2 variations show little correlation with our planet's climate on long, medium and even short time scales... ...I and the first-class scientists I work with are consistently finding excellent correlations between the regular fluctuations of the Sun and Earthly climate.*

This is not surprising. The Sun and the stars are the ultimate source of energy on this planet... ...Solar scientists predict that, by 2020, the Sun will be starting into its weakest Schwabe cycle of the past two centuries, likely leading to unusually cool conditions on Earth... ...Solar activity has overpowered any effect that CO2 has had before, and it most likely will again... ...If we were to have even a medium-sized solar minimum, we could be looking at a lot more bad effects than 'global warming' would have had.' [17]

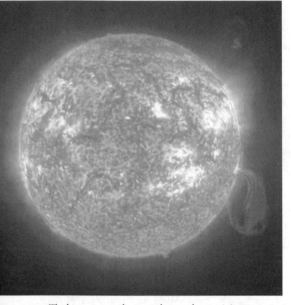

The biggest contributor to climate change..? An increasing number of scientists believe that unless we take solar cycles into the equation, we cannot truly understand what is happening. The Sun may influence far more than is being admitted to by mainstream sources.

NASA data on the very quiet sunspot activity of the most recent cycle and the notable reduction of solar irradiance and radio emissions [page 250] certainly points more towards a cooling process, rather than the opposite. Solar cycles are discussed further in the next chapter. Seemingly every year now, NASA releases new data that suggests that the Sun and its sunspot cycles and fluctuating magnetic fields, which are in the greatest state of unpredictability ever recorded, have a far more profound effect on Earth and its climate than anyone previously thought.

At this point in the debate the traditional evidence of melting ice caps and retreating glaciers, together with requisite tales of drowning polar bears and the suchlike (see the Gore ruling on page 229) are always held up as the final proof of man-made global warming. Ice melt does appear to be rapidly occurring in the north at least, although contrary, if controversial, reports of new ice sheets *forming* elsewhere don't receive the same level of media discussion. Doubters point to increased cloud cover and changing ocean currents stimulated by factors outside of our atmosphere (as proposed by the likes of Calder and Svensmark) as being equally likely to be responsible for the dwindling northern ice, rather than a general warming process. Funded academic dogma prevents broad discussion of such possibilities.

Even government scientists, however, accept that the melting of the Arctic cap (largely just floating pack ice) would not directly or significantly contribute to rising sea levels, despite widely-disseminated scares. The thawing of areas like the Greenland or Antarctic ice sheets would affect the seas more seriously, but the melt rate in these places is far less than at the North Pole and it could take millennia to generate the kind of major water rises often implied. [18] The media, ever simplistic for the sake of a sensational headline, would appear to have us believe otherwise, but exciting and apparently apocalyptic footage of collapsing ice is often attributable to nothing more than standard seasonal thaw.

Despite the mounting evidence for solar influences cooling Earth, a 2006 study in the peer-review journal *Nature* (sometimes accused of being the mouthpiece for official scientific propaganda and a shop window for global warming proponents) concluded that solar changes were 'unlikely' to have much effect on our climate. However, even that piece cautioned the following:

'Apart from solar brightness, more subtle influences on climate from cosmic rays or the Sun's ultraviolet radiation cannot be excluded, say the authors. They also add that these influences cannot be confirmed because physical models for such effects are still too poorly developed.' [19]

By 2013, the models were clearly improving, with prominent NASA writer Dr Tony Phillips stating unequivocally that even 'apparently tiny [solar] variations can have a significant effect on terrestrial climate'.[20] In other words, then, the climate change debate is far from being closed, yet the panic button has already been hit in favor of one theory.

Worriers say we cannot afford to wait to find out for sure what will happen to the climate, and that we must take a chance and act now to save the world from catastrophe—but this is all part of the huge fear and transference of guilt that has been placed upon us, to join all the other spirit-crushing pressures previously discussed. Shouldn't all sides of the debate at least be heard properly before drastic measures are introduced that could have even worse long-term detrimental effects if the mainstream has it wrong? Public doubt concerning the science of climate change should be taken more seriously than it is. People are not as stupid as some would have us believe, and tend to know when something isn't quite right. The polls suggest that the collective psyche (more tangible than is given credit for—Chapter XIV) is touching on an meaningful unease that needs addressing, not dismissing.

'Climategate' and the Media

What is very clear is that a proper debate on the paradoxes of climate science has not been allowed, despite it reaching higher levels of exposure than might have been expected. The official 2009 'Climategate' inquiry of the Science Assessment Panel into the Climatic Research Unit of the University of East Anglia, in which hacked emails appeared to indicate an attempt to dampen evidence that contradicted global warming, concluded that there was 'no evidence of any deliberate scientific malpractice'. However, the actual emails make plain that, at the very least, there was a distinctly disingenuous approach being employed, and a definite attempt to distract attention away from the 'Medieval Warm Period', an era of above-average temperatures in the North Atlantic and Arctic regions around 950-1250 AD that failed to generate any substantial ice cap melt.[21]

Other cover-ups and misrepresentations of potentially embarrassing climate data have been alleged, but the establishment now closes ranks quickly. The hold that a very specific seam of academia seems to have on the mainstream media (the BBC in particular) is so strong that, although global warming dissent has been acknowledged, the space given to it has been limited and the choice of dissenters aired often questionable, focused more on impassioned celebrities or fringe elements rather than the qualified scientists with serious evidence to present. More recently, the rise of the Tea Party in the US has also created the opportunity to unfairly skew attention onto the far-right elements of global warming questioning, concerned more with economics than science.

The Energy Crisis

A few more successive years of falling temperatures will make it far harder to keep the global warming bubble alive and it will be interesting to see just how much longer the official position can stay skewed towards one polarity if temperatures don't begin a substantial—and sustained—rise soon. Some countries are also facing a potential energy crisis within a decade, as carbon-producing power stations are phased out to meet severe greenhouse gas targets. Experts are predicting that replacement technology (some renewables, but much of it nuclear) is unlikely to be ready in time to meet the 'energy gap', and the nuclear option is now looking rather less attractive in the wake of the aforementioned Japanese tsunami. How tolerant families gathered around candles in stone-cold rooms will be towards all the highbrow talk of saving the planet for future generations remains to be seen and may render all the carbon debates redundant. Many people will happily lobby for all the old dirty energies again rather than freeze, in the same way that the austerity mindset has already left some of the higher ideals on the shelf for all the political noise on climate change. Likewise, the developing world, now leaping ahead with new technological industries, appears reluctant to put long term global environmental prospects ahead of the quality of life *now*, as the continued failure of international summits to forge any meaningful pledges makes clear.

Human beings are not used to thinking long-term, and, perhaps unfortunately, there seems little prospect of this changing any time soon. No amount of bleeding-heart Western green thinking and the wish for a return to a world of 'clip-clopping horses' (as one green pundit once eulogized on radio) is going to change the thinking of upcoming civilizations headed in the opposite direction. With only very limited climate protection being predicted to result from even the most drastic carbon emission cuts, other solutions beyond enforced energy fasting and abstinence are therefore going to have to be found to turn things around even if man-made global warming is accepted as a reality. Proponents of 'free-energy' and cleaner technologies, promised by some to be just around the corner but reputedly held back by governments and oil companies (trying to squeeze the last drops of economical control from the formerly dominant mineral slime) claim that such solutions will indeed be forthcoming. Unfortunately, some of the current solutions seem instead to include the much-hailed 'fracking' for shale gas or oil, an only slightly less carbon-rich process promised to bring long years of supply, but one which genuinely risks poisoning drinking water—as has already been seen in the US—and upsetting the seismological equilibrium.[22] Some truthseekers have even suggested the entire global warming scare has been deliberately created to lay a path for these kinds of lucrative 'alternatives', or for the cleaner ones that may eventually follow, but in a way that ensures the industrial-military complexes retain the sole right to develop them.

Common Sense Preservation

In debating and challenging some of the confusing data on climate change, this is *not* to say that we shouldn't be making every effort to protect the planet from pollution and environmental destruction, regardless of where temperature curves do or don't take us. Respecting Mother Nature, preserving the rain forests and cleaning up the air, land and seas with wisdom and a sensible balance of priorities is plainly necessary—and sheer common sense. However, the understandable urgency some green campaigners feel in wanting to avoid dangerous

Questioning global warming does not equate to questioning the need to preserve places like the rain forests or having no concerns over pollution, as is sometimes falsely implied by green dogmatists. Few people deny climate change—it is the man-made global warming model that is challenged.

climate swings has led to an unfortunate situation where people are becoming divided into unhealthy factions and, without question, yet more fear and antipathy is being used to force change instead of encouraging positive forward-thinking.

No sane person questions that the environment and its resources (especially water) must be protected. Dealing with the alarmingly rapid vanishing of wildlife and the increasing acidification of oceans, for example, should be a serious priority. However, all the while man-made global warming is held up by governments and the mainstream as the sole primary issue of our times (besides terrorism) without convincing proof, it remains that people's genuine care for the planet is being abused to justify all manner of heavy taxes, reduced circumstances and restrictive legislation that could turn out to be unnecessary, while leaving potentially more important issues under-addressed. Unless a new clean technology *is* unexpectedly revealed and sanctioned, it is not too difficult to imagine these restrictions eventually manifesting as a general constraint on global movement, as air journeys (Lord Turner of the British Committee on Climate Change has openly called for personal flights to be rationed)[23] and possibly even road trips become prohibitively expensive (and morally frowned upon) to all but the elite few. Note the number of rock stars who flew vast entourages around the world at great expense and with vast carbon outputs to tick us all off about global warming at the *Live Earth* concerts of 2007. Al Gore's 'carbon footprint' is also

rumored to be one of the largest amongst touring celebrities. Yet everyday folk are being discouraged from free movement. Even if global warming is eventually proven and lifestyle restrictions can be shown to be an absolute requirement, the ugly and authoritarian manner by which these changes are currently being forced upon us feels wrong, and a much lighter approach is needed.

What, though, of all the independent scientists and researchers who see natural causes such as solar cycles and cosmic rays (not to mention huge carbon emissions from volcanoes) as being the prime drivers of climate change, be it global warming or cooling? Why are they not listened to more? Tellingly, the natural cause lobby—and this may be key to the current imbalance in the debate—does not offer the political benefits of the man-made greenhouse gas camp; for if in truth we are at the mercy of celestial

Our Earth—a place worth looking after, because there's nowhere else to go. But our desire to save it shouldn't be used to justify dubious restrictions in the name of very uncertain evidence.

cycles outside of our immediate control, then no action on Earth will make much difference to what is going to happen. Financial incentives and social controls would be lost if this were ever admitted, and the risk of panic and despair setting in amongst the populace would become very real. Which is perhaps why the establishment is reluctant to discuss the alternative view on climate change.

The Control Agenda Unfolds

Here, perhaps, is where we begin to see the control agenda unfolding into something concrete. As already touched on, and as the next chapter explores in more detail, what if the true overseers behind the scenes are aware of, or fear, some impending and enormous shift, of which climate change, whatever its real cause, may be a simple precursor? If they even suspect that something might be about to occur which could upset the old order and risk unseating their long-entrenched positions of authority, they would presumably want to insure against this happening. Perhaps this explains the policies of control. We have explored in earlier chapters the prophecies and predictions for these times, which have come through from many sources, psychic, celestial and religious, and are subscribed to by influential political and spiritual leaders. These people will not take any chances on losing their hold on us.

A happy, go-ahead, independent society is much harder to keep under one umbrella of containment, and far harder to manipulate. The conspiracy view holds that to maintain the necessary restraints, every effort must be made to keep us distracted, docile and down, even if that means implementing draconian measures of limitation and surveillance and binding us in a state of fear (the actual title of a 2004 Michael Crichton novel, which heavily questions global warming and posits that the concept was created purely as a social crowbar).[24] For many years, fear of nuclear war, legitimate or not,[25] was plainly used as a political tool, and it appeared to suit authorities for entire generations to grow up in deep terror of imminent incineration. But with atomic apocalypse no longer seen as such a huge threat (although the souped-up campaigns against Russia and the nuclear programs of Iran and North Korea tap into this nostalgia), and with terrorism not quite enough in itself, the warping of climate concerns and the unease over the current global economic crisis may be designed to exacerbate a new all-encompassing fear as a further justification of social restrictions to keep us in our place, as the unfolding 'Agenda 21' project ('green solutions' masking harsh control schemes) seems to suggest. Rationing both travel and the availability of unlimited energy (in the name of saving the planet) would help with this. Meanwhile, restraining access to better health and reducing natural immunity while force-feeding us junk food, junk TV and dubious chemicals, dulls the senses and takes away our spark, leaving a malleable and defenseless population.

Again, could things really be this bad? Let's hope not. But if there is the slightest danger of such an outcome developing, even on a small scale, then it would be wise to look seriously at the possibility and make efforts to prevent such a nightmare from becoming a reality. If, as the name of a leading truth website has it, we are indeed in danger of becoming a 'prison planet', then it is time to stand up for freedom. The last part of this book explores the optimistic view that we can, and will.

Why, however, do things seem to be coming to a head now, of all times? It is necessary at this point, then, to explore more fully the prophecies for the 'New Era'.

THE TRUTH AGENDA: *Legitimate environmental concerns are being abused to create more fear and restriction, setting people against each other and undermining societal cohesion, despite attempts to build 'green' communities. We must clearly preserve our world with enlightened policies, but carbon propaganda threatens to restrict both freedom of spirit and movement, while the panic prematurely compromising our energy infrastructure could plunge us into literal darkness. Global warming has been unfairly presented as an unarguable absolute, when other climate factors may speak of an impending cosmic influence—which may explain why a ruling elite would want to ensure it retains its grip on us all.*

Sunrise from the air, beautiful to see. Yet the Sun could be one of the very factors that could dramatically alter life on Earth, and its current erratic behavior might be part of the changes alluded to in the ancient prophecies for these times.

XII THE NEW ERA

Across the world, a number of ancient cultures have calendrical systems, prophecies or traditions that point very clearly to the notion that the world has entered a 'New Era', one which began back in December 2012. This date was widely misrepresented as an end-of-the-world prediction, but in truth it was always taken by many serious researchers to represent the beginning *of a period of huge global transition and a shift of consciousness, one which would take time to unfold. This means that the significance of the ancient time cycle remains relevant and that the speculation surrounding the prophecies still matters, especially given the recent and clear acceleration of world events. So what exactly might this New Era bring, and what have the predictions said about these times? Whatever transpires, the reality is that the anticipation surrounding the turning of the ancient time cycle has stimulated a new awakening process in many people. Are those dominating forces in places of power aware of the potential for an upsetting of the old order, and therefore trying to create a world that cannot fall from their grasp?*

Millennial Transference

In the 1990s decade running-up to the Millennium, along with the requisite religious fervor and anticipation for the long-awaited Day of Judgement, esoteric seekers began to look for other tangible evidence that might give genuine meaning to all the prophecies and predictions. Curiously, two convincing possibilities duly presented themselves, although the second would take a little longer to percolate.

Most prominently, a sloppy formatting limitation in computer programs raised wide fears of a technological apocalypse, rather than a religious one, in the form of the so-called 'Millennium Bug'. Developed without foresight of commercial computing's rapid proliferation, the standard electronic brain's inability to recognize a new century raised the widely-feared specter that the first tick into the year 2000 might bring a mass-shutdown of an entire civilization, with computers crashing in turn across the time-zones. Although the real Millennium actually occurred in 2001 (2000 technically being the last year of the previous one), it was 2000 that mattered as far as the computers were concerned, as years were generally denoted with just two digits in their core programming. What if they thought '00' meant 1900? What would occur? Doom-laden predictions of power grid meltdowns and frozen databases paralyzing the infrastructure of society were all lugubriously speculated on, sometimes gleefully by the end-timers or extremist green campaigners planning their return to a romantic feudalism. Planes might plummet from the skies and food distribution could grind to a halt. Many larders and cellars were well-stocked by that New Year's Eve, with a wide expectation of the end of life as we knew it.

When the crisis failed to materialize—or enough work was done by panicked programers to avert disaster—a strange kind of restlessness set in amongst those alternately relieved or disappointed. Was that it? No global catastrophe nor heavenly trumpets. While cynics speculated that the whole panic had been a massive scam to promote the sales of new 'Bug-free' hardware, others turned their attention to trying to work out what it was deep down in the collective that still seemed unresolved. A nagging sense of an impending *something* still remained. Had it all just been wild paranoia, or had the echo of another imminent but later event simply been brought forward to the Millennium by our cultural fascination with significant numbers?

At this point, interest began to gather around the second most tangible possibility that might explain all this intuitive anticipation—the prophecies for a New Era,

promised to begin at the end of 2012. Increasingly discussed as the 1990s progressed, their potential significance had been somewhat eclipsed by the millennial angst. With the year 2000 safely cleared, perhaps a greater clarity could now be reached on possible events twelve years later. Thus began the rise in awareness, first amongst the usual demographic of mysteries enthusiasts and truthseekers, then slowly but surely amongst a more general populace, of the '2012' phenomenon, which grew day by day as the significant moment in that year approached. Long tracts

As the Millennium celebrations exploded across the time zones, many breathed sighs of relief—or disappointment—as the much-vaunted computer 'Millennium Bug' failed to bring civilization to its knees. But a sense of expectation still remained.

were written about the many possible scenarios that might unfold, and opinion began to divide into those who expected instant disaster and those who saw it as a far more positive and subtle 'shift of the age' which might take time to manifest fully. Even popular culture latched on, in documentaries and disaster movies, hampering, as much as enhancing, comprehension of something that might have genuine meaning in the real world.

Inevitably, then, when the key cycle-turning date of 21st December 2012 passed without any tangible event, the media, which had gleefully promoted awareness of the prophecies in the immediate run-up to it, scoffed accordingly, while those seekers expecting some kind of instant enlightenment either turned away from the whole phenomenon in abject disappointment or had to reassess their expectations of the New Era and its schedule. The more reflective scholars of the time cycle, however, nodded sagely, now seeing more clearly the knowledge that remained of true value for the period ahead, and what could be left behind as essentially belated millennial angst. For certain, many of the unfulfilled predictions are forgotten at our peril.

The Key Prophetic Elements

The essential component of the New Era beliefs runs thus: a number of ancient cultures, most prominently the Maya (see below), developed complex calendrical systems, which appear to have been based on an observational cycle of some recurring phenomenon, probably astronomical in origin. Although there are some disputes as to the exact date, most reliable researchers (fully taking into account historical alterations to calendars and remembering to include a year zero between 1 BC and 1 AD) agree that this cycle came to a close, and began again, on the winter solstice of 21st December 2012, which occurred—fascinatingly, given the mystical significance which some people attach to these numbers—at precisely 11.11 AM, Universal Time.[1] (Many meditations and tune-ins were held across the world at sacred sites and in spiritual circles at this precise moment to inject positive intention into the collective consciousness, something which can only have done good.)

The same time cycle is recorded by a number of independent cultures around the world, in calendars, folklore and tradition. On the other side of the world from the Maya, for instance, important elements of the same cycle can be found as a prominent part of the King Wen sequence in the *I Ching*, or 'Book of Changes', the Chinese divinatory oracle.

Some of these cultures attached prophecies to this cyclical time-period, which speak of significant changes occurring to the planet and its peoples around or following the time of each calendrical transition. More contemporary sources, divined through spiritual, psychic or other means [Chapter IV] have added their own weight of speculation as to how these changes might manifest. Although no agreement has ever been reached as to exactly what will transpire from hereon, it is hard to dismiss the essential fact that there is an unusual amount of cross-referencing as regards the New Era cycle, which sets the phenomenon apart from the routine cult or evangelical predictions that so often come and go without solid grounds or fulfilment.

The Maya Calendar

The most substantial and oft-referenced source on the ancient time cycle derives from the wisdom of the Maya people, who were most diligent in recording it. In the last decade or so there has been a massive growth of interest, particularly amongst New Agers, in the culture that flourished in what is now essentially Mexico and Central America ('Mesoamerica') between 250 and 900 AD. Despite cultural attempts (not least in Mel Gibson's 2006 film *Apocalypto*) to characterize the Maya as a savage, degenerate race, they were in truth remarkably sophisticated in many ways, and developed highly accurate calendrical systems, apparently based on observations of the sky.

Those who wish to understand the highly complex workings of the Maya calendar must investigate elsewhere, and are referred to the indispensable work of Geoff Stray and John Major Jenkins (see *Appendix 3*). However, in essence, the Maya counts comprise a series of three intersecting systems, the Haab (a 365-day calendar), the

Tzolkin (a 260-day calendar) and, most crucially, the Long Count (a more convoluted calendar of cycles within cycles, most prominently comprising thirteen 'baktuns', or one 'Sun'). The counts originated from the earlier Olmec civilization and were developed as the centuries went by. What matters here is that the exact start date of the all-important Long Count, or 13-baktun Sun cycle, equating to 5,125 of our Gregorian years, has now been accurately calculated based on the workings of all three systems—giving us a precise end point. As Geoff Stray explains:

'It is now clear, after almost a century of disagreement among Maya specialists, that the Creation of the current Sun—the start-point of the 13-baktun cycle—equates to 11th August 3114 BC... ...replaced by the next Creation on 21st December 2012.' [2]

All of which means that we have now entered the next Sun. In itself, this should never have given any more cause for alarm than opening a calendar for a new year would. However, the fascination grew with the many predictions, ancient and modern, associated with this process, leading to much speculation as to what it was about the cycle, beyond its plainly astronomical basis, that was thought important enough to record with such accuracy.

One correlation, as first discovered and outlined by John Major Jenkins in his book *Maya Cosmogenesis 2012*, is very clear. Because of a periodic wobble in the Earth's tilt (which produces the cycle known as 'precession'), every 25,625 years the winter solstice Sun, as seen from our planet, significantly aligns itself over the exact center of the galactic equator, the 'dark rift' of our Milky Way. This is an area where fewer stars are visible due to interstellar dust, but equates to being our viewpoint of the central 'nuclear bulge' of our own galaxy. The Long Count of the Maya is a fifth of this period—5,125 years—and appears to have recorded this process of 'galactic alignment' (as Jenkins calls it). The Sun entered the alignment zone once again in 1980. Because it takes 36 years to precess through this part of the sky, it effectively stood at the precise center of the rift in 1998, but 21st December 2012 was the year specifically defined by the Maya calendar as the special moment for reasons still not yet understood.

Was it just the Sun's movement into a notable position that was recorded in the Maya calendrical systems, with merely astrological and esoteric implications, or was it somehow known that when this point in the galactic alignment process was reached that something more tangible also began to occur? On pages 253-254 we explore some possibilities as to why the Maya may have thought it mattered. But firstly, what are the much spoken-of Maya predictions themselves?

The Maya Prophecies

Despite all the fuss that has been made about the 'Maya prophecies', there is actually remarkably little exact information to be gleaned from true Maya sources about

Maya temple at Chichen Itza, Mexico. Although there are not as many prophecies as people think, the Maya beliefs concerning the New Era are still the most publicized, and the accompanying calendars remain the most complex and best-kept of any ancient system in the world.

what was expected to happen in the new 'Sun'. The clues that do exist, although much held back from circulation by mainstream archaeologists, keen to avoid any doom-mongering taint from mystical New Agers, nonetheless seem to indicate a clear Maya belief that something of great significance would occur. Carvings on 'Monument 6' at Tortuguero in Mexico are the only contemporary references (i.e. made while the Maya were at their height) discovered so far to record what was anticipated to occur at the switchover of the old 'Creation' into the new (on 21st December 2012) and refer to the apparently momentous descent of the 'Nine Support Gods'. Exasperatingly, damage to the carved glyphs denies us a full explanation of what the nine gods would do once here.

The more apocalyptic of the Maya prophecies can be found in much later records, largely in the writings of Chilam Balam, compiled by the 'Jaguar Priests', shaman-seers from Yucatán. Although not written down until the late 1500s, they record (in Maya language, but using European script) the traditional beliefs of the Maya and include the following in the book of *Tizimin*:

'In the final days of misfortune, in the final days of tying up the bundle of the thirteen katuns [baktuns] on 4 Ahau, then the end of the world shall come and the katun of our fathers will ascend on high... ...These valleys of the Earth shall come to an end. For those katuns there shall be no priests, and no one who believes in his government without having doubts... I recount to you the words of the true gods, when they shall come.'

There follows a colorful description of wars waged, destruction, a ravaging of the land and wild weather, during which the nine gods 'arise in sorrow'. Put together with the above references to a loss of faith in governments and priests, and all the not dissimilar themes in St John's Revelation and other religious texts, it's clear to see why some people believe this may indeed be the stage we are at in the world today.

Why, though, should we give credence to the Maya prophecies above other obscure oracles? The meticulous precision with which the time cycle was recorded initially sets it apart from more woolly soothsaying, but it is the remarkable amount of secondary sources that make the New Era prophecies unusually compelling.

Other Historical Predictions

The Aztecs—often mixed up with the Maya but actually a later Mesoamerican civilization that flourished from the 12th century before being destroyed by the Spanish in the 1500s—derived their calendrical systems from the earlier Maya system, but added their own nuances and prophecies, and awaited the return of their god Quetzalcoatl (or Kukulcan), the feathered serpent (believed by some researchers to have been a comet). The famous carved wheel, the Aztec Sunstone or Calendar Stone, for example, represents the five ages of the world, the Aztecs' own take on the Suns of the Maya. Rectangular panels display the four previous Suns, while at the center is shown the fifth and now past era—believed by the Aztecs to have been the very final Sun. [Geoff Stray has claimed that the Sunstone may have been based on the design of an original version with moving parts, and a remarkable animation he has prepared, still available on his website *www.diagnosis2012.co.uk*, as good as proves this.] Were the Aztecs merely wrong, or, again, do modern minds have too simplistic an expectation as to how long the passing of an era really takes?

The Aztecs recorded that each of the previous four Suns ended in some kind of epic disaster—flood; an eclipse accompanied by the descent of flesh-eating demons; volcanoes; and wind. Unfortunately, the demons, or *tzitzimime*, were expected to return again to mark the end of the fifth and last Sun, which means that they, or whatever they really symbolize, could still arrive any year now if a long accuracy allowance is made.

Other cultures, often, though not exclusively, from North and South America, held similar views. The Peruvian Incas predicted that the *pachakuti* or 'turning over' of the world and time would occur in the transition of the cycle, while the Hopi Native Americans of Arizona have been awaiting the arrival of the 'Blue Star Kachina'

Comet Holmes in 2007, colored blue in actuality. At its peak, its gas 'coma' was bigger than the diameter of the Sun. The Hopi believe that the arrival of a blue star heralds great change—was this the very 'star'?

just before the 'Emergence', heralded by a time of the 'great purification'. Many observers believe that the blue-tinged Comet Holmes, which spectacularly entered our solar system in 2007 (its 'coma' gases expanding to a diameter bigger than the Sun), fulfilled the prophecy of the blue star, and some tribal elders believe that the purification process has been occurring since then. Other North American and Mexican tribes have very similar traditions.

If all the prophecies heralded from the Americas, they could, perhaps, simply be written off as word-of-mouth repetition from one original source. Yet, as we have already seen, the ancient Chinese recorded the same precession time cycle in the *I Ching*, and even as far away as New Zealand the Maoris believed that the Earth and Sky, broken apart during the Creation, would begin to come back together again from 2012. This period marks the time when '*Ka hinga te arai*'—'the curtain will fall', or, as a recent rediscovery of the original translation has it, 'the veil will dissolve'. On yet another continent, some African Zulu shamans are expecting the appearance of 'Mu-sho-sho-no-no', a star with a long tail that in previous ages turned the world upside down and caused a deluge (ancient flood stories are rife in almost every civilization's legends). This star was expected to return in the 'year of the red bull', which was 2012. An error, or could a number of significant comets discovered that year have been Mu-sho-sho-no-no? Some researchers have also equated it with Nibiru, the lost planet of the gods [page 86], the imminent arrival of which some say has been covered up by authorities.

This is just a very small selection of the many connected prophecies from all manner of tribes and cultures, which, when calculated into our Gregorian calendar (again, fully allowing for historical adjustments), all seem to focus on the period beginning in 2012 or thereabouts as being of great significance. Many religious texts and cycles, in virtually all the Abrahamic faiths, and in Hindu and Buddhist traditions, have their own associations. Although there is no accordance as to exactly what will transpire or how long it will take to do so—years, decades or centuries?— it seems that the multiple foretellings nonetheless represent an important sense of expectation embedded deep in the collective mind. There have also been more contemporary visions, which may shed light on the New Era phenomenon.

Modern Prophetic Insights

In addition to the historical predictions, there have been all manner of revelations in recent years that point to some kind of significance for these times, many of which have been reached without foreknowledge of the prophecies. A number of people have become cognisant of the period's significance through 'altered state' experiences, either through imbibing hallucinogenic substances or via unplanned shifts of consciousness during out-of-body experiences on operating tables or after head injuries or lightning strikes. From these have come several vivid visions that something huge might be about to occur.

Shamanic experiences have also revealed valuable insights. It was while imbibing the South American hallucinogenic brew Ayahuasca [page 255] in the early 1970s, for instance, that the brothers Terence and Dennis McKenna gained a realization that the *I Ching* represents a fractal 'timewave' of important historical moments (or 'an unfolding pattern of every event that ever happens', as Geoff Stray puts it) —reaching its key infinity point in 2012. The timewave graph, created by taking the

THE TRUTH AGENDA

mathematical content of the *I Ching* and matching it with important historical events, shows peaks of 'novelty' and troughs of 'habit', resembling a fractal mountain range of human developments that, from the late 1960s, curiously starts to descend towards a point of maximum novelty. Based on all the previous information, a computer-predicted projection was that it would suddenly hit the baseline on 17th November 2012 and flatline from thereon as important events simply became the norm. This is close enough to the Maya Creation date to be eerily uncanny—yet at the time of formulating their theory, the McKennas had no knowledge of the ancient prophecies.

The final sequence of the McKenna 'timewave' —the peaks and troughs mark times of historical significance ('novelty') or mundanity ('habit'). Repeating fractal patterns seem to arise from this process, but mysteriously the projected future wave collapsed completely as it approached 2012 [magnified].

We have already seen how a great number of psychics and mediums have received information about the importance of these times. Several entirely unexplained key crop formations have also made direct references to the time cycle,[3] and some claimed UFO abductees such as Jon King [page 48] were given insights that the years around 2012 would be crucial ones for humanity. Those who practice 'remote viewing', in which information on places or people can be gained through clairvoyant techniques (much explored in military experiments), have also tried to divine knowledge of the past and future. However, attempts to view past 2012 often used to fail, as if some kind of psychic barrier prevented insights into the exact nature of the New Era which followed it. Perhaps we will begin to see more clearly now as its years progress.

It is not the place of this book to be a comprehensive compendium of these theories. The curious should read Geoff Stray's seminal *Beyond 2012: Catastrophe or Ecstasy* for that. Although the year has passed, much of the information remains highly relevant. But the impression should be clearly conveyed by these brief examples alone that there does seem to be something oddly mesmerizing about all the intersecting threads that have woven this strange tapestry of expectation.

What, then, is the New Era phenomenon really all about? Will any one very tangible thing ever happen, and if so will it be a positive or negative experience? Will it instead be a growing convergence of world events which will bring people to a new consciousness through an unavoidable but necessary discernment and coping process? Could it all, perhaps, be just so much hysteria, a phantom somehow born through a deeply buried collective awareness of obscure ancient traditions, but with no real substance? Or is a verifiable phenomenon about to make a significant manifestation, knowledge of which has been bubbling up through myth, symbolism and archetype for aeons?

Cosmic Waves

There have been many possibilities put forward to account for what was being recorded by the ancients in the many variations of the time cycle. Most students of prophecy agree that some kind of astronomical factor seems likely, especially given the galactic alignment correlation. Some are betting on esoteric elements coming into play, such as the aforementioned return of the planet Nibiru, but although unsubstantiated sightings and huge cover-ups have been claimed, there don't appear to be any unusually large celestial bodies currently approaching (which surely would have been shouted by amateur astronomers by now, even if authorities kept quiet). Incoming comets and asteroids on huge elliptical orbits, causing gravitational or climate effects, have been cited as more likely agents of change, whilst hyperactive solar cycles and periodic shifts in the Earth's tilt have been equally discussed. However, reasoned explanations as to why the Sun or Earth should by themselves suddenly behave out of character have been lacking. At least until recently.

Of all the theories under discussion, one does appear to keep raising its head, an all-encompassing concept that could explain recent observable changes in our celestial neighborhood. This concerns the idea that our entire solar system, forever in motion with the rest of the Milky Way (and synchronous with the galactic alignment cycle), is moving into an energetically charged region of space.

The persuasive qualities of this hypothesis do not necessarily mean that it is the correct one. However, it would explain many current developments in our region of space and is worth discussion here. The Sun, especially, has been more active in the last decade or so than it has been since records of its activity began—more so, perhaps, than for thousands of years—although it has been going through an uncannily quiet period in recent times, as we shall see. Together with other compelling evidence, cosmic dust levels recorded in ice core samples taken from deep beneath Greenland and Antarctica,[4] and analyzed by Dr Paul LaViolette and other researchers, suggest that we periodically experience the passing of galactic or cosmic 'waves', pulsing out from the center of our galaxy as a result of 'galactic core explosions'. As they transit through

Galaxy NGC 4414, not unlike our own Milky Way. Dr Paul LaViolette believes that energetic pulses periodically emanate from the centers of galaxies, sending out shockwaves that change the behavior of stars as they pass through. We may now be entering such a cosmic wave.

space, it is postulated that these vast shockwaves energetically excite stars, causing an increase in the frequency and intensity of solar flares and giving rise to disrupted sunspot cycles—phenomena which our Sun has been experiencing in recent times.

The wave pattern identified by LaViolette operates on a 26,000-year and/or halfway 13,000-year schedule, and may account for the varying wobble of the Earth's tilt, which creates the cycle of precession and gives us the aforementioned galactic alignment cycle, as well as playing a possible role in a number of mass-extinction events in our prehistory. Calculating on this basis means, happily, that we are not currently due for a major event ('superwave') at this time, but less severe galactic core explosions do seem to occur at more frequent intervals, which are still being studied—a pattern which may be embedded into the ancient calendars. It may be that we are now experiencing the beginning of a transit through one of these lesser—but still significant—waves. (Cosmic wave theory may also account for the supposed coming of the otherwise rather unscientific and misnamed 'photon belt' spoken of in some classic channelled information).

Given that *all* the planets in our solar system have recently been experiencing significant changes (rising temperatures, fluctuating brightness, changes in atmospheric densities and magnetic fields, new thin atmospheres developing around both Mercury and the Moon, and Mars undergoing ice cap melt are just a few of the effects), the behavior of our Sun is a strong candidate as being the common factor here. Scientists who deny that solar cycles can significantly affect the Earth's climate might like to investigate further. But the Sun itself is probably at the mercy of a wider influence, and cosmic waves seem like a good explanation.

The most complex solar coronal mass ejection (CME) yet recorded, 4th January 2002 (seen here in a NASA composite image). The Sun has broken records for activity in recent years, although the current cycle has been unexpectedly quiet.

Solar Activity

Sunspots (areas of intense magnetic activity, which appear relatively darker than the rest of the Sun's surface) run in eleven-year cycles (a period sometimes known as the Schwabe Cycle), peaking in number (solar maximum) at each end of the cycle, and falling back to none or very few (solar minimum) in the middle, as the Sun's natural rotation and other factors give rise to a regular pattern of convection anomalies.[5] Sunspots are associated with the manifestation of flares and 'coronal mass ejections' (CMEs), which throw out voluminous amounts of material and radiation into space, enveloping our entire solar system in a large protective bubble known as the 'heliosphere'. Solar activity can have profound effects on our planet. Particularly strong ejections can cause communications problems on Earth and disrupt electrical power grids. They also generate the *aurora borealis/australis*, or northern/southern lights, at the poles, as charged particles collide in the ionosphere.

Even if the cosmic wave theory is set aside, it remains that the Sun has until recently displayed a sharp upsurge of activity. Occurrences of sunspots have been on a notable rise since they were first properly monitored, with the requisite increase in CMEs and other coronal effects. Although there has been a slight fall in solar activity since the 1960s (in line with the general trend of a rising and falling wider cycle), the overall trajectory has been an upward one. According to David Hathaway of the Marshall Space Flight Center, 'four of the five biggest cycles on record have come in the past fifty years', and on 4th November 2003 the largest flare ever observed (an unheard of 'X-45' in a scale that was never expected to exceed X-20 when it was developed) broke all records and expectations by being more than twice the size of anything

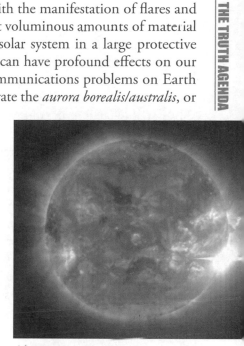

A heavily filtered view of the most powerful solar flare ever seen, 4th November 2003 - an 'X-45' on a scale that only previously went up to X-20. If one of these were to occur while aimed at Earth, our entire power infrastructure could be knocked out.

previously recorded. Given this kind of behavior, could the tribal prophecies of the arrival of stars with long 'tails' and the suchlike be referring not to the coming of a new body into our solar system, but to a changed appearance of our own star?

For some years, NASA was predicting, from computer modelling and statistical analysis of previous solar cycles, that the current 'Cycle 24' would be one of the most active sunspot periods seen in modern times. However, it has instead been very quiet. In 2008, no sunspots were seen on 266 days of the year, the least since 1913, and although activity did then pick up, it remains overall the most subdued cycle since 1823. This led NASA and the National Oceanic and Atmospheric Administration (NOAA) to move the expected peak of the cycle to 2013 and to forecast a 'below-average' number of sunspots, with the caveat that 'even a below-average cycle is capable of producing severe space weather', but when it arrived the peak was still hesitant to get going, leading some scientists to wonder if this was the start of a longer and much quieter wider cycle.[6]

Interestingly, periods of quiet sunspot activity have been associated with very cold spells for Earth's climate. The 'Maunder Minimum' of the 17th century, in which sunspot counts fell to very few for a long stretch, seemed to begin a time known as the 'Little Ice Age', a spate of bitterly cold winters between 1650-1850, the source of all the Christmas card paintings showing skaters on European rivers. Given this, perhaps those academics predicting global cooling rather than global warming [previous chapter] may yet be proved right. In 2009, NASA also released figures that showed a drop in solar irradiance—a 0.02% reduction at visible wavelengths, but a substantial 6% fall in the ultraviolet spectrum—reducing in turn the heating of the Earth's upper atmosphere. Radio emissions from the Sun also fell to their lowest level since 1955.[7] Is this an ongoing trend into another Maunder Minimum-type period— or the calm before a storm, as some scientists think? Huge solar flares can still occur in quiet periods and NASA itself has now given out several stark warnings that the current cycle might produce some particularly dangerous events. Thus alerted to the solar anomalies, even the mass-media has warned of the possibility of a massive flare that could take human society back to a new dark age by knocking out our electricity grids and technological infrastructure with an electromagnetic wave. If something like the 1859 'Carrington Event' flare, which sparked off aurorae across the whole planet, occurred today with our super-reliance on technology, the continued stability of our civilization would be in severe jeopardy. In 2010, NASA launched its 'Solar Shield' initiative to help cope with such an event, and high-level talks were held with Western governments, but the world is nowhere near as prepared as it should be.[8]

Whether it is a period of hugely increased solar activity ahead, or a notable quietening, the likelihood is that we are entering a cyclical anomaly, which is indicative of a noteworthy change in our local celestial backyard, one that may affect all life on Earth. If we are indeed passing through the energetic shock-wave of a galactic core explosion, the theory offers one possibility as to why this change may be so marked, beyond the usual solar cycles. The same process may well be affecting not only us, but our entire heliosphere.

Fluctuations in the Heliosphere

With material from the Sun being ejected to the furthest reaches of the solar system, the protective shell it creates acts as a shield against some of the more unwelcome cosmic rays and radiation pouring out into space from other stars and active celestial bodies. Yet the heliosphere has itself been behaving rather oddly, again reflecting apparent changes in our Sun.

The heliosphere pushes against the interstellar wind like a ship ploughing through the sea. Its passage through space even leaves an energetic bow-wave, with its edge known as the 'heliopause' [see diagram]. Yet Russian studies have shown that the boundary of the heliosphere, the 'termination shock', has increased in thickness by around an astonishing 1000% since the 1960s, suggesting a development of great significance. The Siberian geologist Dr Alexey Dmitriev believes the solar system is currently moving through a 'magnetized cloud of plasma' (presumably part of the cosmic wave), which is adhering to its edge to create the thickening. Dmitriev holds that this plasma (a partially ionized gas with a proportion of free electrons, known as an important 'state of matter') is the cause of so many of the changes we are seeing. He points to a notable increase of plasma in the Earth's ionosphere (the highest layer of our atmosphere), which may be affecting our weather and contributing to an accelerating process of 'geomagnetic reversal' [see below].

Conversely, recent NASA studies have reported that, despite the apparent thickening of the termination shock, the heliosphere itself is weakening at a dramatic rate and thus beginning to shrink in diameter. In 2008, data from the Ulysses spacecraft, which orbits the poles of the Sun, confirmed that the solar wind had decreased in general magnetic pressure by 20% since the previous solar cycle (and by an astonishing 36% in the immediate vicinity of the craft itself), making it the lowest reading since records began fifty years ago. By 2011, it had fallen even lower.[9] As a result of this retraction, the Pioneer and Voyager craft, sent out

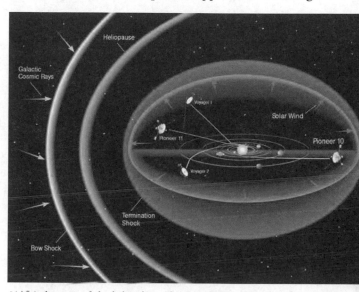

NASA diagram of the heliosphere, the protective bubble around our solar system exuded by the Sun, which ploughs through space creating a kind of bow wave ('bow shock'). In recent years the heliosphere has been shrinking, suggesting that we may be passing through a cosmic wave.

in the 1970s, are beginning to exit the heliosphere far earlier than expected. Even usually cautious NASA scientists have expressed concern that this reduced cosmic protection could make us far more vulnerable to high-energy interstellar influence, and others have speculated that this might be a factor affecting our climate (the latter point played down by official sources, as ever).

Our own local protective fields are not even as secure as was previously believed. Also in 2008, the THEMIS (Time History of Events and Macroscale Interactions during Substorms) fleet of five NASA spacecraft detected a tendency of the Earth's magnetic field to admit solar particles at completely unexpected times—therefore allowing far more in than had been previously calculated. The official NASA website describes the findings thus:

'Our magnetic field is a leaky shield and the number of particles breaching this shield depends on the orientation of the Sun's magnetic field. It had been thought that when

the Sun's magnetic field is aligned with that of the Earth, the door is shut and that few if any solar particles enter Earth's magnetic shield. The door was thought to open up when the solar magnetic field direction points opposite to Earth's field, leading to more solar particles inside the shield. Surprisingly, recent observations by the THEMIS spacecraft fleet demonstrate that the opposite is true. "Twenty times more solar particles cross the Earth's leaky magnetic shield when the Sun's magnetic field is aligned with that of the Earth compared to when the two magnetic fields are oppositely directed," said Marit Oieroset of the University of California, Berkeley, lead author of one of two papers on this research, published May 2008 in Geophysical Research Letters. *Researchers have long suspected that this "closed door" entry mechanism might exist, but didn't know how important it was. "It's as if people knew there was a crack in a levy, but they did not know how much flooding it caused," said Oieroset.'* [10]

All of which seems to add to the view that not only is our local space environment now in a state of great flux, but the limitations of our understanding of it are also being revealed. This leaves the door open to the possibility that so-called 'fringe science', such as cosmic wave theory, may deserve far more serious consideration if we are to understand both what we may be due to go through and what the ancients were perhaps recording.

Geomagnetic Reversal

Another potentially epochal planetary effect, almost certainly related to the phenomena being discussed here (and, again, little reported on in the mainstream), is the fact that the Earth would appear to be in the early stages of what is known as a 'geomagnetic reversal'. This is where the magnetic polarities of the planet make an abrupt switch, reversing their positions. Geological evidence reveals that it has occurred before, apparently on a major cycle of around 250,000 years, with other possible ones occurring at shorter intervals (some believe there was one 13,000 years ago, concurrent with the period the Atlantis legends may originate from, and also— as with the superwave cycle—embodying half a precession period). Calculations reveal that another reversal should therefore be expected any time soon, and the signs are that it has already begun.

The north magnetic pole started to shift its location in 1904, as noted by Canadian scientists from the Geolab group, but since 1974 it has been wandering four times faster, by several hundred kilometers. Researcher Gregg Braden has stated that Earth's magnetic field has fallen by 38% in the last 2000 years and that this rate of decline has risen to an average of 6% per year over the last century. This strongly suggests that 'the magnetic field is dropping at an accelerating rate towards a "zero point" at which the polarity of the Earth will reverse', according to Geoff Stray's report. Stray adds:

'French geologists have found a "large area of reversed magnetic flux" in the ocean off South Africa, which matches computer simulations of imminent reversal. They say that "the magnetic field seems to he disappearing most alarmingly near the poles", and there are "huge whorls" of molten iron beneath the poles that are rotating in a reverse direction, further weakening the field and accelerating the process.'

Meanwhile, in 2008, the Russian news agency *Pravda* revealed that scientists had identified evidence of pole movement in such a fashion that it could contribute to an actual axis shift of the planet, a phenomenon which psychics have often had channelled warnings about, and something also suggested by other researchers. This would give rise to enormous climate changes and earthquake activity:

'Alexander Fefelov, a senior spokesman for the Russian Academy of Natural Sciences, said that planet Earth would have its magnetic and geographic poles relocated during the upcoming years. "Planet Earth on the orbit is a round object in weightlessness. The planet may suddenly change its axial inclination from time to time. It happens once in 23,000 years. The pole displacement angle may reach 30 degrees. The South Pole used to be located in the area of Easter Island before the latest displacement, whereas the North Pole was located in the Himalayas. That is why mammoths, rhinoceroses and sabre-toothed tigers used to inhabit Arctic latitudes. It was a very sudden displacement of poles. Archaeologists still uncover animals with undigested herbal food in their stomachs, which means that the animals died as a result of fast freezing, so to speak," the scientist said.' [11]

Although many analysts of geomagnetic reversal do *not* believe that a magnetic polarity switch will physically alter the tilt or rotation of the planet, it is clear that large effects could still be expected. The temporary collapse of the Earth's protective magnetic fields that would accompany the final stage of a polarity flip (which some believe could occur very quickly—possibly within days or even hours—after a slow build-up of years), could also expose us, however briefly, to a surplus of cosmic rays, with unknown results. In the worst case scenario, any huge electromagnetic pulse (EMP) that might emanate from the Sun during this period (*always* a major risk in any case) could also result in a neutralization of all electrical equipment (including batteries) and a complete wiping of databases, plunging society back into the medieval lifestyle seemingly desired by some people.

All very apocalyptic, then, as the prophecies seem to suggest. Or is it? For it could be that these very kinds of unexplored energetic effects might have a profound—and not necessarily negative—effect on humanity.

Galactic Alignment and Ascension

John Major Jenkins' observation that the Maya were recording the cycle of galactic alignment, in which the Sun, from the perspective of Earth, appears to stand over a particular part of the center of the dark rift of our Milky Way every 5,125 years [page 242], may offer more than just a visual nicety. According to Jenkins, the alignment may also result in a 'field-effect energy reversal'—an energetic resonance and a reversal of our *personal* polarity fields as well as our planet's geomagnetic ones—as the galactic core's magnetic field aligns itself with the Sun. Geoff Stray explains:

'The source of the "energy" field (which includes the electromagnetic spectrum and beyond) is the Galactic Center, and just as water spirals down a plughole in opposing directions in each of Earth's hemispheres, which are divided by the Earth's equator, so our changing orientation to the Galactic Equator will affect us in a similar way. This will be the completion of the "human spiritual embryogenesis" that is measured by the Maya Long Count calendar, culminating in a "pole shift in our collective psyche" and the birth of our Higher Selves.' [12]

Some have misunderstood this to mean that our entire solar system is crossing over the galactic plane, like a frisbee going up and down, but this is incorrect—the alignment in question results purely from the tilt of Earth in relation to the Sun. This, however, is not insignificant, as Jenkins insinuates. In a personal communication to this author, Geoff Stray elaborates:

'During the galactic alignment process, the Earth's axis is pointing in the direction of the Sun, and behind the Sun, to the visual center of the galaxy (not astronomical galactic center—the Sun will be in closest conjunction to that in another 200 years from now). The Earth's magnetic field will thus be aligned towards the Sun. It has just been discovered that there is a huge hole in Earth's magnetosphere... ...I personally think galactic alignment is just a cosmic clock that points to a time-window in which something will happen... ...Of course, this could combine with a huge influx of plasma, as in Alexey Dmitriev's scenario [page 250]—perhaps a huge flare will breach the heliosphere and let in all that interstellar plasma, which will come straight in the hole in the magnetosphere.'

Although such an event did not directly take place on 21st December 2012 as some had envisaged, there seems no reason to believe (especially as precise galactic alignment occurred in 1998) that such a process might not be a more gradual one with an accumulative effect. It would seem likely that there is a link between the original cosmological event that started the Earth's wobble, our magnetic field's consequent periodic alignment with the Sun, geomagnetic reversal and the cosmic wave theory. It seems too much of a coincidence that these might all be falling together by chance. All the discussed phenomena ultimately speak of a cyclical reaction to a changed environment in space. But whichever consequence takes precedence, it seems reasonable to anticipate something within ourselves being affected, and this may have unexpected results.

THE TRUTH AGENDA

Exposure to increased or altered electromagnetic fields can have a number of striking effects on human states of mind, creating mood swings between elation and depression, and even stimulating epilepsy or hallucinations, depending on the dosage. Some researchers believe this to be a result of the brain's pineal gland producing natural amounts of dimethyltryptamine, or DMT, as it responds to energetic changes. DMT is found in plants such as Virola, Psychotria and Acacia, and, depending on the area of the Amazon concerned, whichever DMT plant is locally available is added to the Ayahuasca brew, known for its extreme and sometimes expansive effects on the human mind (as the McKenna brothers explored). The taking of Ayahuasca is now a fashionable venture, with visitors from overseas seeking shamanic experiences.

Dr Rick Strassman, a US professor of psychiatry, has discovered that DMT (or the 'Spirit Molecule') is also produced by the pineal gland during times of extreme physical or psychological trauma, or at significant moments such as birth and death, and that it can result in people having mystical episodes or out-of-body experiences [page 35], where consciousness appears to detach from physicality. This may explain the 'unreal' feeling which can set in whilst experiencing accidents or stressful circumstances, if it is a natural protective mechanism. Debates continue as to

The Ayahuasca brew being prepared in the Peruvian jungle. Ceremony and ritual is an important part of the preparation. Ayahuasca contains DMT, which appears to expand consciousness (or distort it, depending on the viewpoint). But the brain also produces natural quantities of DMT, which can be stimulated by electromagnetic pulses. Could a cosmological event trigger a mass consciousness shift through a DMT response?

whether DMT helps release what some would call the soul from its attachment to matter, or whether it merely produces the hallucinogenic *illusion* of such an experience—but its effect on our consciousness is claimed to be profound.[13]

Strassman and other speculators believe that a huge rush of DMT production in our pineal glands could be stimulated across the entire global population in response to a cosmological energy spike, solar EMP or geomagnetic polarity shift, perhaps resulting in a mass out-of-body experience that affects the entire population of Earth. Given that a change in the geomagnetic field of just twenty 'nanoTeslas' (nT) is enough to trigger epileptic seizures, a major leap caused by unusual solar flares, which can already raise the field by 500 nT, could clearly result in a very dramatic influence on civilization. Perhaps, with the rise of unexplained phenomena and psi effects we seem to have experienced in recent history [Chapter XIV], we are already seeing the beginning of a response, as our solar system approaches a crucial moment.

Tools of Control

Work by neuroscientist Dr Michael Persinger demonstrates that ghost and poltergeist activity notably increases at times of raised geomagnetic activity, either because more appear or because we become more attuned to them.[14] Thus, the literal specter is raised of a world going into mental and physical freefall during an extreme EMP event as the planet physically reacts to the energy shift with quakes and tsunamis, atmospheric auroras shimmer overhead, our pineal glands go into overdrive and we find ourselves unable to discern between the already unusual external reality and the eccentric hallucinogenic visions that may suddenly fill our consciousness. All this would bring the world to its knees as surely as any Millennium Bug.

But will we be brought to our knees—or raised to a higher state of being? A recurring optimistic feature of New Age prognosis and psychically channelled messages has been that the Earth changes will bring with them a 'raising of consciousness' into a 'new dimension'. Many refer to this process as 'Ascension' (although that term can have more specific connotations—see page 310). Some predictions are more specific than others, and they are hard to reconcile with each other in any fine detail, but the general thread is of a movement towards something more advanced than our current psychological and physiological state.

Some sources directly assert that, at the peak of the consciousness shift, those evolved souls of a 'higher' nature will suddenly advance to the 'Fifth Dimension', to enjoy a new life on a less physical and far purer plain of existence (what happens to the rest of us is unclear), while other versions suggest that it will bring a gentler transition as Gaia evolves, with normal life continuing but on an 'improved-frequency' Earth. Detail on how any of these scenarios are supposed to actually occur is usually absent, but, as with the very similar Abrahamic or evangelical aspirations to a 'New Jerusalem' after a period of tribulation (some versions of Ascension seem to be The Rapture without the religious trimmings), they universally seem to offer hope of better things for the faithful or the spiritually aware. All theories, at the least, reflect a feeling that nothing will be quite the same afterwards. Again, some seekers were imagining that all this might transpire on 21st December 2012 and were disheartened to find that the spiritual free lunch they were expecting was not going to be so easily attained. [See *Appendix 1* for further thoughts in this area.]

With all the more (relatively) science-based speculations being considered here, perhaps it is not so outlandish to imagine that passing through a cosmic wave and/or undergoing a changed magnetic alignment with the Sun might result in some lasting effect, which leaves us in a new evolutionary state. If all the DMT-inspired pineal fireworks do result in pushing our brains to new extremes of experience, it is interesting to note that Dr Persinger also observes that during *quiet* times of electromagnetic activity, incidences of telepathy and ESP phenomena seem to rise substantially. In the descent from the peak of the shift, as whatever disruption we might experience recedes and some kind of modified normality sets in until the next cosmological bump, perhaps our species might find itself with enhanced transcendental faculties that remain active, the wilder visions settling down into a new sense of telepathic intuition and communalism. Perhaps, in such a world, those of the old control agendas may suddenly find themselves marginalized and left behind by a civilization liberated from shackles that no longer work in an altered context—which may be their greatest fear. A whole new level of evolutionary adventure may then present itself, rather as Kubrick's *2001: A Space Odyssey* muses. Indeed, the first steps towards understanding the true power of our metaphysical natures may already be taking place, as Chapter XIV outlines.

Balanced Expectations

All this is as maybe—and is, of course, speculative, as such discussion tends inevitably to be. The sifting of all these options should not be taken as any kind of endorsement of their veracity. The Truth Agenda can only be applied partially when faced with something almost entirely nebulous. The cross-referencing calendrical cycles across the globe, together with modern insights (such as the timewave theory), definitely suggest a more substantial basis than is usual in the pantheon of prophecy, and as such they are significant, but the little we have to go on reveals nothing of any solidity. 2012 itself came and went without an obvious climax, after all.

Amongst all the excited speculation, we must also, therefore, be prepared to face the possibility that in the decades ahead we might be looking back at a quieter than expected (if comforting) period without dramatic esoteric occurrences. Perhaps there will have been a few tangible effects, but only very subtle ones. And yet, looking around the world today, there seems to be no doubt that an acceleration of important global events *is* taking place, with seemingly continuous revelations of things previously hidden, huge social upheavals, major geopolitical changes and conflicts, and a sense of spiritual renaissance taking place all at the same time. Perhaps many decades will need to pass before anyone will be able to gain real perspective, but it is a reasonable bet that, sooner or later, these times will indeed be viewed as ones of great change, even if Ascension or transformative solar events don't arrive. Something in the collective consciousness is clearly being abnormally stimulated, whatever the cause.

What, however, of the other day-to-day realities that wider awareness of the New Era phenomenon might bring? For, as stated before, what is more important to the hypothesis being discussed in this book is not whether any of the visions, prophecies and predictions for these times actually come true, but that the *belief that they might* may well be helping to shape the massive control agenda that seems to be so insidious—and very real.

Tying the Threads Together

It can be taken as a given that if those on high (the Illuminati, lizards, ruling elite or whoever may be pulling the strings of control according to the conspiracy theorists) really are motivated by ancient beliefs and occult practices, as the Bohemian Grove rituals and other supporting evidence outlined in this book strongly suggests, then they will be very aware of the New Era predictions. Anticipating the upheavals that might result from a fulfilment of the prophecies, ones which could potentially overturn the established order of their machinations and tip long-term agendas into chaos, it can also be taken as a given that they would do everything in their power to ensure they retained their position at the top. If so, this would seem to make sense of the global control scenario on a number of levels.

Notwithstanding the lure of power for power's sake, which almost certainly plays at least some part in the motivation of the controllers, there does seem to be an urgency to the placing of the chess-pieces that are forming the patterns of today's global politics. Tracing the likely paths do make the notion of a One World Government a feasible ambition. And yet diversity has always been held up as a strength in the past, so why change that now? Could it be that the threat of a planetary catastrophe or psychic shift, making a mockery of borders, has helped to shape the new agenda?

Readiness for Civil Unrest?

Amongst all the predictive speculation, there have been extraordinary claims that a number of countries are expecting civil disturbances on a massive scale. Some truthseekers believe that the Rex 84 (Readiness Exercise 1984) program in the US, for instance, run in the Reagan years to test civil unrest contingency plans, led to the building of around 600 FEMA (Federal Emergency Management Agency) prison complexes, each one designed to hold thousands of inmates. It is claimed they lie empty, waiting... for what? Mainstream pundits have attacked the myths that have built up around the 'concentration camp' assertions, some alleged locations for which, when investigated, have turned out to be nothing more than water-treatment plants or dilapidated World War II internment camps. Yet the belief in these camps persists, and there does seem to be a grain of truth that the US has some worryingly draconian policies in waiting, beyond those already discussed. In a piece otherwise critical of the conspiracy theories, *PublicEye.org*, the 'Website of Political Research Associates', does concede the following:

The Spotlight... *carried the first exclusive story on "Rex 84" by writer James Harrer. "Rex 84" was one of a long series of readiness exercises for government military, security and police forces. "Rex 84"—Readiness Exercise, 1984—was a drill which postulated a scenario of massive civil unrest and the need to round up and detain large numbers of demonstrators and dissidents. While creating scenarios and carrying out mock exercises is common, the potential for Constitutional abuses under the contingency plans drawn up for "Rex 84" was, and is, very real. The legislative authorization and Executive agency capacity for such a round-up of dissidents remains operational.*

The April 23, 1984 Spotlight *article ran with a banner headline "Reagan Orders Concentration Camps." ...The Harrer article was based primarily on two unnamed government sources, and follow-up confirmations. Mainstream reporters pursued the allegations through interviews and Freedom of Information Act requests, and ultimately the Harrer* Spotlight *article proved to be a substantially accurate account of the readiness exercise, although* Spotlight *did underplay the fact that this was a scenario and drill, not an actual order to round up dissidents.'* [15]

This suggests that whilst some of the conspiracy hysteria may be unfounded, plans to combat 'massive civil unrest' do exist—as surely they must (and as the US Army's 1964 'Project Camelot' also explored).[16] Official explanations for the unoccupied camps that *have* been acknowledged in the US imply that they are merely back-up for any unexpected surge of illegal immigrants over the US-Mexican border. But why should such an influx occur and what event might precipitate the movements of such high numbers of people? Is it merely the (possibly over-reactive) worry that global warming and rising sea-levels might displace populations, which could turn up on US borders seeking refuge, or could there be a bigger disaster anticipated, in tune with all the New Era speculation?

With so many US citizens having easy access to guns and other weaponry, and already strong units of local militias and defended communities established around the States, with resistance to proposed gun controls being passionately strong, any destabilizing event could easily see a plunge back into a feudal 'Wild West' situation. It has long been predicted that a new American civil war could erupt in difficult times, and, for all the heroism and good community relations that surely were forged during it, the Hurricane Katrina disaster that hit New Orleans in 2005 exposed the perilous fragility of law and order that manifests when governments hesitate. With the US still struggling to emerge from its worst recession since the Depression of the 1930s, any extra New Era-related ingredients entering the powder-keg might require authorities (in their eyes) to incarcerate—or 'protect'—large numbers of its population.

US Navy air crewmen survey the devastation caused by Hurricane Katrina in 2005. The anarchy that broke out in some parts of New Orleans during the disaster was an example of how quickly society can become unstable when the natural order is disrupted. Are the authorities going to be better prepared in the event of a global 'event'—and is their 'solution' internment camps?

It is likely that most countries will have similar contingency plans (there are also claims of empty British prison camps), and the control agenda that appears to be gripping most Western societies may have at least some of its roots in the fear that the world is about to—metaphorically or literally—turn upside down.

The Astrological Perspective

Statistically, despite science's ongoing refusal to investigate and shallow debunking from celebrity astronomers, astrological cycles *do* appear to have tangible influence on the collective psychological states that generate events on Earth (as the 2006 book *Cosmos and Psyche* by Richard Tarnas, previously seen as a hard-line academic and now predictably marginalized by his alleged peers, makes very clear).[17] Interestingly, even without the prophecies, by itself the astrological component of the period we have now entered would appear to promise social, spiritual and political disruption (and potential healing), and it is worth spending a little time considering this perspective, which may throw some important light on the context of the times.

In the all-important 'birth chart' of the New Era—21st December 2012—we can find many clues to the kinds of developments that can be expected, and indeed have already begun, beyond the more conspiratorial considerations. Helen Sewell D.Psych.Astrol, a psychological astrologer who has made an extensive study of the New Era birth chart, elaborates for this book on the overriding issues of the age:

'When the slow-moving outer planets transit through a sign, everything that sign 'rules' comes into focus and change occurs in those realms. The outer planets—Uranus, Neptune and Pluto—unlike the inner personal planets, represent huge archetypal forces which are difficult for us mere humans to manage. They are like cogs of evolution constantly pushing us forwards to become more conscious. Uranus and Pluto often bring upheaval.

The chart of 2012 determines the next decade or so and shows us that Uranus and Pluto have reached the first of the major 'aspects' (90 degrees) they form together in their dance through the zodiac. Uranus/Pluto cycles begin with a 'conjunction' and last about 127 years, with the most recent cycle starting in the mid-1960s, where it reflected an era of huge change in our social structures. Uranus, striving for Utopia, brings uprisings, revolution, social reform, and rebellion, often in a quite shocking and unpredictable way. He is the truthseeker shining the light of inspired thought onto any given situation (if sometimes with a lack of emotional connection). Uranus spends seven years in each sign and since it has been transiting through the warlike sign of Aries (first entering in 2010), we have most notably witnessed the 'Arab Spring' and much Middle Eastern unrest.

Pluto, the planet of transformation, death and rebirth, has been transiting through the sign of Capricorn since 2008 and will remain there until 2023. Capricorn rules institutions, governments and structures (examples include national health services, education, the monarchy, the police, the armed forces, councils, and the food industry) and almost exactly on cue we have seen the most fundamental changes transpiring in these areas, commencing with the financial institutions and the consequent banking crisis. With its urge for truth, fairness and equality, Uranus has shone a light into Pluto's Underworld, revealing hidden

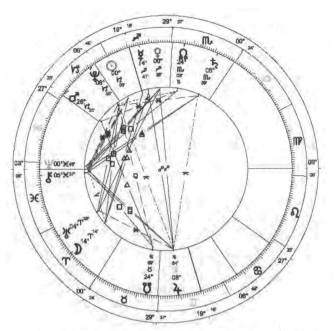

Astrological chart for the birth of the New Era—21st December 2012, 11:11 am, as set for London, UK, home to the '0 degree' meridian.

dark secrets and unearthing them for us all to see.

We have indeed seen an unprecedented exposure of institutional corruption, from Edward Snowden's surveillance revelations to shocking pedophilia scandals, WikiLeaks, political expenses rows and the uncovering of Rupert Murdoch's political influence, to name but a few. Unsavory though they may be, we cannot move forward in our development if these issues remain hidden and unaddressed. Where there is unfair domination and control lurking in the underbelly of society, Uranus will rebel, and we have seen a startling rise in reports from countries where women have been suppressed, with long-overdue public outcries about atrocities being carried out against them. Issues such as the poor treatment of developing-world workers by multinationals is also being brought to our attention, and there has also been exposure of the treatment of other helpless 'victims', whether they be hospital patients or abused children. Through these shameful tragedies it is hoped that more unethical practices that do not fit with a Uranian 'enlightened' worldview will come up out of Pluto's Underworld for conscious review.

In past Uranus/Pluto cycles there have been giant leaps forward concerning fundamental and transformational reform in society—the abolition of slavery and women's emancipation being two examples. When this cycle began in the mid-1960s we saw a lot of unrest that sparked change in society's attitudes. Students stood up and rioted against the Vietnam War, China saw the Cultural Revolution, and women were more liberated with the advent of the contraceptive pill (with Pluto ruling sex and Uranus ruling revolution, it was under their conjunction that the term 'sexual revolution' was coined). Suppressed ethnic minorities were also given more long-overdue equality in these times. Now, Uranus and Pluto's energies are fighting each other, resulting in an epic struggle between the forces of Plutonian control and domination and Uranian love of freedom and equality. The ultimate goal of Pluto in Capricorn (ruling governments) would be a One World Government and global domination. However, it could have a hard task ahead, as it is being severely challenged by Uranus' rebellious and non-conformist stance which will fight to the death while it is transiting through the war-like sign of Aries.

It is also worth noting that nuclear matters have sprung up in the media since these two planets came into square aspect (90 degrees) in 2012, starting with the Japanese Fukushima reactor incident when the words 'Uranium' and 'Plutonium' proliferated in the media. There has also been a lot of talk about countries and their nuclear capabilities from Iran to Pakistan and North Korea. This aspect does not mean that there will be a nuclear conflagration, but because Uranus and Pluto are in such a tension-filled aspect then all things pertaining to these planets will be sharply in focus. Ultimately, it comes down to the level of consciousness that we as individuals or nations have in dealing with these powerful archetypal forces that will manifest the outcome.

Uranus and Pluto's squaring up to each other ends in 2015, but it has been an unusually long-lasting transit indicating an intense period of upheavals around the world. Pluto is about power's rise and fall. For instance, when Pluto transited England's 'Midheaven' (a chart's public status position) in 2012, the world's eyes were focused on the UK for good or ill. The energy, fortuitously, was channelled positively into the Queen's Diamond Jubilee and the Olympics. Those displayed it as a powerful nation, but then shortly after the other side of Pluto arrived, as was demonstrated by damaging pedophile revelations. The US, too, is undergoing a period of big transformation which can manifest as an opportunity to positively review itself with consciousness or, negatively, project fear onto outside threats.

The New Era birth chart has a yod (or 'Finger of God') – a rare and significant triangular configuration composed of Saturn and Pluto with Jupiter at the apex in the sign of Gemini. Jupiter is therefore most significant and this speaks much about the times ahead. Whatever Jupiter 'touches' has its main principle expanded, with consequent negative or positive outcomes. Gemini 'rules' communication and information gathering, and can be witnessed in the rapid expansion of the Internet to a point of information overload and the obsessive quality of people compelled to be constantly in communication with others. Pluto brings an element of compulsion, while Saturn attempts to impose some kind of structure. This is not an easy aspect to manage and is something that will have to be worked on to rein in that 'runaway' quality of unfettered expansion. Positively, of course, the Internet has been the most transformational tool of our times but, again, we are being severely challenged to raise our consciousness to deal with the ethical issues that have arisen. We need to focus more on Jupiter's highest qualities of growth, optimism and a positive vision of the future.

The third outer planet in this chart, Neptune, has returned home to the sign it rules, Pisces, an event last seen 165 years ago, and here we see it powerfully placed with the asteroid Chiron (the Wounded Healer) on the 'Ascendant' (horizon line). Neptune symbolizes the spiritual, our connection to the numinous, deep compassion, suffering and service, and most importantly of all, unconditional love. However, it also 'rules' deception, confusion, illusion and delusion. If we look back at the last time Neptune was in Pisces, in the mid-1800s, we saw a massive resurgence in the spiritual movement and a hungry fascination in the afterlife, to the point that parlor seances were commonplace, and psychic abilities, telepathy, spirit photography and fairies were all being investigated—either genuinely or fraudulently—with great fervor. Over the next fourteen years a reflection of these times *may unfold with a wistful nostalgia for a less materialistic attitude and a new exploration of the different possibilities of an existence beyond the physical. With its conjunction with Chiron, we could well see the collective wounds of the past resurfacing for nations and individuals, so we have the potential at least to heal some of the suffering and move forward into the New Era with compassion. To bear the suffering and not engage with Neptune's weaker tendency to 'escape' from responsibility in the face of difficulty will be our challenge.*

The New Era chart has a very 'real world' feel about it and, though challenging, it is bursting with potential and opportunities for change. The Sun in Capricorn will force us to see the reality of life as it truly is and, as Capricorn is known for its capacity to endure hardship and difficulties like no other sign, we will plough stoically forward knowing there are no short cuts to enlightenment and no free lunches, but that if we prepare the soil well at the beginning of this period and get our house in order, the crop we will eventually reap will be bountiful and good.

The Sun, Mars and Pluto, meanwhile, are also all in Capricorn—the last of the Earth signs—and therefore all things to do with the physical and natural world are also highlighted and up for change. We could well see a continuing rise in earthquakes, volcanic activity, hurricanes and tsunamis, in fact, and geological changes and climate change will be highlighted, especially with Pluto remaining in Capricorn until 2023.

The backdrop to the current shorter cycles of the planets is the changing over from the Age of Pisces to the Age of Aquarius. An 'Age' lasts approximately 2000 years, with a crossover period of a couple of hundred years. Each Age has its gods and it is interesting to note that the last two thousand years saw Christianity arriving on the scene, with which the symbol of the fish (Pisces) is often associated. The new 'god' for the Age of Aquarius will be technology and the mind, and the advancements we have made thus far in the last twenty years are only the baby steps of the adult the Age will become. As the Roman gods of the Age of Aries had to step aside and concede to the Christian God of the Age of Pisces, so too will Christianity and other faiths have to transform or gradually be usurped. 'God' will no longer be seen so much as an external being who controls and manipulates our fate. Instead, through advancements in technology, we ourselves will have the capacity to play 'God' and we will be forced to deal with all the moral dilemmas that come with that.' [18]

Given the obvious grounding in metaphysics and the occult shared by those who may be covertly pulling the global strings, it is almost inconceivable that they would not also be aware of these zodiacal implications for the near future. Even in the more public face of power, Tony Blair's wife Cherie Blair, for instance, is known to have regularly consulted astrologers (which must have influenced Blair himself), as did Princess Diana, while Ronald Reagan allegedly built his entire schedule around astrological advice.[19] Once again (for any doubters of mysticism reading this), what is important here is powerful people's *belief* in such things, regardless of the truth. Sensing any kind of upheaval or trends that might unseat their influence, it stands to reason that the world's secret rulers would want to cling to power at all costs and put into place every kind of control that would help achieve this.

The better news, for those open to the astrological view, is that the roles of Neptune and Jupiter could provide the spiritual balance to all this, Neptune in particular helping with an expansion of consciousness and the 'Ascension' qualities discussed earlier. The general thrust is clear, however—the New Era, by astrology alone, would seem to be a time when the old order of things could change beyond recognition, bringing difficulties but, through them, great transformation.

The Control Agenda Explained?

To summarize... A fear in high places, based on long-studied prophecies and modern predictions, that everything we have known in our recent history may be about to transform or implode, would seem to be a plausible motivation behind the climate of control that has been cranked up so vastly in the last decade. If the agenda is not just about power in its own right, but masks instead an underlying mystic/occult conviction, passed down through endless generations, of a right-to-rule amongst an elite class (or even *believed* to have been passed down), perhaps some sense can be made of the world we live in. History records that when power is so desired, or thought to be an inherent dynastic right, no method of implementation, however deceitful or callous it may seem to the masses, is considered off-limits. If the swarming populations are seen as little more than cattle in the eyes of a pious elite (as emotionally removed as the Nazis were to the Jews), why would we be treated as anything but livestock; animals merely to be herded or slaughtered as necessary? Certainly, any possibility of individuals suddenly evolving on a spiritual level and stepping up to a new, fuller potential would be something to vigorously resist at all costs and curtail by whatever suppressants necessary, be they social, political or chemical. This, at least, is the conspiracy view, the take on life this book has mostly chosen to explore, offered for consideration, not as an absolute.

London's 'Shard' tower, another symbol of money and power dominating a city skyline—and bearing a worryingly uncanny resemblance to the dark towers of JRR Tolkien's Lord of the Rings.

Yet if all this turns out to be the dark fantasy of our inner collective fears and we live not at the mercy of some deeply-preserved occult elite worried about mystic predictions, but merely a group of selfish manipulators milking an economic system they have learnt to play well, is the outcome likely to be very different? Sensing even the vaguest possibility of a forthcoming planetary shift—even if they genuinely think that something like global warming alone might be the disruptor—would they not wish to ensure their continuing monopoly? The Truth Agenda, whichever way it is applied, would seem to reveal unarguable control games, and in the last part of this book we will see how they could be diluted and side-stepped to create a world that benefits the many and not just the few.

The New Era Squared

What of the New Era phenomenon itself? This chapter has examined some of the more credible possibilities to account for it, but there are many other ideas to be explored elsewhere. Are we dealing with a large global shift, or something more introspective; an apocalypse of the heart, rather than the external world? Will we be looking at social upheaval, spiritual upheaval, or both? Are we dealing with a planetary evolution, at the whim of cycles in the heavens, and if so, can we successfully ride with it as it goes?

Shifting skies and incoming weather... What will the New Era bring, and will it manifest environmentally, socially or spiritually—or all of these things?

Some people have scoffed at the New Age pretensions so often associated with the speculation regarding New Eras, with all its talk of transformation and 'raising of consciousness'. After all, would people be feeling quite so elated in the midst of social strife, electromagnetic pulse waves, atmospheric upheaval and earthquakes, whilst simultaneously undergoing traumatizing hallucinogenic experiences? And what does any of this mean to the oblivious millions of the 'developing world', simply trying to survive another day rather than being concerned with the raising of consciousness? The truth is that no-one knows what will happen, nor whether this chapter (or indeed the entire book, along with several other tomes) will come to be seen as an embarrassing footnote of fringe paranoia. Yet the gift of it all has been that the very act of *considering* the possibility of fundamental developments to both humanity and the planet, and waking to the idea that someone might want to hold back our full potential as living beings, is in itself creating a self-fulfilling prophecy of positive change.

Through mere conceptual contemplation of a great shift, many seekers are finding their lives transformed and enhanced in ways they had never before thought possible, and these people are tipping metaphorical lines of dominoes that are having a genuine and uplifting effect on the world. The awakening process initiated by all the speculation is in itself a force to be reckoned with. The realization that truths, both political and metaphysical, have been kept from us and that we may be able to transcend the restrictive view of ourselves that has been so widely fostered, can only be the path to something better, if delusion can be forestalled and everything kept in perspective. Learning discernment and finding perspective are the biggest challenges that these times we find ourselves in bring—and there will be casualties along the way amongst those who cannot find the balance. But if enough minds can keep themselves in a sensible questioning state, achieving a genuinely new level of consciousness and stepping up to a fresh social and planetary responsibility in a mode of true self-awareness, then the entire New Era phenomenon will have been worthwhile, even if years come and go without great drama.

What, though, of the window that began on 21st December 2012, one which failed to bring an instant great upheaval? The doom-mongers who put so much weight on the more devastating predictions might have done well to have remembered the name given to the great turning of the calendrical system by the Maya, whose beliefs above all seem to have captured the popular imagination—they called it 'Creation Day'. So all this, whichever way things transpire, was never about endings, but beginnings. We need to look, then, at ways in which to ensure that something new and good can grow in these times.

The recognition of our inherent power, so often trodden down or distracted from by the system we have become locked into, could balance and neutralize the agendas of those who seem to prefer us weak, and instead offer opportunities to create a pristine culture of hope and vibrancy.

THE TRUTH AGENDA: *The New Era prophecies are unusually cross-referenced by many sources, ancient and modern, and seem to represent an important upwelling from the collective psyche, stimulating an awareness of imminent change. Cosmic forces and alignments may be the bringers of that change but, whether metaphor or reality, the simple self-reflection that knowledge of the prophecies has inspired may in itself contribute to an important developmental stage for humanity. Any road to higher consciousness may be something to be fought against in the eyes of a ruling elite. Its fear of losing the control and privileges maintained for so long might well be the driving force behind the erosion of liberty and programs of suppression. If the coming period does bring huge events, conscious knowledge will surely help us; if it ultimately disappoints, the speculation will still have woken many minds up to wanting to improve their world.*

4

Part Four:
Solutions and Inspirations

To some truthseekers, overt occult symbolism such as the glass pyramid at the Louvre, Paris, suggests a boastful arrogance in the elite's attitude. But what kinds of minds would plan such things, and are they really as infallible and all-knowing as some would have us believe?

XIII   WHO ARE WE DEALING WITH?

Intense speculation on the ruling elite that may be running the world can lead to the presumption that it is all-powerful and infallible. But is it? And do we really understand its motivation? Identifying the human foibles and underlying desires of those who may be planning centralized domination could lead to a greater chance to offset their agendas—if people can break the chains of apathy and step up to the task.

Lifting the Blindfold

So far in this book we have been exploring a hypothesis; what if the world *is* being controlled by a ruling elite putting its own narrow interests and convictions above ours? And what if we are about to undergo a huge change, social, spiritual or cosmological? The exploration of these ideas has thrown up disturbing possibilities and more pieces of evidence to support them than is entirely comfortable. For all this, however, it is still a hypothesis until proven beyond doubt, and the fervent campaigners who believe passionately in every aspect of conspiracy theory's most extreme frontiers would do well to remember this when trying to drive their beliefs home to doubting listeners. A balanced and sensible approach is always more helpful if something is to come across as credible.

However, as has been expressed in earlier pages, if all that this troubled speculation achieves is to help prevent such a grim picture from coming true, or at least reaching full fruition, then it will have served a useful purpose. It is also crucial that a note of optimism is struck as we reach our conclusion. A common and often valid criticism of truthseekers is that their fevered investigations into humankind's worst nightmares can leave some listeners feeling *more* fearful, and risks driving them into a state of disempowered paralysis, putting up the shutters when what is needed is engagement. Yet the unavoidable truth is that looking a potentially tough situation in the eye does mean facing up to disturbing realities that may have been swept under the carpet, for they might require urgent action. Lifting the blindfold even just a little means that we might not run into the approaching wall at such a great velocity. If these pages have left some readers feeling shocked and reeling, the act of simply contemplating such issues may in itself spark a new awakening, whether all the ideas are agreed with or not. Looking twice at the world around us can only be a good habit to cultivate. If the reader has come this far, it is likely that at least some of it has connected.

With that established, this last part of this book steps back from detailed dissection of the symptoms to get a sense of perspective on the overall shape of the central hypothesis. In so doing, some potential solutions and strategies for dealing with it become clearer, as encouraging processes that could help us are identified and examples of past actions that have changed the world for the better emerge as the kind of transformational developments that can occur when enough people stand up to initiate them.

The Elite and its Motivations

Something too often missed in all the conspiracy speculation is the realization that if we are being governed by a secret and powerful elite trying to twist the world to its own ends, then we are still essentially dealing with fellow human beings (putting the ET/reptilian theories aside for a moment). Like every other person on the planet, they must have physical, social and emotional needs, even if the latter faculty may be too easily set aside in the kind of mind that would plan 9/11-type scenarios. The personalities involved must have loved ones of their own, and experience thoughts, feelings and cares in at least some directions—and they eat, procreate and go to the lavatory like everyone else. They also, like most of us in our lives, probably think they are doing the right thing, however much we may see their schemes as misguided.

This is an important point. We all have reasons for doing what we do, and can often justify actions to ourselves in the face of serious challenges from the outside. Hard though it may be to comprehend the motivation of those who might think that wiping out a fair percentage of the population would be a positive move, or who believe that planning wars and economic breakdowns to effect the creation of a unifying world government is an acceptable strategy, the fact is that many seemingly well-intentioned visionaries and academics throughout history have voiced the need for such approaches. This does not make them right, of course, but there is plainly a significant, if small, seam of humanity that believes a bigger picture should be put before the needs of the masses. Those who have expressed support for eugenics and depopulation programs, for instance, often have deep-seated environmental concerns or feel strongly that we have lost our balance with nature and must put the planet's future ahead of the requirements of the common people (as with the attenders of the 1975 conference that seems to have been at least the partial root of the global warming scare—page 230).

One of the most prominent promoters of the term 'New World Order' was the famous and much revered writer H G Wells, who believed passionately that the only answer to global strife would be the creation of the eponymous hierarchy, though he saw it as a long and nebulous process. Writing in his 1940 book *The New World Order*, Wells states:

'There will be no day of days then when a new world order comes into being. Step by step and here and there it will arrive, and even as it comes into being it will develop fresh perspectives, discover unsuspected problems and go on to new adventures. No man, no group of men, will ever be singled out as its father or founder. For its maker will be not this man nor that man nor any man but Man, that being who is in some measure in every one of us.' [1]

The New World Order is clearly not a modern concept, and has roots going back even further than this idealistic vision of it.[2] Some people believe that both World Wars were deliberately coordinated, or at least used, to help bring about a mandate for world government. As early as 1913, writing in his book *The New Freedom*, President Woodrow Wilson made clear that some formidable force already underpinned the commercial, and probably political, infrastructure of the USA:

'Since I entered politics, I have chiefly had men's views confided to me privately. Some of the biggest men in the US, in the field of commerce and manufacturing, are afraid of somebody, are afraid of something. They know that there is a power somewhere so organized, so subtle, so watchful, so interlocked, so complete, so pervasive, that they had better not speak above their breath when they speak in condemnation of it.' [3]

Herbert George Wells in 1943. Famous for novels such as War of the Worlds, *Wells held radical political views and believed that only a 'New World Order' and eugenics could save the world. It is easy to condemn these attitudes, but those who hold them may see themselves as saviors.*

What is striking in H G Wells' writings, however, is his sense of excitement and enthusiasm for the idea of a dominating collective that would put all to rights and avert 'the disastrous extinction of Mankind'. There is no sense of negative intention nor a Malthusian dislike for humanity. Yet at the same time Wells was an advocate of eugenics, writing:

'It is in the sterilization of failure, and not in the selection of successes for breeding, that the possibility of an improvement of the human stock lies.'

This view may seem entirely repugnant, but here is the paradox—the very kinds of people truthseekers tend to single out as the enemies of humanity clearly see themselves as its saviors. It is all a matter of perspective and of where one chooses to draw the moral line.

The philosopher Bertrand Russell openly accepted the inevitability of a One World Government, founded on the basis of hard scientific values, and was disturbingly frank about the society that would result, writing in his 1931 book *The Scientific Outlook*:

'In like manner, the scientific rulers will provide one kind of education for ordinary men and women, and another for those who are to become holders of scientific power.

Ordinary men and women will be expected to be docile, industrious, punctual, thoughtless, and contented. Of these qualities, probably contentment will be considered the most important. In order to produce it, all the researches of psycho-analysis, behaviorism, and biochemistry will be brought into play... ...All the boys and girls will learn from an early age to be what is called 'cooperative,' i.e., to do exactly what everybody is doing. Initiative will be discouraged in these children, and insubordination, without being punished, will be scientifically trained out of them.'

Bertrand Russell, philosopher and Nobel laureate, in 1950. Russell's views on how the future of humankind would evolve into a rigidly-managed hierarchy of 'rulers' and 'plebs' were either shockingly prescient, or are being used today as a working blueprint.

Could this be exactly what is going on today? By 1953, Russell was even more direct. Writing in his book *The Impact of Science on Society*, he states:

'Diet, injections, and injunctions will combine, from a very early age, to produce the sort of character and the sort of beliefs that the authorities consider desirable, and any serious criticism of the powers that be will become psychologically impossible... ...Gradually, by selective breeding, the congenital differences between rulers and ruled will increase until they become almost different species. A revolt of the plebs would become as unthinkable as an organized insurrection of sheep against the practice of eating mutton.' [4]

On the surface, this appears to encourage such a world, rather than condemn it, and such thinking seems outrageous and unacceptable, even if it does come close to identifying the very philosophy that may now be actively shaping our world. However, although it seems difficult, almost distasteful, for some to contemplate, there is a thought to be considered here: What if such thinking were definitively shown to be right? What if humankind's very survival did rest on the notion of more control, not less? What if the choice were demonstrated to be between total destruction through over-population, pollution and over-stretched resources, or a selectively-bred, closely-monitored world that regulated itself and continued on? What if an anarchy-ridden post-apocalypse society could be shown to stand no real chance of survival, whereas a tightly-controlled disciplinarian civilization would? Uncomfortably, in the light of the world's current issues, it can be seen, at least to a small extent, how arguments could be made in these directions when looked at from a certain viewpoint. The problem comes, as ever, with the massive issue of who gets to decide, and the ethics of any subsequent actions. Those in comfortable circumstances looking down from on high must inevitably see things rather differently to those scraping an existence lower down the rungs, at their mercy.

We already hold the power of genetic manipulation in our hands, and it will not be too long before required characteristics of children will be able to be routinely selected and engineered. Also, with life-spans ever-increasing, and our understanding of tissue and brain cell regeneration growing by the year, how long will it be before life can be sustained indefinitely, in full health? When that occurs, the population problem will clearly explode if unlimited access to such power is allowed (that is, if the majority of the population is permitted to survive in the first place). A world of immortals would risk stagnation, but also domination from those who attained the status of immortality first. They would effectively decide who would be offered the gift from thereon. In the end, the gene pool would almost certainly be controlled by such authorities, the new eugenics having arrived through the back door. These issues are already reality, not dystopian fiction. The power of genetic engineering, which is currently changing our food, both animal and vegetable—and thus our entire eco-system, as spliced and altered genes make their way into nature through pollination and cross-breeding (with evils such as 'terminator seeds')—means that humankind has already taken the entire planet's evolutionary destiny into its own hands, and there is no going back. Do those calling the shots have the moral compass to carry such a huge responsibility? Can they serve as the gods they are setting themselves up to be?

In a society of angels, perhaps a charter of rigid regulation, surveillance and genetic population control could be applied with compassion and the wide agreement of a common consensus—but we are nowhere near such a state of being. With the motivation of those governing our world today clearly in question, it seems impossible that the kinds of agendas they appear to be implementing could work in any way other than being a simple attack on the larger percentage of humankind. Without common consensus, whatever the supposedly good intentions that might exist somewhere behind the plans, any attempt to regulate the world by coercion and draconian measures remains immoral. There may be other solutions the elite has not considered in its hermetically-sealed world of privilege and protection, ones that might possibly be constructively and widely discussed if the agenda were thrown open to exposure and public debate.

Openness as Mitigation?

It is an irony that if the ruling elite were to be entirely honest about its actions in some areas, it might find more backing than expected. The public, concerned about energy, might support a long game to foment the creation of Western oil pipelines across the Middle East, for instance, if it was openly declared and decently negotiated, instead of being manipulated into being by suspect wars with false-flag origins. Similarly, an admission that 9/11 was aided by a cabal inside America might shake Western culture for a while, and risk some repercussions, but eventually things would settle into a respect for the new spirit of honesty. The bizarre Bohemian Grove ritual [page 93] might be tolerated as a harmless pageant if it were fully admitted to and taken for granted, instead of being oddly hidden and skirted around. Even the perfect portraits of people standing on the Moon might be a little more acceptable as acknowledged fakes if vulnerabilities were admitted and it was explained why representative shots had to be reproduced to show what we *should* have seen.

The problem with global cover-ups is that they arrive and build up—as deception does so often for all of us—through a lack of honesty largely sparked by the fear of what people might think or do if they were to perceive the true vulnerability within. The elite appears to fear us and our reactions as much as we may fear it [page 318]. Many disingenuous actions are borne of inner psychosis; a lack of trust that other people will understand. Our leaders appear to have got so used to lying and playing deceptive games that they cannot now operate any other strategy. Everything from the banking system to parliamentary administration appears to be based on subterfuge. Right now we are clearly not trusted by those affecting our lives so strongly and as a result we do not trust them. Yet sometimes a declaration of the truth creates unexpected results. Perhaps we are seeing small steps towards this kind of policy in the now blatant gatherings of the Bilderbergs or the defensive excuses given for why blanket surveillance needs to take place, but it still feels hesitant and cowardly. There is a long way to go. Not that some of the elite would care a jot for our trust, nor be remotely bothered about what any of us thinks of their actions.

Wall Street, New York. The banking crisis, which resulted in huge losses and unemployment across the world, revealed deep seams of dishonesty that appear to have become acceptable standard practice.

For readers who may feel that caveats to explain such motivation is too generous to people who maim, kill and deceive to get their way, for whatever reason, it should be noted that there do also appear to be those pulling the strings who simply seek power for power's sake. The lessons of history tell us that selfishness, greed and excited bloodlust cannot be ruled out as prime movers in some cases, at least. And, to acknowledge the not-insubstantial belief in the reptilian agenda, if it were to turn out that this highly exclusive club was indeed the result of a dominating extra-terrestrial gene seeded long ago and being exploited and/or activated by celestial visitors today, then it admittedly might explain why concern for the needs of humanity appears to be as low down the list of its priorities as our general concern for the welfare of livestock is today.

As for what kind of people may comprise the global elite, the well-intentioned and the not-so well-intentioned, most likely we are largely dealing with high-ranking politicians, academics, intellectuals (as with Wells and Russell), monarchies, media moguls, bankers, and very rich families. In other words, all the obvious candidates. Other books go into the detail, so there is little need to explore it here. Most researchers cite the key players as being the likes of Henry Kissinger, Zbigniew Brzezinski, Dick Cheney and assorted US neo-conservatives, figures such as Tony Blair and selected world leaders, political and religious, most US presidents and their hidden sponsors, magnates and corporate and financial leaders, and other moneyed and influential business dynasties like the Rothschilds and the Rockefellers. Thinking along these lines soon enables one to speculate freely on the kinds of characters we are probably dealing with. How much of the grand plan all of them know, however, and whether there are pyramids-within-pyramids amongst even the power structures near the top, is another matter.

Factions Within Factions

The presumption is often made that the very existence of a ruling elite means that those involved must be all-powerful and of one mind, accurately manipulating domino events that hit the required spot every time, all to a predetermined agenda. But this may apportion them an unwarranted infallibility.

There is evidence to show that there *are* factions and disputes within the echelons of those with great influence over our lives. After all, the world is a big and complex place. Even with a general agreement on how it should move forward, the pressures of regional needs and personal biases are almost certain to blur the clarity of purpose from time to time. Going on the word that does sneak out from Bilderberg meetings and the suchlike, it seems that as many disagreements, compromises and negotiations arise there as within any supposedly democratic parliament. If this weren't the case, the meetings would not presumably need to take place, so pre-orchestrated would the scheming be.

As with Masonic and other secret society structures, there is also a pecking order to consider. It is doubtful that all those 'in' on a global conspiracy seeking centralized control would be party to every machination, and certain players may themselves be manipulated from within without realizing it. Some years back, for example, from the outside it appeared that British ex-prime minister Gordon Brown, for all his many loudly-voiced references to creating a 'New World Order', did not have the solid support from above that had protected 'Teflon' Tony Blair in his years of power. Brown seemed destined to be a fall-guy from the start, set up to come to power just as the world economy took a tumble (although he himself had clearly played a part in that—page 73). The question is, did Brown know the full plan? Was he someone faithfully playing a game with a known outcome of outward failure, while secretly ensuring success in an agenda of weakening the UK on the world stage to quicken

THE TRUTH AGENDA

a move towards One World Government, or did he cling on in the genuine belief that all would come right and that he would one day be hailed (however unlikely) as a political hero? (The Freudian-slip Brown made in Parliament that the Labour Party had 'saved the world', in the wake of the economic crash, suggests he had a high opinion of his own role, even if few of his elite colleagues shared it.)[5]

Likewise, when President Bill Clinton found himself under threat of impeachment following the Monica Lewinsky sex scandal, was that all part of a contrived drama, or a sign of factions within factions very genuinely trying to remove him after an unintentional gaffe? And did Richard Nixon go rogue or was he just playing a pre-auditioned role? On a smaller level, when a man in the crowd died after being pushed to the ground by a police officer during the 2009 G20 protests in London,[6] it took all the seemingly contrived focus away from images of a few people smashing a bank window, and suddenly all the headlines became howls about police brutality. Was this an ongoing twist to stir further civil unrest [page 305] or was it (as strongly suspected) something going unexpectedly wrong and changing the script? Does every war and false-flag terror attack really go to plan, or is there as much uncharted error involved as conspiracy?

How organized, then, is this global elite, and is it really as united as some truthseekers give credit for? The evidence suggests that there are chinks in the armor and disagreements within, and weaknesses and unpredictable elements always arise in any grand plan. This offers hope. The foibles of human nature and the sheer universality of chaos theory may ensure that unexpected events and peculiar sidetracks undermine the apparent solidity of the control agenda just when they are least expected. We could therefore be dealing with something far less coordinated than feared—indeed, the wide truthseeker presumption of the elite's potency may make it seem more of a problem than it really is. But can we take the chance of becoming complacent?

Police 'kettling' (forcibly enclaving) protestors at the London G20 protests in May 2009. When a protestor died shortly after being pushed to the ground by a police officer, the media suddenly turned on the authorities. Is this evidence of a coordinated elite strategy to enrage the population further or, as many believe, an unexpected error? How organized can a ruling elite really be?

We have clearly seen, through the application of the Truth Agenda, that certain events and trends do seem to be part of an unfolding pattern that suggests an attempt to engineer a mandate for centralized power. Whilst we must not become petrified into inaction by this, nor, however, should we take the opposite risk of assuming there is no real threat, even if the conspirators are found to be less competent than some believe. Either way, it is important at the very least to call attention to the appalling deeds committed by those at least *trying* to be an all-powerful force.

Consent by Apathy

If plans for world domination are being laid on any level, a simple fact needs to be recognized—that it only goes on because we collectively allow it. Even with obvious governmental deceptions such as the weapons of mass-destruction debacle, such things only continue to occur as widely as they do because too few people stand solidly against them or fully call their leaders to account. Through all the methods discussed in Part Three, we have allowed apathy and the distractions of (apparent) comfort, trivia and electronic entertainment to hold us in our armchairs in the hope that anything dark 'out there' will remedy itself in due course. Voter turnouts for

Did the full advent of television from the 1950s onwards encourage a slow and deliberate trend towards a distracted and apathetic population? More people vote for TV talent contests today than vote for governments.

US and British elections have become perilously low, meanwhile, meaning that some recent governments have come to power with the direct consent of only a tiny minority of the population, with fewer votes than those regularly cast for TV talent shows. As discussed in Chapter VII, this lack of political interest is understandable given past betrayals and the sometimes dubious specimens up for selection, but it also sends out the message that we don't really care how we are ruled, and quietly gives permission to those with driving ambitions to do with us what they wish. After all, if we show so little regard for the democratic process, however flawed it may be, they might conclude that perhaps we won't mind not having one at all.

By becoming so disconnected with what goes on around us in our names, we have not stood up in our collective power—and are therefore as responsible as any global elite for having created the world we live in today. With the consent granted by our passivity, we have watched obvious lies and manipulations take away our strength, resolve and liberty, and have done little or nothing about it. As such, we have given away our personal responsibility. The energy spent complaining loudly but emptily in the bar or bus queue about the shortcomings of today's society, if applied in more proactive and positive directions, could be used to offset the very things being complained about. The problem is that we have been trained to think that we cannot make a difference, when, in truth, we can. The next chapter will explore an unseen mechanism that may offer some hope in this direction, while the final one provides some practical examples of people power, which could lead to genuine solutions.

The truth is that until now, conspiracy or no conspiracy, we have collectively permitted a relatively small group of flawed individuals to foster questionable agendas that affect many lives. That this was able to happen at all is astonishing in itself, but a long game is being played and there is still time to wake up before the final pieces are put into position.

Maintaining the Flame of Optimism

Much of the awakening process that HAS begun has come from the kind of people drawn to be part of the truthseeking community, and there are many players who should be applauded for their selfless efforts to raise awareness. Instead, those often unseen efforts are generally rewarded by undeserved ridicule and sidelining by a culture that has shut its eyes and ears to anything but the skewed vision it is fed by those who prefer to keep us dumb. People who question the status quo are easily neutered in the mainstream by being inanely lumped in with those (i.e. almost nobody) who supposedly believe Elvis is still alive and working in a local McDonald's—false stereotypes created by a media that is all too often either itself controlled, fearful or just lazily stupid. Truthseeker enthusiasm has, without doubt, allowed things to spill over into fanaticism and lack of discernment sometimes and this must be guarded against, but the fact is that there are absolutely vital questions and observations being raised by other very reasonable, very *normal* people, which could make a real and positive difference to people's lives—if ever given a chance. To get that chance, though, however small, these questions will have to be framed in the right way and targeted in the right direction.

We have already seen in Chapter I how accusations of verbal evasion had Barack Obama repeating his inaugural oath the day after taking office to avoid 'conspiracy theories'. With a significant controversy hanging over his very legitimacy due to doubts as to whether he was born in the USA or not (doubts which rumble on with unresolved issues around the genuineness of his birth certificate), Obama's team was bound to be sensitive to the issue, but this was still a remarkable acknowledgment of the growing influence of conspiracy thinking. The concerns over the old-guard powers and secret societies most likely behind the accession of all presidents certainly demand attention, especially with characters like Zbigniew Brzezinski having groomed Obama for his role and maintaining influence in the background. At the same time, this should not be allowed to eclipse the very real hope for something new that shines in the eyes of those who vote for change. If that positive energy is not leached away by the usual distractions, there is genuine cause for optimism because of it,

THE TRUTH AGENDA

though a new realism may be required. The revitalized political enthusiasm sparked by Obama in the 2008 US election made it feel like people were beginning to care again, people who thought that their opinion might count for something this time. The economic crisis caused by questionable banking and complacent (or complicit) politicians had woken people up in a big way to the possibility that they may not have been as well looked after as they believed before. Any tangible disappointment in the new US administration was bound to alert them even further to the reality

that the world is not being run for our collective benefit. With the wide-eyed hopes of so many people heaped on his shoulders, once Obama inevitably became seen as a disappointment, a wider sea-change began to arise in how US citizens perceive the way they are governed. It didn't stop his re-election for a second term, but the enthusiasm had notably waned. Unfortunately, a growing part of the American electorate seems to have reached for knee-jerk far-right solutions in the face of ongoing distress (a pattern also seen in countries like Greece), so more lessons may

Thousands upon thousands line the Washington DC National Mall to witness the inauguration of Barack Obama. Hopes were high for something new from a very new kind of president. Perhaps inevitably, disappointment followed, making some people more alert to seeking less conventional views on the way their lives are governed.

yet be needed before people finally look into a mirror to see where the real power for deeper change resides. In Britain, perhaps, with its long history of unpredictable kings and queens, some good, some very bad, a more entrenched cynicism already set in centuries ago, with its population having far lower expectations for leaders than in the somewhat fresher nation of the USA, but its citizens still seem to act surprised when the foibles of power are uncovered.

However, it doesn't take long for the average person in any country to see through manipulation once obvious anomalies are pointed out. Assuming the masses will always be dumb may be an arrogant and huge mistake on the part of our masters (as Tony Blair discovered when he attempted to feed patronizing spin to the annual conference of the British Women's Institute in 2000, receiving a much-deserved slow-handclap of objection in response).[7] When discussed in an accessible and objective way, the concept of a ruling global elite, which believes that some kind of catastrophic change may be imminent and has thus been implementing a regime

Solutions and Inspirations

of draconian restrictions by nefarious means to ensure it retains control, is nowhere near as far-fetched as it may at first seem to those new to the idea. It is also plain that 'fringe' areas such as UFOs, paranormal phenomena, religious apparitions, visions of the future and ancient prophecies are taken far more seriously by authorities than has ever been admitted. The connection between all these areas, as discussed in previous chapters, *can* be made to sound credible when expressed in balanced tones, and when sensible evidence is presented.

Tones are important. The introduction to this book has already pointed out that extreme conspiracy dogma, passionately but indiscriminately shouted, can repel potential support and plays into the hands of the mainstream's characterization of all alternative thinkers as uneducated tinfoil-hatted fanatics (the hats meant to guard against alien or Illuminati mind manipulation, apparently), a fake conditioning stereotype designed to sideline people with genuine concerns and keep them out of the limelight. Those with the power of insight who can rise above this have a responsibility to convey a user-friendly overview of the control agenda—and check their facts, or be prepared to be corrected with good grace if proven to be wrong. Shouting loudly or preaching only to the converted won't be enough if real change is to be created and critical

Confrontational protest banners at a London peace rally. Striking the right balance between making a robust point and avoiding putting people off through over-zealous in-your-face campaigning is not always easy. Understanding what diverse groups of people will respond to and having empathy for their individual sensitivities can make a big difference in making listeners more open to hearing alternative truths.

mass achieved. Successful outreach requires initial moderation—and compassion. Newcomers can be confused by all the many complex sources of information out there, and may shrink from the at-first shocking alternative viewpoints if not properly acclimatized. Truthseekers themselves need to take this into account, find a sense of balance and exercise real discernment. The habit of questioning absolutely everything can lead to a hubristic assumption that we are *never* told the truth of anything by anyone, but this is to fall too deeply into cynicism and risks pathology. Hearts and minds must be kept open and optimism maintained if true change is to come about, whilst at the same time retaining sensible vigilance.

The uncertain era we live in now provides a unique opportunity for the people with the insights to offer another view—while they can. The ongoing withdrawal of

THE TRUTH AGENDA

liberty and freedom of speech in Western society needs serious addressing and only greater awareness will enable the collective will to create its own catharsis. For that to happen those with eyes to see need to take true responsibility.

The good news is that the weight of numbers believing in something, or changing a viewpoint, may have a far more wide-reaching effect than anyone suspects, as we shall now explore.

THE TRUTH AGENDA: *There may be more than one reason why a world of centralized control would be desired by a ruling elite, and we cannot fully presume to understand from the outside. But no strategy that imposes an undeclared agenda without transparency or choice can be right, and any regime of underhand manipulation must be resisted. To resist successfully, however, those with awareness must hold on to optimism and strike an appropriate tone if they are to be listened to and people awakened so that a self-elected and questionable minority's vision for the world is not allowed to ride roughshod over the needs of everyday people. No elite, of any kind, can be infallible, and this offers hope.*

Solutions and Inspirations

We all like to think of ourselves as individuals—and we are
—yet recent scientific discoveries are making it clear that our
minds, when working together, have a genuine collective effect
on the world, one that could be very powerful if tapped.

XIV   THE POWER OF COLLECTIVE THOUGHT

The belief that minds working together can affect the material world may be more than just New Age rhetoric. Scientific experiments with the power of thought are revealing an all-encompassing mechanism of collective consciousness, the understanding of which may be the key to forging a new world of positive change. Can we step up to the responsibility that proactive use of this process could bring?

What Are We Fighting For?

In Chapter XII we explored the hopes and fears for the New Era. Beyond the obvious astronomical observations, we cannot yet know for sure what kind of recurring event the ancients were indicating in their calendrical systems, but it seems that a significant shift may be on the cards, even if it occurs through the simple self-fulfilment of people's own expectations. A spiritual renaissance is in order, one that could be forged in the fires of social turmoil and the challenging of a stagnant and corrupt establishment (as the astrology alone suggests).

Yet it cannot be denied that, based on past archaeological evidence, perceptible cosmological events on a scale beyond our control would also seem inevitable; if not soon then at some point in the future. This leads the pessimistic to dark musings. Given that our planet has endured catastrophes, climate changes and mass-extinctions several times before, almost wiping the slate clean each time, then where, in truth, is our civilization going? Has the emergence of humankind, seemingly the most advanced intelligence Earth has yet produced, been a statistical quirk born in a time of geological and celestial stability but doomed to falter as most other dominant species have before it? If so, what is the point of trying to better ourselves? Why fight to build a more enlightened civilization, free from fascistic control and complex conspiracies, only to see it knocked down again by cycles outside of our influence?

There are some people who feel helpless in the dual face of cold agendas from powerful elites and pending doom from natural threats, and shrink at the seemingly insurmountable tasks our world must confront if it is to gather itself into something sane and resilient. This fearful stance is all-too-often used to justify a dangerous path of inaction, apathy or religious End Times passivity. The notion that nothing we do or think can make a real difference may also be deeply misconceived.

The Evolution of Consciousness

On a practical level, all we really have in life are the basics—ourselves, our loved ones and the immediate environment around us. For some, this is all that is needed. The pragmatic approach of accepting that reality and making the very best of it to live in the now and enjoy the pleasures and little moments for what they are brings all the meaning they require. It is remarkable how even those who find themselves in situations or environments beyond their making, far from perfection, can often cultivate a sense of well-being from within, their spirits kept high. For others, however, a more profound center is needed; a sense that what they do, what they think and how they live affects a larger canvas outside of themselves. The continuing magnetic pull to religion, however misused it may have become, is evidence of how strong this human instinct is. The belief in the collective power of prayer has motivated the lives of millions (to scoffing from the likes of Richard Dawkins), yet only recently has evidence begun to emerge that there may indeed be a scientifically detectable force behind it.

A Hindu woman at prayer. Scientific experiments with the mind are proving that both individual and collective thoughts can and do alter the environment around us, and that mind-to-mind 'transmission' is a reality, thus entirely supporting the genuine power of prayer.

If it does turn out that our every thought and action is directly affecting the external world on an energetic level, as the experiments described below suggest, then it also follows that over long aeons the human race has been evolving its consciousness to the point where the collective mind may have become a powerful 'entity' in its own right. Perhaps every strife, every debate and painful learning experience, all the pushes and pulls between right and wrong, 'good' and 'evil', have been for a higher purpose after all, as equations resolve (however agonisingly slowly) and the entity (or 'Noosphere', as Pierre Teilhard-de Chardin called it) matures into adulthood.[1] Removed from the long-held and narrow view that we live our lives merely to be judged or played with by lofty deities, be they Olympian, Norse, Hindu or Abrahamic (and all points in-between, which is not necessarily to say they don't exist on some level), we may face instead the reality that a web of consciousness itself is the ultimate force of life, binding us and propelling the universe forward; God by any other name. From this perspective, it may be the experiences and thoughts that somehow imprint themselves into the permanent fabric of the universal mind that are important, rather than the material gains or losses fought for day by day. Edgar Cayce [page 52] would have called the resulting memory-field the 'Akashic Record', a kind of eternal databank through which the universe evolves. All of this means that what occurs here and now *does* matter, because it will count in the future, very much so, regardless of what calamities may appear to befall. How we handle events and what we learn and radiate into the collective consciousness may be the most crucial thing of all.

Arthur C Clarke's 1954 book *Childhood's End* posits the notion that humankind may eventually evolve into something far beyond flesh and blood (as does his and Stanley Kubrick's *2001: A Space Odyssey*).[2] The story concludes with humanity's psychic progeny dissolving the Earth as they move onwards out into the universe, the cradle discarded. We appear to be nowhere near such a stage yet—although some Ascensionists may disagree—and keeping the planet strong and healthy is still our current responsibility (once we agree, based on correctly-assessed evidence, which way that will best be achieved—Chapter XI), but Clarke's parable illustrates that our attachments to the things we think matter most may need some reappraisal. It is our handling of what we have before us now that may determine greatly how quickly we step up the ladder of consciousness.

What, then, is the evidence that we have a tangible psychic evolution before us?

The Power of the Mind

In Dean Radin's influential book *Entangled Minds*, he assesses the oft-dismissed yet astonishingly substantial evidence that the average human mind not only communicates with other minds on a recordable minute-by-minute basis, but that all minds working together generate a collective 'field' (for want of a better term) that can affect material reality.[3] The power of the mind has been tested and speculated on for centuries, yet mainstream science has managed to sideline and dismiss the multiple studies that have been mounted to show that consciousness can and does extend beyond the body and outwards across perhaps unlimited distances. This dismissal is unforgivable in light of the fact that many of these studies have been conducted under rigorous scientific conditions, the methodology painstakingly developed, dutifully tidying up all loopholes or any potential for inaccuracy or vagueness. Indeed, because of the need for scrupulous integrity in the face of mainstream cynicism, many of the experiments have been carried out under strictures more rigidly scientific than most peer-reviewed sciences. Yet still academics refuse to acknowledge the findings, or afford them only the faintest of interest, which soon sees the implications forgotten.

Conducting what is known as meta-analysis—compiling statistical studies of the studies—and factoring in even the widest possible margins of error, Radin demonstrates categorically that science *has* proved that the mind is capable of telepathy (or 'psi' phenomena) and other 'non-local' effects, as the odds against the positive results occurring by chance are simply too huge. Most strikingly, the quantum quality of 'entanglement', in which particles once joined and then separated remain in mysterious and instantaneous communication with each other, can be shown to work at a macro level too. In other words, we are all 'entangled' with each other and the world around us in a way that means we are inseparable from our fellow beings and our environment—and the universe is inseparable from us. The implications of this work are truly colossal, and many students of the 'new physics' are, however reluctantly, coming to the same conclusions.

It is worth a brief resume here of the kinds of effects that have been discovered from the numerous investigations by different researchers into psi phenomena, fully confirmed by meta-analysis:

• Basic telepathy ('transmission' of images, feelings, etc.) can provably occur between certain individuals, and the effect is much stronger when the test participants are known to each other and therefore entangled (i.e. if they are life partners, which says much about the importance of relationships).

• Physical distance between participants can make a difference to psi effects (the further the separation, sometimes the weaker the results), but not always, and 'transmissions' are instantaneous, no matter what distance is involved.

• The instantaneous qualities of psi effects have been confirmed by wiring people up to machines that register brainwaves, skin-resistance, and heart or nervous system reactions. Incredibly, the machines record that separated participants can share identical matching reactions even when only *one* of them is being stimulated (with images or sounds, etc.) and the other is entirely unaware of what is happening to their counterpart. And, fascinatingly, the heart usually reacts *before* the brain. This is all clear evidence of quantum entanglement and also suggests that 'gut reaction' is far more than an empty term.

• Results for psychokinesis (or telekinesis—the ability to influence the movement or behavior of objects) have been less solid, but still show a success rate far beyond statistical chance. Experiments with dice, for instance, have shown that it is possible to influence the general outcome of a series of throws.

These extraordinary findings demonstrate that we live in a world where the pattern of events, relationships and emotional states must be influenced on a continuous basis by these processes, even if they are merely operating at a background level. Perhaps it is not just by mathematical coincidence that we so often know who is at the other end of the line before we pick up the telephone. Maybe we should trust our initial instinctive feelings about people and places more than we do. A run of good fortune when we are in a positive mood could be more than just the perception of a happy-go-lucky mindset. And when the car or lawnmower next breaks down when we are in a bad state of mind, we should perhaps consider the very real influence we may be having on the objects and environment around us.

But if all of this is indeed occurring continuously, what wider effects might it be having beyond our individual lives? The 'collective unconscious', alluded to by the likes of Carl Jung in more esoteric and psychological terms, may be more of an

THE TRUTH AGENDA

everyday reality than anyone has previously suspected, offering a tool that could help the current plight of civilization.

The Global Consciousness Project

Realizing that there must be a larger implication to the web of psi effects, a number of researchers have looked for ways in which such an influence can be tracked and monitored. Here is not the place for a complex study of the workings of consciousness science, and *Appendix 3* gives some necessary pointers for further research. However, open-minded physicists like Dean Radin and Robert Jahn, working at the Princeton Engineering Anomalies Research Laboratory (PEAR) in the USA, have been instrumental in developing fail-safe mechanisms for testing the powers of psi—thus also creating ones for recording collective patterns.

The standard method of reading cards with symbols and pictures and 'transmitting' the images to another person in a different room had produced positive results above statistical chance, but was not considered scientific enough to constitute absolute recordable proof. Tests on the likes of brainwaves and skin responses took things to a higher level, but more was needed. Hence the idea was developed of using computers to produce random binary sequences—entirely meaningless streams of digital ones and zeroes pouring out in an endless torrent. It was established that if a person or persons could, without any physical interaction with the computer, influence the streams into more ordered sequences, this would be a) a fairly infallible test of psi, and b) would be scientifically recordable to the finest degree. Subsequently, the 'Random Number Generator' (RNG) tests have produced the most convincing evidence yet that the mind operates on levels outside of any of the usual restrictive parameters conventional science has superimposed onto it.

It was soon realized that certain individuals could nudge the otherwise chaotic RNG data into desired sequences. Radin writes:

'In the PEAR Lab tests, participants tried to intentionally influence the RNG outputs to drift above *the chance-expected average (they called this the high aim condition, like aiming for heads instead of tails), then* below *chance (the low aim condition, like aiming for tails), and then to withdraw their mental intention entirely to allow the RNGs to behave normally as the baseline or* control *condition.*

From their experiments, Jahn's team reached several conclusions. They found that in all of their experiments using truly random sources, like those based on quantum events, the random outputs tended to match the directions that the participants intended. When wishing for high scores the RNG outputs drifted up, and when wishing for low scores the RNG outputs drifted down. By comparison, no positive results were observed when simulated random numbers were used, like those generated by software algorithms. They estimated that the magnitude of the PK [psychokinesis] effect was approximately equal to 1 bit out of 10,000 being shifted away from chance expectation. While this may

Solutions and Inspirations

seem like a tiny effect, over the entire database this resulted in odds against chance of 35 trillion to 1.' [4]

Further experiments showed that *groups* of people working with the RNGs had even more chance of pushing the sequences into non-random patterns. It was discovered, therefore, that the human mind appeared to have the astonishing capability of creating order from chaos, generating 'coherence', and that an increase of focused minds could affect the outcome. With this remarkable insight, the researchers began to consider whether it might be something that was occurring on a daily underlying level, as a natural output of the ever-evolving consciousness of humanity. This genius stroke of enquiry led in turn to the creation of the now ongoing Global Consciousness Project.[5]

As the years have gone by, an increasing number of RNGs, or 'eggs' as the global models are known, have been placed at several participating locations around the world, streaming out their meaningless sequences for the Global Consciousness Project. Each has its own power source, with no direct connection to the outside world. The latest results are collected from each individual machine at intervals and then compiled. Those results have been profound. It was quickly observed that certain collective events—i.e. when many minds were focused on the same thing at the same time—were producing notable divergences from randomness in the RNG data. The most significant areas of global focus, such as the death of Princess Diana, the Boxing Day tsunami of 2004 and, perhaps inevitably, 9/11, seemed to create the biggest ripples of all. Even bizarre events like the unexpected 'not guilty' verdict in the original 1995 murder trial of actor O J Simpson (transmitted live around the world) generated powerful spikes of coherence in the RNG output.

Four events that had the most dramatic effects on the Random Number Generators (clockwise from top left)—9/11; the 2004 Boxing Day tsunami; The O J Simpson murder trial verdict; Princess Diana's funeral. What these seemingly unrelated occurrences have in common is that they all focused many minds on the same thing simultaneously and sent out psychic ripples across the world.

What this reveals is that the act of strong collective focus seems to throw something out into the wider environment, affecting the workings of material components, such as computers. The generation of data coherence would seem

to show that when we think together, a more ordered universe appears to result—an encouraging thought. Although a very subtle effect in the labs, and the mechanism behind it remains unknown, it has nonetheless become clear that some process is at work, quantum, energetic or esoteric, that is at its most powerful when we are *united*. Exactly how this process can be practically tapped and manipulated is not something promoted by the Global Consciousness Project researchers, who remain cautiously laid back in their observations, but others outside the strictures of (perhaps understandably in this case) having to maintain scientific credibility have been able to speculate more freely.

Taking Back Collective Power

The RNG and other psi experiments seem to reveal a world in which we are incontrovertibly entangled with each other, bound together by more than just societal trends. If the Big Bang theory or all its multiple variations is correct, it must be the case that every piece of matter in the universe was once bound together in a 'singularity'—before being burst apart in a massive expansion. As particle physics has shown, once something is entangled, it is always entangled, no matter what distance is introduced. Should we really be surprised, therefore, at the discovery that we are in a constant state of instantaneous and non-local interaction with each other? This at once vindicates the beliefs of mystics throughout the ages, and supports the reality of the power of prayer. Experiments with prayer using groups and target recipients (chosen groups of hospital patients, for instance) have shown positive results of faster recovery above statistical chance, regardless of which faith or denomination might be doing the praying. [Dawkins attempts to debunk such studies, but the examples he gives in his 2006 bestseller *The God Delusion* are highly selective.][6] The RNG experiments give a clue as to how it is that prayer can be successful. Maybe it is we ourselves—if also interacting with a larger universal collective consciousness that we could recognise as God—who are doing much of the work, rather than the outcome relying solely on the intercession of a higher power.

The realization that working and thinking together has more than just metaphorical consequence potentially grants us much power; but it also gives us great responsibility. If we could learn fully how the process of collective consciousness works, it could be used to great effect, perhaps even to create the Utopia that humanity has aspired to for centuries. However, it also reveals to us how easily such a mechanism could be manipulated for negative purposes. Maybe it has been deployed against us all this time. We have seen how figures in powerful places appear instinctively to be drawn to occult wisdom and the metaphysical realms. Adolf Hitler is said to have famously gathered such knowledge and created massive collective ripples to a terrible effect. With a new and wider awareness of the power of united thinking, could there be a chance to take back a mechanism that was always rightfully ours? In this way we could start to forge a world we actually want, rather than settling for the prepackaged and compromised one we are being handed.

Of course, the implications of a global consciousness field have mixed consequences, for it means that however much we may try to live apart from the big wide world 'out there', we can never truly escape it. The interactive process ensures that we are always being affected, whether we are aware of civilization's worst excesses or not. Becoming a hermit may not be the panacea of isolation it appears. If the collective is being polluted by what certain elements of humankind put into it, then we are all sullied on some level. However, the equal and happier observation is that when we project positivity and live in ways that offset darkness, the mechanism must be such that it cannot do anything but channel that back into the collective too—an effect that must also reach the very people trying to enforce their agendas over the common good.

'Critical mass' is often spoken about in New Age circles, the belief that if enough people take on an attribute then that same attribute is psychically passed on to the entire human race when a certain key percentage of the population is affected. People will often (if sometimes glibly) speak of the 'hundredth monkey' syndrome as an example, supposedly based on experiments with apes on South Pacific islands.[7] It can sound all too loose and easy—yet experiments by dedicated researchers like Dr Rupert Sheldrake, observing the mysterious transmission of behavioral traits amongst animal species (which he calls 'morphic resonance'), do indeed support the view that all life is bound together by some kind of ether or field. The feeding habits of certain bird species, for instance, have been shown to have very quickly changed across the world at rates beyond that dictated by simple behavioral mimicking. Sheldrake believes the methods and information are being passed on through what amounts to being, in the populist view, a collective telepathic field. Perhaps the all-encompassing 'Force' in the *Star Wars* movies is not so far from the reality of what we are dealing with.

This all seems to suggest that the spreading of collective information and abilities is dictated by the weight of numbers alone; but in the human mechanism at least, the focus of intention seems to have equal status when strategically applied.

The Importance of Intention

Despite the apparent evidence that it is the *proportion* of a population focusing on something that produces the largest energetic output into the collective, it is also clear from the effectiveness of propaganda, sparked from on high and spread by the media, that the collective can be easily led, like starlings in a flock. This unfortunate effect has been responsible for much of the state of affairs we have discussed throughout these pages, and we can now see that there is far more to the process than simple word-of-mouth influence. When a certain percentage of the human race is persuaded to believe something, that belief would appear to be transmitted across the entire species through a more esoteric medium than previously suspected. It takes a strong will and a keen level of awareness to break free of the tendrils being bound around each one of us, regardless of our own individual experience.

But there is evidence to show that concentrated personal *intention* can override the critical-mass mechanism. Free-thinkers have fought themselves clear of the popular consensus since time began—otherwise we might still believe the Sun revolved around the Earth today—but it takes dedication and the courage to face risk. Hitler was a negative example of how one man's will was able to lead the collective, made especially susceptible given the dire social circumstances in Germany at the time of his rise. Some dictators achieve their position by force alone, but charisma and the power of personal faith seems to produce the most lasting effect. This is something that plainly demands vigilance. Some personalities seem to have the power to shape the collective to their own will, setting up lines of dominoes and tipping them to their own patterns and design, while others (like Tony Blair) have the ability to mollify the masses in the face of great resistance while employing obvious deception [Chapter VII]. How can this happen given that the more people who think something, the greater effect it produces on the RNGs? Why is it that some individuals are able to push past this process to impose manifestos of their own onto a majority opposition?

Adolf Hitler, 1932, during his ascent to power. Highly focused intention can easily lead the will of the collective, as Hitler clearly demonstrated—or override weak opposition, for all the importance of the weight of numbers in the RNG experiments.

It is an established statistic that sportsmen or teams tend to win home games more often than when playing away. Although much of this can be put down to a familiarity of environment and a generally more relaxed attitude, the clear presence of support from a larger number of fans makes a huge difference. The players are inevitably more puffed up with pride and propelled by expectation. But it has never been entirely understood why the success rate is influenced so greatly. Perhaps the discoveries regarding collective consciousness provide an answer. But how, then, are certain individuals seemingly able to buck this trend?

Some years back, Tim Henman was one of Britain's finest professional tennis players, and achieved good results in tournaments around the world. Yet whenever confronted with the Wimbledon championships, on his own turf so to speak, although he did better there than anywhere else, full success always eluded him. Why should this have been, with an entire stadium and a country full of eager supporters tuning in to will him to the top? Surely, according to the implications of the collective process, Henman should have won Wimbledon at least once?

Famously, in 2001, it was Croatian player Goran Ivanisevic who raised the winning cup at Wimbledon, to everyone's surprise. When Ivanisevic arrived for the start of the tournament, he was considered a rank outsider after a particularly poor season in the run-up, and he had only been entered into the competition as a 'wild card'. So how was he able to make such a comeback, unexpectedly defeating Henman in the semi-finals along the way? Interestingly, from the moment Ivanisevic was first interviewed for the games, he claimed that he felt confident because God 'wanted' him to win [echoes of George W Bush—page 61]. This extraordinary claim was repeated as he made his victory speech. For all the millions willing Henman to beat him, their wishes appeared to have been entirely nullified by one man's faith that God was on his side. History records many other examples of unlikely victories where the power of something greater was invoked. But did God really fix Ivanisevic's matches for him, or was it the personal conviction that saw the player through? Most likely it was the latter, but it makes a point—the numbers game, as far as the collective mind goes, is not a fail-safe mechanism for success. Something more is needed, and that something appears to be the power of intention. Other psi experiments support this view.[8] Projects which have tried to influence the creation of specific crop formation designs using psychic abilities also appear to demonstrate the same principle, with a number of successful outcomes.[9] The late Masuru Emoto, a doctor of alternative medicine, even claimed that the formation of water crystals can be manipulated by telepathic intention. (Emoto's views have been influential in New Age quarters, although his methods and stated results have been the subject of some controversy.)[10]

Of course, it could be that *lack* of faith might also have played a part in Tim Henman's repeated inability to win Wimbledon. Subconscious thoughts are often more powerful than our conscious minds. Perhaps the innate British fear that he might *not* win, for all the bravado on the surface, coupled with an insecurity around the same thing within the player, also helped to prevent his ultimate triumph.

The quality of intention is very important here, and may explain how a global elite has managed to turn the world to its own advantage. Those fomenting the New World Order and all its grand plans must be highly dedicated if they want their schemes to work. It seems that no stone is left unturned along the way, and the cold propensity towards ruthlessness in the name of a glorious cause, sacrificing perhaps millions of lives in the process, risks them becoming invincible. It can't be denied that the adherence to moral scruples, although the higher path and the one that must be taken, can compromise the chances of instant success (although instant success is not the same as lasting success). Apathy, however, has been the biggest neutralizer of our own potency. The icy focus of highly coordinated intent gives the elite the upper hand over a collective mind that has been weakened by distraction and deception, diverted socially and chemically, and compromised by the insidious encouragement of the 'whatever' attitude; the killer of all effective societies. Our own collective power of intent has been eroded down to almost nothingness in a culture that seems no longer to know what it wants, nor is able to agree on what it thinks matters. The intent from the opposition, meanwhile, has grown ever sharper. No wonder things are they way they are.

It is time to wake up and learn how to use both the weight of numbers *and* intention to change this unacceptable situation. We must become as attentive and focused as those who are shaping the world for us to our detriment—and put to positive use a mechanism that could have the potential to, literally, move mountains.

The Proactive Use of the Collective

Is it too far beyond the realm of imagination to contemplate that the practical application of the collective process could, with much greater development and understanding, be used to do more than simply offset the schemes of a ruling elite? With the risk of cosmological catastrophe hanging over us, an apparatus for dealing with that could also be helpful right now.

In the run-up to the Millennium, one rather promising idea was pitched by the popular psychic Uri Geller. With his claims that broken watches can be fixed by collective focus and that cutlery can be physically bent by the power of the mind (both demonstrated on numerous television programs over the years, to savage attacks from skeptics), Geller reasoned that a wider application of these abilities could make a huge difference to the world. His vision was of stadiums and living rooms full of people on the first day of the new century, focusing their minds on... attempting to defuse the world's nuclear arsenals. What better way to start a new Millennium than by cleansing the planet of one threat, at least? Sadly, the idea never came to fruition, but in the pitching of the idea, Geller had hit on a constructive way of new thinking that could be used in a number of directions.

Given that dice rolls can be influenced by the thoughts of individuals, and that objects can be telekinetically manipulated, albeit on rare occasions, it might be worth considering the idea that this gift could be amplified massively by the focused intent of millions of minds, and used to hold back all manner of looming dangers. If dice can be influenced, why not also, say, a killer asteroid or comet heading our way? Were we to be faced with such an imminent disaster (and were we actually to be told of it in advance), would there be any sense in *not* trying it? Could the Sun's erratic behavior

Could the effects of mass-consciousness and telekinesis experiments offer a way out of potential apocalypse scenarios? Could killer asteroids or comets, for instance, actually be repelled by thought?

be calmed by the influence of the collective, for instance? Or the Earth's seismic movements and vulcanism contained?

Experiments with spiritual healing, monitored by RNGs, also show clear signs of successful influence, again backing up the reality of the power of prayer. Dean Radin describes a study conducted by Ryan Taft in which even brain cell growth in flasks was plainly stimulated by focused healing meditations.[11] This remarkable result suggests that the key to universally good health may be something else in our own hands, if we but knew it. Mental well-being has long been associated with physiological resilience. When humanity stops pumping itself full of the drugs and suppressants sold to it by the pharmaceutical giants as the sole solutions, it may find that it never really needed them. In time, even superhero-type regenerative powers might be possible—all without genetic engineering.

These ideas may sound like insane idealism, and perhaps today they are, but the discovery that our minds do appear to influence the environment around us provides a tiny glimpse into a future that could be very different if such techniques were to be investigated and progressed. Perhaps the next revolution will be not technological, but consciousness-based. If the hopes that the human race may find itself with higher psychic faculties in the New Era are realized, this revolution could come faster than we think.

Taking Responsibility

If it does become an irrefutable fact that the power of the collective mind is an integral part of shaping the world we live in, this will place a large responsibility on every person's shoulders. If what we think, what we say, what we watch and how we act is being fed into an all-encompassing matrix, then it joyfully transmits to, or gloomily infects, every other being on the planet, on however small a scale. No-one can sidestep it. As it is likely that the resulting domino effect of this system has been misused against the populace many times, it is clear that we have played a part in allowing this to happen in an even more substantial way than supposed in the previous chapter. Therefore, we truly need to look at how we live our individual lives and identify what we are feeding into the collective—because it makes a difference to everyone else around us. It is time to take greater responsibility for managing the tools that are used to focus the collective attention, and wrestle back control for a more enlightened purpose.

Even aside from gaming and what is available online, a journey through a usual night's television viewing reveals an appalling diet of death, mutilation and misery, all being fed into the ether and dulling down the collective energy. A study in 1992 revealed that the average child of the day had witnessed around 40,000 onscreen murders by the age of 18.[12] The statistic has probably gone up since. This is not a sensible way to live. We have been fooled into thinking that no other entertainment is as exciting as violent conflict, but we had best be sure of how we want to entertain ourselves in future, as it becomes ever clearer that the evolution of consciousness is at stake here in a very direct way. This does not mean that viewing violent imagery will necessarily create copycat crimes (although this does sometimes happen), but it is not hard to see that continual exposure must create an ambience where violence is more likely to occur. The psychic field must also be affected by the near-continual diet of personal conflict and unpleasantness that glues together most television soaps, inciting depression and pessimism if nothing else.

The minutiae of many things we currently take for granted, therefore, may have to change if the collective is to be used to its purest potential. Even the way we conduct our politics may require a major reassessment. Most Western countries today have at least deduced that the best chambers to operate in are ones set in a semi-circular layout—unlike the British Parliament, the oft-claimed 'mother of democracy', which still follows the traditional pattern of opposing benches. This creates an environment that can only encourage head-

The British Houses of Parliament and some of the people governed by its inhabitants. Both the antiquated layout and traditions of this admittedly globally iconic complex are beginning to look somewhat anachronistic in these times of change—and the psychic imprint of everything that has happened there must surely affect the decisions made within its walls.

to-head conflict, instead of inspiring cooperation. With this, Britain has ignored the lessons of legend; even King Arthur spotted that what was needed for positive government was a round table. The distance between the front benches in the Lords and Commons was actually set out with the expectation of conflict, being precisely two sword-lengths *and a bit* to prevent fights breaking out in the days when weapons were as likely to be brandished as words. From these chambers decisions are made which ripple out and affect peoples' lives, yet the edicts and rulings cannot help but be shaped by their environment. More thought may need to go into what lies at the heart of the smallest domino points. As for London's parliaments, perhaps it is time to move out of the old buildings and into fresh premises for the new times before us (although not, preferably, to Strasbourg or Brussels—page 76). It is often said that ghosts have a tendency to linger where the circumstances of their deaths were traumatic, as if the sudden energetic output of the events somehow imprinted themselves into the fabric of the walls and ceilings. Given this, the endless years of corruption, conflict and obfuscation in the old chambers must have an effect on

Solutions and Inspirations

those working within them today, and influence their thought patterns and moods accordingly. It is time for something different.

Echoes From the Future

Another aspect of psi phenomena that has recently come to light is the quality of 'presentiment'. This is an astonishing discovery resulting from the numerous noted experiments, including the RNG readings. It became clear, from analyzing the data on brainwaves, skin responses and heart and nervous system reactions that an unexpected phenomenon was occurring: both participants in any test were registering the recorded changes in response to stimuli a few seconds (sometimes several seconds) *before* the stimulation. Initially considered an error or statistical quirk, it soon became clear that this effect was repeatedly evident in many tests. Presentiment has since been identified in data even from mainstream medical response test results, something previously unnoticed purely because no-one thought to analyze those parts of the data that preceded the stimulant.[13]

The staggering conclusion that can be drawn from this observation is that, on some level, every one of us knows what is about to happen *a short while in advance*. How this works is an unknown, but work it does. Does the mind exist slightly out of time? Does time not operate in the way we imagined, as quantum physics is beginning to suggest? Either way, the psi tests have stumbled upon an incredible ability we never knew we had—the faculty of responding to future events.

Realizing that this must also be occurring on a much greater scale, researchers applied the observation of presentiment to the global RNG data and discovered—breathtakingly—that certain large-scale events were indeed being anticipated by a large section of humanity. The highly significant RNG responses to 9/11 show that the curve into output coherence began a clear two hours before the first of the attacks. That is two hours in which, on some subconscious level, humanity already knew it was in for one of the most momentous days of modern history. The thoughts of those relative few involved in planning the attacks (whoever they were) would be unlikely

The aftermath of the Boxing Day tsunami of 2004 in Sumatra, Indonesia. The devastation caused by the wave was apalling, but the event also created another kind of wave, a psychic one rippling backwards in time to be picked up by humankind in the hours running up to the quake, as revealed by the RNG data.

to have generated such a notable pattern of non-randomness by themselves, unless the power of intention played a part. Most likely, it seems that we collectively felt the echo of a ripple coming backwards in time towards us. Indeed, there are many records of relevant dreams, visions and predictions that occurred across the world in the days and hours before the events of 9/11, which were perhaps very literal receptions of this spontaneous broadcast from the future. Similarly, the 2004 tsunami, which wiped out the coastlines of many countries on the Indian Ocean, also produced a presentiment curve of coherence in the hours before the quake took place, again with preceding dreams and intimations. Animals seemed to pick up on the future echo even more strongly, with many reports of strange behavior and of creatures clearing away from the coasts long before the event.[14] Skeptics say they were simply sensing tremors beyond our senses, but others believe they may be more finely tuned into the presentiment system than we are, as Sheldrake's work might suggest. If the tsunami was a truly natural event (some have claimed the quake was triggered by nuclear tests, as others have asserted that the Japanese tsunami of 2011 was deliberately caused by the HAARP Project [page 70], though there is no definitive proof for this), no intention component could, presumably, have come into the equation.

Time is perhaps one of the least understood qualities of nature, and the 'new physics' is rapidly discovering that many of our previous presumptions about it have been wrong. High energy accelerators have produced particles that seem to travel backwards in time, and the laws of physics do not entirely rule out the possibility of negative flow. We appear on the surface to live our lives in an arrow of time that moves forward, but maybe not everything obeys those rules. If time is a river, flowing generally in one direction, perhaps a disruptive pebble thrown into that river, just as in water, momentarily produces ripples that flow in both directions, before all of them are quickly swept forwards again. It may be that this is what we are picking up on with huge events like 9/11. Some moments may be so big, so devastating to the consciousness of humanity, that they punch larger holes in the river than others. Perhaps, if we could learn to fine-tune the reading of the data, we could even discover how to interpret the echoes from the future—or possible futures—and try to change the events if necessary, or avoid the worst consequences.

Stepping Up to the Task

Alternative physics, then, brings us back to one of the central themes of this hypothesis. Prophecies and predictions about these times are so strong, so ubiquitous, that it is not unreasonable to suppose that what we are collectively tuning into is a particularly large ripple from an occurrence just around the corner, making itself known in the manner described. Except that this time the ripple may be so big that we have been picking up on it for years—centuries, even. Certain sections of human society may have known about this all along and kept it hidden, but maybe now the secret is leaking out. The exact nature of the change everyone seems to feel in their bones still remains elusive, but they sense it nonetheless. Can we alter it or anticipate its worst excesses (if the event turns out to have negative connotations), or can we only confront it as it arrives?

The evolution of consciousness may have been the very thing which is gifting us the ability to 'see' further than we ever have before, and curves of learning and the development of technology are now enabling us to detect the presence of energetic waves, whilst revealing telling transgressions of what were previously seen as the barriers of time. Whatever happens to us, that evolution of the collective mind has been precious, and we must not let it go to waste by giving up hope of improving ourselves. Instead, we could use a new wider awareness of the power of consciousness to help create hitherto unimaginable solutions to break the ancient cycle of mass extinctions and cosmological threats. With that awareness, we could gain an extra faculty that might help us enormously once its full effect is realized.

Rupert Sheldrake—'alternative' scientists such as Sheldrake attempt to push back the boundaries of consciousness research with convincing data, but still meet resistance at every turn.

As things stand, the dogma of establishment science continues to hold back full investigation of this potential gift, and those who challenge the narrow parameters set down by academic scoffers are attacked and ridiculed without their evidence ever being properly addressed. Rupert Sheldrake suffered accordingly when he was invited to speak on his work for the eminent TED (Technology, Entertainment, Design) lecture series, only to find the video of his compelling presentation taken down from the main TED website and YouTube channel because of complaints from mainstream scientists, who accused him of quackery and of debasing 'true' science. (Alternative archaeologist Graham Hancock received the same treatment.)[15] Such unfortunate examples do not encourage the hope that consciousness research will reach wider acceptance any time soon, but the extreme reaction to these new ideas also speaks of a defensiveness that indicates cages being rattled—cages that will one day, sooner or later, surely have to be opened, if shamefacedly and belatedly.

When greater acceptance of collective fields is finally embraced, in some far distant time the extraordinary ability of mind to create coherence might even be applied to the inherent problem of 'entropy' (energy's ultimate propensity towards disorder), which many—though not all—scientists believe will one day dictate a long and dreary end to the universe in a soup of dead particles. But they are surely not factoring in the power of consciousness to seemingly rearrange energy and matter, which might yet provide a mechanism by which entropy is defeated. In several billion years, who knows where the tiny seed of understanding we may just be starting to nurture may take us, together with the unified coherence created by whatever other flickers of sentience the cosmos produces elsewhere in its myriad environments for life.[16]

These exciting processes and the recognition of their potentials stand before us, then, offering huge opportunities for those open-minded enough to grasp them. The Internet has already expanded our ability to share thoughts and experiences with millions of souls across the world in seconds, and combined with future technologies of biological and mind/matter interfacing, with all their dreams and nightmares, the evolution of the collective could take any kind of astonishing turn. Yet already, here today, the combined power we do have, twinned with practical *action* and freed from fear, offers endless possibilities. Thus it is time for all of us to step up to the task of forging the world anew—not a New World Order, but simply a new world. History alone records that when people stand up to be counted, positive change always comes—and showing up for duty is the first step.

THE TRUTH AGENDA: *Astonishing discoveries are being made in the realm of consciousness research, revealing that psychic abilities are not rare gifts, but widely-distributed effects that bind us together on a day to day basis. The realization that collective thought is not an abstract concept but, courtesy of the Random Number Generator experiments, a recordable reality, grants us an insight into hitherto unsuspected powers we may all have available to forge a better world using both the telepathic weight of numbers and the power of intention. With that realization, however, comes greater awareness of the huge responsibility we have to our fellow beings. What we think and do affects everyone else, and what we pour into the collective helps to shape it negatively or positively, as we decide.*

The US Live Aid concert, 1985, one in a network of
simultaneous global events that raised millions for famine
relief and set an example of what can be achieved when
people stand up for a cause and work together positively.

XV   THE POWER OF POSITIVE ACTION

How can we put into practice the lessons learned from serious contemplation of the control agenda, and live a new truth to create a better world, whilst maintaining personal integrity? What does history show us about the possibility of turning around even the most seemingly insurmountable situations through concerted collective effort? Taking the initiative and keeping the flame of optimism alive must now be our primary duty.

Personal Responsibility

A growing theme as these pages have unfolded has been that of taking collective responsibility. Global cover-ups and deceptions only occur because everyone allows them to. But, as the process of collective mind reveals, *personal* responsibility is equally as important. What manifests in the collective is a product of what we do individually. Although it is easy to point the finger at governments and ruling elites for their many misdemeanors, if we are truly honest with ourselves it is likely that we all embody many of the same issues in our own personal lives. Lies and deception occur through fear and the dominance of the ego. Can many of us say we have never once been dishonest in our lives? When we do fall from integrity, we create caveats for ourselves to justify our actions, and the caveats may sometimes even have validity. Those who rule our lives are simply mass-projections of our own inner conflicts and issues. It is often said that we get the leaders we deserve, and there is a truth to this. They represent *us* in more ways than one. We put them there and permit them to stay in positions of influence even after the likes of the weapons of mass destruction debacle. Those we don't vote for, the mysterious elite, Illuminati, ruling class, whatever we choose to call them, still could not function in the way they do without society's tacit consent through apathy. We very often turn blind eyes to the things we fear are occurring, because engaging any more closely invites the possibility of having to do something about it ourselves—and this is where the resolve of many people falters. This is a great shame, because the will to change things is there, but the fear and distractions placed on us tend to dissolve the confidence necessary to stand up and put thoughts into action.

This author once had a conversation with a fellow guest at a party. The guest was bemoaning the surveillance state, speed cameras, the threat of an ID culture and the rise of ridiculous rules regarding the photographing of school football matches. Venturing the suggestion that perhaps he should join the growing movement trying to alert people to such concerns, offering mention of a few websites and publications that might help, I was met with an immediate and dramatic withdrawal of interest. Suddenly, there was a backtracking; the guest's entire demeanor changed. He went as far as to say that actually he wasn't really bothered by any of the things he had just been loudly lamenting and that he didn't think things were really too bad. It would all be alright in the end. Excuses were made and he shuffled away.

This cautionary tale encapsulates the problems faced in trying to create change; many people want it, but are either too scared or too habitually passive to stand up and be counted. Once again, our collective cultural resolve is so much weaker than the highly focused intent of those making the rules for us, that the imbalance of power becomes inevitable. This has to change if the worst excesses of the control agenda are to be avoided.

Facing the Fear of Ridicule

Disenchanted citizens tend not to voice deeper concerns for the world they live in because they fear ridicule from a society that has been trained not to question, brainwashed by a media that pours scorn on anything remotely 'alternative'. Yet the curious fact is that when just one person takes a risk and expresses personal feelings about potential 'other' reasons for the state of things, it is remarkable how many people will then agree with the viewpoints expressed. It doesn't take too long to find someone at work, on the bus, or in the family, who will agree with what may at first seem like an extreme view, though it can take time for the barrier to be broken. At first, there may be a reluctance to engage with the issue, if there is an uncertainty about what will result. Given the confidence, however, that by openly assenting to a supposedly heretical view that they will not be met with mocking humiliation, supportive personal views and anecdotes are often forthcoming, sometimes from unexpected quarters. As a prolific lecturer on unexplained mysteries and cover-ups, the author has witnessed this phenomenon many times—faced with someone risking more ridicule than they are, audience members will often share a view or an experience (often to do with ghosts or UFO sightings) they may never have spoken of before. It is quickly revealed by this kind of admission, or by venturing into unusual personal conversations with friends and colleagues, that society's self-image of 'consensus reality' is entirely false. We live in a world underpinned by mysteries and deceptions, as this book has revealed, but a facade is presented to give the opposite impression, and most of us quietly agree not to rock the boat.

Speakers forum at Britain's longest-running 'alternative' conference, the Glastonbury Symposium [page 370]. Faced with people publicly willing to speak their minds at such events, listeners will often open up about their own beliefs, which can reveal quite a different take to official 'consensus reality'.

To shatter this fraudulent artifice, then, we need to be willing to take risks. We have to step into our real power and learn to face opposition with confidence and courage. So what, if someone doesn't agree with your view on, say, 9/11 or the Moon landings? So what, if you challenge the official version of a major news story and are taken to task on it? A little resilience and obstinacy is called for. The odds are that any returning verbal attack will be based on loosely-held perceptions of the issues rather than genuinely firm knowledge, so why not take a small chance and guess that you will be in possession of more facts than your critics? If you are *not* familiar with those facts, of course, then you are on shaky ground. All truthseekers owe it to themselves to be properly informed on the subject of their passion. Views ranted without foundation are soon rounded on for demolition, and rightly so. But when there is a firm basis for a debate, when one has gathered more information (or at least serious points to raise) than most, conversational authority is often quietly conceded to those whose power of intent, combined with informed argument, radiates clearly. *Un*informed challengers will often back down in the face of supreme confidence, and a strong personal conviction can be admired even by those who disagree with the viewpoint. In a society where most opinions are based on third-hand tabloid sources, ones that the majority of the public know in their hearts aren't reliable, someone who really knows their subject is in good stead.

This is not to say that voicing unusual views in the bar or in the office, in an attempt to air important issues, isn't sometimes going to be an uncomfortable experience. Some listeners will take up the gauntlet and attempt to demolish you with equal conviction, in the same way that this book will doubtless be torn apart by those who have firmly placed themselves into the camp of the mainstream 'consensus' view. But so be it. Questioning convention isn't for the faint-hearted. However, adopting the right tones and being as non-confrontational as possible can make a huge difference. Offer a truth, never attempt to sell it. But if this doesn't work, comfort yourself with the thought that if George W Bush and Tony Blair could get over widely televised criticism and even eventual proof of their connivance in the Iraq war debacle and *still* be voted back in, anyone can handle a little humiliation here and there.

If readers of this book have concluded that a ruling elite is indeed trying to warp the world's needs to its own deceptive manifestos, then our very civilization, our very planet, even our lives, may all be at stake. What price a little philosophical confrontation here and there? For those with eyes to see, it is time to step up to the full responsibility demanded by the simple awareness that a serious debate needs to take place. We have already established that the collective effect of doing this could be massive—but the fight to apply the Truth Agenda to many levels of life now needs to begin in earnest.

Being the Change
Personal integrity is vital in all of this. Trying to make the world a better place whilst living a life full of the same mistakes one is hoping to correct in others can only take a mission so far. None of us is perfect, but we owe it to ourselves to take a good long

look in the mirror before setting out to right the wrongs of others. It is not an easy process, nor one that will ever be fully won; we are only human after all. But a habit of occasionally checking for false projections, correcting even the smallest step into the kind of behavior we may abhor on the outside, is one worth cultivating.

If we are all contributing to a growing entity of shared mind that imprints itself on the universe, it is also our collective responsibility to create a world that operates from a positive center—and this can only be done by operating from the correct place in our own personal center. If some of the more dire predictions of apocalyptic events were to be realized, we might find ourselves in a society that rapidly developed into a dog-eat-dog situation (it is often said we are only two meals away from revolution). The question we must ask ourselves is, do we really want to be dogs? Cultivating a compassionate manner, if resolute and resilient, whilst helping to set up a cooperative network of like-minded people unwilling to fall into anarchy and chaos, could make a huge difference in the event of a global crisis. (The grim but meaningful 2009 film adaptation of Cormac McCarthy's post-apocalypse novel *The Road* offers some interesting meditations on this theme.)

The maintenance of personal integrity also extends to living out our ideals, not just preaching them. So if the crumbling of communities and families is a personal concern, then making active efforts to create strong communities and families should become a priority. If the denigration of speech and the dumbing down of society worries us, then we need to make the effort to use a wider vocabulary and keep ourselves educated and sharp. If political deception creates a pain in our hearts, then we need to live as honestly in our own lives as we can. And so on. Put more simply, universally applying the adage 'be the change you want to see' to all areas of life will stand more chance of manifesting an improved world than not doing so.

Guarding Against Mob Rule

Given the propensity for civil unrest in hard times, the rise of the mob-rule mentality should be actively guarded against. We have seen that it is likely that a social upheaval of some kind could erupt in harder times, as economic conditions and concern over control agendas exacerbate the problem. There will always be those who will use these situations to indulge delightedly in violence and conflict, as we have seen in some 'anti-capitalist' protests. There may also be *agent provocateurs* stirred into the mix by governments which could, increasingly, be looking for convenient excuses to install draconian restrictions on their citizens. When stones were thrown through the window of a prominent executive in the wake of a British banking scandal, for instance, the television coverage as good as announced his home address, seeming to beg for more trouble. It is interesting to note how often the concept of potential rioting is planted into the public mind by politicians and journalists, under the guise of not wanting it. The media thrives on conflict, while the ruling forces want more control, which makes for a powerful mix we should be very suspicious of. In June 2009, then British Conservative leader David Cameron (before becoming prime minister) voiced an expectation of street riots, things that then indeed occurred under his watch, starting with 2010's student protests and accelerating with the oddly nihilistic mass rioting across British cities in 2011. Even mainstream sources questioned why police appeared to deliberately stand back and allow things to conflagrate on the first night, almost ensuring a further spread of anarchy. The bizarre incident of Prince Charles and the Duchess of Cornwall's official car 'accidentally' getting caught up in the 2010 student scuffles and consequently being attacked by protestors was also widely seen as a set-up. US race riots, meanwhile, are often sparked by obviously avoidable police violence. What is going on? Is this social engineering at work to deliberately create civil unrest?[1] Sure enough, new legislation usually follows, giving police greater street powers, with calls made for closer monitoring of online social networking, perceived to be aiding 'criminal action', strongly bringing to mind the classic PROBLEM-REACTION-SOLUTION equation [Chapter V].

Riot police at the G20 protests. The concept of rioting seems to have been increasingly seeded in the public mind in these austerity times. Such events only enable the justification of more extreme draconian laws, and we must guard against a stirred mob mentality.

The catch is that there *is* increasingly good reason to take to the streets—in peaceful protest. Injustice, restricted liberty, misplaced austerity measures, and the outrageous financial abuse of banks and companies (especially those avoiding tax) remain unaddressed to any serious degree, for all the disingenuous talk of 'Big Society' and the suchlike. The new resistance now seems to come from Western 'middle classes' as much as extremist groups. There is a notable unrest (especially amongst the elderly, who have seen hard-earned pensions crumble) in a previously quiet demographic that might have been underestimated. But issues that demand serious protest are often sidelined and perhaps deliberately distracted from, eclipsed instead by social scapegoating, such as the anti-Muslim protests and assaults that followed both the Boston Marathon bombs in April 2013, and the bizarre London street attack a month later, where apparent Islamic fanatics killed and attempted to dismember a soldier in plain sight (leading to many conspiracy allegations).[2] Public horror was, of course, justified if the attacks were what they seemed to be, but blanket venom towards an ethnic minority blamed for a nation's troubles must do nothing but help states breathe sighs of relief, happy to see national ire deflected away from them for a while.

For the issues that do demand serious action, armed revolution and mob rule will not solve anything—instead it might simply play into the hands of those waiting to use all the many civil unrest measures which have quietly accumulated in the wake of the War on Terror. Perhaps the claimed secret internment camps [page 258] may yet find some occupants. We must not make it so easy for any such plans. What is needed now is a rebellion of the heart, not one of hate and anger. Non-violent action has nearly always shown itself to have the longest-lasting effect in fomenting global change, as we shall shortly see. We must stand in the light and look to the highest aspirations if we want to forge a better civilization. But violent protests are often given the most publicity, again raising a suspicion about media motivation.

It has already been noted that some conspiracy theorists believe that Britain is being used as a 'guinea pig', the focus of a huge social experiment in control techniques. It certainly has more surveillance cameras than anywhere else in the world, and sweeping anti-terror laws that have raised many eyebrows. The old historical ties between the US and Britain may explain why the climate of restriction and suppression has seemed especially strong in both countries since 9/11. For a small country, the original 'mother of democracy' still maintains a high profile in accusations concerning the NWO, and it is worth briefly looking at the issues around this.

Manipulating the 'Mother of Democracy'

If believers in the Reptilian Agenda are correct [Chapter V], then the British Royal Family lie at the very heart of the global controlling elite. However, even without the ET element, and for all the torchbearing of the NWO from the US in recent decades, it is very clear that Britain still maintains great prominence in this area. Some people, for instance, think that Britain was specifically chosen to focus the 'energies' at the gates of the New Era in 2012, by being granted the Olympic Games for that year. It was certainly to great relief that the London Olympics passed off without any dire consequence; many truthseekers had feared some kind of false-flag attack.

However, there is evidence that the games may have been used for more subtle psy-ops (psychological operations) purposes. Keen observers feel it was no accident that London won the bid for the 2012 Olympics. It wasn't expected to—Paris was the front-runner, and there were allegations of vote-rigging amongst the Olympic panels. It seems to have been important to someone that the eyes of the world should be on the UK in 2012, and the UK wasn't complaining. The country's jubilation at the news was short lived, though. Just one day after the announcement in July 2005, the 7/7 bombings took place, instantly neutering any pride or joy. Some people believe this was a form of social conditioning. Although thankfully it did not turn out to be a foreshadowing of what might come with the games themselves, it was still a celebration then tempered with a grim recognition of the hard realities of life. A morbid coincidence was noted by many viewers when the mock double-decker, carrying London Mayor Boris Johnson and guitarist Jimmy Page (amongst others) into China's Beijing Olympic stadium as part of the hand-over ritual in its 2008 closing ceremony, mechanically opened up at the top to resemble, rather disturbingly, the exploded 7/7 bus in Tavistock Square. Was this making a point?

Once the 2012 Olympic stadium was completed, New World Order aficionados were struck even more by the marked, and surely intentional, resemblance of both the surrounding lighting gantries and the excessively peculiar single-eyed Olympic mascots to the famous Masonic symbol of the 'Eye of Providence' over the pyramid [page 90]. The nearby 'Orbit' tower, a mess of tangled scaffolding, was also created implicitly (according to Anish Kapoor, its designer) to suggest 'unstability'; a strange message to radiate to the world. Those who fear Zionist agendas had already been drawn by the very odd coincidence of the official '2012' logo spelling the word 'Zion' [page 83] when rearranged even just

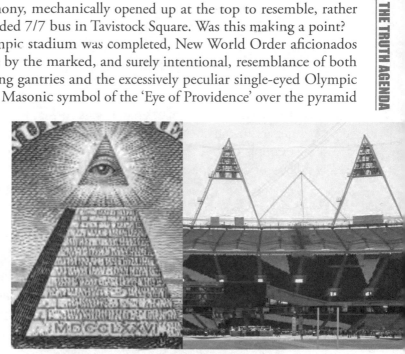

The lighting gantries at the London Olympic stadium (right) bear an uncanny resemblance to the Masonic 'Eye of Providence' (left)—note also the implied Giza-type pyramid structure between the two gantries. Other unignorable New World Order correlations were noted in a number of 2012 Olympic symbols.

slightly. If the ruling elite weren't going to take any action during the Games, they were certainly going to make their presence felt, either as a cynical in-joke or to sully the collective energies of an event that focused much of humanity's attention at the very doorstep of the all-important New Era. But why select Britain to be at the heart of that attention in 2012? Why was the favorite Paris not chosen, say, with all its overt occult architecture and secret society connections, if a full message of elite dominance needed to be delivered? Or indeed the US, so obviously a NWO linchpin?

Misplaced patriotism aside, there has always been something specific about the UK that has made it a world leader in so many areas. Somehow, this little country even managed to create an Empire that spanned the globe, a NWO forerunner. Unfortunately, that empire was founded on slavery and oppression, but the fact that it was created at all was still remarkable. Perhaps it is something in the British psyche—it generally looks outwards and retains a keen awareness of the wider world. Its people are not insular, always seeking outreach, be it through trade, colonization or the spread of pioneering culture (modern music especially). The British don't keep things to themselves. Like US citizens, they may be protective of their borders (hence the EU's exasperation at the UK's reluctance to give away sovereignty, and the apparent program to erode it from the inside), but they *do* always want to talk to the world outside of them. Britain stands between the Americas and Europe and has often provided a bridge between the two, politically and philosophically. It also displays a healthy balance of cynicism and open-mindedness. Despite the impression given in its media, most British citizens *will* listen to unusual viewpoints if backed up by evidence and reasoned debate.

The fact that Britain is seen by some figures in the New Age movement as the 'heart chakra' of the world is interesting. Certainly, it is curious that this country attracts (or generates, depending on one's viewpoint) more crop circles than any other—and this is just one example of some peculiarly British (although often English) mysteries on the boundaries of the inexplicable that have ignited many discussions about the entire nature of reality. For all the inevitable skepticism, the enduring fascination with the crop formations (even by non-believers) is a fine example of national stoicism in the face of opposition. The presence of a network of stone circles and 'earth energy' sites has also attracted many alternative thinkers to the country, and the continuing flirtation with Arthurian myths, stories of Jesus visiting Glastonbury, and belief in fairies and a whole undercurrent of mystical beings that

Britain's Glastonbury Tor, considered by some to be the Isle of Avalon, King Arthur's final resting place. This 'green and pleasant land' is rich with myths, legends and mysteries such as the crop circles, and many people feel that its roots have played a key role in modern global power.

supposedly inhabit the British Isles, seems to add to the feeling of something special residing there. Britain escaped threatened invasion in several conflicts, most notably from the Spanish Armada in the 1500s and from the Nazis in the Second World War, and perhaps there is some underlying esoteric reason for its having been so protected in recent centuries. It would make sense that the roots of modern global power and crucial bloodlines might be found concentrated in such a place. With all the speculation, both social and metaphysical, about the possible turning-points of the New Era, it is curious that the UK played such a major role around the opening of the gateway. Yet at the same time, could it be that the control experiment is being specifically focused there because the British are particularly susceptible, rather than enlightened? It does seem to have been recognized by at least one of the great mystics that there is more to the role of the British than meets the eye. Speaking in Switzerland in 1917, while addressing the issue of secret societies, the Austrian philosopher Rudolf Steiner described 'elements' of the British as being the bearers of 'the consciousness soul', but he also identified their vulnerability to manipulation:

'What is the aim of these secret brotherhoods? They do not work out of any particular British patriotism but out of the desire to bring the whole world under the yoke of pure materialism. And because... ...certain elements of the British people as the bearer of the consciousness soul are most suitable for this, the brotherhoods want, by means of grey magic, to use these elements as promoters of this materialism. This is the important point. Those who know what impulses are at work in world events can also steer them. No other national element, no other people, has ever before been so usable as material for transforming the whole world into a materialistic realm.

Therefore, those who know want to set their foot on the neck of this national element and strip it of all spiritual endeavor—which of course lives equally in all human beings. Just because karma has ordained that the consciousness soul should work here [in Britain] particularly strongly, the secret brotherhoods have sought out elements in the British national character. Their aim is to send a wave of materialism over the Earth and make the physical plane the only valid one. A spiritual world is to be recognized only in terms of what the physical plane has to offer.' [3]

This uncannily accurate foresight would appear to be borne out by today's program of control and the distraction of materialism, which seems so powerful in the UK, at the expense of the numinous. It may also explain why the New Era could be used to make a demonstration of quelling the human spirit there; some citizens may have the 'consciousness soul', but they are also easy to manipulate in certain ways.

So, for every nation that is undoubtedly embroiled in the schemes of today, Britain may have been selected long ago to help sow the seeds of control, with its partial progeny, the US, taking it further. Each country has its own strengths and weaknesses and doubtless all have their own vital part to play in either falling further under the spell of ancient power games, or awakening to the truth and changing the plan.

The Waiting Game

As we are now in the times alluded to for so long in prophecies and visions, any sense of anticipation as to how they might progress needs to be matched with a schedule of proactive action to lay the ground positively. The high hopes dashed by the uneventful passing of the 21st December 2012 date did bring home to some souls the realization that perhaps change needed to be earned rather than just expected, but certain faith communities still seem determined to wait for everything to be done for them. This problem has been endemic amongst certain Christian elements awaiting an imminent Second Coming, and it also compromises a number of groups in the New Age community.

As far back as the early 1990s, psychic channellings were being widely received from an apparently space-faring spiritual collective known as the Ascended Masters. Led by Sananda, reputedly an incarnation of the Christ, and accompanied by the commander Ashtar, Saint Germain and an assortment of holy avatars, the messages generated a popular belief that spaceships were orbiting the planet, waiting to rescue the chosen ones before the predicted Earth changes began in earnest. Vivid predictions of the San Andreas fault demolishing California and of a chain of subsequent earthquakes, volcanoes and hurricanes led many followers to believe the end was nigh. All would be well for the more spiritually-advanced, however, who would be beamed up onto the ships at the crucial time. Except that the time never came—or if it did, no-one noticed. Some devotees had sold their belongings, left partners and quit jobs, and gone into holy exile to wait for their 'ascension'. Presumably they still wait today. Perhaps it was the New Era the channellings were really referring to, but it seemed clear at the time that the changes were expected within the 1990s.

Unfulfilled prophecies have been letting down the devout for generations, and the same disappointment manifested to those who had been anticipating a more direct effect for the key 2012 date. However, the personal purification process the Ascension followers went through might still have counted for something for those who put them into practice there and then. Some seekers, sensibly, used the learning gleaned from *considering* the possibility of huge change as a self-fulfilling program of personal development, similar to that discussed at the end of Chapter XII, and as such they didn't waste their time. Others, however, waited, putting entire lives on hold, abdicating responsibility to improve the world they lived in. The Ascended Masters would put all to rights when they arrived, and who were they to interfere with their plans? Better to sit quietly and wait. And wait.

When it was pointed out that perhaps Ascension wasn't coming after all, new channellings started to come through, which intimated that the rescue program *had* in fact occurred. No-one had noticed though, because the memory of ascended friends and family had been 'erased' from our minds. On one level, this ludicrously unlikely let-out devastated those aghast at having been left behind, but on another it effectively ended the Ascension movement in its initial guise, as people woke up to the possibility that they might just have been led astray by some trickster thought-form. Belief in Ascension, though reduced, is still around today, and has strong resonance with the evangelical Rapture movement, but it mostly seems to have become something more sensibly nebulous and rather less dogmatic.

This phenomenon of being on eternal hold, doing nothing but waiting, is something that occurs in a number of spiritual movements, yet it feels fundamentally wrong. Surely, any higher being would demand some active participation from us to make a better world, rather than just offer salvation on a plate? And for those awaiting the Second Coming, is it unreasonable to consider that Jesus himself might also want some positive change instigated in the run-up to his arrival? Waiting for beings from

The Power of Positive Action XV

above to come down and put everything straight, be they Jesus, Maitreya, Ashtar or all manner of anticipated (unfaked) extra-terrestrial landings, obviously high on the expectation list due to the concerted UFO cover-ups explored in Chapter III, risks becoming yet another excuse not to do anything ourselves to sort things out.

Making a Stand

It is time to make a stand. Regardless of what other powers may be out there watching over us, we cannot take the chance that they really exist or, if they do, that they will be there for us when it counts. WE have to create change, and it has to happen now. Any ruling elite (sometimes blamed for encouraging belief in celestial rescuers) will not be waiting for something else to do its work for it. There are identifiable problems that could be tackled here and now with enough people willing to play their part and make it happen. We must also set our own standards. The supposed testimony of gods and prophets have made it pretty clear over the centuries what is required of us for better lives, and we ourselves are now canny enough to be able to make the choice between right and wrong. The cradle has fallen and we have to stand on our own feet.

Assuming full personal responsibility can be the moment of epiphany. In his 1983 book *People of the Lie*,[4] psychiatrist Dr M Scott Peck cites a lack of anyone taking responsibility as one of the reasons for the appalling 1968 My Lai massacre, in which US soldiers rampaged through a South Vietnamese village, indiscriminately raping and killing hundreds of civilians, mostly women and children. Each participant simply deferred responsibility to another in the chain of command, who then did the same, *ad infinitum*. Few wanted to risk being seen as objectors. So bloodlust reigned and unwisely dehumanized men found themselves doing the unthinkable. In the end, only one military commander was ever prosecuted for the atrocity, and even then Richard Nixon stepped in to reduce his sentence.[5]

This far-from-isolated example says much about the reason why we all too often live under the strictures of evil, or even incompetence—because not enough of us are willing to put our heads above the parapet, to stand up for what is so clearly right. Yet when we do, and the collective takes hold, the successful results can be striking. Perhaps the oft-stated, and yet underestimated, adage (generally attributed to the 18th century political philosopher Edmund Burke) says it best: 'All that is necessary for the triumph of evil is that good men do nothing.'

When people do decide to take a role in shaping their community and environments, extraordinary things can happen. Being proactive in voicing views on both the small and the large things in life, and creatively campaigning for necessary changes, generates a web of focused intent that binds people together more positively and breaks the stagnation of laziness and apathy. Everyone feels better in an active state, and energy expended positively is never wasted. It seems to be a universal law that it comes back a thousandfold in the end, refreshing those who give it. The Random

Number Generator experiments have now shown that such focused activity truly reshapes the world on measurable levels. Far more energy is expended in a much less healthy way enduring yet another heavy night of television in the armchair.

Doing something, anything, even just once a week, could make a substantial contribution to the world. For the truly enthusiastic, US film-maker and political activist Michael Moore recommends that all the people with strong views on the incapability of authorities should stand for election themselves, even on small local councils, so that those on power trips are not always the ones left in charge. Otherwise, writing letters to political representatives, newspapers, councillors or web forums on whatever issues are of concern could nudge the odd domino here and there, at least. Taking part in peaceful protests and spreading leaflets for campaigns is another outlet. They may not get instant results but do transmit the fact that someone cares about the decisions that are made. Joining collectives and organizations of like-minded people can be more influential than working alone, and getting involved with positive local projects, social or environmental, can produce unexpected results (the planned erection of many local microwave masts have been successfully fought this way, for instance, and there are now concerted anti-fracking movements at work). If even that seems too much, just willfully introducing a 'difficult' subject at the bar or across the dinner table might transform at least one person's life. And if there is no possibility of social interaction, then the simple act of changing one's own attitude on a daily basis might feed something good back into the collective. However much or little we choose to do, let us not go passively into our cages.

For the bolder participants, Moore's idea of putting oneself up for even minor elections identifies something important. All the while those who fervently desire power are allowed to dominate the electoral system, the big egos and dangerous climbers most likely to be recruited by the elite will continue to rise to the top, and we will suffer accordingly. Installing a system that compels a certain number of people who do *not* have political ambitions to be part of any vote might at least prevent some of the more dubious manipulated decisions that have colored our view of authorities throughout history. Perhaps one day (with our full idealist glasses on) the technology that already allows the population to vote for their favorite TV singers or entertainers each week, might be broadened to allow us all more of an everyday say in governmental matters. If electronic voting is seen as safe enough to be used for general elections, why should many big ongoing decisions not also be influenced by Internet-referenda, with everyone voting from home on the issues of the day? If that is not practical, laws could be passed to ensure that at least a proportion of every Parliamentary vote has to be cast by members of the public, perhaps being called into the Houses on a jury-service basis. Although the decisions influenced by such a system might be somewhat unpredictable, it would be a truer democracy and would at least ensure far fewer lobbied and partisan decisions. To put things right, then, we may have to take part ourselves in the very systems we feel threatened by.

The Positive Lessons of Recent History

Throughout these pages we have explored the connection between unexplained mysteries, conspiracy theories and future prophecies, trying to see where the truth of it all lies. One thing, it would seem, has become clear; that whatever the underlying reality there does appear to be a concerted effort to control humankind through subterfuge and oppression. For a long time this scheme has been flying 'under the radar', but now it appears to be emerging unapologetically into full sight—a worrying sign that its sponsors are becoming confident of a successful outcome. But this arrogance may have revealed their hand too soon. They may have underestimated the strength of feeling that could be galvanized with enough public consciousness. There is still time to awaken the world to what is going on.

History records many instances when seemingly hopeless situations have been quickly turned around by the sudden rising of awareness and mass action, and it is helpful here to remind ourselves of a few of them:

• In 1989, within weeks, political shift within the Eastern Bloc saw the opening of the border between East and West Germany and the fall of the Berlin Wall. Thousands took to the previously impregnable barrier and stood defiantly on top of it, unable to believe that such an enduring symbol of division and oppression had been rendered impotent overnight. It is true that by this point it was politically and economically convenient for the wall to be removed, but the flood of hope and transformation that ran through the population of the alienated German sides was very real and enabled the change to take place more swiftly and painlessly than might ever have been imagined; in the end, seeing growing bureaucratic delays and painfully slow political manoeuvring, citizens took things into their own hands and the armies stood back. No-one could have foreseen such a development even a year or so before.

Suffragette Emmeline Pankhurst is arrested in London, 1914. The struggle to attain votes for women was hard—but successful. The suffragette movement is one of the best examples of great change achieved through dedication and tenacity, and its motto is timely today: 'deeds, not words.'

• The suffragette movement in the late 19th and early 20th century saw a huge step forward for the rights of women in the West. Arrests, abuse and intimidation failed to douse the spirit of the suffragettes, one of whom (Emily Davison) threw herself under

King George V's race horse to make her point, losing her life in the process. Change did not come easily for the women's movement, but it did come. After slow and reluctant legislative amendments, in the end equal voting rights were won. Finding a candidate one *wants* to vote for is more of the problem today, but it shouldn't be forgotten how hard-won the universal ability to do so was. It took the rise of a large and concerted movement to achieve the end, and the journey wasn't comfortable, but it worked and helped transform the lives of millions.

• The late Nelson Mandela was incarcerated for 27 years and it seemed for a long while that he would die in captivity. Although some critics still believe that his original tactics with the armed wing of the African National Congress did amount to terrorism, perception had changed by the 1980s and Mandela had become a symbol of freedom for the disempowered black majority. Dedicated and relentless campaigning, aided by international awareness, helped push South Africa into unexpected social shift. An upsurge of support humbled and undermined the white minority government and Mandela was released in 1990. Within four years he had become president of South Africa. Few people would have predicted such an astonishing development in such a short time.

• Oppressed Poland saw the unexpected rise in the early 1980s of the dockyard union Solidarity. Breaking all the rules of the then communist regime, and led by the tenacious figure of Lech Wałęsa, Solidarity inspired a huge national freedom movement in the face of violent threats and harsh penalties. Although the union suffered severe repression the flame didn't go out and the dissolution of the Soviet Union (helped in part by the example set by Polish workers) saw the incredible development of a Solidarity-led coalition effectively forming the first post-oppression government, with Wałęsa as its president. Poland had many social problems still, but it was free at last to work out its issues on its own democratic terms—largely because enough people had risked all to make it happen.

• It is easy to be cynical about the now ubiquitous charity bonanzas of today, but the Live Aid concerts of 1985 were a remarkable example of mass consciousness in action. Realizing that the governments of the world were not doing enough to prevent an appalling humanitarian crisis due to famine and conflict in Ethiopia, a conglomerate of rock stars led by Bob Geldof and Midge Ure (whose role is often understated) mounted first an all-star charity Christmas record in 1984 (*Band Aid*), and then the massive network of live concerts around the world on 13 July 1985, led by the London concert in Wembley Stadium and linked by global satellite transmissions. Huge amounts of money were raised to help directly alleviate some of the suffering, while governments dithered and made excuses (although Geldof, and later cohort Bono, have since been accused of becoming NWO puppets). Some researchers believe that the coming together of so much goodwill made a lasting impression on the collective psychic field. The Global Consciousness Project [page 287] wasn't running at that point, but the Random Number Generators would surely have been producing significant results if it had been. Other examples of collective focus, such as the 'Harmonic Convergence' of 1987, which was one of the first global-meditation projects, have been rightly cited as important moments in mass consciousness, but it could be argued that the many millions more involved in Live Aid created the largest wave of compassion and joy to flow through the collective, the first to be stimulated on such a scale by the medium of modern communications—an example of their best use.

• A number of mainly peaceful demonstrations in modern history have created great ripples. Even if the ultimate results have been uncertain or prone to NWO manipulation, as alleged by many truthseekers, the very genuine resolve and positive intent of people who have risked everything, including their

The 'orange revolution' in Kiev, Ukraine, 2004. Although political reversals and conflicts sadly followed in time, with accusations of NWO manipulation, it still remains that when brave people very genuinely risk their lives and livelihoods for freedom it makes an impact which authorities have to rise to and shows what can be achieved when people unite.

lives, to take to the streets in the hope of attaining greater freedom should never be underestimated. Examples of this can be found in the 2004 Ukraine 'Orange Revolution' in Ukraine (reflecting the political color of the democratic movement) where thousands took to the streets to successfully reverse a clearly rigged election, facing tanks and freezing conditions for nearly a month to make their point. Equally, several countries found themselves part of the 'Arab Uprisings', which also saw governments falter in the wake of strong public feeling as city squares filled with brave individuals. Although unfortunate reversals, conflicts and abuses sometimes occur afterwards (as with Ukraine and Egypt), leading to further strife, they nonetheless show that peaceful demonstration *can* make its point as strongly as armed struggle. The lesson perhaps is to not let the fire for reform go out, nor let empty promises from states or opportunistic dictatorial tendencies in supposed replacement governments allow the intent to falter or be diverted. Things certainly don't always work out so well, of course, with the tragic Tiananmen Square events of 1989 being a bad example, but even in China change is occurring. Softly and slowly, dedication and the willingness to take risks eventually undermines even the most rigid edifices of power.

• The Northern Ireland peace process has been a long and very difficult path, and still provokes strong emotions. Yet it is clear that something had to give. After so many deaths, injuries and bereavements on all sides of the divides, the efforts of those who believed a unity of vision could still be forged have paid off. Tony Blair appropriated other people's long efforts to claim credit for himself and used the process to increase his political standing, but there is no questioning the significance of what has been achieved thus far. Who would ever have envisioned, even just a few years before the 1998 signing of the Good Friday Agreement, that hardline unionist Ian Paisley and Sinn Fein leader Gerry Adams would finally be able to sit at a table together, smiling for cameras? Or that the late Paisley would actually become friends with once arch-enemy and IRA member Martin McGuinness? Or that McGuinness would one day shake hands with the Queen? Reaching this point wasn't easy, and much pride and anger has had to be swallowed, but if this situation is not a sign that great change *can* come even in the most dire of circumstances—when enough people put their minds to creating it—then what is? Yesterday's men still keep some of the old emnities going, with occasional attacks, but they have been reduced to the status of small criminal organizations, with little support from the wider community, and it is now unlikely that the 'troubles' of old will return at the same level.

Naturally, more cynical observers interpret a number of the above situations as being conspiracy manipulations in themselves, and there is certainly far more complexity to all these examples than discussed here. But there does comes a point during seismic social shifts where it becomes clear that people are taking matters into their own hands and generating change that seems beyond false engineering. The actions can be misdirected and misused, but the collective energy of the impetus cannot. These few examples show how quickly and how massively the world can (and does) alter for the better with the application of proactive dedication, passion, compassion—and highly focused intent. Facing seemingly insurmountable odds, the steely wall of oppression or authoritative stagnation CAN be taken down when these qualities are stirred and determination is sustained.

There are many more examples of successful and dramatic changes that could be mentioned here; the spread of genetically modified food has been massively held back in the UK by a basic consumer resistance which has said 'no' to overt tinkering with their food, for instance. Sadly, it is now being imposed by lobbied ministers and coming in through the back door courtesy of the best efforts of the Codex Alimentarius 'food safety' body [page 209], but large companies like Monsanto have had to struggle to get this far. On a smaller scale, but thematically related, groups like the British Campaign for Real Ale have helped save a number of independent breweries from bankruptcy by mounting boycotts of pubs that refuse to install local brews at the pumps, along with other actions.[6] Economic pressure alone often sees the will of the people triumph. On the larger scale, peace protests may have made a huge difference to the world, when seen with the long view. The CND marches from the mid-20th century onwards may not have eradicated nuclear weapons, but the fact that so many people made their feelings known may have prevented an even worse proliferation. Likewise, the huge show of feeling around the 2003 invasion of Iraq [Chapter VII] may not have dissuaded the decision-makers to call off the war, but it certainly made it harder for them to achieve their aims without conscience or cause; hence, perhaps, the need to generate the weapons of mass destruction lie and other similarly unfounded scares since. Had those millions around the world not made it clear that the war in Iraq was being perpetrated against their wills, perhaps Western bombs would have started falling on, say, Iran several years ago. All the time that the elite and their elected puppets see that people care, though they may ignore their ultimate wishes, it must, however irritatingly for them, hold back the plans they might otherwise implement to even more devastating effect. Although the surveillance state and the control culture have insidiously crept forwards, they have also been held back more than they might have been if no-one had ever objected, with some of the more extreme proposals having to be at least temporarily rescinded for vote-winning reasons alone.

An Interlude

On a good day, when the Sun is shining outside, the birds are singing and life appears to be going on as normal, it all seems so serene and secure. Things appear easy enough, beyond the usual stresses and strains of the modern world and the complexities of human relationships. Some readers may be having such a nonchalant experience as they peruse this, perhaps in the comfort of their homes or gardens. So what's the problem? Why worry about any of this control agenda stuff?

It is clear that everyday life in some parts of the West, if nowhere else (paradise compared to many places on Earth, it must be said), is not yet *overtly* compromised by the issues examined under the Truth Agenda. The question is, will this last? The very veneer of normality and the relative ease of Western society can keep us distracted from seeing below the surface to the very concerning issues bubbling away underneath, not yet on the boil, but maybe not far off. Even when the news is full of fear and disaster, we still have a general propensity to switch it off and go back into our little worlds of coziness. But with some kind of shift, cosmological or social, possibly on the way, and with signs and wonders in the skies and fields, underlying religious and occult agendas influencing the corridors of power, and the now apparent engineering of an Orwellian society, how long can this deceptively appealing normality be maintained?

An alarm clock is ticking, near to ringing. Many of us are already awake, though, watching the clock from under the duvet. Do we wait for the inevitable heart-thumping shock—or do we get up early while we still can and switch the alarm off, making for a more gentle awakening? It is, after all, the early bird that catches the worm.

Prometheus Unbound

What is the very worst that can happen if we make a stand against any rise, any hint, of a global fascist state? A few unpleasant scenarios come to mind. But perhaps the question that should be asked is—what is the worst that can happen if we do not make a stand? That option paints a picture too bleak to contemplate further, as previous chapters have examined. Which means that there are limited choices in the matter. If we collectively do nothing, we risk losing the freedom we have left and put ourselves at the mercy of forces that may wish to remove us entirely from their world. It may be that the worst fears of the conspiracy theorists are never realized and that they have fallen too far into paranoia. But what if even a few of those fears are founded in a level of reality? Wouldn't it be better to head them off before such plans come to maturity?

We need to put our fears aside and deal with the things we can see in front of us now. If there is something to be done, we must do it, and rise above the threatening darkness—and not expect any thanks. In Greek myth, Prometheus' reward for stealing fire from the gods to enlighten humankind was to be chained up on a rock whereby an eagle pecked out his ever-regenerating liver each day. Hopefully we will not meet quite such a gruesome fate, but the task of trying to enlighten humankind does always seem to have been a somewhat thankless one. Do we want friends in the short term, or an enduring world of freedom? Sacrifices may have to be made. But as many of those involved in the positive history-making events listed above discovered, the resulting dividends can be huge. If time and energy is given in a spirit of service, with no expectation of personal gratification, the rewards deliver themselves in due course. And Prometheus was released from his rock in the end.

Confidence and High Spirits

A commonly-heard lament amongst those with awareness of the issues discussed throughout these pages is the question of whether we should really be bringing children into the world right now, with all its present and coming traumas. But this is a narrow view. From many people's spiritual perspective, souls which incarnate here choose to do so. In that light, if true, what right do we have to halt their journey? Indeed, children of those awake to the issues may be needed more than ever as the grand equation works itself out.

Fear must be replaced with confidence—the confidence that we are astonishing beings with often untapped qualities and the ability to cope with whatever is thrown at us. The irony is that the ruling elite, whatever and whoever it may comprise, clearly recognizes this, when many of those it would dominate don't. It is plain that forces which distract us from our true selves and crush the human spirit with social controls and chemical suppression must do so because they *know how powerful we really are*. Otherwise, why bother? Those in the elite would appear to fear us as much as we may fear them—and there are far more of us.

Some researchers who study the legends of extra-terrestrials visiting Earth in ancient times, with all the tales of the Annunaki, the Nephilim and beyond, believe that humankind was genetically accelerated from ape-like beings (again, shades of *2001*) to be a slave race for the 'gods'. To achieve this, however, through gene control and breeding, it is said that they had to cut us off from our innate connection to the higher spiritual forces, to keep us energetically mute, and thus malleable. Many people believe that we are now regaining those lost faculties through an imminent evolutionary leap and that the battle for the soul of humankind is still being fought. Even if the myths are just myths, the metaphor is clear and the lesson is the same: we are more than we think we are. Hence the fight-back from those who fear us. The gods have lost control and we now have our own power to turn the world from darkness to light, if the will can be galvanized and focused.

There are good grounds for optimism and high spirits are recommended. We must always hold up a light in the shadows. Perhaps Mahatma Gandhi said it best when he wrote:

'When I despair, I remember that all through history the ways of truth and love have always won. There have been tyrants, and murderers, and for a time they can seem invincible, but in the end they always fall. Think of it—always.'

As a final thought, then, if we ever find ourselves asking 'who are we to stand up to all this?', perhaps we should rephrase the question and ask—who are we *not* to?

THE TRUTH AGENDA: *Collective positive action* **works.** *It may take time and dedication, but the rewards are worthwhile—and what will be the price of not challenging tyranny and subterfuge? The ultimate reality probably lies somewhere in the middle of the viewpoints which say that everything is a conspiratorial manipulation, or that nothing is. But valid questions have been asked throughout these pages and either way it is time to step out of fear and stand up for liberty and truth, taking the best from the journey ahead, wherever it may lead us.*

Julian Bell's mural of 18th century rights campaigner Thomas Paine, Lewes, East Sussex, UK

APPENDIX 1

THESE ARE THE TIMES
Facing New Realities in the Alternative World

This piece, updated for this book, originally appeared in the magazine Kindred
Spirit *and is included here as a useful extra, a little dessert, to the main chapters
of* The Truth Agenda. *By exploring how truthseekers can best meet what could
turn out to be the challenging reality of the hoped-for 'new paradigms', it covers
some of the same ground as previous pages but offers a more personalized author's
view and elaborates on some of the themes with a few more insights.*

At the mid-point of the colorful and revolutionary years of the 1960s, I was born in
the historical East Sussex town of Lewes in England, renowned for its huge annual
'Bonfire Night' celebrations. These commemorate the 1605 Gunpowder Plot and
other religious controversies, and more generally celebrate freedom of speech and
political steadfastness—some might say stubbornness. The town has played its part
in history-shaking events (the victory of the barons over King Henry III at the
Battle of Lewes in 1264 helped pave the way to today's democratic parliamentary
systems), and bred some significant personalities over the centuries.

Anyone growing up in Lewes couldn't fail to be aware of the enduring memory
of Thomas Paine, the libertarian and inspirational political writer who lived there
between 1768 and 1774. Paine's impassioned tracts on human rights and the real
meaning of political freedom helped inspire both the American War of Independence
and the French Revolution. He is generally assumed to have cut his teeth as a fiery
debater during his Lewes years, before setting off to help ignite the New World. Paine
was not some thuggish agitator, but an eloquent and artful scribe. Although some
of his views are still fiercely debated today, the sheer pragmatic persuasiveness of the
way he presented his arguments changed the world in a number of areas for which
he is still not given full credit. Indeed, America's Bill of Rights and constitution—
which, if actually operated to their true principles today, might still be excellent
examples of how to run a country—owe much to Paine's influence.

Why, then, is Paine not honoured more in the annals of human achievement?
Probably because throughout his struggles to achieve real liberty, Paine refused to
let go of the ideals of exposing everything to re-examination to find the truth of
a situation. As such, his campaigns against corruption within both the early US
government and the post-revolutionary French republic lost him many former
friends, and his still brave book *The Age of Reason* alienated those allies remaining
by challenging the authority of the Christian religion (though Paine himself was
not an atheist—nor a Freemason, as is sometimes said; conspiracy views on Paine

are generally unfounded). The reward for his Promethean efforts to accelerate humankind's political and spiritual freedom? Just six people at his funeral and the eventual disinterment of his grave, only for his bones to be scattered and lost.

What, though, would Paine have made of today's global situation, a world of mass surveillance, conspiracy, corruption, banker hegemony and obfuscation on just about every level? If nothing else, surely he would rage against the squandered opportunities for enlightenment and the erosion of his cherished liberty that has been much fostered by the very nation he helped to found, especially since the tribulations of 11th September 2001 and its subsequent wars. "These are the times that try men's souls", Paine once famously wrote in the face of the British oppression of America. There are few people today who would not resonate with that statement on some level.

For over twenty-five years, I have been privileged to address audiences of many kinds, sharing information on unexplained mysteries that the average listener probably wouldn't otherwise come across. This began with UFOs, crop circles, earth mysteries, the psychic realms and beyond; areas not generally treated with respect from a media bound to academic hierarchies or the world of material distractions. Over the years it became clear, through my contact with different audiences and researchers, that indulgence in these realms seemed, somehow, always to lead to talk of cover-ups and conspiracies, huge secret agendas and prophecies of Earth changes and consciousness shift, all meshing somewhere in the middle. Soon enough, these began to become a major focus for some presentations, as I tried to coherently draw the connections together. Curiously, this was easier than I had at first anticipated. Although some listeners have been shocked, and one or two outraged, on the whole most audiences seem curious, sometimes even delighted, to have another world-view revealed to them, recognizing the value of identifying areas that never previously quite made sense.

Applying a 'Truth Agenda'—a series of simple but searching questions aimed at any given assumption or sacred cow of history—soon reveals whether we have been told the whole story on any given subject. Mostly, activating this process reveals that we have not. Indeed, interest in the paranormal and belief in the occult—the very things apparently scorned by the mainstream—seems rife at unexpectedly high levels. If not, why do global politicians and corporate leaders turn up each year to attend the 'Cremation of Care' ritual beneath a giant stone owl at California's Bohemian Grove, as even journalist and general skeptic Jon Ronson witnessed for himself (outlined in his bestseller *Them*)? Defenders challenge that it is all a harmless pageant, but the ritual, which sacrifices the effigy of a child, cannot be fully separated from its obviously mystical and, in this case, rather dark origins. Meanwhile, history is nigh littered with conspiracies and engineered agendas. Strange, then, that some people find it hard to believe such things still occur today.

In attempting to translate all this to everyday audiences, at first I expected a backlash. Many groups I address are far from 'alternative'. Determined to try anyway, instead, to my surprise, I began to find more nods of agreement than dissension. It is profoundly unsettling to even consider that we might all have been lied to since time began, thus thrown from the cozy cradle of illusion that says we are lovingly looked after by the powers that be, yet there is also an underlying sense that, deep in our hearts, most of us *know* we live in a different world to the one the media presents us with—we simply distract ourselves just enough not to have to act on it.

Thus encouraged, so was born *The Truth Agenda* as a book. The subtitle *Making Sense of Unexplained Mysteries, Global Cover-Ups and Visions For a New Era* attempts to do precisely that; present a coherent hypothesis to aid understanding of the challenging controversies welling up in the collective today, but without forcing one viewpoint on the reader. Above all, what emerges from this alchemy of intrigues is the quite possible reality—already widely believed amongst alternative thinkers— that a hidden ruling elite may be engineering a global control agenda through the slow but steady formation of a One World Government (the 'New World Order'), using manipulated crises to create a mandate of control. Why? To be ready for the possibility that some kind of imminent cosmological and/or consciousness shift might before too long change everything we have ever known. The elite will want to keep its grip on the masses if that happens. Happily, *The Truth Agenda* has been well received and appears to have helped a few more human beings to find context for these strange times we find ourselves in, whilst also offering hope and constructive solutions to the problems the hypothesis presents.

Oddly, however, although everyday clubs and societies have seemingly been happy to chat through the hidden subjects that need serious illumination if they are to be positively remedied, unexpected resistance—or even complete ignorance of such information—seems to be more present in the 'New Age' realms; strange, perhaps, given its apparent openness to what could be referred to as the 'unusual'. Why should this be?

Lest there be any misunderstanding, I myself have given hefty service in years past to investigating psychic circles, healing ceremonies, channelling sessions and all points between. The living room shrines and workshop spaces which play host to these activities are largely inhabited by kind and caring people, concerned for the future of their planet, and yet a narrowness seems to have evolved in more recent times, one that has seen some seekers turn away from what might be perceived as the harder social and political realities of life, from fear of being tainted by 'negativity'. Though understandable on one level, this approach has also prevented potentially valuable contributors giving of their knowledge and abilities in a way that could actually help resolve the issues of today.

If these, then, are the new times that try human souls, we are also being given another vital chance to examine the *collective* soul. As Paine knew, such opportunities are the crucible in which reinvigorated future choices are born. We live today in an era where much that we have taken for granted is being challenged by huge change in social, political and spiritual paradigms, something long predicted, yet which still seems to have taken many people by surprise. Tax-avoiding companies and financial institutions, for example, now find austerity-smitten protesters lodged in their lobbies, demanding that they pay their dues to society, while others camp out in the streets outside cathedrals to make their point. The lofty seem shocked that the habits of a lifetime are suddenly being exposed for reassessment. Even students, long mute and downtrodden, have found a voice again in the last few years, as has been seen with various protests. Meanwhile, the revolutions that have swept the Arab nations, whether sponsored by our own countries (as many believe) or not, still speak of an upsetting of an old order that has kept the West rich at the expense of human freedom in a manner previously just enough out of sight for us not to feel uncomfortable. Now we are faced with a new reality, one which asks us to evolve a conscience and take on responsibilities long evaded. Apparent Western enthusiasm for the attempted liberation of long-oppressed masses may have to be partnered with a firm-jawed letting go of the benefits with which that oppression has fuelled our comparative paradise (easily available oil being the most visible), if any real change is to result.

New realities, of course, are what those of the alternative or New Age persuasions have been anticipating for long years, albeit in metaphysical terms. The question is, however—with the much-discussed year 2012 now well behind us as we stride firmly into the New Era—are we ready for the potentially hard truth of what that reality might really be, for a while at least? The many channelled messages of Earth changes, arriving photon belts and human disruption that have been pushing through the veil for nigh on a century now seemed almost wistfully fairy tale-like a few years back, like the script of some exciting movie that might be fun to watch, though of course we wouldn't necessarily want to live there. But now we do.

Did anyone honestly believe that the kind of events described in numerous prophecies would happen only on the one grand date of 21st December 2012 (the turning-point of the ancient 5,125-year cycle), and that once past all would be safe and cozy again? Vast change had begun before then, and will continue through these times and beyond. The shifts in the global order we are seeing now, together with climatic and environmental alterations (whatever one ascribes them to) are surely manifestations of what this new reality was always going to be, ones which may yet become enhanced by solar flares, cosmic superwaves, galactic alignments or higher-dimensional forces influencing human consciousness. The self-fulfilling result of so many people changing themselves in anticipation of a shift have ensured that ripples of mass-reassessment have transmitted into the collective anyhow. Whatever cyclical events the ancients may have been recording, the truth would seem to be that the New Era has only just begun and will be with us for the foreseeable future, with different human behavior as its first most telling sign.

Astrology alone makes clear that the Uranus-Pluto cycle (amongst other influences), which began with the conjunction in the mid-1960s and had reached the first challenging square aspect by 21st December 2012, was in itself always bound to bring a clash of power versus freedom. The new rise of protest movements, anti-capitalist or race riots and a new awareness around issues of women's rights and modern slavery have fitted the 'transits' perfectly. The seemingly endless public revelations we have seen since in uncovered surveillance plots, abuse scandals and state cover-ups across the West have been further manifestations of astrological synchronicity. Meanwhile, it is clear that the Arab uprisings were just the start of something that is upsetting many of our previous assumptions about the way our 'global village' works, at home and abroad, although the serious issues around Syria, Iraq and Islamic State have created unexpected and uncertain consequences.

But what of the several New Era predictions that also speak of humankind ascending to a higher state of being? Curiously, there seems to be a wide New Age presumption that this process is going to be *easy*. The much-anticipated free lunch of fifth-dimensional enlightenment that some believers seem to be expecting, where all or some of humankind will suddenly transform or leap to an energetically-enhanced Earth, is an attractive one; but also very nebulous. Few of the speculations offer practical advice on what the reality of Earth changes or energetic metamorphosis might be like to live through.

A number of researchers believe that the Earth's magnetic field is due, possibly at some point during our lifetimes, to temporarily collapse during a cyclic polarity reversal stimulated by hyperactive changes in the Sun, allowing in a surfeit of cosmic energy and solar particles. This unusual exposure could be the very mechanism by which raised global consciousness occurs, according to the theories of researchers like Rick Strassman and Michael Persinger, who study the brain's reaction to altered levels of electromagnetism. However, those hungry for such events often fail to ponder the drawbacks which might also accompany this scenario, i.e. social breakdown, no amenities or food, unforeseen climate effects, extreme weather, increased cancers, trauma and the rest. In other words, people may not be preparing fully to make the best of events that may come. What if astral Masters don't immediately rush to our rescue? What if we are not mysteriously ascended into a state of bliss, but are left in a house with no electricity or running water, unusual radiation falling from a shimmering sky and frightened people panicking outside, albeit ones in an enhanced psychic state?

This is expressed neither to scare nor to be cynical about some dearly-held Ascension beliefs, but simply to inject a more cautious note to those waiting for change to be delivered to them in a pretty ribbon-tied box. It may be, of course, that nothing on these lines ever happens at all, and then dealing with disappointment might become the main task. But those who 'can't wait' for general havoc to arrive (an exclamation oft-heard in alternative circles) may not be considering the true potential of such a situation—and much more than just waiting around may be asked of us, if we are to truly transcend an old, muddled world that most would agree needs a huge leap forward to meet the new social realities and powerful technologies now at its disposal. We may also be asked to look after ourselves for a while, in this physical dimension as much as any other.

Aside from apocalyptic potentials, surely the creation of a new world must require all of us to step up to a new collective responsibility? This means getting on our feet and doing something. The 'new physics' being explored by the likes of the Global Consciousness Project, founded at Princeton University [page 287], and the results of various weighty psi-experiments with computers, make clear that when large numbers of people focus their thoughts in the same direction simultaneously, the energetic environment around us is mysteriously but verifiably reshaped by some remarkable process of mind. Therefore, what we think and feel IS important, and faith in the critical mass effect offers true potential for positively progressing the collective entity of evolving consciousness.

But what we do, not just what we think, must be equally crucial—something too often overlooked by advocates of mere positive thinking. After all, would the recent beginnings of something new, however flawed and manipulated the solutions have proven to be, have come to some nations unless people had taken to the streets to make their feelings known, in a (mostly) non-violent stand? Almost certainly not. Not that mob rule is ever a solution; indeed, it must be avoided at all costs lest ruling elites with hidden draconian control agendas find all the excuses they need to create the Orwellian world they appear to aspire to. But voting with the feet is important, making feelings known, speaking out, peacefully protesting, lobbying those who claim to lead us. Despite its apparent failure in the short-term, if millions hadn't taken to the streets to contest the Iraq war in 2003, for example, there is every chance that our governments would have been raining down bombs on the likes of Iran several years ago. Apathy allows tyranny to breed. The millions of voices across the globe that opposed what happened in Iraq may have helped to prevent worse atrocities in the long run. Though they may appear to ignore our wishes, governments still clearly feel the need to engineer our consent to a certain degree, hence the whole weapons of mass destruction fantasy that led to so much misery, and the build-up of justification for (currently stalled) action against 'rogue states' like Iran. When people stand up in their power, it DOES count (as many historical precedents demonstrate), even if an immediate result isn't forthcoming.

A consciousness shift, then, is a desirable and necessary development. But for the full dividend, we may also have to practically engage too, as Paine realized. This is something that some minds in the alternative world seem resistant to, as if trying to influence an incurable arena, such as politics, full of corruption and questionable motivations, might sully the aura of 'love and light' that is the solution to all things. Indeed, ultimately, these probably *are* the solutions—but in its current dimensional state, our planet also requires action with wisdom, diplomacy and tact, as well as love. If an assailant unexpectedly leaps out and holds a gun to your head, just sending out love and light may not be quite enough to deal with the immediate problem.

A useful analogy is of running, blindfolded, towards a wall. We can stay in a state of blissful unawareness if we choose but, sooner or later, we are still going to hit the wall. Why not just lift the blindfold a little and avoid the painful collision with a hitherto-denied but inevitable reality? Positive engagement with the issues of our times is needed now more than ever. If God helps those who help themselves, then it must surely follow that the New Age gods, the likes of the Ashtar Command, Council of Nine, Arcturans, Pleiadians, or whichever celestial guardians appear to speak to groups through their chosen channels, will also be expecting us to *do* something—not just wait for their possible intervention. Some Christian evangelicals have already heavily fallen prey to disempowerment. After all, why do anything now, when Jesus will soon return to put all to rights? The New Age would do well to avoid this potentially perilous philosophy. Help from 'above' may be needed at some point, but if it is there it is as likely to be an energetic input as a direct materialization, and very probably our hands will be the tools. After all, why should we expect other-dimensional neighbors to do our dirty work for us?

So, we may be stuck with the problems we have until we deal with them. The WikiLeaks revelations, for instance, that appeared at first to shake the world did, in truth, uncover little more than what we knew—that governments lie to each other and to themselves, and that the whole political system is endemically conniving. WikiLeaks, aside from the vagaries of its curious founder Julian Assange, was an important development in that our society was uncomfortably and unusually revealed to itself in a dramatic fashion—thus making it easier to directly tackle— but can anyone really say that they were shocked? And who, at some point, has not been guilty of similar behavior on one scale or another?

Of the myriad of conspiracy scenarios explored by truthseekers, the most urgent and compelling is certainly that 9/11 must have been at least partially coordinated by a perhaps small criminal cabal embedded somewhere within the US administration (and very probably beyond), whatever role Al Qaeda did or didn't play. Impeccable work by the likes of David Ray Griffin and many other sound and respected researchers demonstrates this clearly to those with eyes to see, but it has been allowed to go unvoiced in the mainstream largely because of a complicit, arrogant or blinded media. Hard though it may be to countenance, it is clear we are not being told the truth of what happened on 11th September 2001. Minor anomalies in the official story might be ignored, but blatant misrepresentation and omission of key data in the 9/11 Commission report, retrospectively-edited air traffic control transcripts, reports of explosions inside the twin towers which began even before the first plane hit, seeming contraventions of the laws of physics in the way *three* buildings at the World Trade Center fell, particles of explosive substances found in the resulting toxic dust, and a hole far too small for a Boeing 757 at the Pentagon are just a few areas of concern that seem impossible to easily push to one side, despite the best efforts of scornful journalists. Not for nothing do polls show that around half of the world's population is now prepared to believe that the events of 9/11 were either allowed to happen or deliberately engineered.

Yet, for something that is widely seen as the major stepping stone in the New World Order control program, it is notable that of all the many contentious topics supposedly included in the WikiLeaks documents, 9/11 barely, if at all, featured. It could reasonably be supposed that at least one crucial nugget might be buried in amongst the thousands of documents, either to confirm or deny the official version. That nothing in any direction arose suggests an oddly selective process employed either by WikiLeaks or the media outlets that helped sift the evidence. That, or the leaks themselves were contrived by authorities tacitly keen to allow certain secrets out, but not others. Hence concerns amongst conspiracy theorists that the whole WikiLeaks scenario may in itself have been a contrived manipulation.

But, in its quiet way, the alternative 'spiritual' world may also have been complicit in allowing the deception-led society we find ourselves in today to grow, either by turning too much of a blind eye, in a see-no-evil stance, or by refusing to engage with subjects deemed as dark or 'negative'—a dismissive term too often used to abdicate responsibility towards trying to make a difference. The aforementioned Global Consciousness Project makes clear that massed minds, if bolstered with clear intention, have a significant effect. If the many millions of people who are set on creating a new Earth, aspiring to fifth-dimensional reality or whatever, were to stand as one and gather themselves to actively and positively connect with some of the practical issues that simply have to be dealt with (unless we are all unexpectedly pulled over the rainbow one day), then this planet would be on a far quicker road to redemption. But there is still time.

We can, of course, attend healing circles, hold meditations, pray, tune-in, burn incense and send out love and light to the world, as feels right; all of these things are, without doubt, important focusing points for higher aspirations. But we must also apply the positive intentions behind these practices to the everyday world and be ready to look the true reality of what we may be moving into squarely in the eye. By so doing, we may find within ourselves the proactive energy that has been there all along to help truly prepare ourselves for all possible scenarios (having some spare water, food and toilet rolls ready might not go amiss, for instance, should the Sun flare, the Earth's magnetic field reverse, or even just the world's economy collapse). All that we should have gathered from long years of spiritual learning—working on our own psychology, dealing with personal issues, improving ourselves and therefore those around us for the good of the collective, and campaigning and working for what feels inherently right—needs to be put to good use *now*, not in some maybe-future. Or we can just pack a small bag of crystals, tightly grip our perceived ticket to the Fifth Dimension and wait to be beamed up.

In the midst of all this, we may also need to learn discernment. After all, deception seems to have held humankind in soul slavery all these centuries, so there seems no reason to suppose the same tricks won't be tried again, albeit in different guises. Some concerned quarters are even expecting a faked alien invasion or bogus Second Coming to hasten the creation of the New World Order. It would certainly make sense to the powers that be to attempt to keep us all in our places and maintain the upper hand amidst new paradigms and cosmological shifts, things which might threaten their power-bases. Amongst the signs and wonders of the age will doubtless be new sleights of hand, and eyes and ears may not be enough to know what is real and what is not. But truly self-aware spirits, having genuinely learnt how to discern, will probably know, deep down, when to act, and when to bide their time. That is the challenge that all this consciousness evolution may have been preparing us for all along. The parable of the sower could yet find a new relevance in the exciting and potentially fertile era ahead of us.

These, then, could again be the times that try peoples' souls. If approached wisely, consciously and proactively, they may also be the times that make them.

First published, in its original form, in Kindred Spirit, *issue 111, July/August 2011*

Light at the end of the tunnel...

APPENDIX 2 — Notes

A Note on the Notes

Reading sparse reference-only notes, which require constant flicking between the middle and the back of the book to glue together what is referring to what, can be frustrating, so these notes are written in a prose style and are as self-contained as possible. They also contain some relevant detail that almost made it into the main chapters.

As for the references cited, we now live in an age where the Internet has taken over from libraries, so although books still feature both here and in the *Further Information* section that follows, those without computers must forgive the electronic bias. Unfortunately, some links do vanish after a while (although if this happens, try searching for them at: *www.archive.org*), but all of the ones listed here were live at the time of publication. Today, of course, search engines give access to a huge vat of information on most topics, and many news websites, especially, cover the same events. Discerning the best sources to reference is a time-consuming business of observing the detail and diligence of any report, and involves a degree of gut instinct. So the references here are merely the ones I found helpful—it goes without saying that searches can be run and numerous alternatives will keep readers busy.

Throughout the book, I have tried to access the most mainstream channels where possible, rather than relying on conspiracy databanks, which can be prone to recycling of unreferenced material or over-reactionary filtering. Given the book's repeated theme that information in the mainstream is highly biased and often manipulative, some readers may be puzzled by this. The advantage of such an approach is that if even the official media is tuning into something, however lightly or unwittingly, it serves as an indication that the matter in question must truly warrant investigation and is therefore more likely to alert the attention of those just setting out on the path of questioning consensus reality. This is not to say that truthseeker channels are always inherently unreliable, and they are also included here for some areas, but I denote the type of source used where it is not obvious.

Readers will also note that I sometimes deliberately use *Wikipedia*—the online encyclopedia that anyone can edit—as a reference tool. *Wikipedia*'s notorious inclination to mainstream bias and editing by dubious hands (especially over things like 9/11 or paranormal phenomena) may at first make this seem a strange choice, but the point above stands here too; when even *Wikipedia* hints at doubts in an official version of events, then something interesting is definitely going on (see note 2, Chapter IX, on Waco, for instance). In any case, because of the 'peer-review' editing system, its reporting of 'normal' subjects, at least, is generally balanced and fair, and even with its skeptical takes on more interesting matters it is sometimes good to see what the everyday view on something is before exploring the more conspiratorial channels. *Wikipedia* pages are also very good as a first-stop for useful links that may lead to deeper areas with a bit of web-surfing. Ditto the British BBC News website; many truthseekers are now critical of the BBC, but if one takes some of the reporting with a pinch of salt it still acts as one of the main global windows into what the average household is being fed as reality, and the links are useful.

As for the books mentioned here and in the *Further Resources* section (*Appendix 3*), publication details are generally for first print-runs, in whichever countries, unless otherwise noted. Sometimes it can be hard to define whether these are US or UK editions, but where this is known I state it, and Internet retailers like Amazon make all but the most obscure books pretty easy to find.

It should also be mentioned that the references given for documentaries are usually their home websites, but most of them can also be found on YouTube and Google Video, etc., although these are not always strictly legal. Supporting the original filmmakers (some of whose creations are still free on their websites, but they get advertising revenue from those hitting their sites) obviously helps them to fund further useful works.

I MAKING SENSE OF OUR WORLD

1) Majority of Britons are happy: This perhaps surprising news, ascertained from the first national survey of its kind, is reported in *The majority of British people are happy in spite of gloomy economic news and social disorder over the summer, according to new figures*, 1 December 2011, at: *http://www.telegraph.co.uk/news/uknews/8928174/Majority-of-Britons-are-happy-first-national-survey-finds.html*

2] David Aaronovitch's *Voodoo Histories*: Aaronovitch's conspiracy-debunking book (Jonathan Cape, 2009), subtitled *The Role of the Conspiracy Theory in Shaping Modern History*, is accurately summed up by Ian Kershaw's endorsement of it on the back cover as '[a] witty demolition of numerous conspiracy theories and an analysis of why otherwise intelligent people are so ready to believe in them'. Unfortunately, this claimed analysis seems to plump for the usual lazy view that many conspiracy theorists are inherently anti-Zionist (or worse, anti-Semitic) fanatics, and, in the case of 9/11, evades a discussion of the actual evidence with limp arguments that could be easily knocked down if any details were actually addressed. The book's hardback jacket promises 'to provide ammunition for those who have found themselves at the wrong end of a conversation about moon landings'—on this alone readers should ask for their money back, as Aaronovitch's discussion of this subject amounts to nothing more than a few short general paragraphs that, again, address not one jot of evidence.

3] Polly Toynbee on conspiracies: Polly Toynbee is quoted from her article in *The Guardian*, *A growing state of mind that needs a firm rebuttal—conspiracy theories provide easy answers, but rarely much insight*, 31 August 2005. The full article and a good critical dissection of this piece can be found at: ***http://www.julyseventh. co.uk/july-7-conspiracy-theorists.html***.

4] Obama's inaugural speech: Barack Obama's oath-taking fluff is discussed in Ewen MacAskill's article *Obama retakes oath to quell conspiracy theories*, 23 January 2009, which can be read at: ***http://www.guardian. co.uk/world/2009/jan/23/obama-presidential-oath***. In essence, when Obama repeated back the all-important words, as recited by the chief justice John Roberts, Roberts accidentally (or not, according to the conspiracy version) said 'I do solemnly swear that I will execute the office of president of the United States *faithfully*' [my italics], words which Obama dutifully, if falteringly, repeated. However, what should have been said by both was 'I do solemnly swear that I will *faithfully* execute the office of president of the United States'. A simple misplacement of a single word can mean a lot at such a crucial moment in history—see also comments on page 126 concerning Neil Armstrong's iconic words, spoken as he supposedly first set foot on the Moon.

5] Robert M Gates retained as US Defense Secretary: Obama's unexpected and much-questioned retention of the Republican Robert M Gates as US Defense Secretary is analyzed by Peter Baker and Thom Shanker in the article *Obama Plans to Retain Gates at Defense Department*, 25th November 2008, which can be found at: ***http://www.nytimes.com/2008/11/26/us/politics/26gates.html?hp***.

6] Conspiracy doubts over Obama: In 2009, Alex Jones put out an Internet documentary entitled *The Obama Deception*, which squarely points the finger at Barack Obama's administration as being a full continuation of the New World Order agenda, with no allowances whatsoever made to those who believe Obama himself may want to create positive change from the inside. Download the film from Jones' website ***www.prisonplanet.com***.

The controversies over Obama's birth certificate, oft-dismissed as right wing Republican fantasies yet still not resolved, can be found all over the Internet, but check out ***http://obamacrimes.com*** for the total conspiracy view on it. The name of the website indicates its stance well enough.

7] The WikiLeaks controversy: WikiLeaks has been unquestionably helpful in revealing footage and/or details of appalling Western military atrocities in Iraq and other trouble spots of the world. But some cynics believe that WikiLeaks has also, wittingly or unwittingly, been used to air information that would be awkward, diplomatically speaking, to officially accuse a country of withholding, but which actually suits certain powers—the US especially—to be made public, i.e. the allegedly stronger-than-thought presence of Al Qaeda in Pakistan (thus justifying more open US military forays across the Afghanistan/Pakistan border). It also appears, from the WikiLeaks releases, that the US has been less keen to invade Iran, for instance, than it might seem, with surrounding Arab nations apparently cajoling for action over its nuclear program far more than America. Given the ongoing tough US rhetoric aimed at Iran over the years, some conspiracy theorists see this as a smokescreen, distracting the world's eyes from the true main source of enmity. Was the claimed embarrassment from a number of global politicians at certain WikiLeaks revelations just the price that had to be paid to sneak in handy misinformation amongst real, but not really that devastating, disclosures?

The full implications of the WikiLeaks releases are still unfolding, with more exposés of military and diplomatic information still promised (threatened?). However, the accusations of both rape *and* anti-

Semitism against WikiLeaks founder Julian Assange, who at the time of writing is evading extradition to Sweden (with a passing-on to the US highly likely) by sheltering in the Ecuadorian embassy in London, have blurred the issues, with Assange claiming these are trumped-up vengeance tactics. If the information passed to WikiLeaks *is* in itself a conspiratorial manipulation, is this simply the powers that be having to be *seen* to do something, to keep it all bubbling along, or is it that they actually *do* want him out of the way?

Information on WikiLeaks can be found on its main website at ***http://wikileaks.org***, but the UK newspaper *The Guardian* was also instrumental in channelling much of the initial information into the global mainstream, and its dedicated pages for this can be found at: ***http://www.guardian.co.uk/media/wikileaks***.

II MYSTERIES ANCIENT AND MODERN

1) Were internal ramps used to build the pyramids?: In 2007, Jean-Pierre Houdin, a French architect, proposed an interesting theory, supported by many verifiable observations, that the Great Pyramid (and by implication the others) may have been built using an ingenious system of *internal* ramps and counterweights to hoist the huge blocks into place. This certainly makes more sense than the external ramps theory, for which there is no clear evidence, and if proven to be correct would force an uncomfortable revision of much Egyptological dogma. The initial theory is reported in the piece *Mystery of Great Pyramid 'Solved'*, 31 March 2007, at: ***http://news.bbc.co.uk/1/hi/world/middle_east/6514155.stm***. In the piece, even Egyptologist Bob Brier, tellingly, states:

'This goes against both main existing theories... ...I've been teaching them myself for 20 years, but deep down I know they're wrong.'

A supportive article by Brier explains the internal ramps theory further at: ***http://www.archaeology.org/0705/etc/pyramid.html***. In 2009, BBC 2's *Timewatch* series featured the theory in the program *Pyramid: The Last Secret*, information on which is available at: ***http://www.bbc.co.uk/timewatch/pyramid.shtml***

2) *Giza: The Truth*: Ian Lawton and Chris Ogilvie Herald's book *Giza: The Truth—The Politics, People and History Behind the World's Most Famous Archaeological Site* (Virgin Books, 1999) attempts to objectively assess all the alternative theories of Hancock, Bauval, Gilbert, etc. (see next note and the *Ancient Mysteries* section in *Further Information*), but ends up as a suspiciously partisan advert for orthodox Egyptology, with the one caveat that the possibility of levitation as a building technique is considered. It is worth a read for a round-up of conventional archaeology's views on unconventional theories, but caution is advised for those seeking an unbiased assessment. More information can be found on Ian Lawton's website at: ***http://www.ianlawton.com/gttindex.htm***.

3) The Giza-Orion correlation: The theory that the Giza pyramids were laid out to represent the belt of the constellation Orion received its first full airing in Robert Bauval and Adrian Gilbert's book *The Orion Mystery* (Mandarin Books, 1994). Many have since criticized the detail (especially Lawton and Ogilvie-Herald—see previous note), but the general idea of an astronomical correlation at Giza remains popular.

4) Alternative views on the pyramids: Some interesting facts and figures that serve as a concise compendium of some of the less conventional views on the Giza pyramids can be found at: ***http://www.welcomethelight.com/2009/03/amazing-pyramids-of-modern-times***, from where this quote is taken.

5) Heretical archaeological theories: Some believe that humankind originated millions of years earlier than we are usually told, and claim that important archaeological discoveries proving this have been deliberately kept from us. Those wishing to explore the idea further should explore *Forbidden Archaeology: The Hidden History of the Human Race*, by Michael A Cremo and Richard L Thompson (BBT Science, 1996). At 952 pages, it isn't a light read by any means, but does include some tantalizing evidence to suggest that archaeological cover-ups of 'inconvenient' findings (such as clearly-tooled objects found in supposedly pre-human strata) *do* occur. Michael Cremo's website offers other related titles and information at: ***http://www.mcremo.com/fa.htm***.

6) Crop circle disinformation: George Wingfield's investigation into the non-existence of the press agency that issued the Doug and Dave debunking story led him to believe there might be an MI5 plot in operation,

Notes

as outlined in his article *The Doug 'N' Dave Scam*, *The Cerealogist*, issue 5 (Winter 1991-92), pages 3-6.

7) Ministry of Agriculture crop circle investigation: Interestingly, the department of the UK's ADAS (Agricultural Development and Advisory Service) that discovered soil anomalies beneath crop circles was shut down in mysterious circumstances soon after announcing its results, as recounted in my book *Swirled Harvest: Views from the Crop Circle Frontline* (Vital Signs Publishing, 2003), Chapter 6, *End Game*, pages 43-46.

8) Astronomical crop formations and the Sun: An analysis of the possible connection between astronomical crop formations and Sun cycles can, again, be found in my book *Swirled Harvest: Views from the Crop Circle Frontline*, Chapter 15, *Galaxy Legacy*, pages 123-129.

9) Martian anomalies: The contentious 'Martian trees', which scientists say are mere geological simulacra, are debated at: *http://www.marsanomalyresearch.com/evidence-reports/2010/177/dunes-trees-tech.htm*.
   A very good and long analysis of orbital Mars images which have almost certainly been edited using computer image-'cloning' techniques, seemingly to mask the real surface features, appears to have suspiciously vanished from the Internet along with related discussion of it. A short fragment still remained at the time of writing at: *http://www.youtube.com/watch?v=3wAOOS8bsKA*.

10) Sky spirals: There seems to be no definitive source to recommend on the incredible 2009 luminous spiral that appeared in the Norwegian skies, or indeed the ones which have followed around the world, but an Internet search will turn up every kind of polarized view. The main media outlets naturally swallow the Russian missile story, while alternative sources opt either for HAARP or extra-terrestrials, or take it as a sign of the imminent arrival of the long-promised New Age prophet Maitreya. Some footage of the Norway event and the subsequent Australian spiral can be seen in an extensive montage of fascinating aerial phenomena videos, as reported on mainstream TV, at: *http://www.youtube.com/watch?v=87PRVP4EQAo*.
   A report on the very similar sky spiral seen over Israel and Jordan in June 2012 is reported in *Missile or UFO? Thousands of people in Jordan and Israel witness spinning 'Catherine Wheel' in the sky*, by Eddie Wren, 8 June 2012, at: *http://www.dailymail.co.uk/sciencetech/article-2156388/Missile-UFO-Thousands-people-Jordan-Israel-witness-spinning-Catherine-Wheel-sky.html#ixzz2XcHXheI6*.

III UFOS

1) UFOs and nuclear bases: Robert Salas was a military officer present at the US Malmstrom Air Force Base in 1967 when an unidentified aerial object temporarily rendered the nuclear missiles there inoperable. Since going public about it, Salas has become a regular on the UFO conference circuit, and several ex-officers have backed up his story. Similar occurrences have also been reported at other military bases, and the implications of an outside force that can neutralize nuclear weapons are clearly huge. The details of the Malmstrom event are told in Salas' book *Faded Giant* (BookSurge Publishing, 2005), while a potted version of the account can be read at: *http://www.cufon.org/cufon/malmstrom/malm1.htm*. Salas took part in a 2010 US press conference with other military whistleblowers, shedding more light on this and similar events, which can be watched at: *http://www.youtube.com/watch?v=YqzoC3QPI_E*. The claimed presence of nuclear missiles at the UK Rendlesham base at the time of its own famous UFO sighting has never been officially acknowledged, but is privately confirmed by insiders.

2) The Gary McKinnon extradition case: A straightforward record of British UFO enthusiast Gary McKinnon's battle against extradition, which unsuccessfully attempted to send him to US trial for hacking military computers in search of ET information, can be found at: *http://en.wikipedia.org/wiki/Gary_McKinnon*.

3) The Disclosure Project: Full details of Steven Greer's Disclosure Project, which aims to stimulate UFO-related testimony from military and civil aviation personnel, are available on its official website at: *http://www.disclosureproject.org*.

4) UFOs and animal mutilations: The laser-precision animal mutilations are a disturbing and largely unexplained mystery. Despite many attempts to dismiss the missing organs and/or flesh as the results of natural causes (such as infestations from blow-fly maggots), it is very hard to explain all of the effects in this way, and the many related sightings of strange aerial phenomena take things into different territory. Although many researchers believe that extra-terrestrials are responsible, others believe the UFO connection is a mask for secret military experiments.

The first serious study of the phenomenon was made by Linda Moulton Howe in her book *Alien Harvest* (Littleton/Co., 1989). A concise round-up of the traditional paranormalist view on the animal mutilations can be found at *http://www.crystalinks.com/animal_mutilation.html*, while a more mainstream but perhaps rather too skeptical view is available at: *http://en.wikipedia.org/wiki/Cattle_mutilation*.

5) Dome of the Rock UFO: Skeptics have inevitably attacked the videos of the sparkling light allegedly filmed on 28th January 2011, which is seen to descend to hover for a short while near the golden dome of the famous Jerusalem temple, before shooting off at an astonishing speed to join a group of red lights in the sky far above. However, with at least four videos now available, showing the event from different angles, interest remains, and the reactions indeed raise the slightly disturbing question of what would happen socially and politically if an undeniable mass-sighting occurred in a very religiously-contentious location. See a good montage of three of the videos at: *http://www.youtube.com/watch?v=SuuTVLS6eVg&feature=related*.

6) Project Blue Beam: The idea that the New World Order might try to fake a Second Coming as part of its drive to create a One World Government was popularized by Canadian conspiracy theorist Serge Monast (who died in 1996) in his book *Project Blue Beam NASA* (Presse libre nord-américaine, 1994), but the Internet is full of other researchers' takes on it, including evangelical claims that it will herald the arrival of the Antichrist.

7) Billy Meier's ET-inspired prophecies: Claimed UFO contactee Billy Meier's future predictions are rounded up by Michael Horn in *The Henoch Prophecies from the Billy Meier Contacts* at: *http://www.galactic-server. com/rune/meierpredict.html*. This in itself appears to be extracted from *Nexus Magazine*, Volume 11, No. 5.

8) Jon King's 'Earthshift' schedule: A good summing up of claimed ET contactee Jon King's 'Earthshift' schedule can be found in Geoff Stray's *Beyond 2012: Catastrophe or Ecstasy* (Vital Signs Publishing, 2005), Chapter 15, *UFOs and ETs*, pages 167-169. King's own book, *Cosmic Top Secret: The Unseen Agenda* (New English Library, 1999), fills in his own general views on extra-terrestrial activities.

IV MIRACLES AND PROPHECIES

1) Nostradamus and Mother Shipton's predictions: Geoff Stray gives a good resume of the Nostradamus and Mother Shipton prophecies in *Beyond 2012: Catastrophe or Ecstasy*, Chapter 18, *Nostradamus*, pages 186-193. The basics on Nostradamus can be found at: *http://en.wikipedia.org/wiki/Nostradamus*.

2) Edgar Cayce's predictions: More details on the Cayce prophecies can be found at the website for the Edgar Cayce Association for Research and Enlightenment: *http://www.edgarcayce.org*. A more mainstream (and less partisan) view on Cayce can be found at: *http://en.wikipedia.org/wiki/Edgar_Cayce*.

3) Bar Codes do NOT represent 666: The urban myth that bar codes embody the biblically significant number 666 is, disappointingly for some, convincingly exploded at *Bar Code 1: A Web Of Information About Bar Code* at: *http://www.adams1.com/pub/russadam/new.html*. Asked 'Is there a hidden 666 in bar code?', the website robustly responds with the following:

*'NO! I get this question asked at least once a week. What people really mean is "does UPC found on grocery products have a hidden 666 (mentioned in Revelation 13:16 in the New Testament)?" People have thought that the three guard bars used to specify the start, middle and end of a UPC bar code looked like the bar code sequence for a "6" found in the UPC symbol table... ...These guard bars are not "6" and carry no information. Even if you don't believe that guard bars carry no information and insist on applying the code table, you have to determine whether the digit is on the left side or the right side of the symbol. That's because the sequence of bars and spaces are different depending on whether the digit is on the left of the symbol or the right of the symbol. The LEFT guard bar would have to be **smallest space, smallest bar, smallest space, WIDEST BAR** in order to be a "6". The guard bar on the left is actually **space of undetermined wide** (left side digit must always start with a space element), **smallest bar, smallest space, smallest bar**. That sequence of bars and spaces is undefined and is*

not a "6" even using the table. The middle guard bar is not on the left or the right ('cause it is used to divide the symbol), so it is undefined by the table.'

4) The Bible Code: Michael Drosnin's somewhat doom-laden but influential book *The Bible Code* (Simon & Schuster, 1997), which purports to have found a code of apocalyptic prophecies scattered throughout the Bible, has frightened many readers, but has been savagely attacked by skeptics. An anonymous Amazon review by 'A Customer', which can be read at *http://www.amazon.com/Bible-Code-Michael-Drosnin/dp/0684849739*, sums up the main case against it:

'Researchers Dror Bar-Natan, Maya Bar-Hillel, Gil Kalai and Brendan McKay published an article in the journal Statistical Science, *edited by the Institute of Mathematical Statistics, in which they proved the Bible Code to be non-existent. There is no single, agreed-upon original Bible. Even the oldest versions of the Bible vary from one another. Therefore, any attempt to pick out, for example, every fifth word, would be different for each Bible. Besides, even these versions of the Bible are not the original texts, but highly edited versions of more ancient works. The procedures followed by the Bible Code team were not in compliance with scientific standards because they were repeatedly changed with the goal of finding a code. Such statistical tuning can eventually find a few apparently meaningful codes in any long book, but for every such coherent fragment there is a huge amount of gibberish. The focus on the tiny bit of apparent coherence to the detriment of the huge amount of nonsense is a biased attempt to interpret white noise into a supposedly divine message.'*

Despite this, and despite the slightly self-deflating claim from Drosnin that the predicted events may be avoidable, the book, and its several sequels, have been huge hits with Christian End-Timers in particular.

5) The Virgin Mary and earth energies: Interesting links between Marian apparitions and earth mysteries are made by Richard Leviton in his book *Signs On The Earth: Deciphering The Message of Virgin Mary Apparitions, UFO Encounters, and Crop Circles* (Hampton Roads, 2005). Leviton concludes that natural earth energy 'hot spots' help stimulate connections with other levels of consciousness.

6) The Fatima apparitions of 1917: There are, of course, myriad Internet references to the 1917 Fatima events, many of them inevitably somewhat religiously biased, but I found these ones particularly useful:
http://members.aol.com/bjw1106/marian6.htm
http://www.theotokos.org.uk/pages/approved/appariti/fatima.html
http://en.wikipedia.org/wiki/Our_Lady_of_Fatima

7) George W Bush says 'God' told him to invade Iraq: Ewen MacAskill recounts Palestinian Foreign Minister Nabil Shaath's testimony that George W Bush claimed divine inspiration concerning the invasion of Iraq in the article *George Bush: 'God told me to end the tyranny in Iraq'—President told Palestinians God also talked to him about Middle East peace*, 7 October 2005, which can be read at: *http://www.guardian.co.uk/world/2005/oct/07/iraq.usa*.
   Shaath and Abu Mazen, Palestinian Prime Minister, give on-camera descriptions of their meeting with President Bush in the BBC series *Elusive Peace: Israel and the Arabs*, broadcast on BBC 2 in October 2005. Details can be found at: *http://news.bbc.co.uk/1/hi/programmes/elusive_peace/4268184.stm*.

8) More on Bush and God: Bush also told author Bob Woodward, author of the book *Plan of Attack* (Simon & Schuster, 2004—an account of the administration's invasion of Iraq), that, after giving the order to invade, he went into the White House garden and prayed 'that our troops be safe, be protected by the Almighty', adding 'I was praying for strength to do the Lord's will.'

9) The astrology of George W Bush: The astonishing identical placement of George W Bush's astrological Sun to America's Sun is discussed further in Helen Sewell's article *The Astrology of 2012*, originally published at: *www.diagnosis2012.co.uk/astro.html* and updated slightly at: *http://goldenagetoday.com/departments/golden-age-articles/36-article-page/376-the-astrology-of-2012*. See also note 17 of Chapter XII for general information on astrology, and Helen Sewell's website at *www.astrologicalinsights.co.uk*.

10) Evangelist Ted Haggard: More background on the controversial evangelical preacher Ted Haggard can be found at *http://en.wikipedia.org/wiki/Ted_Haggard*.

11) Jeff Sharlet on Ted Haggard: Haggard and the creeping influence of fundamentalist Christianity in US politics is examined in Jeff Sharlet's book *The Family: The Secret Fundamentalism at the Heart of American Power* (Harper, 2008), from which this quote is taken.

12) Hillary Clinton and 'The Family': Jeff Sharlet's book (see note 11) also claims that Hillary Clinton is a member of one of the 'cell churches' that make up the slightly sinister evangelical 'Family' referred to in the title, which acts as a kind of pyramid-scheme for religious 'dominionists' trying to infiltrate all levels of US society. Further thoughts on this can be found in the article *Hillary Clinton member of "cell church" run by "The Family"*, 4 April 2008, at: *http://www.dailykos.com/story/2008/4/4/133640/8678/994/490211*.

13) Did Tony Blair and George W Bush 'pray together'?: In a famous BBC TV *Newsnight* interview (screened on 6 February 2003) with then Prime Minister Tony Blair in the run-up to the Iraq invasion, the following curious exchange took place between Blair and Jeremy Paxman, the then British TV nemesis of politicians:

PAXMAN: I want to explore a little further about your personal feelings about this war. Does the fact that George Bush and you are both Christians make it easier for you to view these conflicts in terms of good and evil?
BLAIR: I don't think so, no. I think that whether you're a Christian or you're not a Christian you can try to perceive what is good and what is evil.
PAXMAN: You don't pray together for example?
BLAIR: [awkwardly, with a sheepish grin] No, we don't pray together Jeremy, no.
PAXMAN: Why do you smile?
BLAIR: Because—why do you ask me the question?
PAXMAN: Because I'm trying to find out how you feel about it.
BLAIR: [strangely] Possibly.

The full transcript of this interview (and a link to the broadcast), which in any case makes for fascinating reading in the light of the disaster in Iraq that followed and all the later revelations about the deceptions behind it, can be read at: *http://news.bbc.co.uk/1/hi/programmes/newsnight/2732979.stm*.

V GRAND CONSPIRACIES

1) Concerns over vaccinations: Many qualified medical experts have questioned the safety and science of the vaccination program—and some have been unfairly debunked and accused of quackery as a result. Internet searches will reveal a lot of important information that should be read before parents decide (while they still have the power of decision) to allow the immunization of their children.

One of the most thorough questioners has been Trevor Gunn, author of the influential booklet *Mass Immunization—A Point in Question*, first published by Cutting Edge Publications in 1992 and reproduced many times since. Gunn (corresponding on behalf of *The Informed Parent* magazine) contributes an important dialogue with Dr C J Clements EPI of the Global Program for Vaccines and Immunization, identifying some serious issues with immunization propaganda, in a piece entitled *Response to WHO Evidence for Vaccine Safety and Effectiveness*, which can be found at: *http://www.whale.to/m/gunn.html*.

Trevor Gunn has complied some interesting videos on immunization issues on his YouTube page at: *https://www.youtube.com/user/MrTrevorgu*. Some other sources on vaccination concerns can be found in Appendix 2, in the *Health* section.

A concerted effort to debunk MMR questioners has centered around the work of Dr Andrew Wakefield, who produced a 1998 paper in the medical journal *The Lancet* asserting links between the MMR jabs and cases of autism. Subsequent allegations of professional misconduct in his research methods have resulted in Wakefield being vilified in the media (the same media that made screaming headlines of his original findings), but many parents who believe their childrens' autism is directly attributable to MMR continue to support him and Wakefield still fights to clear his name. *Wikipedia*'s view on Wakefield can be found at *http://en.wikipedia.org/wiki/Andrew_Wakefield*, while Wakefield himself mounts a robust defense of his work (defending himself against his arch-nemesis, journalist Brian Deer) in the article *Autism, bowel disease and MMR vaccination: In his desperation, Deer gets it wrong once again*, 9th February 2009, at: *http://www.rescuepost.com/files/deer-response.pdf*.

2) AIDS conspiracy theories: There are too many alternative theories on the possible origins and 'purpose' of AIDS to go into here, but a handy (if largely skeptical) round-up of some of them is available in Juliet Lapidos' report *The AIDS Conspiracy Handbook*, 19 March 2008, at: *http://www.slate.com/id/2186860/*, while a good example of the total conspiracy view can be found at the website *The AIDS Conspiracy*, at: *http://sonic.net/~doretk/ArchiveARCHIVE/Aids/Aids.html*.

3) The overpopulation controversy: The threat of planetary overpopulation is seen by some (including TV naturalist David Attenborough) as one of the major issues of our times, or at least is being promoted as such, raising truthseeker fears that drastic action might be taken by a ruling elite to 'solve' the problem. Typical of such reports was an interview with Professor John Beddington on BBC Radio 4's *Today* program, 19 March 2009, which can be heard at: *http://news.bbc.co.uk/today/hi/today/newsid_7952000/7952148. stm*. Promotion for the interview reads as follows:

'The government's chief scientific officer has warned that a "perfect storm" will occur in the year 2030, with simultaneous shortages of energy, food and fresh water devastating an over-populated planet. Professor John Beddington explains how he reached this conclusion and puts forward his solutions.'

On the other hand, some conspiracy theorists believe the over-population scare is another engineered myth spread to further the control agenda, and there have been claims that the world is nowhere near reaching resources capacity, despite trouble in more densely-populated areas. Some of these views may, of course, be pushed by religious hardliners with an anti-contraception stance, but the arguments are worth a listen. An interesting article on this can be found at: *http://www.lifeissues.net/writers/kas/kas_01overpopulation.html*.

4) Dr Eric Pianka denies advocating mass-extermination: The controversy over Dr Eric Pianka's 2006 lecture to St Edwards University, which some took as a recommendation that a human extermination program should be instigated, is discussed at: *http://en.wikipedia.org/wiki/Mims-Pianka_controversy*. Denying this interpretation, and in an effort to clear his name, Pianka issued a statement on the University of Texas website, which included the following paragraph:

'I have two grandchildren and I want them to inherit a stable Earth. But I fear for them. Humans have overpopulated the Earth and in the process have created an ideal nutritional substrate on which bacteria and viruses (microbes) will grow and prosper. We are behaving like bacteria growing on an agar plate, flourishing until natural limits are reached or until another microbe colonizes and takes over, using them as their resource. In addition to our extremely high population density, we are social and mobile, exactly the conditions that favor growth and spread of pathogenic (disease-causing) microbes. I believe it is only a matter of time until microbes once again assert control over our population, since we are unwilling to control it ourselves. This idea has been espoused by ecologists for at least four decades and is nothing new. People just don't want to hear it... I do not bear any ill will toward humanity. However, I am convinced that the world WOULD clearly be much better off without so many of us... We need to make a transition to a sustainable world. If we don't, nature is going to do it for us in ways of her own choosing. By definition, these ways will not be ours and they won't be much fun. Think about that.'

5) Dr Leonard Horowitz on flu anti-virals: Horowitz's view that it is the anti-virals that are as much the problem as Swine Flu itself was expressed in a presentation given at The Alternative View conference at Heathrow, UK in May 2009. Horowitz's book, *Emerging Viruses: AIDS and Ebola—Nature, Accident or Intentional?* (Healthy World Distributing, 1996), explores the idea that the viruses in question were 'by-products of a genetic engineering program'. His personal website can be found at: *http://www.drlenhorowitz.com*.

6) Side-effects of Tamiflu: The worrying and numerous neuropsychiatric effects reported in people taking Tamiflu, especially children and young adults, which have resulted in suicides and self-harming, appear to be accepted in the mainstream, as discussed in detail in *Wikipedia*'s entry on oseltamivir (Tamiflu) at: *http://en.wikipedia.org/wiki/Oseltamivir*. So why isn't there more of a debate about it in the media? Public fear, as ever, has overridden common sense.

7) UK government stockpiles Tamiflu / Extended Tamiflu lifespan: The news that the UK government spent £100 million on buying up to 50 million doses of Tamiflu at the height of the first swine flu scare can be read in David Rose's article *Tamiflu might not work against swine flu, Government's own scientists warn*, 23 May 2009, at: *http://www.dailymail.co.uk/news/article-1186913/Tamiflu-work-swine-flu-Governments-scientists-warn.html*. Later revelations, amidst even official retrospective questioning, 4 June 2010, *WHO* *swine flu experts 'linked' with drug companies*, can be read at *http://www.bbc.co.uk/news/10235558*.

The very unusual announcement, also in May 2009, that Tamiflu was going to have its shelf-life extended by two years is seen by many as a diversion from the fact that the Swine Flu scare did begin just as the current stocks needed to be used. Did the panic not use up as much as was anticipated? Andrew Jack's short report *Tamiflu can be used past 'sell by'*, 9 May 2009, at *http://www.ft.com/cms/s/0/e96d7460-3c30-11de-acbc-00144feabdc0.html*, states the following:

'The European Medicines Agency said for the first time ever that a medicine could remain safe to use for seven years, in response to concerns of a global shortage of a drug [Tamiflu] that could help prevent and treat a pandemic flu virus. "The recommendation is don't throw it away," a spokeswoman said.

The move may reduce short-term pressure for additional stockpile orders by governments from Roche of Switzerland, which produces the drug.'

8) Donald Rumsfeld and Tamiflu: The claimed flu antidote Tamiflu was developed by Roche Laboratories, and former US Secretary of Defense Donald Rumsfeld (seen by many as a main New World Order operative, and a key architect of the George W Bush Iraq and Afghanistan campaigns) was indeed chairman of Gilead Sciences Inc. when his company bought the patent for Tamiflu in 1996. This has obviously raised suspicions in a number of directions, and Rumsfeld's involvement in the production of the dubious sweetener aspartame (see note 3 of Chapter X) has added to the speculation. A discussion on the truths and myths of the details can be read on the page *The Tamiflu/Rumsfeld Connection*, April 2006, at: *http://urbanlegends.about.com/library/bl_bird_flu.htm*, while another revealing piece on Rumsfeld's profiteering from Tamiflu can be found in Geoffrey Lean and Jonathan Owen's article *Donald Rumsfeld makes $5m killing on bird flu drug*, 12 March 2006, at: *http://www.independent.co.uk/news/world/americas/donald-rumsfeld-makes-5m-killing-on-bird-flu-drug-469599.html*.

9) The Georgia Guidestones: This US stone monument with inscriptions that appear to recommend a massive reduction of the global population, along with other apparent New World Order platitudes, is discussed basically at: *http://en.wikipedia.org/wiki/Georgia_Guidestones*. For a fuller conspiracy view on the stones, have a look at: *http://www.theforbiddenknowledge.com/hardtruth/thegeorgiaguidestones.htm*.

10) The 'Amero' currency: Information on the 'Amero', the claimed single currency that will supposedly one day encompass the USA, Mexico and Canada, can be found at: *http://en.wikipedia.org/wiki/North_American_currency_union*.

11) Doubts over the Federal Reserve: Many conspiracy websites inevitably have something to say about the astonishing illegality of the US Federal Reserve, but for a non-conspiratorial critical take on it, go to: *http://www.abolishthefederalreserve.com*.

Another intelligent and critical piece on President Obama's decision to give yet more control to the Federal Reserve can be read in John Nichol's article *Don't Cede More Economic Authority to Unaccountable Fed*, 18 June 2009, which can be read at: *http://www.thenation.com/blogs/thebeat/444471/don_t_cede_more_economic_authority_to_unaccountable_fed*.

12) *The Money Masters* documentary: Information on the film *The Money Masters*, which takes a highly critical and illuminating look at the history of banking, can be found at its official website: *http://www.themoneymasters.com/synopsis.htm*.

13) House of Lords bribes scandal: The failure of the British House of Lords to properly punish two of its members, exposed by undercover journalists from the *Sunday Times* for the verbal admission that they would accept bribes to influence legislation, was at least partially corrected in May 2009 when Lord Truscott and Lord Taylor of Blackburn were temporarily suspended from the House. Many others think they should have been permanently ejected, but in the mess of the MPs' expenses scandal no-one was going to throw stones in their own glasshouse. These two made the mistake of getting caught—how many other Lords are equally corrupt, however? In 2013, yet more cases were exposed. A good resume of the initial bribes scandal can be read in the article *Britain's House of Lords suspends members in "bribe" probe*, 20 May 2009, at: *http://www.monstersandcritics.com/news/uk/news/article_1478521.php*.

14) 'Common Purpose': Although supposedly a harmless European 'educational charity' that promotes 'leadership and networking development training', many believe the organization Common Purpose masks an attempt to subvert democracy and introduce federalist-EU policies and other murky agendas through a back door. Several websites are now dedicated to exposing it, including the *Stop Common Purpose* website at: *http://www.stopcp.com*. A more concise article calling attention to problems with CP can be found at *http://www.tpuc.org/node/107*, and a full video presentation by CP's most public nemesis, Brian Gerrish, can be downloaded at: *https://www.youtube.com/watch?v=-3DmnovmBIA*.

15) ID Cards: The basics on the issues that surrounded the cancelled UK ID-card scheme can be found at: *http://en.wikipedia.org/wiki/British_national_identity_card*.

16) Implications of an ID society: An excellent fictional account of what could happen in a society entirely based around ID tags and surveillance was featured in a now-rare flash of BBC risk-taking with the series *The Last Enemy*, broadcast on BBC 1 in February-March 2008. The effect of the lead character (played by Benedict Cumberbatch) being deliberately deleted from the ID database, reducing him to the status of a street tramp, gives a chilling demonstration of what could happen to anyone considered 'problematic' by any future fascist state. Details of the series can be found at: *http://www.bbc.co.uk/drama/lastenemy/welcome.shtml*.

In the non-fictional world, human rights campaigner Peter Tatchell interviews 'No2ID' founder Phil Booth on the perils of ID systems and their potential abuses in a video that can be downloaded at: *https://www.youtube.com/watch?v=UqnuXdpl-8s*.

17) Bloodlines of presidents and monarchs: A good compact guide revealing the complex but fascinating genealogical connections between various presidents, politicians and monarchs, with many links and references, can be found at: *http://groups.google.com/group/total_truth_sciences/browse_thread/thread/f3c944726cb1f283*. Amongst the more worrying news from this is that Barack Obama is claimed to be related to Dick Cheney (believed by many to be one of the key architects of 9/11—see Chapter VIII), and that the British Royal Family are descendants of Vlad the Impaler, the cruel 15th century Transylvanian/Romanian tyrant on which Bram Stoker based the character of Dracula!

18) '6000 people run the world': The mainstream exposure that just 6000 people essentially run the world was first revealed in David Rothkopf's book *Superclass: The Global Power Elite and the World They Are Making* (Farrar, Straus and Giroux, 2008). Although largely non-conspiratorial in tone, it manages to identify many of the same people truthseekers point to as being key elements in the One World Government agenda, adding a few celebrities like *U2*'s Bono into the mix as well as identifying other names one might expect, such as Rupert Murdoch and Bill Gates. Interestingly, the book received a fair bit of media coverage from some of the same journalists who usually scoff at conspiracy theories, showing that revelations of what amounts to partisan manipulation can be reportable—but only if couched in certain terms and put through the right intellectual filters. An informative review of Rothkopf's book, by Laura Miller, can be read at: *http://www.salon.com/books/review/2008/03/14/superclass/*. Miller comments:

'Rothkopf announces that he and his researchers have identified "just over 6,000" people who match his definition of the superclass—that is, who have met complicated (and vaguely explained) metrics designed to determine "the ability to regularly influence the lives of millions of people in multiple countries worldwide." These include heads of state and religious and military leaders... ...but the core membership is businessmen: hedge fund managers, technology entrepreneurs and private equity investors.'

19) The US military damage ancient Babylon: News that the US military willfully camped on the ancient site of Babylon, creating untold harm to an important archaeological site, did actually go mainstream. The BBC's coverage of it, *Army base 'has damaged Babylon'*, 15 January 2005, can be found at: *http://news.bbc.co.uk/1/hi/world/middle_east/4177577.stm*.

20) The Tower of Babel: The Tower of Babel quote is taken from *The Bible: Revised Standard Version* (1952).

21) Freemasonry: The Internet is crammed full of conspiracy takes on Freemasonry, naturally, but for a straightforward and fair assessment (which includes critical observations), *Wikipedia*, like it or not, is probably the best starting point for an all-round history: *http://en.wikipedia.org/wiki/Freemasonry*.

22) The mystical layout of famous cities: Greater awareness of occult symbolism being encoded into architecture and city planning was aroused by the publication of Graham Hancock and Robert Bauval's book *Talisman: Sacred Cities, Secret Faith*, Element Books (US), Michael Joseph (UK), 2004.

An informative conversation with Robert Bauval, which makes for a concise insight into the subject, can be read in the article *Robert Bauval: A Man For All Seasons—Conversation with Robert Bauval on the Subject of Egyptian and Masonic Symbolism as Incorporated into the Master Plan of the District of Columbia*, at: *http://www.opencheops.org/page18.htm*.

23) Princess Diana conspiracy theories: There appear to have been people queuing up to assassinate Princess Diana, if the many conspiracy theories doing the rounds are to be believed, and amongst which Mohammed Al Fayed's Prince Philip allegations seem tame in comparison. Although claims that Diana's lineage from the Stuart dynasty was not acceptable to hardline elements from the House of Windsor may not be entirely without foundation, alternative versions involve the belief that Diana's growing involvement in anti-landmine campaigns was an important element (Dodi Al Fayed's mother was the upper class Saudi Samira Khashoggi, sister of major armaments dealer Adnan Khashoggi—perhaps someone in the family didn't want a peacenik at their table), or comprise confused tangles concerning the preservation of specific extra-terrestrial bloodlines.

Seeing the entire assassination set-up as a kind of modern ritual sacrifice, with heavy secret society overtones, others have speculated on everything from Diana's supposed genealogical connections to Mary Magdalene and the Merovingian dynasty, to extraordinary (if darkly entertaining) claims that she was murdered on the orders of Hillary Clinton to prevent Diana being forcibly 'married' in an occult ceremony to then President Bill (!). The problem is that so much has now been stirred into the pot of mythology and partial-truths that Diana's admittedly suspicious death will probably now never be solved, as with the JFK shooting.

Of all the Diana conspiracy books available, the most grounded and convincing is Jon King and John Beveridge's *Princess Diana: The Hidden Evidence* (SPI Books, 2001), which makes clear, if nothing else, that staged car-crashes are indeed a tried-and-tested method of assassination in the intelligence world.

For a detailed resumé, readers are directed to my own book *Conspiracies: The Facts—The Theories—The Evidence* (Watkins Publishing, 2013), which includes a long section on the whole Princess Diana saga.

24) Modern pyramids: Pyramid building now seems to be all the rage again, for good or ill. A wide selection of photos showing recently constructed pyramids from around the world can be found at: *http://www.welcomethelight.com/2009/03/amazing-pyramids-of-modern-times/*.

25) The 'Cremation of Care' ceremony at Bohemian Grove: A mainstream, but balanced and thorough, view of The Bohemian Club and the Cremation of Care ceremony can be found at: *http://en.wikipedia.org/wiki/Bohemian_Grove#cite_note-21*. This article notes that, in response to a heckler who raised the subject of Bohemian Grove at one of his public appearances in 2007, Bill Clinton (laughing) said:

'The Bohemian Club! Did you say Bohemian Club? That's where all those rich Republicans go up and stand naked against redwood trees right? I've never been to the Bohemian Club, but you oughta go. It'd be good for you. You'd get some fresh air.'

26) Mysterious deaths and the Clintons: It is easy to joke about the Clintons, but a glance at the list of their ex-associates and colleagues who have met untimely ends in unusual or unexplained circumstances is a sobering experience. The morbidly curious should look at *The Progressive Review's Arkansas Sudden Death Syndrome*, which lists over 50 people who have fallen into this unfortunate category: *http://www.freerepublic.com/focus/f-news/1142670/posts*.

27) Jon Ronson and Bohemian Grove: Journalist Ronson remains non-committal about the significance of what he saw at Bohemian Grove, but he was impressed enough to base an entire chapter of his bestselling book *Them: Adventures With Extremists* (Simon & Schuster, 2002) on his experience of sneaking into the Cremation of Care ceremony with Alex Jones, as well as showing the footage on the noted Channel 4 documentary.

27) Kenneth Clarke defends Bilderbergs: The remarkable moment when UK MP Michael Meacher forced both Clarke and Labour's Ed Balls to explain to Parliament their involvement in the Bilderberg meetings can be viewed at *Parliament laughs off Bilderberg inquiry*, 11 June 2013, at: *http://www.redicecreations.com/article.php?id=25576*. Both attempt to lightheartedly brush it aside, but their embarrassed squirming is notable.

THE TRUTH AGENDA

VI ONE GIANT LEAP..?

1) JFK's intention to land astronauts on the Moon: President John F Kennedy announced his aims to send men to the Moon by the end of the 1960s in a speech known as the *Special Message to the Congress on Urgent National Needs*, 25 May 1961. The entire text of this very influential speech can be read and heard at: *http://www.jfklibrary. org/Historical+Resources/Archives/Reference+Desk/Speeches/JFK/003POF03NationalNeeds05251961.htm*.

2) Inconsistencies in the claimed visibility of stars: In his book *NASA Mooned America!* (self-published, 1992), Chapter 5, *Star Light—Star Bright*, pages 29-36, Ralph René draws a series of curious comparisons highlighting astronauts' often contradictory statements about either the brightness or dimness of stars as seen from space, and struggles to reach a definitive conclusion on the ultimate truth of the matter. For instance, he quotes Harry Hurt III's book *For All Mankind* (Atlantic Monthly Press, 1988), in which Hurt writes of the Apollo 14 mission:

'The astronauts had a hard time seeing the stars even with the help of a special "monocular" (half a binocular) used to supplement the scanning telescope and the sextant. Due to the absence of an atmosphere to refract and filter light, the stars do not twinkle in cislunar space. Rather, as Stu Roosa puts it, "The stars look like little points of light or fuzzy little dots".'

On the other hand, these kinds of statements need to be contrasted with comments such as this from Apollo 11 astronaut Michael Collins, who writes (describing his thoughts at the time of being in space):

'My God, the stars are everywhere, even below me. They are somewhat brighter than on Earth.'

There are numerous examples, equally at odds with each other, leading many theorists to question the testimony of the astronauts.

3) Virgil 'Gus' Grissom: Astronaut Virgil Grissom's running critique of the Moon program, his subsequent untimely demise in the Apollo 1 fire and his son Scott Grissom's attempts to piece together what happened is discussed at length in Gerhard Wisnewski's worryingly credible book *One Small Step?—The Great Moon Hoax and the Race to Dominate Earth from Space*, Clairview Books, 2007.
   Scott Grissom's public breaking of the news that he believed his father was murdered first appeared in Steve Herz's article *Apollo Astronaut was Murdered, Son Charges* in the US magazine *Star*, issue dated 16 February 1999, and is summed up in a similarly-titled piece by Christopher Ruddy at: *http://www. theforbiddenknowledge.com/hardtruth/astronaut_murdered.htm*.

4) Thomas Ronald Baron's damning report on Apollo safety: Although Baron's final 500-page report on poor safety at North American Aviation (NAA) has never been seen since he and his entire family were killed in a suspicious car crash, his preliminary paper is available to read. This alone makes it clear that the Apollo missions were hardly being planned with the kind of efficacy and diligence surely required to safely get men to the Moon and back. Notes on the Baron affair and the paper itself can be found in Steve Garber's article *Baron Report (1965-1966)*, 3 February 2003, at: *http://history.nasa.gov/Apollo204/barron.html*.

5) James Irwin: The claims that astronaut James Irwin was about to make a public statement exposing the Moon missions as a fraud, but died suddenly before he could do so, were made by one Lee Gelvani (apparently a friend of moon-hoax theorist Bill Kaysing—see *http://billkaysing.com*), who claimed to have been in direct contact with Irwin. However, 'Lee Gelvani' appears to be a pseudonym and no direct proof of his allegations exist.

6) Moon rocks not what they seem: Astrobiologist Andrew Steele's discovery that the lunar sample he was sent for analysis contained obvious earthly particles is reported in Gerhard Wisnewski's *One Small Step?*, Part Two: *The USA*, pages 207-208.
   Meanwhile, the perhaps telling story of the much-treasured 'Moon rock' at the Dutch Rijksmuseum in Amsterdam turning out to be nothing of the sort was widely publicized in August 2009, and a typical report, *Moon rock in museum is just petrified wood*, by Toby Sterling, 27 August 2009, can be found at: *http://www.msnbc.msn.com/id/32581790/ns/technology_and_science-space/*.

7) Laser reflectors on the Moon: Gerhard Wisnewski's revelation that scientists cannot pinpoint the exact location of the laser-reflectors supposedly left on the lunar surface by the astronauts is discussed in *One Small Step?*, Part Two: *The USA*, pages 209-218.

8) Incorrect horizon line behind Aldrin: The impossibility that an aesthetically perfect horizon line could run through 'Buzz' Aldrin's visor reflection to match the real horizon behind him, if taken with a camera at chest height, is incontrovertibly demonstrated in Mary Bennett and David Percy's dense and detailed book *Dark Moon: Apollo and the Whistleblowers* (Aulis Publishers, 1999), Chapter 1, *Photo Call*, pages 40-41.

9) Original Moon videos lost: The astonishing news that NASA had lost the original videotapes of the Moon missions (before suspiciously finding them again in time for the 40th anniversary) was originally published in the Australian newspaper *The Sydney Morning Herald* in the report *One giant blunder for mankind—how NASA lost moon pictures*, 5 August 2006. *Wikipedia's* take on it can be found at: *http://en.wikipedia.org/wiki/Apollo_program_missing_tapes*.

10) Fake space walk photo: The provably-doctored photo of astronaut Michael Collins, taken on a terrestrial training flight but altered to represent a Gemini space walk, features prominently in Collins' 1974 autobiographical book *Carrying the Fire: An Astronaut's Journeys* (republished 2001 by Cooper Square Press). Curiously, the same shot is cut out *again* and superimposed over 1970s spacey artwork on the original cover.

11) Fake 'Moon golf' photo: The obviously montaged shot of Alan Shepard and companion supposedly playing golf on the Moon is analyzed and taken apart (literally) bit by bit by Mary Bennett and David Percy at: *http://www.aulis.com/nasa12.htm*. The book in which the photo features is *Moon Shot: The Inside Story of America's Race to the Moon*, by Al Shepard and Deke Slayton (Turner Publishing Inc., 1994).

12) Ed Mitchell's ET claims: The first interview in which astronaut Edgar Mitchell claimed that NASA and the US authorities had covered-up evidence of ET activity was made on *Kerrang Radio*, 23 July 2008, and can be heard at: *http://www.youtube.com/watch?v=RhNdxdveK7c*.

The *Daily Mail's* take on the story, *Apollo 14 astronaut claims aliens HAVE made contact—but it has been covered up for 60 years*, can be read at: *http://www.dailymail.co.uk/sciencetech/article-1037471/Apollo-14-astronaut-claims-aliens-HAVE-contact--covered-60-years.html*.

Mitchell has gone on to be very vocal on this issue, leading some to acclaim him as the whistleblower everyone has been waiting for, while others are suspicious, fearing that his claims may in themselves be a set-up of some kind.

13) Radiation hazards in space: Radiation is the 'show stopper' in the manned exploration of space, according to Mary Bennett and David Percy, who use it as one of the key arguments against the official story of the lunar missions in *Dark Moon*. Chapter 3, *Radiant Daze*, pages 77- 114, sifts many of the issues. Ralph René also discusses the problem at length in *NASA Mooned America!*, Chapter 15, *Sunstroke*, pages 125-136.

14) Were the space suits radiation-proof?: Given the high doses of radiation in space and on the lunar surface, one might reasonably expect that the astronauts' space suits were radiation-proof. Yet no fully-protective suit has yet been devised that can handle prolonged exposure in a terrestrial radiation zone (i.e. in a Chernobyl-type disaster), let alone a space-bound one—raising further questions about how the astronauts survived on the Moon.

15) 'Health Penalties' for Mars Missions: In an interview entitled *Should astronauts risk their health for Mars mission?* on the BBC News website at *http://www.bbc.co.uk/news/science-environment-22727305*, 1 June 2013, Dr Kevin Fong ('former NASA scientist and director of the Center for Space Medicine at University College, London'), warns of 'health penalties' for astronauts bound for Mars. The BBC text reads:

'Scientists have confirmed that astronauts sent on missions to Mars would have an increased risk of developing cancer because of high levels of radiation. The findings came from a study by NASA's unmanned Curiosity Rover mission which counted the number of high-energy space particles striking it on its eight-month journey to the planet. The data suggested humans would experience radiation doses that go beyond what is currently deemed acceptable for a career astronaut.'

16) Marcus Allen: One of the most high-profile NASA challengers, and UK publisher of *Nexus Magazine*, Marcus Allen has appeared widely on television and radio, managing to disarm even British TV rottweiler Jeremy Clarkson. A full video presentation by Allen can be watched at: *https://www.youtube.com/watch?v=LVR2WTK20Ig*.

17) Jack White's Moon photo analysis: The late Jack White's exhaustive and very convincing deconstruction of the NASA lunar image bank can be sifted through at *http://aulis.com/jackstudies_index1.html*, and is almost impossible to peruse without feeling at least slightly shaken afterwards. Amongst more obvious anomalies, White also identifies peculiarities such as photographic prints of the Apollo 11 mission seen lying on the foot of the Apollo 15 lander (a horizontally-flipped version of NASA photo reference AS11-40-5948)—something never explained, and other items that presumably wouldn't be able to survive the harsh lunar environment of high-temperature sunlight in a vacuum without some serious curling if nothing else. Gerhard Wisnewski demonstrates the same problem in *One Small Step?*, Part Two: *The USA*, pages 158-159, in which a print photograph showing the family of Apollo 16 astronaut Charles Duke can be seen lying on the lunar surface, apparently unaffected in any way. Leaving an unframed print photograph in even terrestrial sunlight for a short time will soon affect it, so how did those on the Moon stay so pristine?

18) Pete Conrad's 'spotlight' comments: Pete Conrad's curious commentary on the Sun resembling a 'super-bright spotlight' is quoted from Mary Bennett and David Percy's *Dark Moon*, Chapter 1, *Photo Call*, page 27.

19) Did Yuri Gagarin really go into space?: There is good evidence to suggest that a number of manned space flights were secretly attempted by the Russians before the famed Gagarin mission, but that the cosmonauts involved were either killed or injured. Some researchers believe that in wanting to claim a first and realizing that the US might officially achieve the feat of manned spaceflight before them, the Soviet authorities used air officer Gagarin as a publicity front until real cosmonauts could eventually make it into space. Not as unlikely as it sounds, Gagarin only had a few flying hours' experience when he was chosen, and his observations about the historic flight were notably inconsistent with the official claims. Photos of him allegedly sitting in the capsule appear to have been doctored, and it seems slightly odd that no camera was used to look outwards into space during the flight to record such an incredibly important moment. Gagarin himself was said to have been injured in a fall from a balcony just six months after his supposed feat and suffered behavioral problems thereafter. He reportedly died in a mysterious military plane crash in 1968. No plane wreckage was ever photographed or publicly exhibited, and it is said that hardly anything of Gagarin's body was left—yet the flight suit that identified him was supposedly discovered in treetops nearby.

Gerhard Wisnewski writes at length about the Gagarin anomalies and other Soviet cover-ups in *One Small Step?*, Part One: *The Soviet Union*, but a brief resume (from a somewhat evangelical source) can be found at *http://www.biblebelievers.org.au/gagarin.htm*, and reports the following:

'On 12 April 2001, the Russian senior engineer Mikhail Rudenko, at the Experimental Design Office 456, in Khimki in the Moscow region, admitted in Pravda *that three cosmonauts had died in space before Gagarin was sent up, namely Alexei Ledovskikh (1957), Serenti Zhaborin (February 1958), and Andrei Mitkov (flight attempt January 1959).'*

On top of this astonishing announcement, it is rumored that an additional seven cosmonauts were lost in pre-'Gagarin' flights, with Italian radio hams claiming to have picked up plaintive SOS messages from Russian personnel that could only have come from space.

20) John F Kennedy instructs NASA to cooperate with the Soviets: The remarkable memorandums in which President Kennedy orders NASA to set up joint missions with the Soviet Union, releasing the CIA's UFO files into the bargain, are discussed by Michael Salla PhD in the article *Kennedy linked US-USSR space missions with classified UFO files*, 27 May 2009, at: *http://www.examiner.com/x-2383-Honolulu-Exopolitics-Examiner%7Ey2009m5d27-President-Kennedy-linked-joint-lunar-missions-with-classified-UFO-filed*.

21) Barack Obama blocks new NASA Moon landings: Obama's sudden withdrawal of support for the Constellation project and any immediate plans for a state-funded return to the Moon is reported in Jonathan Amos' piece *Obama cancels Moon return project*, 1 February 2010, at: *http://news.bbc.co.uk/1/hi/sci/tech/8489097.stm*.

VII WEAPONS OF MASS DECEPTION

1) The Suez crisis: A good timeline of the 1956 Suez crisis, which reveals many of its more dubious aspects, is available at: *http://www.bodley.ox.ac.uk/dept/scwmss/projects/suez/suez.html.*

2) The 'fake bin Laden' video: The Osama bin Laden seen in the alleged '9/11 confession' video is widely considered not to be the real man and the footage is debunked at many websites, including *http://www. welfarestate.com/binladen/surprise/* and *http://www.911lies.org/fake_bin_laden.html* (this also covers the interesting fact that bin Laden was never listed on the FBI's 'wanted' list for perpetrating 9/11).

3) Turkmenistan-Afghanistan-Baluchistan oil pipeline?: A good forum discussion, putting forward the pros and cons of the theory that the US wants a major oil pipeline running through these regions, hence some of its recent military strategies, can be found in the thread *Free Baluchistan*, started 6 April 2005, at: *http://www.moonofalabama.org/2005/04/free_baluchista.html.* Another piece, which gives some clarity on the matter, Alex Bigham's *Why Baluchistan Matters*, 4 July 2006, can be found at: *http://www.guardian. co.uk/commentisfree/2006/jul/04/whybaluchistanmatters.*

4) Increased opium production in Afghanistan: The huge rise in opium production in Afghanistan since Western troops arrived has been widely-acknowledged in the media, if sheepishly ignored by politicians, leading many observers to wonder what the motive is in having allowed this to occur. Two good mainstream sources on this can be read at: *http://news.bbc.co.uk/1/hi/world/south_asia/6239734.stm* and *http://www. independent.co.uk/news/world/asia/the-big-question-why-is-opium-production-rising-in-afghanistan-and- can-it-be-stopped-960276.html.* For a more conspiratorial report, making direct links to 9/11, see also: *http://www.veteranstoday.com/2010/10/16/gordon-duff-when-will-the-crimes-of-911-end/*

5) Ron Suskind's revelations on the Iraq war: Ron Suskind has been an important mainstream challenger of the official record of the events leading up to the 2003 invasion of Iraq, and his revelations that WMDs were already known not to exist there deserve more attention. Information on Suskind is available at: *http://en.wikipedia.org/wiki/Ron_Suskind.*

More recent leaks firmly back-up Suskind's discoveries, with the 2009 exposure of certain Whitehall e mails making clear that both politicians and bureaucrats knew full well that the all-important 'dossier' was being (at the very least) over-enhanced to prop up an otherwise shaky case for war. Nigel Morris writes candidly on the deception in his article *Secret emails show Iraq dossier was 'sexed up'—Intelligence chiefs criticized 'iffy drafting' of key document*, 13 March 2009, at: *http://www.independent.co.uk/news/uk/politics/ secret-emails-show-iraq-dossier-uwasu-sexed-up-1643960.html.*

6) Norman Baker MP on David Kelly: Norman Baker's investigation into the shameful David Kelly affair and the weapons inspector's very dubious death is one of the very rare conspiracy theories to go mainstream without blanket ridicule, largely because of Baker's high-profile as a British Parliamentary reformer and an outspoken (for an MP) liberty campaigner. Some see his conclusion that Iraqi dissidents alone killed Kelly as a polite evasion of possible deeper truths, but going public with such views was still a brave move for a man in his position. Partly as a result of Baker's revelations, it is now hard to find too many people willing to believe the official 'suicide' verdict on Kelly's demise, despite UK government attempts in 2010 to squash this by basically restating old (and unconvincing) evidence, but just more loudly.

Baker's bestselling book *The Strange Death of David Kelly* (Methuen Publishing, 2007) is the main source to go to, but for a concise version of his findings, the article *Why I know weapons expert Dr David Kelly was murdered, by the MP who spent a year investigating his death*, 20 October 2007, is a good round-up and can be read at: *http://www.dailymail.co.uk/news/article-488667/Why-I-know-weapons-expert-Dr-David- Kelly-murdered-MP-spent-year-investigating-death.html.*

A video of Norman Baker presenting his findings in a lecture can be seen at: *https://www.youtube.com/ watch?v=TXLXhiJfFv4.*

7) Dr David Kelly's medical records to be withheld for 70 years: Lord Hutton's highly suspicious order that Kelly's medical records, including the post mortem report, be barred from public release until the end of the 21st century is reported well in Miles Goslett's article *David Kelly post mortem to be kept secret for 70 years as doctors accuse Lord Hutton of concealing vital information*, 25 January 2010, at: *http://www.dailymail.*

co.uk/news/article-1245599/David-Kelly-post-mortem-kept-secret-70-years-doctors-accuse-Lord-Hutton-concealing-vital-information.html.

8) Brian Haw's Parliament protest: In what must be one of the longest-running unbroken anti-war protests in history, the late British peace campaigner Brian Haw managed to keep his impassioned, if unsubtle, information stalls on the Iraq war and other recent Western military ventures standing at the edge of London's Parliament Square (opposite the Houses of Parliament) for nearly a decade from 2001. In raising awareness of sanctions and bombings on Iraq even before the WMDs were used to justify a full war two years later, Haw met a continual onslaught of police intimidation and attempted legislation to move him, but public support, court cases and legal loopholes enabled him to stay for years before his death in 2011. Find out more about Haw's impressive tenacity at *http://en.wikipedia.org/wiki/Brian_Haw*. His work's legacy is continued today at: *http://www.brianhaw.tv*. The right to protest in Westminster has been massively curtailed in recent years, so Haw's long success was particularly satisfying, while poignant.

VIII 9/11

1) 9/11 tenth anniversary polls: The anniversary year saw a number of global polls which revealed that something approaching half the world's population now had some kind of doubt as to whether they had been told the whole truth about 9/11. For instance, a British ICM poll, conducted on behalf of Reinvestigate 9/11, concluded that 'of those who expressed an opinion 37% agreed that rogue elements in the American intelligence services may have made a decision prior to 9/11 to allow a terrorist attack to take place'. In France, doubts were more robustly expressed, with an HEC poll revealing 'that 58% have doubts compared to 31% percent who accept the official story. Half suspect that US authorities deliberately allowed the attacks to take place while a third suspect they were implicated in the execution of 9/11.' The polls are discussed at: *http://www.911truth.org/article.php?story=20110909085546680*.

2) Did the FBI aid the 1993 WTC bombing?: The chilling testimony of agent Emad Salem that the FBI deliberately supplied live explosives to the perpetrators of the 1993 WTC bombing has not received the coverage it demands, not even amongst 9/11 truth campaigners. Information on Salem is available at: *http://en.wikipedia.org/wiki/Emad_Salem*.

3) Lack of airplane debris at the Pentagon: The strange absence of obvious plane wreckage inside or outside of the Pentagon was noted by several reporters and eye-witnesses at the time. Quotes such as 'there's no evidence of a plane having crashed anywhere near the Pentagon' (James McIntyre, CNN News), 'I don't recall at any time seeing any plane debris' (April Gallop, Pentagon staff survivor), 'There weren't seats or luggage or things you find in a plane' (Judy Rothschadl, documentary maker) and 'I got in very close, got a look early on at the bad stuff. I could not, however, see any plane wreckage' (John McWethy, ABC News) are typical statements. McWethy was one of the first to coin the phrase that the plane had 'basically, vaporized', a view entirely encouraged by official sources since—and something quite impossible in the circumstances. The debris that has been identified from photos seems not to be from a Boeing 757 [page 150]. Quotes extracted from David Ray Griffin's *Debunking 911 Debunking* (Olive Branch Press, 2007), Chapter Four, *Debunking 9/11 Myths*, pages 269-270.

4) Taxi driver claims surrounding Pentagon damage was 'planned': When interviewed by 9/11 truth campaigners and challenged about anomalies concerning the claimed position of his cab on the day, a taxi driver who was on the roads near the Pentagon when it was attacked appears to crack and state 'it was planned'. At first reluctant to speak, when pressed the driver implies that surrounding damage in the local area (lightpoles, etc.) was somehow arranged in advance. If the interview is genuine and the cab driver is who he says he is (there are claims that his wife works for the FBI), this very curious evidence deserves more exposure. A video of the interview, entitled *Cab Driver Involved In 9/11 Pentagon Attack Admits "It Was Planned"* can be seen on YouTube at: *http://www.youtube.com/watch?v=kvyQOvVwjqc&feature=youtu.be*.

5) NIST's shotgun tests: The bizarre revelation that NIST (National Institute of Standards and Technology) conducted its supposedly 'scientific' analysis of how fireproofing might have been removed from steel supports at the WTC by firing shotgun rounds at metal plates in plywood boxes is reported in David Ray

Griffin's *Debunking 911 Debunking*, Chapter Four, *Debunking 9/11 Myths*, page 251.

6) Fire temperatures should not have weakened steel supports: The quoted statistics on the temperatures needed to weaken steel, as set against the probable maximum temperatures of the fires in the twin towers, are based on data produced by the 9/11 Commission's own Thomas Eagar, professor of Materials Engineering and Engineering Systems at MIT, as quoted in the article by R Herbst BAAE, ME, *Mysteries of the Twin Towers: A Survey of Available Evidence on the Collapse of the World Trade Center Towers*, 12 February 2009, point 5.2.3, *Refutation of Early Fire and Heat Theories*, which can be found at: ***http://www.seattle911visibilityproject.org/rwtcpdf.pdf***.

7) Steven E Jones & Richard Gage: The calibre and qualifications of those questioning the physics of 9/11 is now very high, and the work of Dr Steven Jones and Richard Gage has been important in alerting the upper echelons of physicists and architects (respectively) to the unignorable anomalies in the observable processes of the WTC's destruction. Yet there have been attempts to denigrate the reputations of Jones and Gage as a result of their high-profile work for the 9/11 truth movement, with Jones being suspended from his teacher's position at Brigham Young University as a result, before taking early retirement. To dispel any doubt about their credentials, here are their official biographies:

STEVEN E JONES: Jones earned his bachelor's degree in physics, magna cum laude, from Brigham Young University in 1973, and his Ph.D. in physics from Vanderbilt University in 1978. Jones conducted his Ph.D. research at the Stanford Linear Accelerator Center (from 1974 to 1977), and post-doctoral research at Cornell University and the Los Alamos Meson Physics Facility. [***http://en.wikipedia.org/wiki/Steven_E._Jones***—see also ***http://911scholars.org***]

RICHARD GAGE: Richard Gage, AIA is the founding member of ae911Truth.org [Architects and Engineers for 9/11 Truth]. *He has been a practicing architect for 20 years and has worked on most types of building construction including numerous fire-proofed steel-framed buildings. He is employed with a San Francisco Bay Area architecture firm and has most recently performed Construction Administration services for a new $120M High School campus including a $10M steel-framed Gymnasium. Most recently he worked on the Design Development for a very large mixed use urban project with 1.2M sq.ft. of retail and 320K sq.ft. of mid-rise office space—altogether about 1,200 tons of steel framing.* [***http://www.ae911truth.org***]

8) Delayed release of the WTC blueprints: The blueprints for the WTC were mysteriously held back from circulation until 27 March 2007, when they were finally, and revealingly, released, as discussed at: ***http://stj911.org/press_releases/blueprints.html***.

9) Thomas Eagar on support columns: MIT professor Thomas Eagar's view that the remaining support columns at the WTC should have been enough to hold the towers up is, interestingly, quoted from *Without Precedent: The Inside Story of the 9/11 Commission*, by Thomas Kean and Lee H Hamilton, with Benjamin Rhodes (New York, Alfred A Knopf, 2006)—a book written by the main authors of the official 9/11 Commission report!

10) Richard Gage demonstrates flawed physics in the official 9/11 story: A video presentation by architect Richard Gage, *9/11: Blueprint for Truth*, which by itself nails the case that the WTC could not possibly have fallen due to natural collapse, can be downloaded at: ***http://www.ae911truth.org***.

11) Human remains found several blocks from the WTC: The discovery of new body parts on a New York skyscraper rooftop as long after 9/11 as 2006 (demonstrating to doubters the sheer propulsive force exuded in the destruction of the towers, far more than a simple collapse could generate), is reported in Amy Westfeldt's article *9/11 human remains found on skyscraper rooftop*, 6 April 2006, at: ***http://www.mg.co.za/article/2006-04-06-911-human-remains-found-on-skyscraper-rooftop***.

12) More evidence of propulsive forces at the WTC: Rick Siegel's documentary *911 Eyewitness*, based on his own amateur footage of the WTC collapses taken from across the Hudson at Hoboken, spends some time analyzing the physics of the extraordinary force apparently employed. Some truth campaigners have criticized the film's scientific reliability and take issue with Siegel's belief that helicopters seen hovering near the towers are in some way responsible for their falls. Nonetheless, there are some interesting observations here, including seismic readings on rumbles and deep booms heard on his soundtrack shortly before the towers fall (suggesting large explosions taking out the infrastructure), although these remain as yet unverified by cross-referencing with other footage. Information on the film can be found at: *http://www.911eyewitness.com*.

13) Pulverization of all objects in the WTC debris: The testimony of Robert (Bobby) Gray, crane operator in the clear-up operation at the WTC, that even filing cabinets and other office equipment didn't appear to survive the tower collapses, is quoted from his co-authored book (with Glenn Stout, Charles Vitchers and Joel Meyerowitz) *Nine Months at Ground Zero: The Story of the Brotherhood of Workers Who Took on a Job Like No Other* (Scribner, 2006).

14) Dr Judy Wood: Dr Wood is one of the key proponents of the theory that energy technology of some kind was used to destroy the twin towers, and is author of *Where Did the Towers Go?: The Evidence of Directed Free-Energy Technology on 9/11* (The New Investigation, 2010). She has garnered a strong following amongst some truth campaigners. Wood's own website at *http://drjudywood.co.uk* describes her thus:

'*Dr Judy Wood earned a Ph.D. Degree from Virginia Tech and is a former professor of mechanical engineering. In the time since 9/11/01, Dr Wood has conducted a comprehensive forensic investigation of what physically happened to the World Trade Center site on 9/11.*'

Some supporters of Wood's theories are adamant that these ideas are incompatible with the nano-thermate model, leading to some unfortunate and unhelpful clashes at truth gatherings. Other researchers disagree and consider that both kinds of technology might have been employed to bring down the towers. Further interesting 9/11 energy theories and general conspiracy information can be found at Andrew Johnson's website *http://www.checktheevidence.com/cms*.

15) Thermite found in 9/11 dust: A good résumé of the discovery of thermitic particles in the dust near Ground Zero—effectively proving the presence of explosives at the WTC on 9/11—can be read in Gregg Robert's article *Scientists Find Unignited Explosive Residues in WTC Dust: Red/Gray Chips Match Advanced Thermitic Materials Developed in US Government Labs*, 22 April 2009, at: *http://www.ae911truth.org/info/57*.

16) Toxic dust deaths from 9/11: The scandal that rescue workers and the public were admitted back into the WTC disaster area long before it was safe to breathe the contaminated air has been widely discussed in the US media. It seems the authorities were keen to get nearby Wall Street back up and running again so that the economy wasn't held back, but people have died for it. One of many articles decrying the situation, Paul Krugman's *Dust and Deception*, 26 August 2003, can be read at: *http://healthandenergy.com/dangerous_9_11_dust.htm*, while Penny Little's film on the issue, *911: Dust and Deceit*, can be downloaded at: *http://www.911dust.org/*.

17) Fire Captain witnesses explosions: Fire Captain Karin Deshore's testimony of 'popping' explosions at the WTC is quoted from David Ray Griffin's *Debunking 911 Debunking*, Chapter Three, *The Disintegration of the World Trade Center*, page 177.

18) Firemen silenced about 9/11: Paul Isaac's depressing claim that NYC firemen have been forbidden by fire authorities from discussing their witnessing of explosions at the WTC is reported in an article by Randy Lavello, *Bombs in the Building*, at: *www.prisonplanet.com/analysis_lavello_050503_bombs.html*. Encouragingly, the creation of Firefighters for 9/11 Truth seems at last to be taking a stand against this situation—see *http://firefightersfor911truth.org*.

19) More on the 1993 WTC bomb: The (official) story of the 1993 bomb that attempted to bring down the WTC can be read at: *http://en.wikipedia.org/wiki/World_Trade_Center_bombing*.

20) More on Rick Siegel: See note 12 above.

21) WTC Janitor's testimony: Janitor William Rodriguez's reporting of the bomb blast in the basement just before the first plane hit the WTC is quoted from Greg Szymanski's article *WTC Basement Blast and Injured Burn Victim Blows 'Official 9/11 Story' Sky High*, 24 June 2005, at: *www.arcticbeacon.com/24-Jun-2005. html*. Rodriguez, who became a major campaigner for 9/11 truth, has his own website at: *http://www. william911.com*, where details of his DVD *What Really Happened on 9/11?* can be found.

22) Light aircraft hits NYC tower block: A report on the plane that hit a New York apartment block on 12th October 2006, entirely failing to raise fears that the building might collapse due to the subsequent fires, can be read in Ed Pilkington and Andrew Clark's report *Manhattan plane crash reawakens spectre of 9/11—Baseball star's aircraft flies into apartment block/Fighter jets scrambled as smoke pall hangs over city*, at: *http://www.guardian.co.uk/world/2006/oct/12/usa.edpilkington*.

23) Demolition experts' WTC 7 observations: Demolition experts' remarks that the video of the fall of WTC 7 (played to them without foreknowledge of where the footage was taken) must have been showing controlled demolition at work are recounted in David Ray Griffin's *Debunking 9/11 Debunking*, Chapter 3, *The Disintegration of the World Trade Center*, pages 200-201.

24) Fire Captain reports warning of WTC 7's demise: Fire Captain Michael Currid's report that he had been warned by Mayor Giuliani's Office of Emergency Management that WTC 7 was 'a lost cause' and ordered to evacuate is quoted in Dean E Murphy's *September 11: An Oral History* (Gale Group, 2003), pages 175-176.

25) Barry Jennings reports early evacuation and explosions in WTC 7: City Housing Authority worker Jennings' claim that he and colleague Michael Hess entered the emergency command center in WTC 7 only to find it already evacuated by 9.03am, together with their subsequent experiencing of explosions inside the building, are described by Jennings himself in an interview with Dylan Avery (director of the influential *Loose Change* films on 9/11 [page 357], which can be seen at: *http://www.youtube.com/watch?gl=GB&v=VQY-ksiuwKU*. A timeline of Jennings' account can be read at: *http://www.historycommons.org/entity.jsp?entity=barry_ jennings_1*. The BBC *Conspiracy Files* program on WTC 7 distorted Jennings' testimony, twisting the timeline and implying that no-one else witnessed the claimed explosion.
   Jennings died of unknown causes in 2008, age 53, leading to inevitable conspiracy speculation that an important eye-witness had been done away with, as discussed in Joe DeFranceschi's piece (with subsequent forum comments) *Barry Jennings, Key 9/11 Witness Dies*, 17 September 2008, at: *http://www.groundreport. com/US/Barry-Jennings-Key-9-11-Witness-Dies*.

26) Remote control used for 9/11 planes?: The notion that enforced remote control might have been used to guide the planes in on 9/11 may once have seemed far fetched, but today's wide usage of US military drones and the fact that the supposed Al Qaeda hijackers were reported by their flight schools as being such poor pilots (as with Hani Hanjour—page 149) make it something that has to be considered. Some good information links on this can be explored at: *http://911research.wtc7.net/resources/web/remote.html*.

27) 9/11 Commission director's friendship with Condoleezza Rice: Philip Zelikow's all-too-close links with then US Secretary of State Condoleezza Rice—hardly making the 9/11 Commission an 'independent' inquiry—can be explored at: *http://www.antiwar.com/sperry/index.php?articleid=2209*.

28) Was Flight 77's cockpit door ever opened?: It has been widely reported in the conspiracy world that the Flight Data Recorder (suspiciously, the only one 'recovered' from 9/11) for the plane which allegedly hit the Pentagon shows that the cockpit door never opened in the air, casting doubt on the hijack scenario. Some counter that if it had been accessed with a key by a flight attendant instead of the cockpit crew hitting the release button, it might not show up in electronic records, but uncertainty still surrounds the issue, especially as many believe that it was not Flight 77 that impacted the Pentagon. A report on this, *Flight 77 Cockpit Door Never Opened During 9/11 "Hijack"*, by Sheila Casey, 13 January 2010, can be found at: *http://www. sodahead.com/united-states/flight-77-cockpit-door-never-opened-during-911-hijack/question-821961/*.

29) Editing and misrepresentation of air traffic control tapes: The inconsistencies and apparent subsequent altering of the NORAD air traffic control transcripts and recorded conversations from 9/11 constitute some of the most serious and glaring problems of the official account, but to do them any justice here would take up another quarter of the book. Instead, readers are once again directed to David Ray Griffin's essential book *Debunking 9/11 Debunking*, in which the entire first chapter, *9/11 Live or Distorted?*, is taken up with exploring the NORAD transcript issues in fine and shocking detail, between—tellingly—pages 27-94.

30) Norman Mineta's report on Dick Cheney: Norman Mineta's discarded yet crucial testimony to the 9/11 Commission regarding the very strange 'do the orders still stand?' incident with Dick Cheney, by which it seems that a plane was being deliberately allowed to approach the Pentagon, is recounted at: *http:// en.wikipedia.org/wiki/Norman_Mineta*. However, this report also mentions an entirely different—and totally contradictory—retelling of the incident later made in the *Washington Post*, 22 January 2002, in which a more heroic slant is put on the actions allegedly taken in the Presidential Emergency Operating Center, suggesting yet another rewriting of history taking place.

31) A K Dewdney's cell phone experiments: Science writer A K Dewdney's experiments with cell phones (mobiles) in aircraft, which determined that none of the alleged cell calls from Flight 93 could possibly have been made in that way, can be read in detail at: *http://physics911.net/projectachilles*. The general anomalies and all-round strangeness of the calls allegedly received by relatives of the hijacked victims is discussed in another article by Dewdney at: *http://physics911.net/cellphoneflight93*.

32) Barbara Olson's claimed calls from Flight 77: David Ray Griffin's critique of the contradictions inherent in the claims that Barbara Olson made calls to her husband Ted from Flight 77 is quoted from his article *Ted Olson's Report of Phone Calls from Barbara Olson on 9/11: Three Official Denials*, 1 April 2008 (and very much *not* an April Fool's gag), at: *http://www.globalresearch.ca/index.php?context=va&aid=8514*.

33) Rice denies warnings of planes-as-missiles: Condoleezza Rice initially denied that intelligence warnings had ever been given that planes might be used as missiles in a terrorist attack. However, when presented with evidence that such warnings *were* given, this was her response to the Independent National Commission on Terrorist Attacks Upon the United States (the 9/11 Commission) on 13 May 2004:

'I think that concern about what... we might have known was provoked by some statements that I made in a press conference... ...And I said, "No one could have imagined them taking a plane, slamming it into the Pentagon"—I'm paraphrasing now—"into the World Trade Center, using planes as a missile." ...I probably should have said, "I could not have imagined," because within two days, people started to come to me and say, "Oh, but there were these reports in 1998 and 1999. The intelligence community did look at information about this." To the best of my knowledge, Mr Chairman, this kind of analysis about the use of airplanes as weapons actually was never briefed to us.'

34) Air Force One threatened?: The story of presidential airplane Air Force One being threatened with destruction, initially publicized on 9/11 before being quietly withdrawn, is discussed at length in Webster Griffin Tarpley's [no relation to David Ray Griffin] book *9/11 Synthetic Terror: Made in USA* (Progressive Press, 2005), Chapter IX, *"Angel is Next"—The Invisible Government Speaks*, pages 272-310.
   Tarpley believes the use of the code-word 'Angel' to describe Air Force One in the threatening message allegedly received by the White House on 9/11 is evidence that the terrorism of that day was firmly home-grown, because the likes of Al Qaeda would not have known such codes. Tarpley holds that this was the moment Bush was brought into the confidence of the neo-con plotters he claims were the architects of 9/11 (led by Dick Cheney). Tarpley's intimation is that if Bush hadn't agreed to go along with their plans, then Air Force One might not have returned from its trip that day.

35) US poll shows a majority believes 9/11 was allowed to occur: In addition to the anniversary polls discussed in Note 1 of this chapter, on 23 November 2007, Kevin Crowe and Guido H Stempel III of the Scripps Howard News Service website (*www.scrippsnews.com/node/28533*) reported the following result from a poll taken from 'a national survey of 811 adult residents of the United States' conducted by Scripps and Ohio University:

'Nearly two-thirds of Americans think it is possible that some federal officials had specific warnings of the Sept. 11, 2001, terrorist attacks on New York and Washington, but chose to ignore those warnings.'

36) George Monbiot on 9/11 truthers: 'Green' pundit Monbiot's borderline-offensive and clearly uninformed views on 9/11 questioners can be read in his article *9/11 fantasists pose a mortal danger to popular oppositional* *campaigns*, 20 February 2007, at: *http://www.guardian.co.uk/commentisfree/2007/feb/20/comment. september11*. As a typical media response to very valid questions about 9/11, this pitifully ignorant and dismissive piece by itself illustrates why the issue will never receive a proper airing in the mainstream media.

IX   THE WAR ON LIBERTY

1) Pearl Harbor conspiracy: A useful résumé of Pearl Harbor conspiracy theories, *Pearl Harbor: Mother of all Conspiracies*, is available at: *http://www.geocities.com/Pentagon/6315/pearl.html*.

2) The Waco siege: The idea that the fires at the Waco siege of 1993 were deliberately caused by FBI officers was initially dismissed as fringe paranoia. However, the release of the documentary *Waco: The Rules of Engagement* in 1997 (directed by William Gazecki) and its subsequent nomination for an Academy Award, together with the emergence of other credible sources, saw a growth of mainstream awareness that the situation may well have been contrived by the authorities, leading even *Wikipedia's* current entry at the time of writing (*http://en.wikipedia.org/wiki/Waco_Siege#See_also*) to state the following:

'Mainstream media tended to discount the critical views presented in early documentary films, because they were seen as coming from the political fringes of the right and left. This changed in 1997, when professional film makers Dan Gifford and Amy Sommer produced their Emmy Award winning documentary, Waco: The Rules of Engagement. *This film presents a history of the Branch Davidian movement and, most importantly, a critical examination of the conduct of law enforcement, both leading up to the raid and through the aftermath of the fire. The film features footage of the Congressional hearings on Waco, and juxtaposition of official government spokespeople with footage and evidence often directly contradicting the government spokespeople. The documentary also shows infrared footage demonstrating that the FBI likely used incendiary devices to start the fire which consumed the building and that the FBI did indeed fire on, and kill, Branch Davidians attempting to flee the fire.'*

3) Anomalies in the Oklahoma bombing: A concise report on the evidence that other forces must also have been at work to wreak the devastation seen in the Oklahoma City bomb of 1995 can be found in the article *The Oklahoma City Bombing: Were there additional explosive charges and additional bombers?* at: *http:// whatreallyhappened.com/RANCHO/POLITICS/OK/ok.html*.
  Further evidence of anomalies in the official Oklahoma story are discussed in Ambrose Evans-Pritchard's article *Did agents bungle US terror bomb?* at: *http://whatreallyhappened.com/RANCHO/POLITICS/OK/ok2.html*.

4) Authorities involved in Moscow apartment bombs?: Emmy-award winning journalist John Sweeney's illuminating, if disturbing, allegations that Russian authorities were involved in setting up the bombs that destroyed Moscow apartments in 1999 (supposedly placed by Chechen extremists) can be read in his article *The Fifth Bomb: Did Putin's Secret Police Bomb Moscow in a Deadly Black Operation?*, 24 November 2000, at: *http://cryptome.info/putin-bomb5.htm*.
  The issue is discussed in further detail in my book *Conspiracies: The Facts—The Theories—The Evidence* (Watkins Publishing, 2013) under the section *Other Modern False-Flag Events?*, pages 195-197.

5) The Gulf of Tonkin incident: A good account of the spurious Gulf of Tonkin incident, which helped spark the Vietnam conflict, can be found at: *http://en.wikipedia.org/wiki/Gulf_of_Tonkin_Incident*. However, whilst it is now accepted that the events never happened as reported, an apologist culture has arisen in which it is claimed the incident was misrepresented not to politically mislead anyone, but, as *Wikipedia* has it, 'to cover up honest intelligence errors'. This view was highlighted by National Security Agency historian Robert J Hanyok to the *New York Times*, which can be read in Shane Scott's article *Vietnam War Intelligence 'Deliberately Skewed,' Secret Study Says*, 2 December 2005, at: *http://www.commondreams.org/headlines05/1202-06.htm*. Needless to say, many truthseekers do not accept this tamer justification of the cover-up.
  Once again, readers are directed to my book *Conspiracies: The Facts—The Theories—The Evidence* (Watkins Publishing, 2013), *The Gulf of Tonkin Incident*, pages 84-87.

6) *The Power of Nightmares* TV series: Adam Curtis' courageous and excellent BBC 2 television series *The Power of Nightmares: The Rise of the Politics of Fear*, which exposed the fact that much of what we are told about 'Al Qaeda' is modern myth-making spread by Western sources to create disproportionate fear of Middle

Eastern terrorism, was broadcast in late 2004. The series reveals the real Al Qaeda to be a mass of squabbling factions incapable of the organization required to constitute the huge threat it has been presented as. *The Power of Nightmares* was later transmitted in various countries, but never, perhaps notably, in the US.

Much praised at the time, and at one point re-cut for an edited cinema version (which was shown at the 2005 Cannes festival, but never distributed thereafter), it has vanished from circulation in recent years and has never been officially released on DVD, leading many to wonder why (although Curtis cites copyright clearances for the many archive clips used as being one of the problems). Unofficial DVDs and downloads have been widely distributed around truthseeker networks. Detailed information on the series is available at: *http://en.wikipedia.org/wiki/The_Power_of_Nightmares.*

7) Former French Foreign Minister on UK involvement in Syria: The surprisingly candid claim from Roland Dumas on a TV show—that Britain (and, by association, the US) was interfering in Syria even before the civil war—has disturbing, if not entirely surprising, implications. A report, *Britain prepared for war in Syria two years before the crisis flared up, France's former FM says,* 14 June 2013, is available at: *http://sana.sy/eng/22/2013/06/14/487527.htm.* The exact quote from Dumas states:

'I was in Britain two years ago, and I met British officials, some my friends... they admitted that they were up to something in Syria.'

8) The US Patriot Act: A good critique and deconstruction of the draconian Patriot Act can be found in constitutional attorney John W Whitehead's article for The Rutherford Institute, *How Liberty Dies: The Patriot Reauthorization Act,* 13 June 2005 (from where the given quote comes), at: *http://www.rutherford.org/articles_db/commentary.asp?record_id=343.*

9) Attempts to create a 42-day detention law: The House of Lords' defeat of the proposed 42-day detention period for suspected terrorists is well reported in the article *House of Lords deals fatal blow to 42-day terror detention plans,* 14 October 2008, at: *http://www.timesonline.co.uk/tol/news/politics/article4938637.ece.*

10) *Private Eye* **magazine:** The semi-satirical magazine *Private Eye* has become required reading in the UK for its endless uncovering of corruption and intrigue within local and national authorities, as well as inside the media infrastructure. It has gained a worldwide reputation. However, its frustrating inability to believe that the very conspiracies it revels in reporting at those levels could possibly be happening at a global scale, its constant characterization of conspiracy theorists as moronic reprobates or, worse, far-right fanatics, and its endless crusade against alternative medicine, reveals a deep and frustrating seam of ex-public school conservatism (small 'c') at its editorial core, which compromises its supposedly subversive credentials for many. Truthseekers reading *Private Eye* for vital information therefore suffer exasperating swings between fascination or laughter, and wanting to throw the thing out of the train window in rage. Anyone curious to share this experience can find out about the magazine at: *http://www.private-eye.co.uk.*

11) 82-year old activist forcibly removed from conference/Terrorism Act abuses: The disgraceful incident that saw British veteran Labour party activist Walter Wolfgang evicted from the 2005 party conference by security heavies under a misuse of anti-terrorism laws is reported by the BBC in the article *Labour issues apology to heckler,* 28 September 2005, at: *http://news.bbc.co.uk/1/hi/uk_politics/4291388.stm* and analyzed more deeply by Nick Assinder in the piece *Wolfgang highlights deeper disquiet,* 29 September 2005, at: *http://news.bbc.co.uk/1/hi/uk_politics/4293502.stm.*

The revelation that, of 1,721 arrests under the Terrorism Act between 2007-2008, only 73 were for actual terror offences, can be read in Robert Verkaik's article referenced in note 16 of this chapter. News that UK Home Secretary Theresa May would bend the Terrorism Act to stop potential protestors at Prince William's wedding to Kate Middleton on 29 April 2011 is included in Chris Greenwood's piece *Government to consider banning face coverings to deter anarchists during Royal wedding,* 29 March 2011, at: *http://www.dailymail.co.uk/news/article-1370841/Royal-wedding-Government-consider-banning-face-coverings-deter-anarchists.html.*

12) Attempted restrictions on photographing the police: The new law, which could have been used to prevent British civilians from taking photographs of the police and other enforcement personnel if held to the letter, was brought in under Section 76 of the Counter Terrorism Act in 2009. Press photographers staged a mass protest in response, as reported in Victoria Bone's article *Is it a crime to take pictures?,* 16

February 2009, at: *http://news.bbc.co.uk/1/hi/uk/7888301.stm.*

The government legalese employed very vague wording that was feared could have been abused to prevent legitimate filming of police misbehavior, such as that which occurred during the G20 protests, when one Ian Tomlinson died shortly after being deliberately pushed over by an officer. The footage of this moment, together with discussion of the fallout from it, can be read in the article *Video reveals G20 police assault on man who died*, 7 April 2009, at: *http://www.guardian.co.uk/uk/2009/apr/07/video-g20-police-assault.* No prosecutions were attempted for the filming of this, and later qualifications of the law in question appeared to back away from further risks of legal action. (Some PR tact was clearly required for the G20 incident, although another factor here might have been that the police didn't want to draw attention to the fact that many of the anti-riot officers were—quite illegally—not wearing identification numbers.)

The Terrorism Act 2000 can be read about at: *http://en.wikipedia.org/wiki/Terrorism_Act_2000.*

13) CCTV doesn't prevent crime: A useful US journalistic view on the ineffectiveness of CCTV as a crime-prevention tool in the UK can be read in Marcus Baram's article *Eye on the City: Do Cameras Reduce Crime?—NYPD Readies 3,000 Surveillance Cameras; Have They Worked in Other Cities?*, 9 July 2007, at: *http://www.abcnews.go.com/US/Story?id=3360287&page=1.*

14) Governments monitor electronic communications: The announcement that a centralized UK government database monitoring the population's e-mail and Internet movements would be scrapped, in favor of asking communications firms to make records available to authorities, is reported in Dominic Casciani's article *Plans to monitor all internet use*, 27 April 2009, at: *http://news.bbc.co.uk/1/hi/uk_politics/8020039. stm?b.* The 2014 'Counter Terrorism and Security Bill' is debated at: *http://www.independent.co.uk/voices/comment/theresa-may-is-gradually-building-a-surveillance-state-in-bitesized-chunks-9884245.html*

The 2013 revelations that the US PRISM system had been effectively spying on everyone since 2007 anyway generated enormous coverage, with none of the official excuses, claims or counter-claims covering for the fact that basically Big Brother really had arrived, as conspiracy theorists had long claimed. (No-one gave them any credit when the story broke, of course.) There are endless sources available, but a good summary of the essentials can be found at *The Guardian*'s report, *NSA Prism program taps in to user data of Apple, Google and others*, 7 June 2013, at: *http://www.guardian.co.uk/world/2013/jun/06/us-tech-giants-nsa-data.*

A good article on the precursor to PRISM, the ECHELON 'signal interception' system, is available at: *http://whatreallyhappened.com/RANCHO/POLITICS/ECHELON/echelon.html.*

15) Impending regulation of the Internet: There are numerous pieces out there outlining the current threats to the continuing freedom of the Internet, but a good video summing-up of the issues, *The Death of the Internet?*, can be found at: *http://uk.youtube.com/watch?v=G5RQrxkGgCM.*

16) Troops surround Heathrow: The never-explained incident in which tanks rolled up to surround London's Heathrow airport in 2003 was reported in the moment by the BBC in the article *Heathrow threat real says Blunkett*, 14 February 2003, at: *http://news.bbc.co.uk/1/hi/uk_politics/2758753.stm.* In the continuing absence of any given reason for the sudden arrival of troops at a major UK airport, it is likely this was simply an exercise in maintaining public fear in the earlier years of the War on Terror. If we were genuinely being protected from something, it seems strange for even the basic nature of the threat never to have been revealed.

17) Few convictions after terror arrests: The official figures announcing that hardly anyone arrested under British terror laws is ever convicted are reported well in Robert Verkaik's article *Just one in eight terror arrests ends with guilty verdict, admits Home Office*, 14 May 2009, which can be read at: *http://www.independent.co.uk/news/uk/home-news/just-one-in-eight-terror-arrests-ends-with-guilty-verdict-admits-home-office-1684580.html.*

18) Anomalies of the 7/7 bombings: A round-up of the key issues surrounding doubts over the official story of the London 7/7 bombings can be found at the July 7th Truth Campaign's website at: *http://www.julyseventh.co.uk/july-7-truth-campaign-flyer.html.*

An interesting 2006 documentary that outlines many of the problems with 7/7, *Mind the Gap*, can be watched at: *http://www.officialconfusion.com/77/index.html*, while another, shorter, film, *Ludicrous Diversion*, is also worth seeing at: *http://google.com/videoplay?docid=4943675105275097719.*

19) Terror exercises on 7/7: Peter Power's astonishing claims that terror exercises were taking place at the very locations of the bombs on 7/7 are dissected at: *http://www.julyseventh.co.uk/july-7-terror-rehearsal.html.*

20) The bus at Tavistock Square on 7/7: A claimed survivor of the London bus bombing, Daniel Obachike, has controversially stated that two cars appeared to deliberately block the path of the bus up the Euston Road, necessitating a diversion that led to its entering Tavistock Square, where the explosion then occurred. Obachike also asserts a number of anomalies concerning the strange behavior and injuries of certain bystanders outside the bus, and states that what appeared to him to be intelligence operatives seemed to be already present in the Square, as if expecting an event. Some have challenged the reliability of Obachike's testimony, which remains uncorroborated—however, it can be read in his book *The 4th Bomb—Inside London's Terror Storm* (Floran Publishing, 2007). A precis of the claims can be found in Steve Watson and Alex Jones' article *7/7 Bus Bomb Survivor Describes "Agents" at Scene in Immediate Aftermath*, 29 January 2007, at: *http://www.infowars.net/articles/january2007/290107Exclusive.htm.*

21) The shooting of Jean Charles De Menezes: The disheartening refusal of the judge to allow an 'unlawful killing' verdict in the case of Jean Charles De Menezes, shot on 22nd July 2005 at point-blank range on the London Underground under (false) suspicion of being a terrorist, is reported by Helen Pidd in the article *No charges over De Menezes shooting—Police officers will not face trial over killing of Brazilian they mistook for a suicide bomber, says Crown Prosecution Service*, 13 February 2009, at: *http://www.guardian.co.uk/uk/2009/feb/13/police-no-charges-de-menezes-shooting.*

22) Taser-related deaths: The unacceptable blanket use of 'Tasers' (electronic stun guns), now all too often being used by police around the world in unnecessary situations, has led to many deaths, where the victims' constitutions have been unable to withstand high-voltage electric shocks, often ineptly deployed. Human rights organization Amnesty International states the following at *http://blog.amnestyusa.org/tag/taser/:*

'The controversy surrounding Tasers is well-documented. Between July 2001 and August 2008, Amnesty International studied more than 334 deaths that occurred after police-use of Tasers. So many of the deaths were needless. Police frequently used Tasers inappropriately, especially considering that in well over 90% of the cases, the person on whom the Taser was used did not even have a weapon. Medical examiners have cited Taser as a primary or contributory cause of death in at least 50 cases.'

The same article goes on to describe a new and worrying Taser 'shockwave' device that will be able to electrocute entire crowds at once. Science-fiction this isn't, and things haven't improved in recent years. More Amnesty information on Tasers, with further links, can be found at *http://www.amnestyusa.org/us-human-rights/taser-abuse/page.do?id=1021202.* See also: *http://en.wikipedia.org/wiki/Taser.*

23) Ambiguous knife crime statistics: The much-claimed increase in knife-crime remains unproven, despite all the media coverage, leading to confusion, but an inevitable deepening of fear in the population. It is hard to know what is really going on, and the stats don't seem reliable in either direction. Two British articles are worth reading in this regard, Elizabeth Stewart's *Knife crime 'not increasing'*, 13 May 2008, at *http://www.guardian.co.uk/uk/2008/may/13/ukcrime.boris*, and Knife Crime Facts UK at *http://www.insight-security.com/facts-knife-crime-stats.htm.*

X CAGING THE HUMAN SPIRIT

1) The effects of Health and Safety restrictions on children: The findings that too-rigorous risk-assessment restrictions are harming children is reported in James Slack's article *Health and safety 'extremists' damaging children's development*, 11 November 2007, at: *http://www.dailymail.co.uk/news/article-493019/Health-safety-extremists-damaging-childrens-development.html.* The piece includes this quote:

'Author Alan Pearce has also collated examples of extreme health and safety rules for his book, Playing It Safe: The Crazy World of Britain's Health and Safety Regulations. *These include swings being removed in one playground in case children were blinded by the sun, and pupils being banned from cycling to school because local roads were too narrow.'*

2) Criticisms of alternative medicine: A critique of the manipulatively selective way biologist and arch-skeptic Richard Dawkins dismisses alternative medicine trials is contained in an interview with doctor-turned-'punk-scientist' Dr Manjir Samanta-Laughton at: *http://www.i-c-m.org.uk/news/news/*. See also *http://www.punkscience.com*.

3) The claimed dangers of aspartame: The much-criticized artificial sweetener aspartame (often marketed as NutraSweet and also available under other names) seems to have sneaked itself into so many foodstuffs and drinks now (especially, but far from exclusively, diet drinks), that it is hard to get away from without close scrutiny of tiny-print ingredients on packaging. Authorities insist that it is safe to use, and yet there is huge evidence from studies that it has great potential dangers for human health, and some countries have attempted to ban or restrict it. Good links on the controversial issues surrounding aspartame can be found at: *http://www.dorway.com*.

One area of suspicion that leads some people to question the impartiality of the decisions that led to the general acceptance of aspartame (even from bodies such as the World Health Organization) is the fact that one-time US Secretary of Defense Donald Rumsfeld was chairman of G D Searle & Company when it was helping to develop aspartame, and actively pushed for its approval through his political connections. A useful quick guide to Rumsfeld's aspartame connections can be read at: *http://www.newswithviews.com/NWVexclusive/exclusive15.htm*. Rumsfeld, of course, also owns major stocks in the company that owns the patent for the controversial flu 'antidote' Tamiflu (see page 71 and also notes 6-8 of Chapter V).

4) Codex Alimentarius' controls on health supplements: An excellent source of detailed information and links concerning the Codex Alimentarius food safety body and its recommended controls on vitamins and health supplements can be found on the website of the Alliance for Natural Health at: *http://www.anhcampaign.org/campaigns/codex*. A precise list of the restrictions and how they affect different countries is available at: *http://www.anhcampaign.org/campaigns/freedom-health-choice*.

A comprehensive video presentation on Codex Alimentarius by Robert Verkerk of the ANH can be found at: *https://www.youtube.com/watch?v=aPqkggzD_fg*.

See also the National Health Federation's Codex resources page at: *http://www.thenhf.com/page.php?id=128*

5) Conventional medicine is the main cause of death in the US: The staggering statistic (compiled by *The Journal of the American Medical Association*) that an average of 783,936 deaths occur each year due to the effects of prescribed drugs and medical misdiagnosis, along with other remarkable figures, is referenced and summed up well in Rebecca Sato's article *Is the US Fighting the Wrong War on Drugs?*, 16 January 2008, at: *http://www.dailygalaxy.com/my_weblog/2008/01/is-the-us-fight.html*.

6) The dangers of fluoride: So many studies have cast doubt on the effectiveness and/or safety of fluoride that one has to question the motive of its continued introduction into global drinking water supplies. To pursue this policy without proper investigation is sinister at worst, and stupid at best. One good fluoride link is given in *Appendix 3*, but another very good resource for multiple web links on the problems with fluoride can be found at: *http://www.eves-best.com/fluoride-dangers.htm*.

7) MMR vaccine to be made compulsory in the UK?: In June 2009, Sir Sandy Macara, former chairman of the British Medical Association, called for the MMR jab to be made a necessary requirement for all children attending state schools—or they should be excluded from the system. A number of MPs backed the call and television coverage gave virtually no space to opposers. This was reported with the usual emotional blackmail and entirely unproven statements implying that recent measles outbreaks in the UK were due to the one in four children who remain unvaccinated due to parents' concerns. Graham Satchell's report, *Call to Make MMR Jab Compulsory*, 2 June 2009, can be found at: *http://news.bbc.co.uk/1/hi/health/8078500.stm*.

Vaccination has long been mandatory in some states of the US and other countries, but compulsory programs have still not yet arrived in the UK, though it is an ever-present threat even in a nation that boasts of 'free choices'. Readers are referred to note 1 of Chapter V for general references to vaccination issues.

8) The Unfair Commercial Practices Directive: Although many spiritualist mediums reacted with anger and dismay over the potential discrimination that could be caused by full implementation of the Unfair Commercial Practices Directive, others have taken a more moderate line on it, such as the articles *New Legislation for UK Spiritualists*, 10 March 2008, at: *http://www.spiritualist.tv/news/mar08/new-law.html*, and *Astrology, that EU Directive and Consumer Law*, by Roy Gillett, *Transit* journal, July/August 2008, pages 16-18, which contend that only truly fraudulent or misrepresentative practitioners have anything to fear. Nonetheless, there is a worrying degree of ambiguity in the wording of the new directive that could be misused if so desired, and it reduces the status of any alternative religion or therapist to being merely that of a merchant—which might be more acceptable if all religions were treated equally, but the singling-out of certain spiritual practices is plainly discriminatory.

It has been contended that the previous Fraudulent Mediums Act of 1951 (which the 2008 directive effectively replaced) already compelled the required disclaimer 'for entertainment purposes only' in some cases. However, the Unfair Commercial Practices Directive changes the emphasis of responsibility. A posting from 'Jack of Kent' on the *Bad Psychics* forum on 21 March 2009 at *http://moh2005.proboards.com/index.cgi?board=conpow&action=display&thread=4739&page=5* lays the issues out a little more clearly:

'The new regulations are in many ways an advance on the old Fraudulent Mediums Act. Under the FMA, the prosecution had to prove fraud (which is difficult to do at law, as the Serious Fraud Office often find out); and even if fraud was proved, then entertainment was a complete defense. There were few prosecutions under the FMA. Indeed, the ineffectiveness of the FMA worked to the credit of Psychics; the argument was that, as there were no prosecutions, an unprosecuted psychic was legitimate.

Under the new regulations, there is no need for the prosecution to show fraud—just that consumers could be misled regardless of the trader's intent—and entertainment is not now an automatic defense. Psychics charging for their "services" will be treated like a double-glazing salesperson. So, as long as Psychics are clear and accurate in their "commercial practices" then their exposure to legal risk is low under the new regulations.

On the other hand, exploiting people who are vulnerable (which presumably includes those who are bereaved) is an "aggressive" unfair commercial practice under the regulations. It is not yet clear whether this is being enforced against Psychics by Trading Standards. However, by shifting the focus from the intention of the (fraudulent) medium to the effects (or likely effects) on the consumer, the new regulations have taken the legal context for dealing with dodgy Psychics into an entirely new direction. I think it is too soon to see if Trading Standards will allocate their (limited) resources to scrutiny of commercial psychics. It may well be that there is no general crackdown. But it is new and significant that they are now to be treated just as traders.'

9) Brian Gerrish on the destruction of communities: Readers are referred to note 14 of Chapter V for references to Gerrish's views on the EU's Common Purpose initiative. However, he also believes, on a more extreme level, that authorities are taking children from their parents and putting them into 'care' for reasons that are unclear or unnecessary (beyond obvious abuse cases), making them *more* vulnerable to abuse, and sees this as a) a terror tactic designed to show what the state can do if anyone steps out of line, and b) as a further method of breaking up families, and thus communities, to weaken UK society's resistance to more centralized control.

Many of Gerrish's views are disseminated and/or echoed in the controversial newspaper and website the *UK Column*, which can be found at: *http://www.ukcolumn.org*.

10) Children on Ritalin/Antidepressants: The shockingly high statistics of children—particularly in the USA—being put on the drug Ritalin, together with the many known detrimental side effects, are discussed in a series of informative articles at: *http://www.ritalindeath.com*. The name of the website (run by parents who believe their son died due to administration of the drug) gives a clue to its general stance. See also *http://www.guardian.co.uk/society/2010/jun/11/antidepressant-prescriptions-rise-nhs-recession*.

XI THE GREEN DILEMMA

1) Transition US/Transition Town initiative: The 'Transition' movement, which encourages communities to become less dependent on transport and energy infrastructures and more focused on local initiatives, especially environmental ones, began in Totnes, Devon, UK, in 2007 and now has a US and international network. The US website is at: *http://www.transitionus.org* and UK at: *http://www.transitionnetwork.org*.

Transition, for all its obvious good intentions, has attracted critics for its rigid adherence to green dogma. An example of the conflicts that have arisen can be found in a fascinating debate, *Peak Oil: Myth or Reality?* (recorded for Glastonbury Radio) between truthseeker Ian R Crane, Transition Town founder Rob Hopkins and interviewer Ross Hemsworth on 18 March 2008. Hear it at: *http://www.revver.com/video/752266/ peak-oil-myth-or-reality-recording-from-glastonbury-radio-part-one/*. This in itself was a follow-up to a live debate of the same title between Crane and Forest Row Transition Town spokesman Mike Grenville for this author's Changing Times organization that took place on 4 September 2007, discussed by Crane at: *http://www.wellsphere.com/raw-food-article/from-ian-crane-if-you-missed-i/162640*.

2) Public doubts over global warming: Despite an obvious international concern about climate change in general, opinion polls reveal that faith in man-made global warming as the cause is nowhere near as strong as the media and governments would usually have us believe, as was demonstrated in a 2014 US survey reported in Seth Motel's article *Polls show most Americans believe in climate change, but give it low priority*, 23 September 2014, at: *http://www.pewresearch.org/fact-tank/2014/09/23/most-americans-believe-in-climate-change-but-give-it-low-priority*. 'Most' may believe in it, but a large minority don't, or they at least question the causes, as this article acknowledges:

'In Pew Research's 2014 Political Typology survey, about six-in-ten Americans (61%) said there is solid evidence that Earth's average temperature has been getting warmer over the past few decades, compared with 35% who disagreed. And most who believe the Earth is warming said it is primarily due to human activity (40% total), while 18% of the public said there is warming mostly because of natural environmental patterns..'

An earlier survey reported by the BBC in *'Skepticism' over climate claims*, 3 July 2007, at *http://news.bbc.co.uk/1/hi/sci/tech/6263690.stm* found the following about the views of the British public:

'The Ipsos Mori poll of 2,032 adults—interviewed between 14 and 20 June—found 56% believed scientists were still questioning climate change.' This poll prompted a typical response, quoted in the same piece:

'Royal Society vice-president Sir David Read said: "People should not be misled by those that exploit the complexity of the issue, seeking to distort the science and deny the seriousness of the potential consequences of climate change".'

In other words, to many academics the trend of continuing doubt is merely evidence of deliberate distortion and of people being 'misled' (and not caring, which is untrue)—not the fact that the evidence for man-made global warming is still unclear and confusing, even to some qualified climatologists. For all the bombardment of fear tactics, significant public doubt clearly still remains over the issue.

3) Do 'nearly all' scientists believe in global warming?: Some of the very dubious methods by which it is made to seem—falsely—that most scientists agree on the reality of man-made global warming are uncovered in James Taylor's article *Global Warming Alarmists Caught Doctoring '97-Percent Consensus' Claims*, 30 May 2013, at: *http://www.forbes.com/sites/jamestaylor/2013/05/30/global-warming-alarmists-caught-doctoring-97-percent-consensus-claims*. Taylor writes:

'Global warming alarmists and their allies in the liberal media have been caught doctoring the results of a widely cited paper asserting there is a 97-percent scientific consensus regarding human-caused global warming. After taking a closer look at the paper, investigative journalists report the authors' claims of a 97-percent consensus relied on the authors misclassifying the papers of some of the world's most prominent global warming skeptics. At the same time, the authors deliberately presented a meaningless survey question so they could twist the responses to fit their own preconceived global warming alarmism.'

4) Nigel Lawson questions global warming: Ex-UK cabinet minister Nigel Lawson's book *An Appeal to Reason: A Cool Look at Global Warming* (Gerald Duckworth & Co Ltd, 2008) logically questions the man-made global warming hysteria and political reactions to it, suggesting that even if global warming were eventually proven to be real, the proposed policies currently being implemented to deal with it are the wrong ones. The book has received high praise in many quarters for its well-reasoned (as the title would suggest) arguments, but Lawson has inevitably been lambasted by green campaigners intent on forcing unrealistic carbon reduction targets in the face of much evidence that other strategies would be better at tackling general climate change. His advocacy of shale 'fracking' has divided former supporters, however.

5) Ex-UN environmental adviser questions global warming: The book by scientist-turned-warming-skeptic Peter Taylor, *Chill: A Reassessment of Global Warming Theory* (Clairview Books, 2009), is an excellent and scientifically presented summary of his reasoning, warning that we may instead be heading for global *cooling*.
 A full interview with Taylor from 2011, outlining his credentials and criticisms of 'green' bodies and global warming propaganda, can be heard at: *https://www.youtube.com/watch?v=PzgqTCrCC4k*.

6) *The Chilling Stars* book: Henrik Svensmark and Nigel Calder's book *The Chilling Stars: A New Theory of Climate Change*, which challenges man-made global warming, was published by Icon/Totem Books, 2007.

7) *The Great Global Warming Swindle* documentary: British TV's controversial Channel Four program *The Great Global Warming Swindle* was first broadcast in March 2007 and stirred up huge—and mostly closed-minded—angry reaction from predictable quarters. Although the minor inaccuracies and claims of context-bending were widely used against it, these were as nothing compared to the spurious and ill-informed criticisms of the program that did the rounds in the green community afterwards. Not that this stopped *The Great Global Warming Swindle* being nominated for the Best Documentary Award at the 2008 Broadcast Awards, and Channel Four reported that phone calls it received about the film were '6 to 1' in favor of it. Either way, the program acts as a good round-up of some of the key issues in the debate.

Wag TV, the production company, encountered much prejudice even before its broadcast. An extended version of the film is now available on DVD ('despite the strenuous efforts of those who support the theory of global warming to prevent its release', according to Wag TV), or it can easily be found online, including at: *http://www.youtube.com/watch?v=YtevF4B4RtQ*.

Television regulator Ofcom's detailed official ruling on *The Great Global Warming Swindle*, which essentially supported the veracity of the program, can be read at: *http://www.ofcom.org.uk/tv/obb/prog_cb/obb114/*.

8) The British High Court's ruling on *An Inconvenient Truth*: The full UK High Court ruling on the nine major inaccuracies in Al Gore's film *An Inconvenient Truth* can be read at: *http://www.newparty.co.uk/articles/inaccuracies-gore.html*, from which this adjudication is quoted.

9) Founder of the Weather Channel threatens to sue Al Gore: Weather Channel founder John Coleman's threat to sue Al Gore in a US court of law for his claims on global warming gets a mainstream airing in the piece *Weather Channel Founder: Sue Al Gore for Fraud*, 14 March 2008, at: *http://www.foxnews.com/story/0,2933,337710,00.html*.

10) Doubts over 'carbon credits': The concerns over the effectiveness or honesty of the suspect 'carbon credits' scheme, designed to allow industries to pollute in exchange for supposedly instigating environmental projects, are voiced well in Nick Davies' article *Abuse and incompetence in fight against global warming—Up to 20% of carbon savings in doubt as monitoring firms criticized by UN body*, 2 June 2007, at: *http://www.guardian.co.uk/environment/2007/jun/02/energy.business*.

11) Global temperatures in decline: Despite first 2010 and then 2014 being claimed as the warmest years on record (with only the tiniest of increments in 2014, proclaimed in the news as devastating evidence—to the bemusement of those who actually read the figures), the still relevant general decline of global temperatures in recent years is discussed by *World Climate Report* in the article *Musings on Satellite Temperatures*, 8 January 2008, at: *http://www.worldclimatereport.com/index.php/2008/01/08/musings-on-satellite-temperatures/*.

For a more conspiratorial take on matters, Paul Joseph Watson's article *No Global Warming Since 1998 as Planet Cools Off*, 4 April 2008, doesn't pull its punches, and can be read at: *http://www.prisonplanet.com/articles/april2008/040408_cools_off.htm*.

Not much had changed by 2012, hence David Rose of the *Daily Mail* also weighs in with the self-explanatory *Global warming stopped 16 years ago, reveals Met Office report quietly released... and here is the chart to prove it*, 13 October 2012, at: *http://www.dailymail.co.uk/sciencetech/article-2217286/Global-warming-stopped-16-years-ago-reveals-Met-Office-report-quietly-released--chart-prove-it.html#ixzz29G6SOUPo*.

Come 2013, the by now vocal climate skeptic James Delingpole was cementing the *Daily Mail*'s stance with *The crazy climate change obsession that's made the Met Office a menace*, 10 January 2013, at: *http://www.dailymail.co.uk/news/article-2259942/The-crazy-climate-change-obsession-thats-Met-Office-menace.html*, claiming (to savage attacks from warming believers):

'Without fanfare—apparently in the desperate hope no one would notice—[the Met Office] has finally conceded what other scientists have known for ages: there is no evidence that 'global warming' is happening. The Met Office quietly readjusted its temperature projections on its website on Christmas Eve. Until then, it had been confidently predicting temperature rises of at least 0.2 degrees per decade, with a succession of years exceeding even the record-breaking high of 1998. Its latest chart, however, confirmed in a press release earlier this week, tells a very different story: no more global warming is expected till at least 2017.'

12) Scientists admit to slower warming, but hold to models: By spring 2013, climate scientists were clearly feeling under fire, admitting to a slower rate of warming than thought, but still refusing to back down, as illustrated by Matt McGrath's piece *Climate slowdown means extreme rates of warming 'not as likely'*, 19 May 2013, at *http://www.bbc.co.uk/news/science-environment-22567023*, in which University of Oxford scientist Dr Alexander Otto is quoted accordingly:

'"We would expect a single decade to jump around a bit but the overall trend is independent of it, and people should be exactly as concerned as before about what climate change is doing," said Dr Otto. Is there any succor in these findings for climate skeptics who say the slowdown over the past 14 years means global warming is not real? "None. No comfort whatsoever," he said.'

13) Australian geophysicist claims global cooling: Australian geophysicist and astronautical engineer Philip Chapman's predictions that we are entering a period of global cooling can be read in the article *Sorry to ruin the fun, but an ice age cometh*, 23 April 2008, at: *http://www.theaustralian.news.com.au/story/0,25197,23583376-7583,00.html*.

14) 1975 conference begins global warming scare?: Marjorie Mazel Hecht's account of the US government-sponsored event, *The Atmosphere: Endangered and Endangering*, is quoted from her article *Where the Global Warming Hoax Was Born*, and can be read in full at: *http://www.21stcenturysciencetech.com/Articles%202007/GWHoaxBorn.pdf*.

The same website hosts another scientifically credible and devastating demolition of global warming hysteria in an article by Zbigniew Jaworowski, a senior advisor at the Central Laboratory for Radiological Protection in Warsaw. *CO_2: The Greatest Scientific Scandal of Our Time* can be read at: *http://www.21stcenturysciencetech.com/Articles%202007/20_1-2_CO2_Scandal.pdf*.

15) Hole in the ozone layer: The recent relative quietness on the once end-of-the-world scenario feared due to the hole in the ozone layer, supposedly caused by man-made CFCs (chlorofluorocarbons), used in refrigeration and propellants, speaks volumes. It is considered by many that the hole is a natural function of the planet and that it opens and closes due to entirely normal cycles. A good summing-up of the issues involved can be found in Robert G Williscroft PhD's article *The Great Ozone-Hole Hoax* (in itself a sample chapter from his book *The Chicken Little Agenda—Debunking Experts' Lies*, Pelican Publishing, 2006), which can be found at: *http://thrawnrickle.argee.net/2006/11/08/ch-2--the-great-ozonehole-hoax-part-2-of-8.aspx*.

16) The fake documentary *Alternative 3*: Made by Anglia Television and broadcast on the British ITV network in June 1977 (and shown once since in New Zealand), *Alternative 3* made a convincing case that top scientists were secretly preparing to abandon Earth due to impending climate change. Supposedly intended to be shown as an April Fool's program, but delayed in broadcast due to industrial action, showing it in a normal slot was bound to cause confusion. Consequently, despite the almost immediate revelation that it was a hoax, many people remained convinced that the show was a double-bluff that masked a genuine plan. The first two 'alternatives' given in the program can't help but raise eyebrows today, given the current conspiracy concerns: 1—eliminate a large proportion of the world's population. 2—build huge underground shelters for governments to survive the changes—something numerous truthseekers believe is really happening. The third alternative was to escape to Mars. The continuing speculation on the show is laughed at by skeptics but, whatever else, it certainly did help create a new fear of climate change that has been built on since. Information on *Alternative 3* can be found at: *http://en.wikipedia.org/wiki/Alternative_3*, while a classic full-on conspiracy take on it can be explored at: *http://www.thule.org/alt3.html*.

Another supposed spoof, this time a book, *Report From Iron Mountain* (Dial Press, 1967), stirred similar controversy over its origins. Purporting to be a secret report from a government panel recommending the deliberate creation of wars and the encouragement of the fear of alien threats, amongst other scares, to keep society in line, it was later claimed as a hoax by author Leonard Lewin, but some believe this was a double-bluff. Information on the book can be found at: *http://en.wikipedia.org/wiki/Report_from_Iron_Mountain*.

17) Canadian geologist also claims global cooling: The opinions of professor of geology and director of the Ottawa-Carleton Geoscience Center, R Timothy Patterson, that imminent global cooling is more likely to occur than global warming, due to weak Schwabe cycles in the Sun, are recorded concisely in the *Investor's Business Daily* article *The Sun Also Sets*, 7 February 2007, at: *http://ibdeditorial.com/IBDArticles*.

aspx?id=287279412587175, and expressed more fully in a *National Post* article by Patterson himself, *Read the Sunspots: The mud at the bottom of B.C. fjords reveals that solar output drives climate change—and that we should prepare now for dangerous global cooling*, 20 June 2007, at: *http://www.nationalpost.com/story. html?id=597d0677-2a05-47b4-b34f-b84068db11f4&p=1*. More information on Patterson, who has impressive credentials, can be found at: *http://en.wikipedia.org/wiki/Tim_Patterson*.

18) Sea level rise: There are many contradictions inherent in the data that supposedly shows significant rises to be occurring due, in part at least, to man-made global warming. The fact is that no-one is sure what is going to happen. Many of the problems are well-discussed at: *http://www.skepticalscience.com/sea-level-rise.htm*. Until coastlines do begin to vanish under water, and all the while California keeps hosting beach parties, the general public, at least, will probably remain dubious about sea level rise. Certainly, the data is far from settled. We shall see.

19) *Nature* says climate effects from cosmic sources cannot be excluded: *Nature*'s reluctant admission that the possibility of climate effects resulting from cosmic rays or solar ultraviolet radiation 'cannot be excluded' (despite the study appearing to state the opposite) appears in the article *Variations in solar luminosity and their effect on the Earth's climate*, by P Foukal, C Frohlich, H Spruit and TML Wigley, Nature, 14 September 2006. The findings are summed up on the UCAR (University Corporation for Atmospheric Research) website at: *http://www.ucar.edu/news/releases/2006/brightness.shtml*.

20) Solar variability and climate: Dr Tony Phillips' quoted article, *Solar Variability and Terrestrial Climate*, 8 January 2013, is available at: *http://science.nasa.gov/science-news/science-at-nasa/2013/08jan_sunclimate*.

21) The 'Climategate' scandal: The Internet is, of course, full of opposing and defending sources on the leaked 2009 emails from the Climatic Research Unit of the British University of East Anglia (which, at best, come across as sneakily unpleasant, despite the official absolution given to the authors), but some of the main offending comments are summed up well in climate skeptic James Delingpole's blog, *Climategate: the final nail in the coffin of 'Anthropogenic Global Warming'?*, 20 November 2009, at *http://blogs.telegraph. co.uk/news/jamesdelingpole/100017393/climategate-the-final-nail-in-the-coffin-of-anthropogenic-global-warming/*, while more detailed critiques and extracts can be found at: *http://www.climategate.com/*. For a more balanced overview and details of the later adjudications, *http://en.wikipedia.org/wiki/Climatic_ Research_Unit_email_controversy* gives the picture well enough, if erring inevitably on the defensive.

22) The dangers of 'fracking': Fracking for shale gas (or oil) is currently being sold to many countries as a copious source of energy that will keep the lights on and reduce energy prices. However, aside from studies that show gas prices only fall in countries as large and viable as the US as a result, the dangers of long-term water contamination (high-pressure water with chemical additives is part of the process), the desecration of the landscape, and claims of small earthquakes occurring near drilling sites, convince many people that it just isn't worth it, as some American citizens, in particular, have discovered. Fracking problems are discussed well at: *http://www.earthworksaction.org/issues/detail/hydraulic_fracturing_101#.VG3ePq7uYXQ*

23) Lord Turner says flights should be rationed: A summary of Lord Turner's desire to see limits put on individuals' flights can be read in John Swaine's piece *Flights could be rationed, says environment tsar Lord Turner—Families could see the number of flights they can take rationed in order to cut greenhouse gas emissions, Gordon Brown's "environment tsar" has warned*, 6 February 2009, at: *http://www.telegraph.co.uk/travel/ travelnews/4536352/Flights-could-be-rationed-says-environment-tsar-Lord-Turner.html*.

24) Michael Crichton's *State of Fear*: The late Michael Crichton's novel *State of Fear*, in which fear of global warming is used to create a worldwide mandate of industrial and political control—precisely what many people believe is occurring today—was published by Harper Collins in 2004. Although mainly fictional, Crichton's non-fictional footnotes and appendices make very clear his doubting views on global warming, leading to the book to be used as a supportive tool by other global warming skeptics. This in turn actually led to Crichton (before his death in 2008) being called before the US Senate Committee on Environment and Public Works on the invitation of supporter Senator Jim Inhofe, only to find himself being lambasted by the likes of Hillary Clinton for 'muddy[ing] the issues around sound science'. More on Crichton's novel and the subsequent controversy can be read at: *http://en.wikipedia.org/wiki/State_of_Fear*.

Jim Inhofe himself once described global warming as 'the greatest hoax ever perpetrated on the American people', and as such did not win himself many political friends before the rise of the Tea Party, but he was one of the first voices in Congress to raise objections to its growing obsession with global warming. On the other hand, his hardline right-wing views and close ties to oil and gas industries (*http://en.wikipedia. org/wiki/Jim_Inhofe*) cloud the issue for many, providing unhelpful ammunition to greens who claim that all questioners of man-made global warming are 'working for the other side', which is generally nonsense.

25) Is a nuclear war actually possible?: Former New Zealand airline pilot Bruce Cathie's books *The Energy Grid—Harmonic 695: The Pulse of the Universe* [*The Investigation into the World Energy Grid*] (Adventures Unlimited Press, 1997) and *The Harmonic Conquest of Space* (Adventures Unlimited Press, 1998) put forward the intriguing idea that an all-out nuclear war is an impossibility. This hangs on Cathie's theory that the Earth is surrounded by an energetic 'harmonic grid' that requires the forces needed to create a nuclear explosion to be activated only at very specific times and places. A review of *The Energy Grid* by Kenneth James Michael Maclean at: *http://www.amazon.com/Energy-Grid-Harmonic-Universe-Investigation/dp/0932813445/ref=pd_sim_b_1* sums up the theory thus:

'[Cathie] *asserts the impossibility of nuclear war, because, he claims, a nuclear device, in order to detonate, must be placed not only in a precise geometric position relative to the Earth, but also to the Sun, and that the timing of the detonation is crucial. He says that all of the possible places and times for nuclear explosions have been worked out by the governments of the Earth in advance! This from a man who predicted beforehand the dates and times of the French nuclear tests at Mururoa Island in the South Pacific in 1968.*'

Cathie's extraordinary claims to have accurately predicted the times and places of many nuclear tests, if true, suggest the almost relieving idea that the whole global 'nuclear holocaust' scenario was yet another hoax used for political gain and social control, and that such a disaster could never have happened. Needless to say, Cathie's views have been attacked as extreme eccentricity, but they are worth hearing.

Bruce Cathie's official website can be found at: *http://www.brucecathie.com*, and a video presentation, *Bruce Cathie—Calculating an Atomic Bomb Test: Bruce Cathie explains why we can't have a nuclear war*, can be downloaded at: *http://www.livevideo.com/video/ConspiracyCentral/4985FBA692174AF2A9A3613BF66A9625/bruce-cathie-calculating-an-.aspx*.

XII THE NEW ERA

1) The Maya end-point and 'adjusted' calendars: Many arguments long-raged through the prophecies community concerning the exact end-point of the current Mayan 'Creation', with the majority settling on 21st December 2012. However, some argued for 23rd December 2012 and others even disputed the *year*, with some now claiming 2019 as the key moment to come. Part of the problem comes with those who have adapted the Maya calendar to create their own idealized versions of it, causing much confusion. One such version is the 'Dreamspell' calendar and was developed by the late prominent researcher José Arguelles to work with his own theories on the Maya prophecies; another was recalculated by Carl Calleman, who believed 28th October 2011 to be the end point. These edited versions may or may not have merit, but cannot be said to be the true 'Maya Calendar', as they are all-too often referred to.

Geoff Stray's *Beyond 2012: Catastrophe or Ecstasy*, (Vital Signs Publishing, 2005) pretty much nails these arguments once and for all (see especially Chapter 19, *The New Age*, pages 203-207, together with numerous other clarifications throughout Stray's book). Despite the ubiquity of 'adjusted' calendars, most researchers are happy that 21st December 2012 was the most definitively accurate of all the calculated end-points. See also the many debates on Stray's website at: *http://www.diagnosis2012.co.uk*.

The exact time of the 2012 Winter Solstice, meanwhile—11.11 a.m. precisely, Universal Time—has been the source of endless fascinated speculation, with many ascribing universal significance to the appearance of these numbers throughout life, especially the influential US mystic Solara, whose website can be found at: *http://www.nvisible.com*. The strange 'coincidence' that the Maya end-point fell with these digits at the center of it all is yet one more intrigue of the New Era phenomenon.

2) Geoff Stray on the Maya end-point: Geoff Stray's quote about the now (almost) agreed end point of the Maya calendar comes from his book *2012 in Your Pocket* (Straydog Books, 2008 [UK], 4th Dimension Press, 2009 [USA]), a handy notebook derivation of *Beyond 2012*. Another of Stray's books, which is useful in understanding the Maya calculations, is *The Mayan and Other Ancient Calendars* (Wooden Books/ Walker & Company, 2007).

3) Crop circles with New Era connotations: Formations with connections to the ancient time cycle are fully explored in *Beyond 2012*, Chapter 16, *Crop Circles*, pages 172-182. See also my book *Vital Signs: A Complete Guide to the Crop Circle Mystery* (SB Publications, 1998/2002 [UK], Frog Ltd, 2002 [US]).

4) Ice core samples suggest 'galactic superwaves': The work of Dr Paul LaViolette in identifying cosmic dust from ice core samples, which he uses to support the galactic superwave theory, is explained in his book *Earth Under Fire* (Starlane Publications, 1997). It is also summed up (as ever) throughout Geoff Stray's *Beyond 2012*, especially Chapter 7, *Astronomical Claims*, pages 89-92.

5) Sunspots: A good basic explanation of sunspots is available at: *http://en.wikipedia.org/wiki/Sunspot*.

6) NASA predictions of solar activity for Cycle 24: In 2006, NASA was predicting big things for the Sun in the run-up to 2012, as outlined in the article *Scientists Predict Big Solar Cycle*, 21 December 2006, at: *http:// science.nasa.gov/headlines/y2006/21dec_cycle24.htm*. However, by 2009, due to the very late and quiet start of Cycle 24, NASA and the National Oceanic and Atmospheric Administration (NOAA) had revised this prediction, forecasting the peak to occur in May 2013 and with the expectation of a below-average number of sunspots, as explained in the article *New Solar Cycle Prediction*, 29 May 2009, at: *http://science.nasa.gov/ headlines/y2009/29may_noaaprediction.htm*. In fact, even by May 2013 it was still fairly quiet, and unclear whether Solar Maximum had been reached or not, leading NASA to revise its prediction yet again to wonder if we might be in an unusual double-peaked cycle, as discussed by Dr Tony Phillips in his article *Solar Cycle Update: Twin Peaks?*, 1 March 2013, at: *http://science.nasa.gov/science-news/science-at-nasa/2013/01mar_ twinpeaks*. Cycle 24 is currently looking to be the quietest cycle since records began in 1750.

7) Sharp fall in solar output: The slightly perturbing 2009 finding that solar irradiance, ultraviolet and radio emissions were falling at an unusually fast rate was announced by NASA in the article *Deep Solar Minimum*, 1 April 2009, at: *http://science.nasa.gov/headlines/y2009/01apr_deepsolarminimum.htm?list1123206*.

8) Predictions of 'solar superstorms'/NASA's Solar Shield Project: In 2009, the possibility of a huge solar flare destroying the infrastructure of civilization, if simply through the effect on power grids, went mainstream. *New Scientist* magazine began the trend in issue 2700, 21 March 2009, with Michael Brooks' article *Gone in 90 Seconds*, and this was followed (in the UK) by Michael Hanlon's rather less subtle *Daily Mail* article *Meltdown! A solar superstorm could send us back into the dark ages—and one is due in just THREE years*, 19 April 2009, at: *http://www.dailymail.co.uk/sciencetech/article-1171951/Meltdown-A-solar-superstorm- send-dark-ages--just-THREE-years.html*. Many other global mainstream pieces have followed since— nearly always a sign that something big may be welling up.

In summer 2010, NASA held high-level meetings with scientists and politicians from around the globe (including several Defense Secretaries) to warn them of the potential dangers from increasingly large solar flares due around the 2013 peak of the current Cycle 24, as reported well in Andrew Hough's article *Nasa warns solar flares from 'huge space storm' will cause devastation*, 14 June 2010, at: *http://www.telegraph.co.uk/ science/space/7819201/Nasa-warns-solar-flares-from-huge-space-storm-will-cause-devastation.html*. This summit obviously made a big impression on the then UK's Defense Secretary Liam Fox, who presented the concerns to the British parliament that autumn (if mixed in with somewhat distractive side-issues about the likes of Iran detonating nuclear weapons in space), as subsequently reported by James Kirkup and Andrew Hough in their piece *Solar flares could paralyze Britain's power and communications, Liam Fox says*, 17 September 2010, at: *http://www.telegraph.co.uk/science/space/8009635/Solar-flares-could-paralyse- Britains-power-and-communications-Liam-Fox-says.html*.

Following this, in October 2010, NASA, in one of its more beneficial modes, set up its 'Solar Shield' project, an initiative to encourage development of new power grid systems across North America to better withstand electromagnetic pulse waves (EMPs) from the Sun—another clear sign of its genuine concerns in this area. NASA's official press release on this, *Solar Shield: Protecting the North American Power Grid*, by Dr Tony Phillips, 26 October 2010, can be read at: *http://science.nasa.gov/science-news/science-at-nasa/2010/26oct_solarshield/*.

In June 2011, Administrator of NASA, Charles F Bolden, posted up a very frank video to NASA employees, imploring them to be more ready for an unspecified 'emergency'. NASA played it down, but it is widely wondered if Bolden might have been referring to coming solar flares. The clip can be seen at: *http://www.youtube.com/watch?v=zyKopmPV0PQ*

An article with useful links on solar storms, *A History of Massive Solar Storms: What Does History Tell Us About The Coming Solar Storms?*, by John P. Millis, Ph.D, can be found at: *http://space.about.com/od/sunsol/a/History_Of_Solar_Flares.htm.*

Hollywood is also worth watching for indications of concerns deep in the collective. In 2009, Alex Proyas' film *Knowing* (starring Nicolas Cage), despite lukewarm reviews, did well at the global box office and posits the notion of a massive solar flare extinguishing life on Earth. In fact, the film, often genuinely shocking in places and seemingly playing on evangelical End Times and Ascensionist themes, captures well the apocalyptic zeitgeist of the age, and its success says something about the contemporary mood in these areas.

9) Decrease in the solar wind: The striking decrease in the solar wind is reported in the article *Ulysses Reveals Global Solar Wind Plasma Output at 50-Year Low*, 23 September 2008, at: *http://www.jpl.nasa.gov/news/news.cfm?release=2008-178.*

A slightly newer relevant piece, *What has happened to the Sun? Solar wind speed drops to near 50-year low*, 2 September 2011, is available at: *http://theextinctionprotocol.wordpress.com/2011/09/02/what-has-happened-to-the-sun-solar-wind-speed-drops-to-near-50-year-low.*

10) Earth open to more solar particles than previously thought: The news that the THEMIS spacecraft had detected an unsuspected propensity for the Earth's magnetic fields to let in solar particles at completely unexpected times was first reported in the piece *Sun Often "Tears Out A Wall" In Earth's Solar Storm Shield*, 16 December 2008, at: *http://www.nasa.gov/mission_pages/themis/news/themis_leaky_shield.html.*

11) Russians say actual pole shift could occur: The Russian Academy of Natural Science's somewhat apocalyptic view that a geomagnetic reversal could physically change the tilt of the Earth's axis is reported in *Pravda's* happily-titled article *Displacement of Earth's magnetic poles may turn planet into giant Hiroshima*, 23 October 2008, at: *http://english.pravda.ru/science/earth/23-10-2008/106612-magnetic_poles-0.*

12) The effects of galactic alignment: Geoff Stray's explanation of what could happen during the galactic alignment process is quoted from *Beyond 2012*, Chapter 1, *The Maya Calendars*, pages 23-24. In his book *Maya Cosmogenesis 2012* (Bear & Company, 1998), John Major Jenkins puts it thus:

'The "energy" field emanates from Galactic Center and includes the entire electromagnetic/photon field in which our planet exists. There are dimensions of subtlety within this field—the telluric or astral realms—extending beyond the physical forces of science to include spiritual planes... If we imagine this field as being similar to the lines of force surrounding a magnet, we can understand that our changing orientation to this field has immediate consequences, and little to do with cause-and-effect transmission of energy between us and Galactic Center. We are instead in a relationship of resonance with our source, one that connects us deeply within to each other, and, in fact, to all other beings in this galaxy... I would like to emphasize that the Galactic Equator—the precise edge of our spiralling galaxy—is the Zero Point location of the turnabout moment in the cycle of precession. This World Age shift occurs when the solstice Sun crosses over the Galactic Equator.'

13) Rick Strassman's DMT theories: Strassman's potentially crucial findings on the brain's natural production of dimethyltryptamine (DMT) are outlined in his book *DMT: The Spirit Molecule—A Doctor's Revolutionary Research into the Biology of Near-Death and Mystical Experiences* (Park Street Press, 2001). His personal website is: *http://www.rickstrassman.com.*

14) Dr Michael Persinger on geomagnetic activity and ghosts: Information on Persinger can be found on his webpage at: *http://oldwebsite.laurentian.ca/neurosci/_people/Persinger.htm*, while his impressive CV and a list of published books and papers can be found at: *http://oldwebsite.laurentian.ca/neurosci/_files/MAP%20CV%202005.pdf.*

15) Secret concentration camps and civil order contingencies?: *PublicEye.org's* analysis of the alleged secret concentration camps and the Rex 84 program is quoted from the article *The Right-Wing Roots of Sheehan's "Secret Team" Theory* at: *http://www.publiceye.org/rightwoo/rwooz9-14.html.* To read a total conspiracy view of the US concentration camps furore, which includes some common sense challenges in the forum that follows it to some of the more extreme claims, have a look at *US Concentration Camps—FEMA and the Rex 84 Program*, thread started 14 June 2004, at: *http://www.abovetopsecret.com/forum/thread59023/pg1*.

The related US civil order program 'Operation Garden Plot' is also worth perusing. A comprehensive article on this, by Frank Morales, *US Military Civil Disturbance Planning: The War at Home*, 5 August 2000, can be read at: *http://cryptome.info/0001/garden-plot.htm*.

16) Project Camelot: The basics on the US Army's 1964 'Project Camelot', the goal of which was 'to assess the causes of violent social rebellion and to identify the actions a government could take to prevent its own overthrow', can be found at: *http://en.wikipedia.org/wiki/Project_Camelot*. (To avoid confusion, web surfers looking for other sources should be aware that many unrelated conspiracy websites have appropriated the title 'Project Camelot' without any direct connection to the original program.)

17) Astrological cycles and the evidence for astrology: In a world where astrology had not been sidelined by scoffing intellectuals who refuse look at the compelling statistical evidence for a genuine effect of astrological influences on both psychological profiles and global events, Richard Tarnas' book *Cosmos and Psyche: Intimations of a New World View* (Barnes and Noble, 2006) would be seen as a crucial tool for understanding historical cycles and where we are headed today. As it is, the book has attracted little interest in academic circles, but has at least gained respect amongst serious students of astrology. Information on the book can be found at its official website: *http://www.cosmosandpsyche.com/index.php*.

Those curious to know what the actual evidence is to support the veracity of astrology are advised to start with John Anthony West's book *The Case for Astrology* (Viking Adult, 1991), which effortlessly demolishes most of the allegedly 'scientific' arguments against the art and provides a good round-up of important statistical studies carried out by the likes of Michel and Francoise Gauquelin. Skeptics have long attacked the Gauquelin studies as flawed, but most of these objections are based on widely-spread *myths* about the studies, rather than the facts. A good article that sets the record straight on the Gauquelin findings (which are by no means the only ones to support astrology's relevance), by Ken Irving, *Misunderstandings, Misrepresentations, Frequently Asked Questions & Frequently Voiced Objections About the Gauquelin Planetary Effects*, can be found at: *http://www.planetos.info/mmf.html*.

In the opinion of some researchers, astrology can only fully be explained in terms of thought-forms being projected into the collective consciousness, something which the scientific work of Dean Radin and others is making more likely as a possibility [Chapter XIV]. However, those looking for a more reductionist but still semi-supportive view on astrology might like to read the books of Percy Seymour, especially *The Scientific Proof of Astrology* (Quantum/Foulsham, 2004). A respected astronomer and astrophysicist, Seymour believes that fluctuations in the Earth's magnetic field, caused by the planets moving through the solar wind, may affect brain development in the womb, thus accounting for recurring personality traits amongst people born at certain times. Seymour's theories can only go so far in accounting for all the claimed attributes of astrology, but they do identify some possible real-world components to explain the cycles. This may explain why belief in astrology simply will not go away despite all the best efforts of naysayers like Richard Dawkins and TV astronomer Professor Brian Cox, who stubbornly stonewall any engagement with such evidence, espousing 'Newtonian' principles—conveniently forgetting that Sir Isaac Newton was himself an astrologer.

18) Helen Sewell astrology: This piece was written directly for this book. More information and articles from Helen (who studied with the renowned Liz Greene) can be found at *www.astrologicalinsights.co.uk*.

19) World leaders use astrology: In an article on Percy Seymour (*Star Movements Can Influence Us: The Planets may control your future after all*, 16 May 2004, which can be read at: *http://www.astrology.co.uk/news/percy.htm*), Jonathan Leake of the *Sunday Times* points out that astrology has been used by several prominent politicians to influence decisions (we have already noted Tony Blair's wife's interest), stating:

'Among the powerful who have admitted consulting astrologers to make decisions are Ronald and Nancy Reagan, who allowed the astrologer Joan Quigley to dictate the presidential agenda, including the take-off times for Air Force One. Reagan's chief of staff reportedly had a color-coded calendar around which he was expected to organize the President's schedule: green for "good" days and red for "bad". Even Margaret Thatcher once told MPs: "I was born under the sign of Libra; it follows that I am well-balanced."'

Some may argue that the very last point was not such good proof that astrology works (!), but it is clear that the subject, like many other supposedly 'occult' practices, is taken perfectly seriously by many in high places.

XIII WHO ARE WE DEALING WITH?

1) H G Wells on the New World Order: The entire text of Wells' 1940 book *The New World Order* can be read at: *http://www.theforbiddenknowledge.com/hardtruth/new_world_order_hgwells.htm*. It is clear that Wells was an idealist, which may have clouded his morals at times, but it is also plain from this and much of his writing that he did passionately care about the future of humankind in his own way.

2) The origins of the New World Order: An excellent timeline charting the development of the NWO, D L Cuddy's *A Chronological History of the New World Order*, can be found at: *http://www.constitution.org/col/cuddy_nwo.htm*. Another good guide is available on the webpage *The New World Order (NWO)* at: *http://www.anomalies.net/object/io_1174433802417.html*.

3) Woodrow Wilson warns of a secret dominating force in the US: President Wilson's comments are from his book *The New Freedom: A Call For the Emancipation of the Generous Energies of a People*. Originally published in 1913, it can be freely downloaded in full at: *http://www.gutenberg.org/ebooks/14811*.

4) Bertrand Russell on science and world government: These and other disquieting quotes from the likes of Russell and other intellectuals advocating control by stealth, suppression and drugs for the good of humankind, can be found on the webpage *Exposing the NWO* at: *http://www.uscrusade.com/forum/config.pl/noframes/read/1562*.

5) Gordon Brown 'saves the world': British prime minister Gordon Brown's priceless Parliamentary gaffe in which he claimed Labour had 'saved the world' is discussed in Martin Kettle's *Crash Gordon 'saves the world'*, 10 December 2008, at: *http://www.guardian.co.uk/commentisfree/2008/dec/10/gordon-brown-save-world-pmqs*.

6) Man dies at G20 protests: See note 12 of Chapter IX for details of this incident.

7) Blair slow-handclapped by the Women's Institute: Tony Blair's excruciatingly embarrassing but fully deserved drubbing at the hands of the Women's Institute annual conference is discussed in the article *WI gives Blair hostile reception*, 7 June 2000, at: *http://news.bbc.co.uk/1/hi/uk_politics/780496.stm*.

XIV THE POWER OF COLLECTIVE THOUGHT

1) The Noosphere: The belief of Pierre Teilhard-de Chardin, a paleontologist and Jesuit priest, that the mass-consciousness of humankind was evolving into a merged state of being with the planet, forming a 'layer' that he called the 'Noosphere', is outlined well in Geoff Stray's *Beyond 2012*, Chapter 12, *Fringe Science*, pages 140-141.

2) *Childhood's End* by Arthur C Clarke: The late Clarke's seminal and very influential novel, which envisages the ultimate evolution of humankind into a race of higher (if unreachable) telepathic entities, was first published by Harcourt in 1953 and remains in print today. A summary is outlined in full at: *http://en.wikipedia.org/wiki/Childhood's_End*. Clarke (who became increasingly attached to plots based only on hard science as the years went by, and thus grew rather less interesting) updated the book in 1990 to allow for recent scientific developments, but the essential story remains intact.

3) Dean Radin's *Entangled Minds*: This straightforwardly-written and very convincing assessment of evidence for psi phenomena (full title: *Entangled Minds: Extrasensory Experiences in a Quantum Reality*) was published by Paraview Pocket Books in 2006. This in itself picks up on themes from Radin's previous book *The Conscious Universe: The Scientific Truth of Psychic Phenomena* (HarperEdge, 1997), which won the 1997 Book Award from the Scientific and Medical Network. See also Radin's website at: *www.deanradin.com*

4) Dean Radin describes the RNG experiments: Radin's description of the Random Number Generator studies is quoted from *Entangled Minds*, Chapter 9, *Mind-Matter Interaction*, page 154.

5) The Global Consciousness Project: The ongoing latest results of this extraordinarily important and ongoing study of mass consciousness can be read on its website at: *http://noosphere.princeton.edu/*. Given its obvious veracity and potential cruciality, why isn't this kind of science also being taught in schools?

6) The power of prayer: There have been many scientific studies that have produced positive results to show that prayer can work (despite what Richard Dawkins very selectively reports in *The God Delusion*, Bantam, 2006). Readers are recommended to search the Internet for the evidence, but a good starting point is Debra Williams' article *Scientific Research of Prayer: Can the Power of Prayer Be Proven?*, which can be read at: *http:// www.plim.org/PrayerDeb.htm*. See also *Time to Prescribe Prayer?*, *Fortean Times* (FT271), February 2011.

7) 'Hundredth Monkey' syndrome: The 'hundredth monkey' effect is often widely quoted in New Age circles as proof of collective consciousness. The story is that colonies of apes being studied on a Japanese island in the 1950s began to wash their sweet potatoes before eating them. When a certain critical mass of monkeys was reached (one hundred being a metaphorical round-up), the same behavior was suddenly reported amongst apes on other, entirely separate, islands, as if the new ability had been somehow 'transmitted'. However, despite the wide popularity of the concept, skeptics have rounded on the original story as being much misquoted and misunderstood, and doubt now surrounds the details. Nonetheless, later and better documented studies of collective animal behavior by the likes of Dr Rupert Sheldrake [Chapter XIV] have demonstrated that such a 'transmission' capability may well exist, so even if the original hundredth monkey story itself is dismissed, the concept still seems to embody a general truth.

The monkey controversy is discussed at: *http://en.wikipedia.org/wiki/Hundredth-monkey_effect*.

8) The power of intention: Many experiments into the power of psychic intent have been conducted over the years, but Lynne McTaggart's *The Intention Experiment* (Harper Element, 2008) is probably a good place for a résumé, together with its accompanying website *www.theintentionexperiment.com*.

9) Psychic experiments with crop circles: Attempts to influence the creation of specific crop circles with the power of the mind have thrown up some interesting results over the years, with several claims of success after meditations or visualizations carried out under controlled conditions. This author took part in such experiments in the early to mid-1990s, with intriguing results that were recorded in the book *Quest For Contact: A True Story of Crop Circles, Psychics and UFOs* (Andy Thomas and Paul Bura, SB Publications, 1997). The late Paul Bura elaborates on his experiences in *Stepping to the Drummer* (Bosgo Press, 2000).

10) Masuru Emoto's water crystal experiments: The work of the late Emoto, in which the power of thought was claimed to influence the formation of ice crystals into specific patterns, is another much-quoted piece of 'proof' for psychic influences (largely in the New Age realms, and promoted widely in the not uninteresting 'alternative' 2004 semi-documentary *What the Bleep Do We Know?*). Skeptics have inevitably attacked the work as being seriously flawed. It can't be denied that there are many unanswered questions—no full description of the applied methodology has ever been forthcoming and, as far as anyone can tell, no-one else has managed to reproduce the exact same experiments, despite unsubstantiated claims.

Assuming that a real psychic or vibrational effect *is* occurring, big questions still arise; for instance Emoto pointed out that 'Heavy Metal' music, when played to water, produced irregular and unpleasant crystal structures, whereas classical music produced beautiful ones. However, taking the quantum observer effect into account, along with Emoto's obvious distaste for Heavy Metal, how can it be ensured that he was not himself psychically affecting the outcome of the experiment? This is not to dismiss all of Emoto's findings, but clearly more detailed research needs to be conducted before his methods can be used as proof of anything.

Emoto's website can be accessed at: *http://www.masaru-emoto.net/english/e_ome_home.html* and his best-known book is *The Hidden Messages in Water* (Beyond Words Publishing, 2004).

11) Dean Radin on healing experiments: Radin's findings regarding the effect of mind on healing processes and brain cells are outlined in *Entangled Minds*, Chapter 11, *Gaia's Dreams*, pages 185-191.

12) Children exposed to TV murders: The shocking result of a 1992 survey in the *Journal of the American Medical Association*, which found that around 40,000 onscreen murders had been witnessed by the average 18-year old, is discussed in the article *Violence in the Media*, at: *http://www.enotes.com/violence-media-article*.

13) 'Presentiment' in the RNG experiments: Dean Radin reports at length the astonishing evidence that human beings can sense the future in *Entangled Minds*, Chapter 10, *Presentiment*, pages 161-180.

14) Animals sensed the 2004 tsunami: The news that animals seemed to have picked up on the imminent and devastating tsunami long before it arrived is reported in Maryann Mott's piece *Did Animals Sense Tsunami Was Coming?*, 4 January 2005, at: *http://news.nationalgeographic.com/news/2005/01/0104_050104_tsunami_animals.html*.
   A rather more skeptical but still interesting take on the story can be read in Roger Highfield's article *Did They Sense the Tsunami?*, which can be read at: *http://www.telegraph.co.uk/scienceandtechnology/3337851/Did-they-sense-the-tsunami.html*.

15) Rupert Sheldrake and the TED lectures: A good round-up of the situation around the cowardly withdrawal of Sheldrake's presentation (along with Graham Hancock's) from TED's main website is available in Henrik Palmgren and Elizabeth Leafloor's piece *TED: Some ideas TOO fascinating—Hancock, Sheldrake's censored talks*, 21 March 2013, at: *http://www.redicecreations.com/article.php?id=24281*.

16) Will entropy end the universe?: The theory that the Second Law of Thermodynamics, which could dictate that nature's ultimate tendency towards energetic disorder will mean a gradual 'winding down' of the universe into a long, moribund twilight state is just that; a theory, one that is much debated and disputed in the scientific world. Yet it is too often presented by mainstream physicists as an absolute, seemingly in an attempt to depress people into submission. The astrology-baiting astronomer Professor Brian Cox, for instance [see note 17 of Chapter XII], managed to devote a whole episode of his 2011 BBC series *Wonders of the Universe*, widely broadcast around the world, to promoting the 'heat death' hypothesis, without even once mentioning that many scientists disagree with it.
   Even the usually conformist *Wikipedia* acknowledges that the debate is far from closed (*http://en.wikipedia.org/wiki/Heat_death_of_the_universe*), which says much, and a good dissertation arguing the pros and cons of it all, *Entropy and the Universe*, by Sebastian Bleasdale, can be found at: *http://www.chiark.greenend.org.uk/~sbleas/creative/entropy/*.

XV THE POWER OF POSITIVE ACTION

1) Politicians predict/seed the idea of street riots: Then British Conservative leader David Cameron's 2009 warnings of civil unrest are reported in Andrew Porter and James Kirkup's article *Deceit over cuts will lead to riots', says David Cameron: Britain faces "riots on the streets" if Gordon Brown's "dishonesty" over public spending enables him to win the next election*, 29th June 2009, at: *http://www.telegraph.co.uk/news/newstopics/politics/5690836/Deceit-over-cuts-wil-lead-to-riots-says-David-Cameron.html*. Student riots hit London streets accordingly soon after Cameron's accession to Prime Minister in 2010, followed by wide city rioting in 2011. Interestingly, a Labour minister, Hazel Blears (just before being singled out for criticism during the MPs' expenses row), had also warned of similar unrest a few months before Cameron's own prophecy, as reported in James Chapman's article *Recession could spark riots and civil disorder, minister warns*, 30th April 2009, which can be read at: *http://www.dailymail.co.uk/news/article-1174955/Recession-spark-riots-civil-disorder-minister-warns.html*.
   Were these genuine fears being voiced, or was some kind of seed being planted in the public consciousness?
   The questionable circumstances under which Prince Charles and the Duchess of Cornwall's official car was 'mistakenly' taken too near the London student protests of December 2010, meanwhile, written off as a police 'blunder', are summed up in Ross Lydall and Justin Davenport's article *Camilla hit by rioter through car window as protesters attack royals*, 10 December 2010, at: *http://www.thisislondon.co.uk/standard/article-23905622-student-protest-mob-attacks-charles-and-camilla-on-fees-riot.do*. The conspiracy world widely considers that the royal car was deliberately allowed to become caught in the trouble, thus falling under siege, to create a media story that would distract (as it did) from the genuine issues of the protestors, and further foment the concept of mob unrest in the public mind.
   As for the 2011 riots, which ripped across several UK cities between 6-10 August as an initial reaction to the police shooting of unarmed Tottenham man Mark Duggan but soon sprawled into a general orgy of opportunistic anarchy and looting, many truthseekers observed that the situation appeared to have been deliberately allowed to conflagrate. This view was even voiced (to conditioned audience jeers) by a woman on BBC 1's *Question Time* in the days after, which can be watched at: *http://www.youtube.com/watch?v=Sbe95TEFOSQ*.

2) The killing of soldier Lee Rigby: The very odd street murder of military drummer Lee Rigby outside the Royal Artillery Barracks in Woolwich, London, on 22 May 2013 by two apparent Muslim fanatics (in claimed revenge for UK action in Afghanistan and Iraq) raised many questions amongst truthseekers. The lack of blood on the ground from what we are told was an attempted beheading seemed anomalous, and the assailants did not attempt to run away but stood and ranted to passers-by until the police arrived. The Woolwich attacks sparked several reprisal assaults against British mosques and protests from the likes of the English Defense League, leading to accusations that this was all a social conditioning set-up of some kind, either through Manchurian candidate-type mind control, or a state-sponsored staging.

The mainstream account can be read at *http://en.wikipedia.org/wiki/Death_of_Lee_Rigby*, but for the conspiracy take on it, which draws parallels with the also-odd Boston marathon bombings just a few weeks before, read Femi Fani-Kayode's article *CONSPIRACY THEORIES: The Woolwich Killing—More Questions Than Answers*, 24 May 2013, at: *http://omojuwa.com/2013/05/conspiracy-theories-the-woolwich-killing-more-questions-than-answers-femi-fani-kayode*.

3) Rudolf Steiner on the British: Steiner's words were spoken on 15 Jan 1917 in Dornach, Switzerland and are included in the series of lecture transcripts published as *The Karma of Untruthfulness—Secret Societies, the Media, and Preparations for the Great War Vol. 2* (Rudolf Steiner Press, 2005, p.133).

In a personal communication to this author, Steiner scholar Terry Boardman clarifies the lecture's comments on the British, making some interesting comments on the continuing influence of old bloodlines today:

'By 'grey magic', Steiner meant such things as newspapers, publishing and various forms of propaganda (including political speeches in and out of Parliament, articles, etc.)—'the media' of that time. In my presentations [on Steiner] *I emphasise the word 'elements' to draw attention to the fact that he was NOT saying that EVERYTHING about Britain and the British was eminently suitable to promote materialism, but that there were certain elements within the British national makeup that could be used to do this.*

In the same course of lectures Steiner focuses on what happened at the time of Henry VII and Henry VIII, especially the latter, when a new, more commercially-minded aristocracy replaced much of the older aristocracy. Steiner pointed out that a number of the aristocrats who were prominent in ruling circles in Britain in his own time could trace their lineage back to Tudor times. One thinks of the Cecils, Russells, Howards, etc. In very recent times, we've seen Michael Ancram and Theresa Villiers to name but two on the Tory front bench, and the remaining hereditary Tory Lords are led by Viscount Cranbourne: the families of these three all go back to the court of James I. I think the point is that there have always been a number of families and heads of institutions that regard themselves as being responsible for the nation—as constituting the nation, in fact. The rest of us are essentially servants and foot-soldiers.

This was certainly the case at the time of the Great War and may arguably still be true.'

4) Dr M Scott Peck's *People of the Lie*: *People of the Lie: The hope for healing human evil* (Century Hutchinson, 1983), Scott Peck's psychological analysis of what constitutes evil in the modern world, is a valuable contribution to a long-running debate, although the book's announcement that the author had recently converted to Christianity didn't go down so well with some of his previous admirers, who felt it colored his ability to retain a detached view. New religious admirers, however, were, of course, won.

5) The My Lai massacre: This shocking blot on US military history, which saw many innocent Vietmanese civilians indiscriminately raped and killed, is discussed well at: *http://en.wikipedia.org/wiki/My_Lai_Massacre*.

6) Pub boycotts: In this author's British birth town of Lewes, East Sussex, one of the key central 'pubs' (bars), under the influence of its new corporate owners, made the mistake of throwing out the beer of a famous Lewes-based brewery from the pumps. The resulting furore made any previous local protest on anything at all seem mild by comparison. It even made national headlines (see Tim Minogue's article *Last orders*, 23rd March 2007, at: *http://www.guardian.co.uk/uk/2007/mar/23/britishidentity.travel*). A several-month boycott—complete with protesting picketers at the doors of the pub in question—decimated clientele to the point where the owners had to relent and the brew was restored. This is a fine lesson that people power *does* work. At the same time, it's disturbing that it takes the sudden absence of good alcohol to really kick people into action... If that same resolve could be universally applied to rather larger matters, we might all get somewhere.

Go to it!

APPENDIX 3 — Further Resources

A Note on These Resources

Appendix 2 includes most of the works referenced during research for this book, and gives clear pointers for those seeking more on the subjects covered within these pages, but a few at-a-glance sources of key information are rounded-up here for convenience. Be aware that this is just a very small selection to act as a starting point for further investigation. Readers should also note that my listing of these books, websites and documentaries is not necessarily an endorsement of their full content. Discernment, as ever, will be required.

I have emphasized the sources on 'general conspiracy' and 9/11, as the two are inextricably linked in many people's minds. With the blatant anomalies of 9/11 being seen by many as the most vulnerable and potentially exposable global manipulation in recent history, it warrants particular scrutiny.

GENERAL CONSPIRACY

Books (alphabetically by authors)

William Cooper: Sometimes known as Milton William Cooper or Bill Cooper, if you want to go back to the source that in many ways began the current trend of fascination with conspiracy theories, Cooper's book *Behold a Pale Horse* (Light Technology Publications, 1991) is pretty much it. Not an easy read by any means, and controversial for including risky discussion of the ever-incendiary and hoaxed *Protocols of the Elders of Zion*, it nonetheless started many seekers down the line of New World Order speculation, with all the traditional elements, and therefore has become an important icon in its field. Cooper was shot dead by Arizona police in 2001 after some kind of firearms struggle (see *http://en.wikipedia.org/wiki/Milton_William_Cooper*), leading, perhaps appropriately, to his death becoming the subject of yet more conspiracy theories.

David Icke: Most of Icke's substantial works cover similar ground, but with gradual shifts of emphasis and additional material as each book goes by. Most are long and very detailed, but if you want to know the general ins and outs of who most conspiracy theorists think is responsible for what and where, his books are definitely the place to start, even if one doesn't agree with the more contentious views (reptilians, etc.). Their (non-religious) spiritual content is often underemphasized by truthseekers, so the books are not all gloom and doom and do offer ways out of the problems. Readers are advised to begin with one of his more all-encompassing titles, *The David Icke Guide to the Global Conspiracy (And How To End It)* (Bridge of Love, 2007), and work outwards from there.

Jim Marrs: Marrs began very much down the ET investigation route, but gradually expanded into other subjects, as many mystery researchers do, becoming one of the more prominent writers on the global control agenda. His books act as a good US take on modern conspiracy thinking, and there are several titles to choose from. *Rule by Secrecy* (HarperCollins, 2002) and *The Terror Conspiracy: Deception, 9/11 and the Loss of Liberty* (Disinformation Company Ltd, 2006) probably cover the general ground best. *Alien Agenda: Investigating the Extraterrestrial Presence Among Us* (HarperTorch, 1998) pulls together the big picture on UFOs and alleged US government knowledge of extra-terrestrials.

Jon Ronson: Ronson is considered a non-committal lightweight in the conspiracy world at best, and a skeptic at worst (he has, disappointingly, dismissed 9/11 truthers), more interested in quirky people who believe in conspiracies than in the conspiracies themselves, but it can't be denied that some of his books have taken several subjects into the mainstream (such as the Bohemian Grove rituals) in a way that others have failed to achieve. They also act as a handy, if wafer-thin, glimpse into darker areas for those nervous about getting in too deep. Ronson is best known for *Them: Adventures With Extremists* (Simon & Schuster, 2002), but the follow-up, *The Men Who Stare at Goats* (Picador, 2005), is an interesting delve into the dubious world of US military experiments with psychics, remote viewing and 'unconventional' interrogation techniques (made, unwisely, into a jokey film in 2009).

Websites (alphabetically)

www.davidicke.com

Icke's illuminating insights and often darkly humorous thoughts on the latest global events and the selective way they are reported are always worth reading on his news page, which can be a tonic in times of obvious social manipulation. Whatever anyone thinks of Icke and his more extreme views, a website like this needs to exist, and is excellently presented.

www.ianrcrane.com

Information on Ian R Crane's ongoing and striking live presentations dedicated to uncovering the hidden side of key current issues, with many downloads of past lectures available, is regularly posted here, together with articles, news and opinions.

www.nexusmagazine.com

The monthly publication *Nexus Magazine* has been one of the longest-running and most consistent exposers of cover-ups, and expounds alternative views on everything from conspiracies and metaphysics to health and science. Its head office is based in Australia, but the magazine is available in several international editions, and information on all of them can be found at this website.

www.prisonplanet.com
www.infowars.com

The websites run by truthseeker Alex Jones, and the main stops for the total conspiracy view on current affairs, with a strong US bias. The strident tones can be too much for newcomers, but even if readers don't go with all of it, it can't be denied that the dramatic presentation serves well the sites' laudable aim of unapologetically blasting open the control agenda for public exposure.

www.redicecreations.com

This sublime web-radio station (hosted with balance and intelligence by founder Henrik Palmgren) and substantial information site provides perhaps the best overall glimpse into the main alternative issues of the day, endlessly updated with comprehensive interviews of the key researchers.

www.rense.com

Jeff Rense is another important player in exposing the tools of global manipulation, and the site always gives numerous links to fringe views on the important topics of the moment.

www.truthagenda.org

This author's own website, including news, upcoming lecture dates and presentations to watch, along with biographical details. Information on the annual Glastonbury Symposium conference in the UK (co-hosted by Andy), meanwhile, can be found at *www.glastonburysymposium.co.uk*.

Documentaries

Exploring the above websites will provide links to numerous documentaries on conspiracies of all kinds, freely available on the Internet, but four stand out as good starting points. Nearly all can be seen on their home sites, but otherwise are easily found on You Tube or Google Video.

The hard-hitting *Terrorstorm: A History of Government Sponsored Terrorism*, by Alex Jones, sums up the feelings of many truthseekers about the War on Terror and its apparently contrived causes. The newest 'final cut' version can be downloaded from Jones's website listed above.

For a good insight into how international banking is used as a key component of global control, *The Money Masters* is crucial viewing, and can be seen at: *http://www.themoneymasters.com/synopsis.htm*.

For the best all-round guide to the conspiracy view of the current state of the world, the much-praised *Zeitgeist* trilogy is a mind-blowing trip through the hidden history of control agendas and much more, summing up the issues well (including an excellent section on 9/11 in the first entry) and offering solutions on making a better world. They are long and detailed, but well worth the journey, although the religiously devout should beware, as the initial part is highly critical of both the origins of religion and its misuse through the ages. All three *Zeitgeist* films can be watched (or ordered as DVDs) at their official website at: *http://www.zeitgeistmovie.com*.

Another documentary worth watching is *Thrive*, which covers similar ground to *Zeitgeist* in some ways, but throws in things like free energy, climate debates and crop circles along with all the general conspiracy stuff, making for an interesting overview. Green activists hate it, and the *Huffington Post* describes its stance as 'a reactionary, libertarian political agenda that stands in jarring contrast with the soothing tone of the presentation', which will either put some readers off or immediately make them want to watch it. Find the movie easily on YouTube or DVD, or go to the official website at: *http://www.thrivemovement.com*.

Meanwhile, although fictional and not a documentary, most conspiracy theorists point to the 2005 movie *V for Vendetta* as being the nearest Hollywood has come to making a radical statement about the way the world may really be run. Produced and written by the brothers Laurence and Andrew Wachowski (who also created the not irrelevant *Matrix* films) and inspired by the more complex graphic novel by Alan Moore and David Lloyd (Vertigo, 1995, which in itself is a recommended read), *V for Vendetta* is set in a near-future fascist Britain and seems increasingly relevant as the years go by. The down side of it is that it appears to support terrorism (which this author most certainly does not) and it has been attacked by critics for that, but if this can be overlooked there are many salient lessons in the film. Given its strong anti-establishment tone (although anti-fascist might be a more accurate term), the fact that the producers obtained permission to shut the roads around Whitehall and film for three nights outside the Houses of Parliament now seems astonishing. The now popular wearing of stylized Guy Fawkes masks at liberty events, in honour of the central character, 'V', was directly inspired by this ultimately uplifting, if ideologically ambiguous, film, which is a must-see for anyone concerned about the current control trajectory. Good information and discussion of the film can be found at: *http://en.wikipedia.org/wiki/V_for_Vendetta_(film)*.

V: *'There is something terribly wrong with this country, isn't there? Cruelty and injustice, intolerance and oppression. And where once you had the freedom to object, to think and speak as you saw fit, you now have censors and systems of surveillance coercing your conformity and soliciting your submission. How did this happen? Who's to blame? Well certainly there are those more responsible than others, and they will be held accountable, but again, truth be told, if you're looking for the guilty, you need only look into a mirror. I know why you did it. I know you were afraid. Who wouldn't be? War, terror, disease. There were a myriad of problems, which conspired to corrupt your reason and rob you of your common sense. Fear got the best of you, and in your panic you turned to the now High Chancellor... ...He promised you order, he promised you peace, and all he demanded in return was your silent, obedient consent...'*

9/11 — Books

David Ray Griffin: As a respected academic (feeling obliged by his Christian faith to turn his attention to a glaring immorality he felt he could no longer ignore), Griffin is the most important attribute that the 9/11 truth movement has, always remaining fully grounded and steadfastly adhering to the discussion of hard facts. A stickler for detail, his flawless analyses leave no stone unturned, and no discontinuity or defect of logic gets by him. If the Western cartel that appears to have operated on 9/11 isn't worried by the astonishingly convincing case against the official story that Griffin has laid out in his ever-growing series of books on the subject (eleven full tomes to date), it should be. Where he speculates, he does so carefully and clearly denotes this, but mostly the books stay firmly in the realm of dissecting the known. Anyone who can read Griffin's works and afterwards still believe *every* facet of what he calls 'the official conspiracy theory' (i.e. the assertion that Al Qaeda acted alone) is either in a state of extreme denial or in a coma.

Griffin's first and best-known 9/11 book, *The New Pearl Harbor: Disturbing Questions about the Bush Administration and 9/11* (Olive Branch Press, 2004) has essentially been superseded by the semi-sequel/update *The New Pearl Harbor Revisited: 9/11, the Cover-Up and the Expose* (Olive Branch Press, 2008), which acts as Griffin's best all-round guide to the anomalies of 9/11. However, more dedicated students sometimes choose *9/11 Ten Years Later: When State Crimes Against Democracy Succeed* (Haus Publishing, 2011), a good updated overview, or *Debunking 9/11 Debunking: An Answer to Popular Mechanics and Other Defenders of the Official Conspiracy Theory* (Olive Branch Press, 2007) as their main defense tool, for its robust addressing of media and government attempts to demean and debunk questioners of the official story. Those who want to hear Griffin take apart almost line-by-line the official 9/11 inquiry should read *The 9/11 Commission Report: Omissions And Distortions* (Olive Branch Press, 2004)—the subtitle tells you all you need to know about the book's take on it—while *The Mysterious Collapse of World Trade Center 7: Why the Final Official Report About 9/11 is Unscientific and False* (Interlink Publishing Group, 2009) is pretty much the definitive word on the Building Seven controversy. As a wider commentary on the way states treat conspiracy theorists and attempt to silence them, *Cognitive Infiltration: An Obama Appointee's Plan to Undermine the 9/11 Conspiracy Theory* (Olive Branch Press, 2010), comes highly recommended—the title tells the story. In essence, every Griffin book on 9/11 is worth reading, and completists should also seek out *9/11 Contradictions: An Open Letter to Congress and the Press* (Interlink Publishing Group, 2008) and *Christian Faith and the Truth Behind 9/11: A Call to Reflection and Action* (Westminster John Knox Press, 2006).

Other authors: It is not Griffin alone who has important things to say about 9/11, and there are many books out there by various authors which make for valuable research. However, among these I would particularly cite Ian Henshall and Rowland Morgan's *9/11 Revealed: Challenging the Facts Behind the War on Terror* (Robinson Publishing, 2005), Ian Henshall's solo sequel *9.11: The New Evidence* (Robinson Publishing 2007), Webster Griffin Tarpley's *9/11 Synthetic Terror: Made in USA* (Progressive Press, 2005), and not forgetting David Icke's delightfully-named *Alice in Wonderland and the World Trade Center Disaster: Why the Official Story of 9/11 is a Monumental Lie* (Bridge of Love, 2002), which, although now inevitably dated, was one of the first books out there to challenge the official story. In this regard, Thierry Meyssan's *9/11: The Big Lie* (originally published in France, 2002, and in the US by Carnot USA Books, 2003) is another important early entry. Dr Judy Wood's *Where Did the Towers Go?* (The New Investigation, 2010), meanwhile, proposes the controversial 'energy device' theories. The late Michael Ruppert's *Crossing the Rubicon: The Decline of the American Empire at the End of the Age of Oil* (New Society Publishers, 2004) is also worth reading, although it borders more on straight geopolitics.

9/11 — Websites

There are now so many 9/11-questioning websites out there that it is almost impossible to keep track of them. But the ones run by academics and professionals in their field, who *know* about buildings, airplanes and fires, and the way they should behave, are probably the most important, because they carry weight beyond the usual conspiracy channels. Here is a selection of sites that will keep readers seriously in the loop of the latest 9/11 revelations, and include some very important articles, scientific studies, videos and interviews, which make up an unquestionable case that a fully independent reinvestigation is essential. Something has hit a spot in the collective, which cannot be ignored forever. Most titles in the following (alphabetical) list are self-explanatory, but clarifications are given where not:

www.911blogger.com
www.911building7.co.uk (Martin Noakes' 9/11 campaigning song)
http://911forum.org.uk
http://911research.wtc7.net
http://911scholars.org (Scholars for 9/11 Truth)
www.911truth.org
www.ae911truth.org (Architects & Engineers for 9/11 Truth)
www.CSI911.info
http://drjudywood.co.uk (energy device theories)
http://firefightersfor911truth.org
www.journalof911studies.com
www.l911t.com (Lawyers for 9/11 Truth)
http://patriotsquestion911.com
http://pilotsfor911truth.org
www.stj911.com (Scholars for 9/11 Truth & Justice)
www.visibility911.com
www.v911t.org (Veterans for 9/11 Truth) [Soldiers]
www.william911.com (William Rodriguez, WTC janitor)
www.wtc7.net
http://www.youtube.com/watch?v=uSBYdRRuLxI (*9/11's a Lie*—song by 'The Freebies')

Documentaries

Many good 9/11 documentaries are available, too many to list here, but searches through the websites will soon reveal them. However, although later findings and research have now dated some of the detail, many truthers still maintain that the best starting point for newcomers is Dylan Avery's obscurely-named but hugely influential *Loose Change II*. This replaced a first version, and *Loose Change Final Cut* came along after, but the third installment, although valuable, is essentially a different and more detailed film and takes too much knowledge for granted to really be for beginners. Go for the mark two version first. The issues are necessarily simplified to get it into an easily accessible format, and debunkers have attempted to attack it for this, but it makes all the points it needs to without at any point being disingenuous. *Loose Change II* was, after all, the documentary that really burst open the gates for the 9/11 truth movement, with its circulation via the Internet and DVD-copying networks quickly becoming massive. The official website *http://www.loosechange911.com* tends to default to the final version of the film, but the second one is easily found on YouTube and Google Video.

For the best dissection of the issues around the highly questionable collapse of the towers at the WTC, however, *911 Mysteries Part 1—Demolitions* is excellent, calmly presenting the viewer with almost indisputable observations regarding the footage of the destruction, analyzing the physics as it goes. Part 2 never materialized, but this film does enough by itself. The documentary is ubiquitous online and is also available on DVD (as are all the following titles).

Another excellent scientific analysis, by Richard Gage of Architects and Engineers for 9/11 Truth, *9/11 Explosive Evidence—Experts Speak Out*, uses qualified professional knowledge to expose major flaws in the official explanation as to why the twin towers fell. Essential viewing.

Less focused on the science of the events, but representing an important element of the truth campaign, the film *9/11: Press for Truth* tells the story of the 'Jersey widows', a group of partners and wives of 9/11 victims who campaigned for an official investigation into the attacks, only to see the subsequent 9/11 Commission entirely fail to answer their key questions about how the events came to pass.

In a not dissimilar vein, but more global in its coverage, Dean Puckett's documentary about the 9/11 truth movement, *The Elephant in the Room*, demonstrates the intense feelings and dedication of campaigners in the US and UK and is an impressive reminder that the 9/11 issue isn't going to be dropped by those concerned anytime soon.

OTHER GENERAL INFORMATION

A small but useful selection of books on other subjects covered in these chapters are listed here (in alphabetical order of subject), together with a tiny but helpful scattering of websites from what is obviously a huge pool—again, many further links can be followed from most of them.

ANCIENT MYSTERIES

Books: Christopher Dunn's *The Giza Power Plant: Technologies of Ancient Egypt* (Bear & Company, 1998) is one of the best-expressed alternative theories on the title's subject, while the works of Graham Hancock are also particularly strong in reassessing mysteries such as the pyramids and other ancient artefacts, taking them out of traditional archaeology's narrow confines and speculating more freely, but in a scholarly fashion. His best-known book is probably *Fingerprints of the Gods* (originally Crown, 1996, updated by Century, 2001), but *Heaven's Mirror: Quest for the Lost Civilization* (Michael Joseph, 1998, co-authored with Santha Faiia) and *Keeper of Genesis: A Quest for the Hidden Legacy of Mankind* (Arrow Books Ltd, 1997, co-authored with Robert Bauval), amongst other works, all provide insights into a different view of ancient history. Bauval and Adrian Gilbert's *The Orion Mystery* (Mandarin Books, 1994), which first proposed the much-debated Giza/Orion correlation, is also worth reading, although Lynn Picknett and Clive Prince's book *The Stargate Conspiracy: The Truth about Extraterrestrial Life and the Mysteries of Ancient Egypt* (Berkley Trade, 2001) puts an interesting spin on things, claiming that the likes of Hancock, Bauval and Gilbert are fronting a secret consortium that is actively planning for the imminent return of ancient god-like beings. Meanwhile, the multi-volume 'Earth Chronicle' books of the late Zecharia Sitchin, beginning with *The Twelfth Planet* (originally published 1976, current edition Harper, 2007), though much criticized by skeptics, purport to tell the hidden story of humankind's history as a genetically-engineered slave race (as Sitchin interprets it), its themes derived from ancient Sumerian and other supportive texts. Whatever their veracity, the books have been influential and pretty much gave birth to the modern speculation on the return of the 'Annunaki' and the lost-planet 'Nibiru'.

Websites:
www.gizapower.com (Christopher Dunn)
www.grahamhancock.com
www.mcremo.com (Michael Cremo—*Forbidden Archaeology*)
www.robertbauval.co.uk
www.sitchin.com

CLIMATE CHANGE (ALTERNATIVE THEORIES)

Books: We have already seen that ex-UK chancellor Nigel Lawson's *An Appeal to Reason: A Cool Look at Global Warming* (Gerald Duckworth & Co Ltd, 2008) puts a sensibly argued and pragmatic case that the policies being pursued to deal with perceived global warming are misplaced and damaging, ecologically and economically, even if its existence were to be proven. Henrik Svensmark and Nigel Calder's book *The Chilling Stars* (Icon Books/Totem Books, 2007) actively proposes a different model of climate change based on the theory of cosmic influences causing worldwide cooling, not warming, while on a similar theme Peter Taylor's book *Chill: A Reassessment of Global Warming Theory* (Clairview Books, 2009) is an excellent and informed proposal of the cooling scenario. Other sources include Mitch Battros' *Global Warming: A Convenient Disguise* (Earth Changes Media, 2007), which, together with his earlier volume *Solar Rain: The Earth Changes Have Begun* (Earth Changes Press, 2005), points to the Sun as being the major driver of climate change and other effects, not greenhouse gases. Meanwhile, Canadian environmentalist Lawrence Solomon's impressively scholarly *The Deniers: The World Renowned Scientists Who Stood Up Against Global Warming Hysteria, Political Persecution, and Fraud (*And those who are too fearful to do so)* (Richard Vigilante Books, 2008) focuses on the surprisingly long and eminent list of climatologists and scientists who challenge the global warming theory. How so many qualified people can take a stand against it and not be listened to, while the likes of Al Gore – an ex-politician, not a scientist—gets his film shown in schools, is still a mystery. Roy Spencer's *Climate Confusion: How Global Warming Hysteria Leads to Bad Science, Pandering Politicians and Misguided Policies that Hurt the Poor* is a lighter read, but ably deconstructs the myths and indeed confusions of misplaced climate fear-mongering.

Websites
www.drroyspencer.com
www.dsri.dk/~hsv/ (Henrik Svensmark)
www.earthchangesmedia.com (Mitch Battros)
www.globalwarminghoax.com
www.green-agenda.com ('Agenda 21', etc.)
www.urban-renaissance.org (Lawrence Solomon)

CONSCIOUSNESS/PSI STUDIES

Books: For a balanced and calmly presented assessment of the impressive evidence that human minds are inextricably linked in some kind of collective energetic process, continually communicating by instantaneous 'non-local' means and producing unexpected 'psi' phenomena, Dean Radin's *Entangled Minds: Extrasensory Experiences in a Quantum Reality* (Paraview Pocket Books, 2006) puts the firmest of cases, based on provable science, not New Age speculation. A good round-up of Radin's and many other researchers' work into collective psi effects, while speculating more openly on the implications and possibilities the recognition of a truly proactive collective consciousness could bring (based on the concept of the 'Zero Point Field'), can be found in Lynne McTaggart's *The Field: The Quest for the Secret Force of the Universe* (updated edition, Harper Paperbacks, 2008). Rupert Sheldrake is another researcher who has made important steps in bridging the divide between science and metaphysics (though he would never call it that). His 'morphic resonance' theory to account for collective species development has been very influential. In terms of exploring consciousness and psi effects, the best Sheldrake starting points are probably *The Sense of Being Stared At (and other unexplained powers of the human mind)* (Crown Publishing Group, 2004), and *Seven Experiments That Could Change the World* (Inner Traditions, 2002), but his recent provocative title *Science Set Free: 10 Paths to New Discovery* (Deepak Chopra, 2013—more grittily retitled *The Science Delusion* in the UK) is a crucial and intelligent challenge to the academic dogma surrounding conventional science.

For the fundamentalist hard-science adherents for whom even these very grounded books push the envelope too much, Bruce Rosenblum and Fred Kuttner's *Quantum Enigma: Physics Encounters Consciousness* (Oxford University Press, 2008) should placate. An exploration of straight (if there is such a thing) quantum physics, its balanced and cautious analysis of the role consciousness appears to actively play in shaping reality still makes the point that the New Physics now needs to look outside of its old parameters to embrace a new understanding of the importance of mind. Meanwhile, those interested in the transformative effects of natural dimethyltryptamine in the brain, and what stimulates its production, are again directed to Rick Strassman's *DMT: The Spirit Molecule—A Doctor's Revolutionary Research into the Biology of Near-Death and Mystical Experiences* (Park Street Press, 2001).

Websites
www.deanradin.com
http://noosphere.princeton.edu (Global Consciousness Project)
www.rickstrassman.com
www.sheldrake.org (Rupert Sheldrake)
www.theintentionexperiment.com (Lynne McTaggart)
www.whatthebleep.com

CROP CIRCLES

Books: The earliest books are still some of the best, with Colin Andrews and Pat Delgado's *Circular Evidence* (Bloomsbury, 1989) and the Ralph Noyes-edited *The Crop Circle Enigma* (Gateway, 1991) providing good insights into the initial development of the phenomenon. In later years, the most balanced and informative book, free of unhelpful 'croppie' generalizations, has been Eltjo Haselhoff's *The Deepening Complexity of Crop Circles: Scientific Research and Urban Legends* (Frog Ltd, 2001), which makes an excellent case for a non-human cause, using sensible empirical reasoning, while Michael Glickman's *Crop Circles: The Bones of God* (Frog Ltd, 2009) is a valuable entry from the veteran geometer and researcher. More recently, Eva-Marie Brekkesto's *Crop Circles: History, Research & Theories* (Wessex Books, 2011) gives a very good overview. Readers may also like to investigate my own *Vital Signs: A Complete Guide to the Crop Circle Mystery* (SB Publications 1998/2002 [UK], Frog Ltd, 2002 [US], kindly described more than once as 'the definitive guide', or *An Introduction to Crop Circles* (Wessex Books, 2004/2011), which is a more concise, newer manual.

Websites
www.bltresearch.com (scientific analysis)
www.cropcircleconnector.com
www.kornkreise-forschung.de (also known as *www.cropcirclescience.org*)
www.lucypringle.co.uk (photos and research)
www.swirlednews.com (archive articles edited or written by this author)
www.ukcropcircles.co.uk

GEOPOLITICS

Books: Generally outside the realm of conspiracy theory, but still incisively questioning of political corruption and global intrigues, a few titles are particularly relevant. Any political non-fiction by the late Gore Vidal is worth reading, but two shorter books were particularly picked up on by truthseekers in the wake of 9/11 (although Vidal appears to accept the official line on it), *Perpetual War for Perpetual Peace or How We Came To Be So Hated*, and *Dreaming War: Blood for Oil and the Cheney-Bush Junta* (both by Thunder's Mouth Press, 2002). Someone who did go on to question 9/11 and become very active in truth campaigning is Annie Machon, whose book *Spies, Lies and Whistleblowers: MI5, MI6 and the Shayler affair* (Book Guild Ltd, 2005) is an exposé of her time as a British MI5 officer, detailing a number of dubious British plots, including an attempt to hire Al Qaeda to assassinate the Libyan leader Colonel Gaddafi. (Her then partner David Shayler was sent to prison for trying to reveal what he and Machon considered to be immoral actions.) David Rothkopf's book *Superclass: The Global Power Elite and the World They Are Making* (Farrar, Straus and Giroux, 2008) has already been mentioned, as has Norman Baker's *The Strange Death of David Kelly* (Methuen Publishing, 2007—although this could almost be in the conspiracy section), but other works of interest include Ron Suskind's *The Way of the World: A Story of Truth and Hope in an Age of Extremism* (Harper, 2008), which uncovers the corruption behind the 2003 invasion of Iraq amongst other revelations, and John Pilger's *The New Rulers of the World* (Verso, 2003) and *Freedom Next Time: Resisting the Empire* (Nation Books, 2007), which demonstrate the massive issues around loss of freedom due to globalization and aggressive Western trade and military policies. Likewise, any work by noted academic Noam Chomsky tells much the same story; *Manufacturing Consent: The Political Economy of the Mass Media* (Pantheon, 2002) exposes the way politicians exploit a complicit media to manipulate the public, and *Failed States: The Abuse of Power and the Assault on Democracy (American Empire Project)* (Holt Paperbacks, 2007) takes apart the then George W Bush administration's aggressive policies, the legacy of which lingers on today. However, Chomsky's admittedly puzzling inability to even consider the 9/11 inside-job view has infuriated many truthseekers, who cannot understand why such a keen critic of US government corruption refuses to investigate further, leading to accusations that he has been 'got at'. Perhaps Chomsky and people like him just can't bring themselves to face *that* depth of pessimism about their rulers. This caveat probably covers most of the authors listed in this geopolitics section, not to mention US film maker/political agitator Michael Moore, whose 2004 documentary *Fahrenheit 9/11* is very good for making things like the business connections between the Bush and bin Laden families more than clear (and in general is well worth watching), but shies away from questioning 9/11 itself. Frustrating though their reticence in some areas can be, in the end it is a matter for individuals where they want to go with their views, but at least there are people in the mainstream exposing any of the darker levels at all.

THE TRUTH AGENDA

Websites
www.chomsky.info
www.johnpilger.com
www.michaelmoore.com
http://www.pitt.edu/~kloman/vidalframe.html (Gore Vidal)
http://www.ronsuskind.com/about

HEALTH

Books: The threat to the free availability of natural health products is discussed at length in Scott Tips' *Codex Alimentarius: Global Food Imperialism* (National Health Federation, 2007), a compendium of crucial articles which anticipated all-too-well the now biting restrictions. In regard to vaccinations, Trevor Gunn's *Mass Immunization—A Point in Question* (Cutting Edge Publications, 1992) and Wendy Lydall's *Raising a Vaccine Free Child* (AuthorHouse, 2005) have already been cited as important reading, while Neil Z Miller's *Vaccines: Are They Really Safe and Effective?* (New Atlantean Press, revised edition 2008) is another vital contribution. In terms of adult health, and the questionable pharmaceutical solutions often pushed on us above other options, Lynne McTaggart's *What Doctors Don't Tell You: The Truth About The Dangers Of Modern Medicine* (Avon, 1999) is a seminal title and encompasses many of the problematic issues without blanket condemnation of conventional methods. Meanwhile, both the work of Dr Joseph Mercola and the many books of Philip Day (it's impossible to pick out one) embrace alternative methods of keeping healthy and avoiding the likes of cancer and arthritis by maintaining healthy diets and eating specific foods, and have been sworn to by many who have followed the advice – see the websites below.

Websites
www.anhcampaign.org (Alliance for Natural Health)
www.credence.org (Philip Day)
www.fluoridation.com (excellent resource on fluoride issues)
www.informedparent.co.uk
www.mercola.com (Dr Joseph Mercola)
www.thenhf.com (National Health Federation/Scott Tips)
www.wddty.com (Lynne McTaggart)

NASA CONSPIRACY

Books: We have already seen that two books are particularly prominent on this subject: Gerhard Wisnewski's *One Small Step?—The Great Moon Hoax and the Race to Dominate Earth from Space* (Clairview Books, 2007) is the most real-world case yet presented that the evidence for the lunar missions may be faked, while Mary Bennett and David Percy's *Dark Moon: Apollo and the Whistleblowers* (Aulis Publishers, 1999) is a denser, more esoteric take on it, but still makes for vital reading (see also the accompanying 2000 documentary *What Happened on the Moon?*—details can be found on their website below). Ralph René's self-published book *NASA Mooned America!* (1992) is equally uncompromising in its deconstruction of the lunar claims, and Philippe Lheureux's *Moon Landings: Did NASA Lie?* (Carnot USA Books, 2003) offers a more simplistic, but handy round-up of the main issues. Taking a rather different line, but worth a look for a balancing view, is Richard Hoagland and Mike Bara's *Dark Mission: The*

Secret History of NASA (Feral House, 2007), which postulates that NASA *did* go to the Moon, but that they covered up evidence of ET structures they found there. Hoagland (formerly a NASA staff member) was one of the first promoters of the 'face on Mars' photos from the 1977 Viking mission, and still claims (despite vigorous NASA debunking based on later photos) that Mars is also covered in ancient structures we are not being told about. The authors assert (as do Bennett and Percy) that the power infrastructure of NASA is riddled with secret society and occult undercurrents.

Websites
www.aulis.com (Mary Bennett & David Percy)
http://billkaysing.com
www.enterprisemission.com (Richard Hoagland)
www.moonmovie.com

THE NEW ERA

Books: Though the big date has gone by, Geoff Stray's *Beyond 2012: Catastrophe or Ecstasy* (Vital Signs Publishing, 2005) remains a key source on things which may yet come to pass and contains excellent information of continuing relevance (although beware two inferior imposter books, which have appropriated its title—make sure it's the Stray version you read). John Major Jenkins' work *Maya Cosmogenesis 2012: The True Meaning of the Maya Calendar End-Date* (Bear & Company, 1998) is still also interesting reading, and was the first serious book to alert wider attention to the beliefs of the Maya people, while defining the galactic alignment process.

Websites
www.alignment2012.com (John Major Jenkins)
www.diagnosis2012.co.uk (Geoff Stray)
www.greatdreams.com/2012.htm

UFOS & ETS

Books: UFOs and government cover-ups of them are well-assessed in Timothy Good's seminal works *Above Top Secret: The Worldwide UFO Cover-Up* (Sidgwick & Jackson Ltd, 1987), *Beyond Top Secret* (Pan Books, 1997), and his update, *Need to Know: UFOs, the Military and Intelligence* (Pan Books, 2007). The alien abduction phenomenon is assessed very intelligently by John E Mack in *Passport to the Cosmos: Human Transformation and Alien Encounters* (Crown, 1999), while Whitley Strieber's *Communion* (Avon, 1988) and its sequels give good first-hand accounts of his claimed experiences with ETs. Stanton T Friedman and Don Berliner's *Crash at Corona: The U.S. Military Retrieval and Cover-Up of a UFO* (Marlowe & Co., 1997), meanwhile, describes itself as the 'definitive study' of the Roswell incident, and appears to be generally treated as such. [See also the Jim Marrs entry under *General Conspiracy*.]

Websites
www.earthfiles.com (Linda Moulton-Howe)
www.realufos.net
www.ufocasebook.com
www.ufoevidence.org

PICTURE CREDITS
Image authors and/or sources as below—all other photos by Andy Thomas

Page 10 (and front cover), montage by Jason Porthouse & Andy Thomas. / US military drone ('RQ-4 Global Hawk unmanned aircraft') photo: Bobbi Zapka, USAF. Source: Wikimedia Commons, public domain. / Astronaut photo: NASA. Public domain. / Silhouetted figures and Sun photos: Mark Sewell (thanks also to Katie Sewell and friends). [Other individual photos in the montage credited below.]

Page 12, filming of the BBC's *The One Show*. Photo: Helen Sewell.

Page 13, Barack Obama's inaugural oath. Photo: Petty Officer 1st Class Chad J McNeeley, US Navy (*http://www.defenselink.mil/homepagephotos/homepagephotos.aspx?month=200901*). Source: Wikimedia Commons, public domain.

Page 17, Egyptian temple. Photo: Heather Thomas.

Page 24, The White House, Washington DC. Photo: Tony & Ann Woodall.

Page 28, Giza monuments. Photo: Daniel Mayer. Source: Wikimedia Commons, under the GNU Free Documentation License (*http://commons.wikimedia.org/wiki/Commons:GNU_Free_Documentation_License*).

Pages 30-31, Giza pyramids. Photos: Heather Thomas.

Pages 32-34, aerial crop circle photos. Photos: Andreas Müller (*http://www.kornkreise-forschung.de*).

Page 36, crystal skull. Photo: Jordan Thomas.

Page 37, Norway sky spiral. Photos: Beate Kiil Karlsen.

Page 38, Area 51, 1968. Photo: USGS Aerial Imagery. Source: Wikimedia Commons, public domain.

Pages 40-42, Little A'le'inn, Groom Lake Road and Area 51 sign. Photos: Mike Oram.

Page 44, black triangle UFO, 1990. Photo: J S Henradi (*http://www.abduct-anon.com/AUTHENTIC %20PHOTOS.htm*). Source: Wikimedia Commons, public domain.

Page 47, UFO, 1952. Photo: Central Intelligence Agency (*https://www.cia.gov/csi/studies/97unclass/p69. gif*). Source: Wikimedia Commons, public domain.

Page 52, Edgar Cayce, 1910. Author unknown. Source: Wikimedia Commons, public domain.

Page 54, Revelation mural. Painting by Matthias Gerung. Source: Wikimedia Commons, public domain.

Pages 57-58, Fatima images, 1917. Authors unknown. Source: Wikimedia Commons, public domain.

Page 62, George W Bush meets Pope John Paul II. Photo: Eric Draper, United States Federal Government. Source: Wikimedia Commons, public domain.

Page 72, Georgia Guidestones. Photo: 'Ptkfgs'. Source: Wikimedia Commons, public domain.

Page 73, George Orwell, 1933. Photo: Branch of the National Union of Journalists (c/o *http://www. netcharles.com/orwell/*). Source: Wikimedia Commons, public domain.

Page 75, Canary Wharf by night. Photo: Dave Pape. Source: Wikimedia Commons, public domain.

Page 76, Strasbourg Parliament. Photo: Cédric Puisney. Source: Wikimedia Commons, public domain.

Page 81, micro-chipped cat. Photo: Joel Mills (*http://en.wikipedia.org/wiki/User:Joelmills*). Source: Wikimedia Commons, under the GNU Free Documentation License (*http://commons.wikimedia.org/wiki/Commons:GNU_Free_Documentation_License*).

Page 87, Sumerian seal/Annunaki. Author unknown. Source: Wikimedia Commons, public domain.

Page 88, Tower of Babel. Painting by Pieter Bruegel. Source: Wikimedia Commons, public domain.

Page 89, Egyptian needle. Photo by Ronald Thomas.

Page 90, The Washington Monument. Photo by Tony & Ann Woodall.

Page 92, One Canada Square, Canary Wharf. Photo: Matt T (*http://commons.wikimedia.org/wiki/User:Matt.T*). Source: Wikimedia Commons.

Page 93, Bohemian Grove Cremation of Care ceremony 1907. Photo by Gabriel Moulin. Source: Wikimedia Commons, public domain.

Page 94, Bohemian Grove stage area, 2004. Photo: 'Aarkwilde'. Source: Wikimedia Commons, under the Creative Commons Attribution-Share Alike 3.0 Unported (*http://creativecommons.org/licenses/by-sa/3.0/deed.en*).

Page 95, Operation Ivy nuclear test, 1952. Photo c/o NARA (National Archives and Records Administration). Source: Wikimedia Commons, public domain.

Page 95, St John of Nepomuk. Painting by Luigi Crespi. Source: Wikimedia Commons, public domain.

Page 97, Alex Jones addresses the anti-Bilderberg festival, Watford, UK, 2013. Photo: Martin Noakes.

Page 99, World Trade Center. Photo by Tony & Ann Woodall.

Pages 104-126, Moon mission and other NASA images. All photos: NASA (National Aeronautics and Space Administration). Public domain.

Page 128, lunar lander conceptual art. Painting by NASA. Public domain.

Page 132, Armored vehicle in Bagram, Afghanistan, 2006. Photo: Dexter D Clouden, US Army (DOD 061027-A-5420C-041). Source: Wikimedia Commons, public domain.

Page 133, bin Laden. Photo c/o FBI (Federal Bureau of Investigation). Source: Wikimedia Commons, public domain.

Page 135, Saddam Hussein, 2004. Photo: US Army (DOD 040701-O-9999X-008). Source: Wikimedia Commons, public domain.

Page 137, Marines Firing M198 Howitzer at Umm Qasr, Iraq, 2003. Photo: Matthew J Decker USMC (DOD 030324-M-9933D-002), US Army. Source: Wikimedia Commons, public domain.

Pages 142 & 144, World Trade Center. Photos by Tony & Ann Woodall.

Pages 146 & 148, Pentagon after strike. Photos: Cpl Jason Ingersoll, US Army. Source: Wikimedia Commons, public domain.

Page 149, still (4 of 8) from CCTV purporting to show Flight 77 striking the Pentagon. Video c/o Department of Defense (*http://www.defenselink.mil/pubs/foi/index.html*). Source: Wikimedia Commons, public domain.

Page 150, exit hole in Pentagon. Photo: Jocelyn Augustino. Source: FEMA (Federal Emergency Management Agency). Public domain.

Page 152, Flight 175 strikes the south tower. Photo: 'TheMachineStops'. Source: Wikimedia Commons, under the Creative Commons Attribution 2.0 License (*http://creativecommons.org/licenses/by/2.0/*).

Page 152, World Trade Center burning. Author unknown. Source: Wikimedia Commons, public domain (*http://memory.loc.gov/pnp/ppmsca/02100/02121/0012v.jpg*).

Page 154, wreckage at 'Ground Zero'. Photo: Larry Lerner. Source: FEMA. Public domain.

Page 156, lattice remains at Ground Zero. Author unknown. Source: FEMA. Public domain.

Page 157, fireman clearing WTC dust. Photo: Andrea Booher. Source: FEMA. Public domain.

Page 162, aerial view of WTC 7 as tower collapses. Author unknown. Source: FEMA. Public domain.

Page 163, WTC 7 burns. Photo: Arquelio "Archie" Galarza (*http://www.fema.gov/pdf/library/fema403_ch5. pdf*). Source: FEMA. Public domain.

Page 164, aerial view of Ground Zero. Author unknown. Source: FEMA. Public domain.

Page 165, smoke plume as WTC 7 collapses. Author unknown. Source: Courtesy of the Prints and Photographs Division, Library of Congress (*http://hdl.loc.gov/loc.pnp/ppmsca.02121*). Public domain.

Page 167, Mohamed Atta al-Sayed. Author unknown—driver's license photo. Source: FBI (*http://www. fbi.gov/pressrel/penttbom/aa11/11.htm*). Source: Wikimedia Commons, public domain.

Page 169, debris on roof of WTC 5. Author unknown. Source: FEMA. Public domain.

Page 172 (two images), crash site of Flight 93. Author unknown. Source: US Government. Public domain.

Page 176, 9/11 'Tribute in Light'. Photo: Derek Jensen (Tysto). Source: Wikimedia Commons, public domain (*http://commons.wikimedia.org/wiki/File:Wtc-2004-memorial.jpg*).

Page 180, Liberty Bell, Philadelphia. Photo: Tony & Ann Woodall.

Page 182, Pearl Harbor, 1941. Photo: Lloyd C Duncan. Additional source and credit info from the National Archives, US District Court for the District of Hawaii. Source: Wikimedia Commons, public domain.

Page 184, Oklahoma bomb, 1995. Photo: Staff Sgt. Preston Chasteen, US Army (*http://www.defenselink. mil/multimedia/*). Source: Wikimedia Commons, public domain.

Page 188, Guantanamo Bay, 2002. Photo: credited to Ron Sachs/CNP/Corbis, but may be part of a sequence taken by Petty Officer 1st class Shane T McCoy, US Navy. Source: Wikimedia Commons, public domain.

Page 197, Brighton bomb, Grand Hotel, 1984. Author unknown (uploaded by 'D4444n' at *http:// en.wikipedia.org/wiki/User:D4444n*). Source: Wikimedia Commons, under the GNU Free Documentation License (*http://commons.wikimedia.org/wiki/Commons:GNU_Free_Documentation_License*).

Page 199, passengers escape smoke on 7/7. Photo: Adam Stacey (*http://moblog.co.uk/view.php?id=77571*). Source: Wikimedia Commons, under the Creative Commons Attribution 2.5 License (*http:// creativecommons.org/licenses/by/2.5/*).

Page 202, advanced M26 Taser stun pistol. Photo: US Army (*http://www.pica.army.mil/PicatinnyPublic/ highlights/archive/FastTrack.asp*). Source: Wikimedia Commons, public domain.

Page 204, tablets. Photo: Sage Ross (*http://en.wikipedia.org/wiki/User:Ragesoss*). Source: Wikimedia Commons, under the GNU Free Documentation License (*http://commons.wikimedia.org/wiki/Commons: GNU_Free_Documentation_License*).

Page 208, herbal medicines. Photo: Øyvind. Source: Wikimedia Commons under the Creative Commons Attribution-Share Alike 3.0 Unported (*http://creativecommons.org/licenses/by-sa/3.0/deed.en*).

Page 211, post-WWII US poster promoting vaccination against diphtheria. Artist unknown (*http://www. nationalarchives.gov.uk/imagelibrary/medical/03.htm*). Source: Wikimedia Commons, public domain.

Page 213, Edwardian spiritualists, Chicago, Illinois, 1906. Photo: *Chicago Daily News* (DN-0003152—*Chicago Daily News* negatives collection, Chicago Historical Society). Source: Wikimedia Commons, public domain.

Page 215, sunrise by minaret. Photo: Heather Thomas.

Page 217, couple watching television. Photo: Miguel Pires da Rosa. Source: Wikimedia Commons under the Creative Commons Attribution-Share Alike 2.0 Generic License (*http://creativecommons.org/licenses/by-sa/2.0/deed.en*).

Page 222, cooling towers. Photo: Helen Sewell.

Page 224, smoke stacks. Photo: Alfred T Palmer. Source: Wikimedia Commons, public domain.

Page 232, the Sun. Photo: NASA. Public domain.

Page 236, the Earth, photographed by the Galileo probe, 1990. Photo: NASA (*http://www-pm.larc.nasa. gov/triana/Earth.galileo.jpg*). Catalogued by Jet Propulsion Lab of the United States National Aeronautics and Space Administration (NASA) under Photo ID: PIA00728.

Page 249, fireworks over Sydney Opera House, Australia. Photo: Chris Greenberg (*http://www.whitehouse. gov/news/releases/2007/09/images/20070908-1_p090807cg-0360-515h.html*), United States Federal Government. Source: Wikimedia Commons, public domain.

Page 243, Maya temple, Chichen Itza. Photo: Lee Anderson.

Page 244, Comet Holmes. Photo: Rick Jackimowicz. Source: Wikimedia Commons, public domain.

Page 246, the McKenna timewave. Diagram by Geoff Stray, from *Beyond 2012: Catastrophe or Ecstasy*, Vital Signs Publishing, 2005.

Page 247, Galaxy NGC 4414 (Hubble Image). Photo: NASA, The Hubble Heritage Team, STScI, AURA. Public domain.

Pages 248-249, solar CME/flare. Photos: NASA. Public domain.

Page 251, the heliosphere. Artist unknown. Source: NASA (*http://www.nasa.gov/centers/ames/news/releases/2001/01images/Pioneer10/pioneer10.htm*). Public domain.

Page 255, Ayahuasca being brewed. Photo: Debbie Marriage.

Page 259, Hurricane Katrina damage, Pensacola, USA. Photo: Larry W Kachelhofer, US Navy (*http://www.navy.mil/view_single.asp?id=27629*). Source: Wikimedia Commons, public domain.

Page 261, astrological chart for 21st December 2012 (set for the UK). Chart prepared by Helen Sewell, using *Solar Fire* software.

Page 271, H G Wells, 1943. Author unknown—c/o the Youssuf Karsh collection at the Library and Archives, Canada. Source: Wikimedia Commons, public domain.

Page 272, Bertrand Russell, 1950. Photo: Nobel Foundation (*http://nobelprize.org/nobel_prizes/literature/laureates/1950/russell-bio.html*). Source: Wikimedia Commons, public domain.

Page 276, London G20 protests, 2009. Photo: Charlotte Gilhooly. Source: Wikimedia Commons, under the Creative Commons Attribution 2.0 License (*http://creativecommons.org/licenses/by/2.0/*).

Page 277, family watching television, 1950s. Author unknown. Source: Wikimedia Commons, under the Creative Commons Attribution-Share Alike 2.0 License (*http://en.wikipedia.org/wiki/Creative_Commons/*).

Page 279, crowds at Barack Obama's inauguration. Photo: Senior Master Sgt Thomas Meneguin, US Air Force (*http://www.defenselink.mil/dodcmsshare/homepagephoto/2009-01/hires_090120-F-6184M-007a.jpg*). Source: Wikimedia Commons, public domain.

Page 284, Hindu woman at prayer. Photo: © Claude Renault (*http://www.flickr.com/photos/clodreno/39525690/*). Source: Wikimedia Commons, under the Creative Commons Attribution 2.0 License (*http://creativecommons.org/licenses/by/2.0/*).

Page 288 montage: Pentagon on 9/11. Photo: Cpl Jason Ingersoll, US Army. Source: Wikimedia Commons, public domain. / Tsunami striking Malé, the Maldives, 2004. Photo: Sofwathulla Mohamed (*http://www.darkmoon.mv/wave/*). Source: Wikimedia Commons, public domain. / O J Simpson visiting US troops during Operation Desert Shield. Photo: Gerald Johnson (*http://www.dodmedia.osd.mil/DVIC_View/Still_Details.cfm?SDAN=DNST9103444&JPGPath=/Assets/Still/1991/Navy/DN-ST-91-03444.JPG*), US Army. Source: Wikimedia Commons, public domain. / Princess Diana's funeral procession, 1997. Photo: Paddy Briggs. Source: Wikimedia Commons, public domain.

Page 291, Adolf Hitler, 1932. Author unknown (c/o/Deutsches Bundesarchiv [German Federal Archive]). Source: Wikimedia Commons, public domain.

Page 292, asteroid strike. Painting: Don Davis (*http://www.donaldedavis.com/PARTS/allyours.html*). Source: NASA. Public domain.

Page 296, 2004 tsunami. Photo: Michael L Bak, US military (*http://www.defenseimagery.mil/imagery.html#guid-5e24f570d0bc5a851ac2182993e5d33b5f8ff005*). Source: Wikimedia Commons, public domain.

Page 298, Rupert Sheldrake. Author unknown. Source: Wikimedia Commons, public domain.

Page 300, Live Aid USA, 1985. Photo: 'Squelle'. Source: Wikimedia Commons, under the Creative Commons Attribution 3.0 License (*http://creativecommons.org/licenses/by-sa/3.0/*).

Page 305, riot police at G20 protests. Photo: Chris Brown. Source: Wikimedia Commons, under the Creative Commons Attribution 2.0 License (*http://creativecommons.org/licenses/by/2.0/*).

Page 307, London Olympic stadium lighting. Photo: 'jeffowenphotos'. Source: Wikimedia Commons, under the Creative Commons Attribution 2.0 License (*http://creativecommons.org/licenses/by/2.0/*).

Page 308, Glastonbury Tor, Somerset, UK, as seen from Beckery, 2006. Photo: Palden Jenkins.

Page 313, Emmiline Pankhurst arrested outside Buckingham Palace, 1914. Author unknown. Source: Wikimedia Commons, public domain.

Page 313, 'Orange Revolution' protests. Author unknown (*http://maidan.org.ua/news/view.php3?site=maidan&bn=maidan_foto&key=1101124510*). Source: Wikimedia Commons, under the GNU Free Documentation License (*http://commons.wikimedia.org/wiki/Commons:GNU_Free_Documentation_License*).

Page 320, Thomas Paine mural, Lewes, East Sussex, painted by Julian Bell (c/o Francis Kyle gallery, *www.franciskylegallery.com*).

Page 372, Egyptian temple pillar. Photo: Heather Thomas.

With the exception of the noted public domain or licensed images, authors retain full copyright on the featured photographs, which have been reproduced here with their kind permission.

INDEX

THE TRUTH AGENDA

Terrorism, 19, 67, 68, 79, 83, 84, 134, 174, 194, 195, 197, 198, 200-203, 205, 237, 352
Tesla technology, 70
Texas, USA, 70, 92
Texas Academy of Sciences, 70
Thatcher, Margaret, 197, 364
Them, 95, 322
THEMIS (Time History of Events and Macroscale Interactions during Substorms), 251, 252, 363
Thermite, 156, 157
Tiananmen Square, Beijing, China, 315
Time anomalies/time travel, 47, 297, 298
Times Square, New York, pic 26
Timewave, 245, pic 246, 257
Tinfoil hats, 280
Tips, Scott, 210
Tizimin, book of, 243
Tolerance Acts, 213
Tolkien, JRR, 264
Tomlinson, Ian, 353
Tories—see Conservative Party
Tortuguero, Mexico, 243
Totnes, Devon, 356
Tower of Babel, 87, pic 88, 340
Tower Hamlets, London, UK, 92
Toynbee, Polly, 22, 23, 332
Tragedy & Hope, 74
Transition Towns, 225, 356
Transylvania, 340
Treaty of Lisbon, 77
Trilateral Commission, the, 68, 96
Truscott, Lord, 339
Truth campaigners (general), 80, 189, 225, 269, 312
Tsunami (Indonesian, 2004), pic 288, pic 296, 297
Tsunami (Japanese, 2011), 226, 234, 262, 297
Tunisia, 25
Turkmenistan, 133, 345
Turner, Lord, 235, 360
21st Century Science & Technology, 230
21st December 2012, 15, 35, 48, 239, 240-243, 254, 256, 260, pic 261, 266, 309, 324, 325, 361
Twitter, 219
2001: A Space Odyssey, 120, 257, 285, 319
2012 prophecies (specific), 49, 51, 245

UFO contactees/abductions, 45-49, 53, 56, 246
UFOs, 11, 31, 39-49 (with pics), 58, 59, 87, 122, 127, 280, 302, 311, 322, 335, 344
UK (specific), 12, 13, 25, 78, 79, 131, 135, 137, 141, 178, 197, 218, 234, 325, 352
UK Column, 356
UK Independence Party (UKIP), 76
Ukraine, pic 315
Ulysses space probe, 251, 363
UN (United Nations), 135, 209, 227
Underground shelters (secret), 359
Unfair Commercial Practices Directive, 212, 355, 356
Uniformed Fire Officers Association, 165
United Airlines, 173
United States Air Force (USAF), 43
University of East Anglia, 233
University of Portsmouth, 108
University of California, 252
University of Texas, 338

Unmanned space probes, 108, 109, pic 116, pic 251, 252
Uranus/Pluto astrological cycle, 260-262, 325
Ure, Midge, 314
US constitution, pic 180, 188
US Department of Defense, 161
US Federal Reserve, 74
US National Institutes for Health, 231
US Navy SEALS, 133, 134
US Secret Service, 162
US Senate Committee on Environment and Public Works, 360
USA/North America/Americans (specific), 12, 13, 23, 43, 45, 53, 63, 64, 73, 74, 78, 101, 104, 107, 127, 129, 130, 133-135, 137, 141, 150, 173-175, 180, 186, 187-189, 192, 198, 209, 219, 234, 244, 259, 271, 273, 278, 307-309, 321, 322, 332, 340, 368
USAF (United States Air Force), 43, 44
USS Liberty, 16, 183
USSR—see Soviet Union

Vaccinations, 69, 71, pic 211, 337, 355
Valerian, 209
Van Allen belts, 123
Vapor trails, 70
Vatican, the, 33, 57, 59-62, 65
Venus, 43, 63
Verkerk, Robert, 210, 355
Veterans' Day parade, pic 64, pic 130
Vietnam War, 101, 261, 311, 351
Villiers, Theresa, 368
Violence in TV and games, 217, 218, 294, 295
Virgin Mary, pic 50, 55-57 pic 60, 61, 336
Virginia, USA, 120
Visor Consultants, 199
Vitamins, high-dose, 207, 209, 210
Vlad the Impaler, 340
Volcanoes, 236, 294, 310
Voodoo Histories, 20, 332
Voyager space probe, pic 251
V2 Missiles, 127

Waco siege, 183, 331, 351
Waco: The Rules of Engagement, 351
Wakefield, Dr Andrew, 211, 337
Wałęsa, Lech, 314
Wall Street, New York, pic 274, 348
Wallonia, Belgium, 44
War (general), 67, 68, 138, 185, 189, 243, 270
War on Terror, the, 13, 25, 48, 78, 130-133, 141, 143, 178, 180, 185-187, 191, 197, 198, 201, 203, 306, 353
Warminster, Wiltshire, UK, 43
Warsaw, Poland, 359
Washington DC, USA, pic 24, pic 90, 91, 171, pic 279
Water crystal experiments (Emoto), 292, 366
'Waterboarding' torture, 188
Watergate scandal, 16, 131
Watford, UK, 97
WCPO-TV, 172
Weapons of Mass Destruction (WMDs), 124, 131, 134-139, 141, 277, 345
Weather Channel, 229, 358
Weiss, Philip, 96
Wells, H G, 77, 270, pic 271, 275, 365
West, John Anthony, 364
Westminster, London, UK, 140, 295

Please note that the Index does not cover *Appendix 3 (Further Resources)* or *Picture Credits*.

Appendix 2 (Notes) is covered, although article, book or website names (and their authors) are not generally listed for that section.

Also by Andy Thomas

CONSPIRACIES
The Facts — The Theories — The Evidence

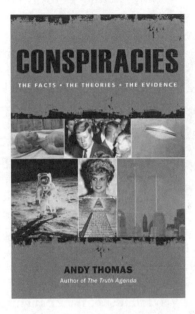

JFK, Watergate, The Gunpowder Plot, Princess Diana, Dr David Kelly, 9/11, The Moon Landings, Chemtrails, HAARP, False-flag Attacks, ETs, The New World Order and far beyond... Since the political intrigues of the Roman Empire, nearly every significant event of the last 2,000 years has sparked off a conspiracy theory.

Andy Thomas sifts through the evidence of more than 30 major conspiracies and sets them against the social and psychological factors that have prompted them to spread. Thematically arranged, the accounts are stripped of unfounded opinion and presented factually but accessibly, dramatically highlighting the core issues in a timely and meticulously-researched overview.

If readers enjoy *The Truth Agenda*, then *Conspiracies* fills in important details on related matters and adds many more layers to crucial subjects for our times. Published in the US, UK and Australia by Watkins Publishing, the book is available from most online retailers, and bookshop chains. Find out more about *Conspiracies* at *www. truthagenda.org*, or on the publisher's website at *www.watkinspublishing.com*.

THE AUTHOR

Andy Thomas is one of the world's leading authors and lecturers on unexplained mysteries and global cover-ups.

Andy is author of many books, including *Conspiracies: The Facts—The Theories—The Evidence*, and *Vital Signs*, which has been widely described as the definitive guide to the crop circle controversy and was nominated for *Kindred Spirit* magazine's Best Book award. *The Truth Agenda* has been acclaimed as the best available overview of paranormal mysteries and conspiracies.

Andy has written for many publications, and regularly contributes to *Nexus Magazine*. He is also author of several books about his historical birth town of Lewes in East Sussex, England, once the residence of inspirational writer and libertarian Thomas Paine and site of the world's largest annual Guy Fawkes celebrations.

A very active lecturer, Andy is renowned for giving striking live presentations, and speaks extensively across Britain and in many parts of the world, including America, Australia, Brazil, Peru and various European countries. He is also co-presenter of The Glastonbury Symposium, the UK's longest-running and largest annual alternative conference, as well as being co-founder of the Changing Times group, which holds regular events on alternative views and truth issues.

Andy has made numerous radio and television appearances around the world, including TV spots on NBC's *Caught on Camera*, The History Channel, National Geographic Channel, and the BBC.

Information on Andy, with news, reviews, videos, Facebook/YouTube links and details of lectures, can be found at The Truth Agenda *website:*

www.truthagenda.org

COVERT WARS AND THE CLASH OF CIVILIZATIONS
UFOs, Oligarchs and Space Secrecy
By Joseph P. Farrell

Farrell continues to delve into the creation of breakaway civilizations by the Nazis in South America and other parts of the world. He elaborates on the advanced technology that they took with them at the "end" of World War II and shows how the breakaway civilizations have created a huge system of hidden finance with the involvement of various banks and financial institutions around the world. He continues to look into the secret space programs used by the breakaway civilization and the clash of civilizations—a virtual secret war going on around us. He investigates the current space secrecy that involves UFOs, suppressed technologies and the hidden oligarchs who control Earth for their own gain and profit.

358 Pages. 6x9 Paperback. Illustrated. $19.95. Code: CWCC

COVERT WARS AND BREAKAWAY CIVILIZATIONS
By Joseph P. Farrell

Farrell delves into the creation of breakaway civilizations by the Nazis in South America and other parts of the world. He discusses the advanced technology that they took with them at the end of the war and the psychological war that they waged for decades on America and NATO. He investigates the secret space programs currently sponsored by the breakaway civilizations and the current militaries in control of planet Earth. Plenty of astounding accounts, documents and speculation on the incredible alternative history of hidden conflicts and secret space programs that began when World War II officially "ended."

370 Pages. 6x9 Paperback. Illustrated. $19.95. Code: BCCW

HAARP
The Ultimate Weapon of the Conspiracy
by Jerry Smith

The HAARP project in Alaska is one of the most controversial projects ever undertaken by the U.S. Government. At at worst, HAARP could be the most dangerous device ever created, a futuristic technology that is everything from super-beam weapon to world-wide mind control device. Topics include Over-the-Horizon Radar and HAARP, Mind Control, ELF and HAARP, The Telsa Connection, The Russian Woodpecker, GWEN & HAARP, Earth Penetrating Tomography, Weather Modification, Secret Science of the Conspiracy, more. Includes the complete 1987 Eastlund patent for his pulsed super-weapon that he claims was stolen by the HAARP Project.

256 pages. 6x9 Paperback. Illustrated. Bib. $14.95. Code: HARP

WEATHER WARFARE
The Military's Plan to Draft Mother Nature
by Jerry E. Smith

Weather modification in the form of cloud seeding to increase snow packs in the Sierras or suppress hail over Kansas is now an everyday affair. Underground nuclear tests in Nevada have set off earthquakes. A Russian company has been offering to sell typhoons (hurricanes) on demand since the 1990s. Scientists have been searching for ways to move hurricanes for over fifty years. In the same amount of time we went from the Wright Brothers to Neil Armstrong. Hundreds of environmental and weather modifying technologies have been patented in the United States alone – and hundreds more are being developed in civilian, academic, military and quasi-military laboratories around the world *at this moment!* Numerous ongoing military programs do inject aerosols at high altitude for communications and surveillance operations.

304 Pages. 6x9 Paperback. Illustrated. Bib. $18.95. Code: WWAR

SECRETS OF THE UNIFIED FIELD
The Philadelphia Experiment, the Nazi Bell, and the Discarded Theory
by Joseph P. Farrell

Farrell examines the now discarded Unified Field Theory. American and German wartime scientists and engineers determined that, while the theory was incomplete, it could nevertheless be engineered. Chapters include: The Meanings of "Torsion"; Wringing an Aluminum Can; The Mistake in Unified Field Theories and Their Discarding by Contemporary Physics; Three Routes to the Doomsday Weapon: Quantum Potential, Torsion, and Vortices; Tesla's Meeting with FDR; Arnold Sommerfeld and Electromagnetic Radar Stealth; Electromagnetic Phase Conjugations, Phase Conjugate Mirrors, and Templates; The Unified Field Theory, the Torsion Tensor, and Witkowski's Idea of the Plasma Focus; tons more.
340 pages. 6x9 Paperback. Illustrated. $18.95. Code: SOUF

NAZI INTERNATIONAL
The Nazi's Postwar Plan to Control Finance, Conflict, Physics and Space
by Joseph P. Farrell

Beginning with prewar corporate partnerships in the USA, including some with the Bush family, he moves on to the surrender of Nazi Germany, and evacuation plans of the Germans. He then covers the vast, and still-little-known recreation of Nazi Germany in South America with help of Juan Peron, I.G. Farben and Martin Bormann. Farrell then covers he development of new energy technologies including the Bariloche Fusion Project, Dr. Philo Farnsworth's Plasmator, and the work of Dr. Nikolai Kozyrev. Finally, Farrell discusses the Nazi desire to control space, and their connection with NASA, the esoteric meaning of NASA Mission Patches.
412 pages. 6x9 Paperback. Illustrated. $19.95. Code: NZIN

SAUCERS, SWASTIKAS AND PSYOPS
By Joseph P. Farrell

Farrell discusses SS Commando Otto Skorzeny; George Adamski; the alleged Hannebu and Vril craft of the Third Reich; The Strange Case of Dr. Hermann Oberth; Nazis in the US and their connections to "UFO contactees." Chapters include: The Nov. 20, 1952 Contact: The Memes are Implants; George Hunt Williamson and the Baileys; William Pelley and the American Fascists; The Messages from "ET"; The Venusian and "The Bomb"; Adamski's ETs and Religion: The Interplanetary Federation of Brotherhood and the "Übermensch ET"; Adamski's Technological Descriptions and Another ET Message: The Danger of Weaponized Gravity; Adamski's Retro-Looking Saucers, and the Nazi Saucer Myth; more.
272 Pages. 6x9 Paperback. Illustrated. $19.95. Code: SSPY

VIMANA:
Flying Machines of the Ancients
by David Hatcher Childress

According to early Sanskrit texts the ancients had several types of airships called vimanas. Like aircraft of today, vimanas were used to fly through the air from city to city; to conduct aerial surveys of uncharted lands; and as delivery vehicles for awesome weapons. Childress takes us on an astounding investigation into tales of ancient flying machines. In his new book, packed with photos and diagrams, he consults ancient texts and modern stories and presents astonishing evidence that aircraft, similar to the ones we use today, were used thousands of years ago in India, Sumeria, China and other countries. Includes a 24-page color section.
408 Pages. 6x9 Paperback. Illustrated. $22.95. Code: VMA

ANCIENT ALIENS ON THE MOON
By Mike Bara
What did NASA find in their explorations of the solar system that they may have kept from the general public? How ancient really are these ruins on the Moon? Using official NASA and Russian photos of the Moon, Bara looks at vast cityscapes and domes in the Sinus Medii region as well as glass domes in the Crisium region. Bara also takes a detailed look at the mission of Apollo 17 and the case that this was a salvage mission, primarily concerned with investigating an opening into a massive hexagonal ruin near the landing site. Chapters include: The History of Lunar Anomalies; The Early 20th Century; Sinus Medii; To the Moon Alice!; Mare Crisium; Yes, Virginia, We Really Went to the Moon; Apollo 17; more. Tons of photos of the Moon examined for possible structures and other anomalies.
248 Pages. 6x9 Paperback. Illustrated.. $19.95. Code: AAOM

ANCIENT ALIENS ON MARS
By Mike Bara
Bara brings us this lavishly illustrated volume on alien structures on Mars. Was there once a vast, technologically advanced civilization on Mars, and did it leave evidence of its existence behind for humans to find eons later? Did these advanced extraterrestrial visitors vanish in a solar system wide cataclysm of their own making, only to make their way to Earth and start anew? Was Mars once as lush and green as the Earth, and teeming with life? Chapters include: War of the Worlds; The Mars Tidal Model; The Death of Mars; Cydonia and the Face on Mars; The Monuments of Mars; The Search for Life on Mars; The True Colors of Mars and The Pathfinder Sphinx; more. Color section.
252 Pages. 6x9 Paperback. Illustrated. $19.95. Code: AMAR

ANCIENT TECHNOLOGY IN PERU & BOLIVIA
By David Hatcher Childress
Childress speculates on the existence of a sunken city in Lake Titicaca and reveals new evidence that the Sumerians may have arrived in South America 4,000 years ago. He demonstrates that the use of "keystone cuts" with metal clamps poured into them to secure megalithic construction was an advanced technology used all over the world, from the Andes to Egypt, Greece and Southeast Asia. He maintains that only power tools could have made the intricate articulation and drill holes found in extremely hard granite and basalt blocks in Bolivia and Peru, and that the megalith builders had to have had advanced methods for moving and stacking gigantic blocks of stone, some weighing over 100 tons.
340 Pages. 6x9 Paperback. Illustrated.. $19.95 Code: ATP

THE ENIGMA OF CRANIAL DEFORMATION
Elongated Skulls of the Ancients
By David Hatcher Childress and Brien Foerster
In a book filled with over a hundred astonishing photos and a color photo section, Childress and Foerster take us to Peru, Bolivia, Egypt, Malta, China, Mexico and other places in search of strange elongated skulls and other cranial deformation. The puzzle of why diverse ancient people—even on remote Pacific Islands—would use head-binding to create elongated heads is mystifying. Where did they even get this idea? Did some people naturally look this way—with long narrow heads? Were they some alien race? Were they an elite race that roamed the entire planet? Why do anthropologists rarely talk about cranial deformation and know so little about it?
250 Pages. 6x9 Paperback. Illustrated. $19.95. Code: ECD

ORDER FORM

10% Discount When You Order 3 or More Items!

One Adventure Place
P.O. Box 74
Kempton, Illinois 60946
United States of America
Tel.: 815-253-6390 • Fax: 815-253-6300
Email: auphq@frontiernet.net
http://www.adventuresunlimitedpress.com

ORDERING INSTRUCTIONS

✓ Remit by USD$ Check, Money Order or Credit Card

✓ Visa, Master Card, Discover & AmEx Accepted

✓ Paypal Payments Can Be Made To:

    info@wexclub.com

✓ Prices May Change Without Notice

✓ 10% Discount for 3 or More Items

SHIPPING CHARGES

United States

✓ Postal Book Rate { $4.50 First Item / 50¢ Each Additional Item

✓ POSTAL BOOK RATE Cannot Be Tracked!
    Not responsible for non-delivery.

✓ Priority Mail { $6.00 First Item / $2.00 Each Additional Item

✓ UPS { $7.00 First Item / $1.50 Each Additional Item

    NOTE: UPS Delivery Available to Mainland USA Only

Canada

✓ Postal Air Mail { $15.00 First Item / $3.00 Each Additional Item

✓ Personal Checks or Bank Drafts MUST BE

    US$ and Drawn on a US Bank

✓ Canadian Postal Money Orders OK

✓ Payment MUST BE US$

All Other Countries

✓ Sorry, No Surface Delivery!

✓ Postal Air Mail { $19.00 First Item / $7.00 Each Additional Item

✓ Checks and Money Orders MUST BE US$
    and Drawn on a US Bank or branch.

✓ Paypal Payments Can Be Made in US$ To:
    info@wexclub.com

SPECIAL NOTES

✓ RETAILERS: Standard Discounts Available

✓ BACKORDERS: We Backorder all Out-of-
    Stock Items Unless Otherwise Requested

✓ PRO FORMA INVOICES: Available on Request

✓ DVD Return Policy: Replace defective DVDs only

ORDER ONLINE AT: www.adventuresunlimitedpress.com

10% Discount When You Order 3 or More Items!

Please check: ✓

☐ This is my first order   ☐ I have ordered before

Name			
Address			
City			
State/Province		**Postal Code**	
Country			
Phone: Day		Evening	
Fax	Email		

Item Code	Item Description	Qty	Total

Please check: ✓

☐ Postal-Surface	Subtotal ▶
☐ Postal-Air Mail (Priority in USA)	Less Discount-10% for 3 or more items ▶
	Balance ▶
	Illinois Residents 6.25% Sales Tax ▶
☐ UPS (Mainland USA only)	Previous Credit ▶
	Shipping ▶
	Total (check/MO in USD$ only) ▶
☐ Visa/MasterCard/Discover/American Express	

Card Number:

Expiration Date: **Security Code:**

✓ SEND A CATALOG TO A FRIEND: